Mexico's Politics and Society in Transition

A project of the
Latin American Program
of the Woodrow Wilson International
Center for Scholars

Mexico's Politics and Society in Transition

edited by

Joseph S. Tulchin
Andrew D. Selee

BOULDER
LONDON

Published in the United States of America in 2003 by
Lynne Rienner Publishers, Inc.
1800 30th Street, Boulder, Colorado 80301
www.rienner.com

and in the United Kingdom by
Lynne Rienner Publishers, Inc.
3 Henrietta Street, Covent Garden, London WC2E 8LU

Library of Congress Cataloging-in-Publication Data
Mexico's politics and society in transition / edited by Joseph S. Tulchin and Andrew D. Selee.
Includes bibliographical references and index.
ISBN 1-58826-128-X (alk. paper)
ISBN 1-58826-104-2 (pbk. : alk. paper)
1. Mexico—Politics and government—1988– 2. Mexico—Economic conditions—1994– 3. Mexico—Foreign economic relations. I. Tulchin, Joseph S., 1939– II. Selee, Andrew D.
JL1281.M497 2002
320.972—dc21
2002069821

British Cataloguing in Publication Data
A Cataloguing in Publication record for this book
is available from the British Library.

Printed and bound in the United States of America

The paper used in this publication meets the requirements
of the American National Standard for Permanence of
Paper for Printed Library Materials Z39.48-1984.

5 4 3 2 1

Contents

Part 2 The Economics of Change and the Challenge of Development

Part 3 Mexicans Abroad

Part 4 Conclusion

Acknowledgments

This book grew out of a joint project on Mexico run by the Woodrow Wilson Center's Latin American Program and the Council on Latin American and Iberian Studies at Yale University, supported by a generous grant from the William and Flora Hewlett Foundation.

In May 2000, the Wilson Center and Yale University sponsored a conference, "Mexico at the Millennium," which was an important step in the evolution of the book. The editors are particularly grateful to Gilbert Joseph and Beatriz Riefkohl at Yale University, David Lorey at the Hewlett Foundation, and Amelia Brown, Heather Golding, and Allison Garland at the Wilson Center for helping to make the conference possible. Most of the authors presented initial versions of their chapters at the conference, revised them, and then, because of the dynamic developments in Mexico over the past two years, revised them again. We appreciate their efforts. We would also like to acknowledge several presenters and commentators at the conference whose comments during the meeting influenced the development of this book in significant ways: Jesús Reyes Heroles, Adolfo Gilly, Erica Pani, Gustavo Vega, Victoria Murillo, Carlos Hurtado, Santiago Levy, José Luis Orozco, Guadalupe González, Rafael Fernández de Castro, Yemile Mizrahi, and David Brooks.

During the preparation of the manuscript, several colleagues lent invaluable assistance. Yemile Mizrahi, Alejandra Vallejo, and Cynthia Arnson commented on parts of the manuscript; Lía Limón, Craig Fagan, and Marianne Benet provided critical research; and Allison Garland, Carlisle Levine, Marianne Benet, Marisol Corral, Priyanka Ananda, and Samantha Newbold helped edit the final manuscript. We are grateful to all for their help in bringing the book to fruition.

Prologue: Toward a New Bilateral Relationship

Jorge G. Castañeda

Mexico is undergoing a far-reaching process of reform and renewal. The federal elections held on July 2, 2000, showed the degree of maturity attained by the country's political institutions. For the first time in seven decades, an opposition candidate became president as a result of free, fair, and uncontested elections. This marked the end of an era of authoritarianism and corporate politics. More important, it also signaled the beginning of a new relationship between Mexican society and its government, a relationship based on trust, accountability, and the rule of law.

Mexico's democratic change has also paved the way for new and more creative forms of cooperation with our partners abroad. The years since the end of the Cold War have seen intense, wide-ranging, and confused debates about the nature of international relations. A lack of long-term strategic vision has characterized all nations' foreign policy thinking, and the crucial challenges that we face as we build new bridges and relationships in the Western Hemisphere are no exception. Based on our rich and diverse national identities, the nations of the Americas must strive to exploit their similarities and articulate long-term national interests that will mutually reinforce each nation throughout the continent. It is in this context that we have a unique opportunity to reaffirm and multiply the ties that bind Mexico to other countries and regions of the world.

Evidently, Mexico's primary scope of action is the Americas. A wide margin for constructive engagement exists today throughout the Western Hemisphere. Thus, all American nations must engage in those issues in which we all have a fundamental stake: the preeminence of negotiation over the use of force; a common concern for the causes of global peace and security; a commitment to aggressively, responsibly, and jointly confront the nontraditional security threats that have arisen in the post–Cold War world; the need to rethink international financial institutions; and the importance of sustainable and long-term economic development that bridges inequality in the region and within our societies.

I believe that the North American community must be more than trade: it is becoming a larger reality as the peoples, the economies, and the environments of Mexico, the United States, and Canada become increasingly intertwined. The North American Free Trade Agreement has represented an ambitious effort to redefine North America's role in the hemisphere and in the world arena. It has given a long-term perspective to our relationship. However, there is much more our countries can do together. We must go one step beyond, first by widening and deepening our cooperation, and second by reviewing the existing hemispheric architecture to ensure that we have mechanisms to address those issues that are specific to our three countries. In those trilateral, regional, and global issues where we share common goals, interests, and agendas, Mexico, the United Sates, and Canada must work together.

The United States already occupies a place of unique importance in Mexico's international agenda, as closer forms of exchange and cooperation have developed over the past few years. Since the late 1980s, profound changes have occurred in Mexico, the United States, and also the international arena. Mexico and the United States are now uniquely placed to harness the challenges of the current international system and, at the same time, play a defining role in shaping the post–Cold War world.

The growing ties between Mexico and the United States imply an increasing need to jointly and constructively address issues that affect both countries, particularly those related to migration, organized crime, and environmental degradation. In the past, efforts to increase cooperation between the governments of Mexico and the United States have sometimes been hampered by a history of misunderstandings and even mistrust. A great deal has been achieved in recent years on both sides of the border in order to overcome these obstacles and to deepen and widen the relationship between both governments.

Relations between both countries have shifted dramatically: from neighborly distance to active engagement, and from fragmented and occasional attention—mostly derived from the intermittent crisis *du jour*—to the systematic articulation of cooperation mechanisms and day-to-day dialogue.

Arguably, there has never been a more auspicious time for Mexico and the United States to work together on the basis of a full, mature, and equitable partnership for prosperity.

First, a full relationship requires that both countries constructively engage not only on all the issues of the bilateral agenda but also on regional and global issues that are relevant to each other, regardless of whether they have a direct impact on bilateral interests. Yet this greater interconnectedness means more than increasing our efforts to jointly, constructively, and responsibly deal with some of the most pressing issues of our bilateral agenda such as migration flows and transnational organized crime. It also requires that we address issues such as the structural reforms needed to guarantee long-term sustainable growth and economic convergence between our two countries, the protection of human rights, the advancement of democracy throughout the world, and the situation in Colombia. Evidently, reaching understanding and achieving consensus between two democratic nations—as Mexico and the United States are today—is harder than in the past, when Mexico's authoritarian rule sometimes made things easier, but it certainly provides for a more solid and long-standing relationship.

Second, a mature relationship means that both countries can explicitly refer to their common perceptions and agreements as well as to their differences and disagreements, regardless of whether these are on bilateral issues, such as border infrastructure and trucking disputes, or regional issues, such as Cuba and the Kyoto Protocol. Maturity also means that if disagreements do occur—as they can and most probably will in a relationship as complex as this one—the long-term objectives of the bilateral agenda will not be jeopardized. Maturity requires that transparency become the name of the game. Mexico and the United States must be willing to fully assume the responsibilities of their decisions: there must be no embarrassing agreements to hide and no carefully disguised or glossed-over disagreements.

And finally, an equitable relationship entails the need to foster growth and development in order to narrow the divide—social, environmental, and even digital—that separates our societies. There is an array of economic instruments at the disposal of both nations that must be brought to bear in order to address the needs of the lesser-developed areas and the most vulnerable groups in our societies. Moreover, regardless of the asymmetries that continue to exist between Mexico and the United States, both governments must engage each other, fostering and deepening trust along the way. The best means by which both countries can work toward this goal is widening and deepening cooperation through permanent and predictable engagement and confidence-building, thereby eliminating surprises and discarding unilateral actions, such as the drug certification process. Cooperation between Mexico and the United States is not a nicety; it is a necessity.

This new partnership hinges on the distinct possibility of improved relations between Mexico and the United States and is based on a new attitude of mutual respect and cooperation. The previous claim cannot be dismissed as an expression of wishful thinking. The newfound legitimacy and self-assuredness of the Mexican government has been acknowledged both at home and abroad. The winds of change that are sweeping through Mexico have been perceived by many as laying a more stable and solid foundation on which to build a new relationship with the United States.

In their effort to attain a full, mature, and equitable relationship, Mexico and the United States face four crucial challenges. First, they must have the ability to deal with border issues in an imaginative, constructive, and joint fashion. Second, both countries must learn to live and interact with the increasingly active Mexican-American communities in the United States, as well as to benefit from their great potential in business, politics, and culture. Third, they need to strengthen institutional mechanisms as a means of handling this complex bilateral relationship. Fourth, policymakers must prevent the use of the bilateral relationship as a sword in the fencing matches of domestic politics. We must be able to convey the right message about the stakes involved in this unique bilateral relationship and the crucial importance that each country has for the other.

Aware that there are no simple solutions to overcoming these challenges, President Vicente Fox and President George W. Bush have made a momentous head start in this process. Their first three encounters (in Guanajuato, in Quebec, and in Washington, D.C.) have set the tone and direction of relations for the coming years. Both presidents are committed to building an authentic partnership for prosperity that will allow Mexico and the United States to go beyond the limitations of the past and seize the unprecedented opportunities that lie before us.

The timely publication by the Woodrow Wilson International Center of this long-overdue volume on Mexico and Mexico-U.S. relations will no doubt enrich the ongoing policy dialogue between Mexico and the United States and thus contribute to promoting greater understanding and cooperation between our two nations.

Introduction

Joseph S. Tulchin and Andrew D. Selee

Mexico and the United States have never been closer. Although the two countries are neighbors that share a 2,000-mile border, that proximity was in the past often the source of pain and distrust. Today, however, Mexico has also become the leading trade partner of the United States after Canada. Since Mexico and the United States joined with Canada to create the largest free trade area in the world (the North American Free Trade Agreement, or NAFTA), the economies of the two countries have become increasingly intertwined, and what happens in one country inevitably affects the other. Equally important, around 21 million Americans, almost 8 percent of the population, trace their heritage to Mexico, including 7–8 million who were born on Mexican soil.[1] Latinos in the United States, two-thirds of whom are of Mexican descent, have taken unprecedented leadership in the media, the labor market, business, academia, and politics. Contact and coordination between the governments of the two countries are complex and increasing. Links among individuals, businesses, and civil society organizations on both sides of the border are dense and growing. Political relations between the two countries, which in the past have often been distant, are now closer than ever. Today, it is critically important for people in the United States to understand what is happening in Mexico. This book will help make that possible.

Mexico is undergoing a period of remarkable change. Its political system, which was dominated by a single party for more than seven decades, has become open and competitive. The president, once all-powerful, has found his power checked by the growing authority of Congress and the courts, which in turn have become increasingly responsive to citizen pressure. The press, once largely controlled by the government, has won newfound freedom. This has stimulated public debate and dialogue among Mexicans about their country's future to an unprecedented degree, including debates around gender, ethnicity, and development and equity. At the same time, Mexico's economy, once largely closed and state-directed, has become one of the most open economies in the developing world. Since 1990, Mexico has multiplied its total trade with the rest of the world six times, and trade now accounts for one-third of gross domestic product (GDP).[2] In addition, Mexicans living in the United States have also come to play a visible role in the political, social, and economic life of both countries. Once shunned and persecuted, they are increasingly courted by politicians on both sides of the border for their votes and resources.

These dramatic changes, though recent, emerge out of several decades of social and political struggle, cultural transformation, and institutional change. There are, of course, watershed moments that mark these changes: President Vicente Fox's election in July 2000, which set in motion a changing of the guard from seventy-one years of single-party rule; the start of NAFTA in 1994, which marked Mexico's integration into the world economy; and the agreement in principle in 2001 between President Fox and President George W. Bush to negotiate a comprehensive migration agreement. However, these transforming moments have been driven by smaller, incremental changes. Social and political organizations gradually opened spaces for greater political openness and competition. Successive economic crises forced changes in economic policy and led to a gradual integration into world markets. Mexicans abroad slowly grew in influence in the social, political, and economic fabric of their communities of origin and in their new home communities.

These changes are not without conflict and problems. Mexico's democracy is far from consolidated. Remnants of the authoritarian past remain embedded in clientelistic relationships between politicians and citizens; impunity has yet to be addressed for wrongs committed in the past; and some security and intelligence organizations do not appear to be fully accountable to civilian oversight. Moreover, the various institutions of government are still learning how to function effectively and coordinate with each other in an era where the president is no longer all-powerful and the contours of the new relationships among institutions are still emerging. At the same time, however, even though Mexico's entrance into the world economy has brought increased economic growth, it has done little to improve the well-being of the majority of Mexicans. The income gap between the wealthiest and the poorest citizens is increasing, which could have dire consequences for democratic governance. And although the influence of Mexican migrants on both sides of the border is growing, little has been done as yet to grant them voting rights in Mexico or, for those who are undocumented, legal status in the United States.

Despite these shortcomings, the changes that have taken place in Mexico's politics and society are dramatic, even breathtaking. Mexico has embarked on a transition from which it is hard to imagine turning back. Every struggle for change in Mexico, every success, and every failure will have a profound impact on the United States. For that reason, it is important for us to be aware of what is happening in our neighboring country to the south and how this transforms our bilateral relationship.

Mexico's Democratic Transition

President Fox's election is the culmination of two decades of political change in Mexico that has led to the emergence of new democratic institutions and organizations. For more than fifty years, from 1929 to the early 1980s, Mexico had a largely unchallenged one-party regime. However, the economic changes of the 1980s and 1990s created dissatisfaction with the ruling party and provided opportunities for opposition parties and civic organizations to challenge the regime. By harnessing public opinion within Mexico and around the world, these groups were able to force the regime to institutionalize procedures for fair and mostly equitable elections and ultimately to unseat the party in power, first locally and then nationally. These changes have gone far beyond institutionalizing fair elections, however. They have led to a gradual democratization of many aspects of Mexican political life, including the media, government-society relationships, and federal-state relations. In turn, this has allowed issues of social and economic exclusion, labor relations, indigenous and women's rights, and the role of subnational governments to emerge at the forefront of public debate.

Democratic transitions are often uneven and contradictory, and Mexico is no exception. Many of the key institutions of Mexican society—and the relationships among them—are slow to change. Congress, the judicial system, state and local governments, and political parties, all of which were established within a system of strict hierarchical authority, are learning to operate in a new era of more horizontal and dispersed political power. Institutions that were designed to reinforce and preserve an authoritarian state, such as the armed forces and the intelligence services, are being forced to redefine their role. Citizens, whose opinions and demands were restricted to authorized channels of political participation, have been redefining their relationship to the state and inventing new strategies for democratic participation.

Not all of these changes occur at the same speed or in the same way, and the new rules are not always clearly drawn. Moreover, some authoritarian political leaders and public officials who feel threatened by the changes taking place are attempting to retrench and resist. In this context, an increasingly competitive, transparent, and democratic system coexists with enclaves of untouchable power, violations of human rights, corruption, patronage politics, and prohibitions on uncovering past wrongs. Mexico, therefore, faces the challenge of developing a framework of formal and informal institutions that can support its new democratic political system and strengthen the capacity of citizens to make demands on the state. It also faces the challenge of balancing the desire for consensus and harmony with the need to account for past wrongs, especially corruption, human rights abuses, and other illicit activities.

The Mexican political system that remained relatively stable from 1929 until the 1980s was based on containing and mediating conflict among diverse competing regional and class interests within a single ruling party. The Institutional Revolutionary Party (PRI) was created in the tumultuous aftermath of the Mexican Revolution (1910–1920) to coordinate and regulate the various factions and regional leaders who had emerged during the revolution. It incorporated most of the social forces in the country, including, officially, the major labor unions, peasant organizations, professional associations, and, unofficially, business and military leaders. The party was based on the ideology of revolutionary nationalism, a broad set of ideas about Mexican nationalism and social justice that could be adjusted to suit the needs of the administration in power. Perhaps most important, the system revolved around its one fixed element, the presidency, which was instilled with metaconstitutional powers to maintain the political arrangements among different sectors and individual leaders.[3]

The PRI also became the vehicle for a series of patronage networks that mediated between citizens and the state and channeled collective action toward ends that were localized and fragmented and thus did not challenge the control of political elites. Citizens contested government policy, but they usually did so through the official organizations within the party or in small independent groups that petitioned the state on local grievances. The National Action Party (PAN) and a few other small political parties competed in elections, with limited success. Occasionally social movements emerged to raise concerns on local issues, although few seriously challenged the hegemony of the PRI. Exceptions, such as the student movement of 1968, the railroad workers' strike of 1958, and several rural rebellions in Morelos and Guerrero, were violently suppressed.[4] The PRI preferred to co-opt when it could and adapt when necessary. It tolerated considerable contestation on specific decisions related to resource allocation, but it did not tolerate challenges to its power as a party or to major national policy decisions.[5]

This political system survived into the 1980s largely because Mexico's strong economic growth and stability created benefits that could be distributed throughout society, even if unequally. The economic crises of the 1980s and 1990s, however, took their toll on the system. Under Mexico's structural adjustment plans, government expenditures fell sharply in the 1980s and remained low in the 1990s.[6] Carlos Elizondo (Chapter 1) argues that the slimmer state was less able to mediate conflicts or maintain its patronage networks. Moreover, GDP growth, which had averaged 6 percent a year over three decades, suddenly slowed to an average of 1.1 percent in the 1980s and 2.7 percent in the 1990s.[7] Real wages dropped 40 percent between 1983 and 1988 and fell even farther in the mid-1990s.[8] Dissatisfaction with the PRI and the government became widespread.

Growing frustration with the government's economic policy and the lack of political space contributed to the rise of new forms of political and civic mobilization in the 1980s and 1990s. In 1983, the PAN won several local elections in Mexico's northern states. In 1985, dozens of independent citizens' organizations emerged to respond to the massive earthquake in Mexico City. Many of these organizations became the base for the political opposition to the PRI in the capital. In 1988, Cuauhtémoc Cárdenas and several other PRI leaders left the ruling party and mounted a significant challenge in the presidential elections of that year. Cárdenas probably won a majority of the vote, but official returns gave the victory to the PRI's Carlos Salinas de Gortari. In 1989, the PAN won its first governorship, which was followed by several other gubernatorial victories in the early 1990s. In Chiapas, indigenous peasants staged an uprising on New Year's Day 1994, under the banner of the Zapatista National Liberation Army (EZLN), in response to centuries of discrimination, political exclusion, and violence.[9] At around the same time, local and national civic organizations formed a prodemocracy coalition, Alianza Cívica, which mobilized more than 18,000 electoral monitors in the 1994 elections to combat voting fraud.

The political and social opposition also benefited from the increasing sensitivity of the Mexican government to outside scrutiny. In the 1980s and 1990s, the Mexican government was eager to show the outside world that it was a nation of laws in order to attract needed investments and demonstrate that it was an equal partner in NAFTA. Groups as different as Alianza Cívica, the PAN, and the EZLN used this sensitivity to increase the pressure for change in the Mexican political system.

The government's search for legitimacy in the face of pressure from the opposition political parties, Alianza Cívica, the EZLN, and other forces in society led to the creation of an electoral board, the Federal Electoral Institute (IFE), in 1994, with wide-ranging authority to set the rules for elections and a series of independent electoral tribunals to resolve disputes.[10] The IFE proved to be a key element in establishing free and fair elections. This set the stage for the congressional elections of 1997, in which the PRI lost its absolute majority in the Congress for the first time while Cárdenas and his left-of-center Democratic Revolutionary Party (PRD) won the mayor's race in Mexico City. This was also the precursor for the 2000 elections in which the PAN's Vicente Fox defeated the PRI's Francisco Labastida for the presidency by a comfortable majority.

Fox's election signals an important shift in Mexican politics. Previously the president had been the central element of the one-party political regime, with his authority serving to mediate disputes among all other political leaders at the national and state levels. Today, however, Mexican politics is fragmented as never before. No party holds a majority in either house of Congress; the president belongs to the PAN; the PRI controls a majority of state governorships; and the PRD governs the capital. In this fragmented polity, it appears that the metaconstitutional powers of the presidency, already somewhat weakened under President Ernesto Zedillo (1994–2000), are eroding even more, which precipitates further shifts in the relationship among the various institutions of politics and government. However, these adjustments have not always been smooth.

The relationship between the Congress and the executive branch was particularly difficult at the beginning of the Fox administration. Until 1997, the first year that the PRI lost its majority in the Congress, the legislators traditionally followed the dictates of the president. Since then, Congress has become an increasingly important player in national political life, often staking out positions quite different from those of the president. However, during the Fox administration to date, the Congress seems mired in factional disputes among and, at times, within parties and has moved very slowly on most major items of legislation. Moreover, the increased authority of the Congress has not been matched by a professionalization of the body. Members of Congress are not eligible for reelection, which reduces their accountability to constituents and their ability to develop legislative skills. As a result, many members seem to see their time in the Congress as a trampoline to other public offices rather than a long-term commitment to policymaking. Nonetheless, the concept of "no reelection" is one of the most sacred tenets of the Mexican Revolution, so this is quite difficult to change despite the interest of many legislators in doing so.

The stalemate in Congress and its rocky relationship with the president also derive in part from realignments going on within the three main political parties. Previously, the PRI's identity had been based on its privileged relationship with the state. It was created more to administer power than to contest it. Adapting to its role as an opposition party has led to indefinition in its ideology and platform and infighting among its leaders. The PAN and PRD both developed as opposition parties, determined to wrest power from an authoritarian system. The PAN has struggled to adjust to its new role as the party in power and often seems to act as though it continued to be in the opposition. Many traditional PAN leaders are distrustful of President Fox, who joined the party only in the 1980s after a career in business. The PRD, by contrast, which played a decisive role in securing the electoral reforms that have made democracy possible, suffered a crushing defeat in the 2000 elections with the emergence of Vicente Fox as the leading anti-PRI candidate. This defeat has left the PRD internally divided and looking for a common platform and leadership to reignite the party's electoral hopes.[11]

During the first year of the Fox administration, the president sought consensus among the major political forces and was often accused of not getting much done. In particular, the government minimized the need for investigating past wrongs committed under previous administrations. As this book goes to print, there are signs that this strategy may be changing. In particular, the administration has shown signs of responding to concerns on human rights by releasing several high-profile prisoners considered by national and international human rights groups as prisoners of conscience.[12] The administration has also taken steps to investigate acts of corruption and human rights abuses committed in previous administrations. Comptroller General Francisco Barrio has announced an investigation into illegal contributions—perhaps as much as $120 million—from the state-owned oil company and oil workers union to the PRI's 2000 presidential campaign. Similarly, at the end of 2001, pressure from citizen organizations forced an investigation by the attorney general's office into killings and forced disappearances that took place in the 1960s and 1970s. It is unclear how far these investigations will go. The debate over how much the administration should seek consensus versus the need to account for past wrongs has finally come to the forefront. It is less certain whether it will remain there.

The relationship between the federal, state, and municipal governments also has undergone a considerable change. Since the 1980s, Mexico's subnational governments have been gaining increasing responsibilities and, in some cases, the resources to carry them out. Although the country is nominally a federation and strong regional identities persist, Mexico has been in reality a highly centralized state since the end of the 1800s. As recently as 1988, almost 90 percent of public expenditures were controlled by the federal government. The process of slimming the state convinced national leaders to transfer some functions, including partial responsibility for education, health care, and social welfare, to the state governments. Moreover, the growth of opposition parties in state and local governments led to increased demands by these governments for more taxation authority and increased federal transfers of funds. By 1998, these subnational governments controlled 29.1 percent of public resources, and additional new responsibilities were transferred to municipalities in 1999 with the passage of a major constitutional reform.[13] In many cases, federal transfers of resources contain detailed conditions as to their use, so subnational governments remain weaker than the total expenditures might indicate. Moreover, not all states and municipalities have the same capacity to raise revenue or administer services effectively. In theory, federal transfers are based on formulas that compensate poorer subnational governments that cannot raise as much revenue locally and may have greater needs; however, in practice the formulas do not always compensate adequately for these disparities and contain historical biases toward major urban areas.[14]

Decentralization has also produced contradictory results for democratic governance. On the one hand, it has created new opportunities for democratic participation at local and state levels, particularly in some urban municipalities. These include participatory planning processes in some urban areas, citizen boards to oversee small community investments, and other innovative strategies to engage citizens. Since the 2000 election, state governors have emerged as an increasingly forceful political force. Although they still largely remain divided along party lines, they have begun to stake out common positions on a few issues. In a country that was strongly centralized for decades, these developments suggest a gradual opening of politics. On the other hand, decentralization is also having the contradictory effect of bolstering authoritarian tendencies in some subnational governments. Leaders who control local political machines have used their greater authority and resources to further entrench themselves, especially in rural areas with vast income disparities. The PRI was created in part to solve the problem of regional factionalism in Mexico. The fragmentation of political power with the end of the one-party regime may have paved the way for the resurgence of regional political elites. The growing strength and autonomy of the federal court may be able to counteract some of the more egregious attempts by subnational leaders to circumvent democratic procedures, but this matter will also require continuous vigilance from national authorities and citizens.[15]

Indeed, the growing strength and independence of Mexico's court system is one of the most striking features of the current process of democratization. Historically, the Supreme Court had largely followed the dictates of the president and rarely, if ever, exercised its power to resolve constitutional questions. The Supreme Court showed an unusual degree of independence under President Zedillo and, since Fox's election, has accepted a series of cases with important constitutional implications that would have been unthinkable a few years before. These have included cases related to federalism, labor law, and indigenous rights. Nonetheless, it is still unclear how far this newfound power to decide constitutional questions extends. Moreover, the advances in independence and integrity made by the Supreme Court have not necessarily been reflected in changes throughout the judicial system, and much remains to be done to strengthen and professionalize lower courts and make their operations more transparent.

Although the increasing independence of the courts has been a hopeful sign, the relative autonomy of the armed forces from civilian control presents a cause for concern. The military continues to be involved in areas of domestic security that are normally reserved for the police, and there are signs that the armed forces have been—and may continue to be—involved in human rights abuses. Raúl Benítez Manaut (Chapter 2) notes that the armed forces played a crucial role after the Mexican Revolution in ensuring cohesion and promoting national development. With their withdrawal from formal politics in the late 1940s, the armed forces negotiated a de facto pact with the civilian authorities: their unconditional support for civilian government in exchange for considerable autonomy of the armed forces from civilian control. Unlike most countries in Latin America, Mexico never suffered a military coup after this pact, and the armed forces remained a bulwark of the PRI-led regime. The government's response to the indigenous uprising in Chiapas, rural rebellions in the state of Guerrero, and the rise of drug cartels in the 1990s gave the armed forces increased prominence in public life. However, the advent of democracy has presented difficult challenges to Mexico's secretive military. Benítez observes that the armed forces' traditional role as a guardian of the political order is no longer consistent with a democratic society. The redefinition of the armed forces' role, however, depends on the willingness of the president to enforce civilian oversight as well as the peaceful resolution of social unrest in rural areas where the military has been given the role of imposing order.

Redefining the formal institutions of governance is only one dimension of Mexico's transition to democracy. A sustainable democratic system needs a vibrant web of social relations and autonomous organizations that generate ideas, keep government accountable, introduce new voices to the political system, and generate horizontal linkages among citizens.[16] Autonomous social organizations also help citizens break down or avoid relations of patronage that keep them tied to the fate of specific political leaders. Historically, most social organizations in Mexico had official or unofficial ties to the ruling PRI. They could often obtain some measure of independence on specific local issues but not on major questions of policy. Social discontent with the worsening economic conditions of the 1980s and the increasing political space afforded by the declining capacity of the government and the PRI to co-opt dissent helped fuel the emergence of hundreds of autonomous social and political organizations. Many organizations that had been part of the PRI or maintained a close relationship with it also began to gain greater margins of autonomy.[17] This is particularly important for the ability of the poorest sectors of society to break free of clientelistic relationships and make claims directly on the government as citizens.

Katrina Burgess (Chapter 3) analyzes the evolution of the labor movement, which historically was tied closely to the state and was one of the pillars of the PRI. As a result, the unions traded their autonomy for a measure of influence in state policy. Workers were generally required to belong to PRI-affiliated unions, whose leaders negotiated deals with businesses and the government on their behalf. Labor unions won some benefits for unionized workers, but they avoided outright confrontation and often accepted conditions that were less than optimal for workers at the government's request. Labor boards were stacked against independent unions and rarely ruled in their favor.

This state-labor alliance began to unravel in the 1980s and 1990s as government austerity measures lowered real wages and alienated traditional labor constituencies. As a consequence, the small independent labor movement grew dramatically and adopted more confrontational strategies. Even PRI-affiliated unions began to experiment with more confrontational tactics. With the PRI no longer in power, the traditional alliance between the state and labor appears to have come to an end. Both the PAN and the PRD have put forth proposals for labor-law reforms that seek to democratize labor relationships, weaken the large unions, and give autonomy to labor boards. Similarly, in 2001 the Supreme Court struck down provisions of the Federal Labor Law that allowed for closed shops, which had helped the large PRI-affiliated labor union to maintain its monopoly of representation in many businesses. Burgess argues that the challenge for labor—as for many other civic organizations—is to find a balance between autonomy and influence in this new era.

In recent years, indigenous organizations have played an important role in Mexico's democratic opening and in redefining their relationship with the state. Mexico's native peoples make up 10–15 percent of the population and have some of the highest indicators of poverty in the country.[18] Indigenous organizations originally began to gain prominence in the 1970s, and they gained increased visibility after the Zapatista rebellion in the southern state of Chiapas in 1994.[19] The 1996 peace negotiations between the Zapatista rebels and the Mexican government provided an opportunity for indigenous leaders throughout the country to meet and develop a common agenda. The negotiations ultimately produced the San Andrés Accord, which grants native peoples a measure of self-governance within their communities.[20] President Zedillo's administration signed the agreement but refused to send it to Congress to be enacted into law. President Fox's first act after his inauguration was to send the agreement to Congress in December 2000. Congress, however, made several changes to key provisions of the agreement, and the bill that emerged was roundly rejected by the Zapatistas and many other indigenous organizations as insufficient. The peace process has remained suspended as a result. However, for the first time Mexico has recognized that indigenous peoples are entitled to specific rights of self-governance, even if these are more limited than many activists would wish.

Indigenous rights legislation is only the beginning of a much larger process of including indigenous communities as full participants in Mexico's development. Rodolfo Stavenhagen (Chapter 4) argues that the Chiapas conflict is "Mexico's most important unfinished business" and that Mexico can be considered truly democratic only when indigenous peoples are fully included in the nation's political and social agenda. He suggests that changes in the laws are likely to help but that the government also needs to address power structures and racist ideologies that maintain the exclusion of indigenous communities.[21] The real challenge will be to make the new rights accorded to indigenous communities effective so that they expand the influence that these communities have on the range of policies that influence them and on the political system itself. Ultimately, this will need to include the ability to control resources, make decisions on self-government, and access state resources for their development.

In recent years, women's organizations in Mexico have had an increasing influence on the role of women in the political, social, and economic life of the nation. Marta Lamas (Chapter 5) notes that gender inequality and violence against women permeate Mexican society. Nonetheless, she argues that rising education levels for women, access to birth control, and struggles for gender equity have led women to strengthen their role in the workplace and in politics. Women now constitute 32 percent of the country's workforce, and they have held high-profile positions in government and politics. Still, they continue to be marginalized in management and in many important spaces of decision-making. Women's activism has been motivated by a context of both machismo and economic inequality, and these dual influences have led women to link questions of economic justice with gender concerns. Moreover, women are increasingly linking demands for democracy in the country with demands for democracy at home. The struggle for women's rights, like the indigenous movements, has benefited from international networks and from Mexico's general move toward greater integration with the wider international community.

Despite the emergence of new civic movements for civil and political rights, as well as the growing autonomy of some traditional PRI-affiliated organizations, civil society in Mexico remains, on balance, highly fragmented and weak. The corporatist structure of the PRI, which dominated social and political relations for decades, has patterned state–civil society relations in ways that have persisted beyond the PRI's hold on power. Ilán Bizberg (Chapter 6) suggests that although social movements organized effectively to challenge the hegemony of the one-party regime, they do not appear to be strong enough to shape the process of democratization and the consolidation of a new political regime. Many of the poorest sectors of society remain tied to organizations of the PRI, and these are likely either to form new alliances with the government in power or simply wither away slowly. Bizberg stresses that a strong and autonomous civil society is critical to the consolidation of a democratic state, but he is skeptical that the current administration understands the importance of strengthening civil society. Although the guarantee of free and fair elections has laid the groundwork of a democratic system, the reconstruction of society and its relationship to the state will help determine the depth and durability of democracy in Mexico.

The Challenge of Development with Equity

Mexico's economy has undergone a profound transformation since 1982. This restructuring has stabilized macroeconomic indicators and seems to have provided some protection against dramatic economic crises in the future, but it has come at the cost of the stagnation of real wages and a growing inequality. The restructuring of the Mexican economy was set in motion by the need to find new strategies to generate investment and growth; the pressure of external lending agencies, which bailed out the flailing economy on condition the government change its policies; and the rise of a new political elite, largely educated in the United States, with a different vision on economic policy. The Mexican government's decision to negotiate NAFTA and to join the World Trade Organization (WTO) has solidified the shift in economic policy.

According to Manuel Pastor and Carol Wise (Chapter 7), three themes have characterized Mexico's economic reform strategy since 1982: the effort to maintain macroeconomic stability; a sharp shift to trade-led development; and a failure to address the "distributional fallout" from the reforms. The debt-backed, state-led growth that characterized the 1950s, 1960s, and 1970s (with 7 percent, 8.6 percent, and 7 percent growth, respectively) could not be sustained in the economic conditions of the 1980s and 1990s. Deep structural reforms in the 1980s sought to remake the Mexican economy by privatizing state companies, encouraging foreign investment, and embarking on export-led growth.

The reforms were partially successful. According to Pastor and Wise, after a series of economic crises and minimal growth in the period 1980–1995, the economy grew by an average of 5.5 percent in the period 1995–2000. However, a closer look shows that most growth has been related to the *maquiladora* sector (foreign-owned manufacturing enterprises), which is concentrated primarily on the northern border, whereas micro-, small-, and medium-sized enterprises have remained stagnant. Similarly, overall wages for workers have also remained stagnant. Real per capita gross national income increased by only 4 percent between 1980 and 2000. At the same time, inequality increased dramatically. The middle sectors of the distributional pyramid lost even more than the poorest sectors, which may explain part of their exodus from the PRI.

Stephen Clarkson (Chapter 8) argues that Mexico's economic reform was imposed both from without and from above. By joining NAFTA and the WTO, Mexican political leaders of the late 1980s and the 1990s ensured that the economy would be profoundly restructured. International trade agreements penetrate deeply into the nation-state, changing aspects of the legal, judicial, and administrative orders. These agreements have direct effects, by superseding existing law and forcing changes to comply with internationally agreed norms; contingent effects, as practices and norms of trade become defined through successive dispute resolutions; and supranational effects, as international bodies develop new rules that affect their members. These processes have a particularly strong effect on a medium-sized country like Mexico, and they help establish an irreversible process of trade integration.

Within the context of these changes, Mexico's rural sector is suffering through one of its worst crises in recent decades. Kirsten Appendini (Chapter 9) observes that rural poverty grew from 49 percent to 53 percent in the 1990s while migration to the United States also increased. Annual average agricultural GDP growth was less than half of that for nonagricultural GDP growth. Despite a dramatic agricultural restructuring initiative in the early 1990s to encourage export agriculture, there have been no noticeable results from this process. She argues that the greatest asset of Mexico's rural producers is their social capital and that they have largely managed to stay afloat in an era of limited state support by creating producers' associations to transport and sell their products at more favorable rates. Indeed, participatory approaches that harness the potential for social organization among Mexico's poorest communities—both rural and urban—may be one of the keys to a successful strategy for reducing poverty. Moreover, Mexico's poor rural and urban communities urgently need credit, infrastructure, and training in order to produce and compete effectively in the market. The risk of social unrest in rural areas of Mexico will likely remain high as long as there is no clear strategy to address poverty.

To address poverty effectively, President Fox and the Congress will need to carry out a substantial fiscal reform. Carlos Elizondo (Chapter 1) notes that Mexico generates tax revenues of 10 percent of GDP, significantly less than it should given its size and level of development. Fiscal reform will be a significant challenge, however, because taxpayers do not necessarily believe that additional taxes will improve government services to them. Therefore, he argues, increased tax revenue will need to be coupled with concerted efforts to increase the efficiency and effectiveness of government expenditures so that people can see palpable results of their tax contributions. However, the nature of the fiscal reform is a thorny issue. The easiest approach to raising revenue is to raise the value added tax or apply it to currently exempt items (food and medicine). Nonetheless, this could have a highly regressive effect on incomes. Creative strategies need to be devised that strike a balance between more efficient collection of tax revenues already mandated and new taxes that do not have an adverse effect on the poorest sectors. At the end of 2001, the Mexican Congress passed a fiscal reform measure designed to raise 1.2 percent more of GDP in taxes by raising taxes on luxury items. This is a promising step (though as with all tax bills, it contained a confusing mix of provisions, some of which are highly counterproductive), but more will clearly need to be done to raise state revenues.

Perhaps Mexico's greatest challenge is to find a comprehensive development strategy that generates both growth and equitable distribution of resources. Gustav Ranis (Chapter 10) argues that Mexico has made considerable strides in recent years by implementing sound macroeconomic policies and clear regulations for foreign direct investment. International agreements make future major policy shifts unlikely, and savings rates have improved. All of this augurs well for Mexico's long-term economic growth. Meanwhile, the Fox government must find a way to address Mexico's unequal distribution of wealth by investing in education, research and development, and in small and medium businesses. Banking and labor market reforms are also pending tasks. Ranis suggests that providing local governments with increased taxation authority would benefit development. To date, decentralization has primarily meant the devolution of responsibilities to the state and local governments without the fiscal authority necessary to raise revenues for these responsibilities.[22]

Mexicans Abroad

On the margins of governments and formal institutions, considerable interchange already exists between Mexico and the United States. Stephen Pitti (Chapter 11) notes that the growth of the Mexican and Mexican-American populations in the United States, along with their ties to people and places in Mexico, have created a Mexican community that transcends the border between the two countries. Ideas, identities, and cultural practices flow and are reshaped within this transnational community. These ties bind specific towns and villages in Mexico to the places where Mexican migrants settle in the United States and, more generally, provide a mechanism for cultural interaction between the two countries.

Increasingly, political action is also taking on a transnational character. Unions have built ties across the border, as have some indigenous organizations and nongovernmental organizations. Although these transborder civil society networks are at an incipient stage, they suggest the possibility of increased coordination in the future.[23] During the 2000 elections, all the major parties actively courted Mexicans living in the United States, and many returned home to vote. Three Mexicans living in the United States even ran for Congress, with one of them winning. Similarly, in 2001 a Mexican living in the United States won the mayor's race in Jerez, Zacatecas.[24] At the same time, U.S. politicians with roots in Mexico have played leading roles in efforts to improve the bilateral relationship.

The Fox administration has sought to tap into the new dynamics of formal and informal exchange among Mexicans on both sides of the border. President Fox has created a special office to serve as a liaison with Mexicans abroad. This initiative has been designed to encourage Mexicans in the United States to invest in their communities of origin, as well as to find ways of improving the treatment of Mexican migrants in the United States. Until the 1990s, the Mexican government, for the most part, had no policy on Mexicans abroad. There was a slight shift in the 1990s with the creation of the Paisano program to assist returning migrants and timid steps taken in the Mexican consulates in the United States to serve as watchdogs for the rights of migrant workers.

However, the Fox administration has taken these efforts to another level. On several of his trips to the United States, President Fox has traveled to cities with large Mexican immigrant populations specifically to meet with Mexicans there. These efforts clearly have an instrumental objective in trying to generate investment and political support from Mexicans and Mexican Americans in the United States, but it also represents a reassertion of the Mexican government's sense of responsibility to its citizens who live outside the country.

Mexican migration to the United States grew rapidly in the 1980s and 1990s as economic crises and increased poverty drove Mexicans to search for work in the north. Robert Bach (Chapter 12) argues that the United States and Mexico need to develop innovative new approaches for managing migratory flows. Drawing on his experience as executive associate commissioner of the INS, he suggests that current enforcement strategies are outmoded and do little to alter the natural patterns of supply and demand. An alternative strategy should include targeted economic development programs to Mexican communities that are a major source of out-migration; the implementation of a campaign for fair wages for farmworkers; an amnesty for undocumented migrants already in the United States; and the development of new bilateral law enforcement partnerships to reduce the flow of migrants.

Many of the proposals that Bach advances have been reflected in recent discussions between the U.S. and Mexican governments. The two governments agreed in early September 2001 on a broad framework that included some form of legalization for undocumented workers already in the United States who could prove a solid work history; a temporary worker program for cyclical workers from Mexico in agriculture and key service industries; greater Mexican enforcement of the border, including a concerted campaign against migrant smugglers; a U.S. commitment to address the elevated number of migrant deaths at the border; and some form of development assistance to regions in Mexico that have high concentrations of out-migration. Negotiations on a bilateral migration agreement were slowed by the September 2001 terrorist attacks on the United States, which led to a reorientation of U.S. foreign policy priorities. However, both sides remained committed to achieving an agreement of some kind on migration. The politics of achieving a compromise acceptable to both sides—including multiple interest groups in both countries—will take a considerable degree of negotiating skill. In the context of the increasing concern in the United States with terrorism, it becomes even more important to regularize the flow of undocumented workers in order to focus enforcement efforts more carefully on potential terrorist threats. At the same time, the heightened concern about terrorism makes it difficult to get a useful discussion of compromise solutions in the U.S. Congress.

Toward a New Partnership with Mexico

The migration agreement is one of several items on an increasingly busy bilateral agenda between the United States and Mexico, an agenda that also includes security cooperation, trade, development, agriculture, and energy. We argue in the Conclusion that the increasing influence of Mexican Americans and Mexicans in the United States, as well as the growing interdependence in trade matters, have contributed to a bilateral relationship that is much deeper and more stable than before. Equally important, the process of democratization in Mexico has given the current Mexican leadership significant credibility in international affairs and allowed it to assume a more active foreign policy. The Fox administration has engaged the United States assertively in bilateral negotiations and pursued multilateral engagements through the United Nations, the Organization of American States, and other institutions. Mexico has emerged from its traditional reluctance to commit itself abroad to become an important agenda-setter in bilateral affairs and a key link between North America and Latin America.

The increased relationship between Mexico and the United States does not mean that the two countries always share common interests; indeed, there are a range of issues on which their governments' positions diverge considerably. However, there is a growing understanding on both sides of the importance of finding common areas of agreement and institutional mechanisms to address areas of disagreement. Mexico cannot be ignored by the United States. Growing ties—both official and unofficial—link our destinies as never before. The purpose of this volume is to describe the significant changes occurring in Mexico and how they shape the relationship between two countries that were once described as "distant neighbors"[25] Today these neighbors are closer than ever and their destinies are increasingly intertwined.

Notes

1. U.S. Census Bureau, "The Hispanic Population in the United States." *Current Population Reports* (March 2001).

2. Trade statistics from the International Monetary Fund, *Direction of Trade Statistics Yearbook* (Washington, D.C.: International Monetary Fund, 1997 and 2001). Figures for trade as a percentage of GDP (1996 figures) from Guadalupe González, "Foreign Policy Strategies in a Globalized World: The Case of Mexico," in Joseph S. Tulchin and Ralph H. Espach, eds., *Latin America in the New Interational System* (Boulder: Lynne Rienner Publishers, 2001), p. 155.

3. Wayne A. Cornelius, *Mexican Politics in Transition: The Breakdown of a One-Party-Dominant Regime* (La Jolla: University of California–San Diego, Center for U.S.-Mexican Studies, 1996), p. 35; Kevin Middlebrook, *The Paradox of Revolution: Labor, the State, and Authoritarianism in Mexico* (Baltimore: Johns Hopkins University Press, 1995), pp. 6–8; Wayne A. Cornelius and Ann Craig, "Houses Divided: Parties and Political Reform in Mexico," in Scott Mainwaring and Timothy Scully, eds., *Building Democratic Institutions: Party Systems in Latin America* (Stanford: Stanford University Press, 1995), p. 517.

4. Many of these suppressed social movements were formative experiences for the leaders who emerged to challenge the PRI's hegemony in the 1980s and 1990s. On clientelism and patronage: Cornelius, *Mexican Politics in Transition,* p. 52; and Middlebrook, *The Paradox of Revolution,* p. 10. On modes of contestation, see Jeffrey Rubin, "Decentering the Regime," in Joe Foweraker and Ann L. Craig, eds., *Popular Movements and Political Change in Mexico* (Boulder: Lynne Rienner Publishers, 1990).

5. The government allowed more representation by opposition political parties in the Congress in the late 1970s, but this was calculated so as to shift increasing opposition into institutional channels while maintaining a PRI majority.

6. Government spending fell 6.9 percent between 1983 and 1988 and then remained constant as a percentage of GDP from 1989 to 1996. Nora Lustig, *Mexico: Remaking of an Economy* (Washington, D.C.: Brookings Institution, 1998), pp. 80–81, 211.

7. World Bank, *World Development Report* (Washington, D.C.: World Bank, 2000), p. 295.

8. They recovered somewhat at the end of the 1990s with a period of sustained growth from 1997 to 2000. Lustig, *Mexico,* pp. 68–69; Enrique Dussel Peters, *Polarizing Mexico: The Impact of Liberalization Strategy* (Boulder: Lynne Rienner Publishers, 2001), chapter 3.

9. Specific direct causes of the Zapatista uprising included falling coffee prices, the elimination of government credits for small rural producers, unresolved land tenure claims, and pervasive discrimination. The region of Chiapas where the rebellion had its strongest support, the Lacandon Forest, had also undergone a dynamic process of organization through successive migrations and the mediating influences of the Catholic Church, Protestant churches, and leftist groups. See Neil Harvey, *The Chiapas Rebellion: The Struggle for Land and Democracy* (Durham, NC: Duke University Press, 1998).

10. The IFE was created in 1990 by an act of Congress, but it was tightly controlled by the government, and chaired by the interior secretary, until a major reform in 1994 gave it virtual autonomy under the leadership of a nonpartisan citizens' electoral council.

11. For a more elaborate description of the changes taking place within the political parties in Mexico, see Yemile Mizrahi, "The Fox Admnistration After One Year in Power," *Woodrow Wilson Center Update the Americas: Mexico,* No. 3 (February 2002), Woodrow Wilson Center Latin American Program.

12. These included General José Francisco Gallardo, first imprisoned after he suggested that the army appoint a human rights ombudsman, and two prominent environmental activists, Rodolfo Montiel and Teodoro Cabrera, in the state of Guerrero, who were accused of links to a guerrilla army. All three had been adopted by Amnesty International as prisoners of conscience, and the Inter-American Commission on Human Rights had forcefully recommended their release.

13. Data taken from Carlos Martínez Assad and Alicia Ziccardi, "Límites y posibilidades para la descentralización de las políticas sociales," in Rolando Cordera and Alicia Ziccardi, *Politicas sociales al fin del milenio: descentralización, diseño y gestión* (Mexico City: Miguel Angel Porrúa, 2000), and Yemile Mizrahi, "Veinte años de descentralización en México: un proceso de arriba hacia abajo," in Phil Oxhorn, Joseph S. Tulchin, and Andrew Selee, eds., *Decentralization, Civil Society, and Democratic Governance* (unpublished manuscript), n.d.

14. John Scott, "Descentralización, focalización y pobreza en México," in Cordera and Ziccardi, eds., *Políticas sociales.*

15. See, for example, the December 2000 issue of *Letras Libres* for a debate on the past and future of *caciques* (local authoritarian leaders) in Mexico, especially the articles by Lorenzo Meyer and Alan Knight.

16. There are several schools of thought on the importance of civil society. Some emphasize its importance in building shared norms and practices among citizens (social capital). Others, including Ilán Bizberg in Chapter 6, emphasize the role of civil society organizations in generating new ideas and expanding citizenship rights. Other approaches look at the link between an active civil society and government's accountability to citizens. For a useful analysis of these arguments and their interrelationship, although focused on the United States, see Mark Warren, *Democracy and Association* (Princeton, NJ: Princeton University Press, 2001).

17. Jonathan Fox, for example, describes the increased autonomy of indigenous social organizations in the state of Oaxaca and shows how a combination of reformist political leadership, outside nongovernmental organizations, and internal leadership and capacity helped these organizations gain greater margins of autonomy. "The Difficult Transition from Clientelism to Citizenship," *World Politics* 46, no. 2 (January 1994): 151–184.

18. Indigenous peoples of fifty-nine ethnic groups make up at least 10 percent of the country's population. Adult illiteracy in indigenous communities is more than four times the national average, and the mortality rate for preschool-age children is almost three times the national rate. Instituto Nacional Indigenista and the World Bank, "National Profile of the Indigenous Peoples of Mexico" (Mexico City: Instituto Nacional Indigenista, 1997). According to former PRI deputy Enrique Ku, only eight of Mexico's 620 members of Congress are indigenous. "Solo ocho legisladores representan a 10 millones de índigenas," *La Jornada,* September 25, 2000.

19. On New Year's Day 1994, a group of masked insurgents, representing dozens of communities in eastern Chiapas, took control of five small towns and one major city and declared war on the Mexican government. The armed conflict between the rebels and the government lasted only twelve days before a cease-fire was declared, but the peace process has dragged on without end since then. On the Chiapas conflict, see Harvey, *The Chiapas Rebellion.* On the history of the indigenous movement, see Jorge Hernández Díaz, *Etnicidad, poder y nación* (Oaxaca: Universidad Autónoma Benito Juárez de Oaxaca, 1993).

20. In particular, the agreement grants indigenous communities a right to use their traditional governance practices in internal matters and to have a say in decisions about the use of natural resources and in development and education policies.

21. Similarly, *The Economist* notes that the legal changes "would mainly formalise what happens already" in terms of indigenous self-governance, though it would also give the communities greater leverage in decisions on the use of resources from and for the communities. "Mexico's Indians, One Nation or Many?" *The Economist,* January 20, 2001, pp. 33–34.

22. Mizrahi, "Veinte años de descentralización en México."

23. See Jonathan Fox, *Assessing Binational Civil Society Coalitions: Lessons from the Mexico-U.S. Experience* (University of California–Santa Cruz, Chicano/Latino Research Center, Working Paper No. 26, April 2000).

24. His election was later overturned based on technical considerations, but his campaign showed an increasing involvement of Mexicans residing in the United States in Mexican politics.

25. Alan Riding, *Distant Neighbors: A Portrait of the Mexicans* (New York: Knopf, 1985).

PART 1

The Politics of Change

1

After the Second of July: Challenges and Opportunities for the Fox Administration

Carlos Elizondo

Since the early 1990s, Mexico's political institutions have undergone a profound transformation. What was an authoritarian system based on the centrality of a president with the discretionary power to punish his enemies, reward his friends, and allocate most political positions—including the choice of his successor—has been substituted with a more limited presidency and strong electoral institutions with the capacity to ensure a fair and legal election. The last step in this process of change was the defeat of Institutional Revolutionary Party (PRI) candidate Francisco Labastida in the July 2, 2000, elections.

This chapter explores the challenges that face the administration of Vicente Fox. In the first section, Fox's victory is analyzed and the short-term challenges to his presidency are discussed. In the second section, some of the structural dilemmas that must be confronted by President Fox are addressed.

The Election

For nearly seventy-one years the PRI, under three different names, was capable of achieving thirteen peaceful transfers of presidential power. Since 1934, this took place every six years through constitutional elections of dubious quality. However, in 2000 clean and uncontested elections gave the National Action Party (PAN) candidate, Vicente Fox, the presidency. Although Fox's victory was greater than anticipated by most analysts, he fell short of winning an absolute majority (see Table 1.1).

Fox is the first non-PRI president in seventy-one years. Even more

Table 1.1 Presidential Election

Candidates	Votes	Percentage
Vicente Fox, Alianza por el Cambio	15,988,740	42.52
Francisco Labastida, PRI	13,576,385	36.10
Cuahutémoc Cárdenas, Alianza por México	6,259,048	16.64
Others	1,779,750	4.73
Total	37,603,923	100

Source: Federal Electoral Institute (IFE), www.ife.org.mx.
Note: Others include blank votes, unregistered candidates, Gilberto Rincon (PDS), and Manuel Camacho (PCD).

significant, for the first time in the history of Mexico, where coups and revolutions have initiated most major changes, the final burial of the old regime through a transfer of power between political parties took place as the result of citizens peacefully casting their votes. Neither heroism from the opposition defending the vote nor violation of citizens' rights by the party in power marked election day. It was just a normal election, as occurs in more advanced democracies, without significant irregularities. Minutes after the last electoral booths closed, exit polls reported by the most important TV and radio newscasts informed Mexicans who had won.

It finally became evident that the electoral institutions, which were built upon more than twenty years of gradual reforms and demanded by an increasingly strong opposition, made a PRI defeat possible as the electorate opted to vote for change. The electoral reform of 1996, which brought about a constitutional reform that enjoyed the support of all the parties in Congress, ensured that votes were counted with the utmost care. The controls probably have no parallel in world history. The electoral process of July 2000 was far more equitable than in the past in terms of money as well as access to the media (Tables 1.2–1.4).

In spite of the deep mistrust that many Mexicans, in particular those who intended to vote for the opposition, had for the country's electoral institutions prior to the election (see Table 1.5), the autonomous Federal Electoral Institute (IFE) demonstrated in the end that each vote counted. President Ernesto Zedillo quickly accepted the defeat of his party, congratulated the future president of Mexico, promised to collaborate in the transition of administrations, and even suggested he would try to convince the PRI to collaborate, a very difficult task indeed.

Table 1.2 Federal Public Budget for the Political Parties Provided by the IFE in 2000

	Millions of Pesos	Percentage
Campaign expenditures	1,469.0	100.0
Alianza por el Cambio (PAN-PVEM)	443.3	30.2
PRI	445.7	30.3
Alianza por México (PRD-PT)	501.4	34.1
Others	78.6	5.4
Ordinary activities	1,469.0	100.0
Alianza por el Cambio (PAN-PVEM)	443.3	30.2
PRI	445.7	30.3
Alianza por México (PRD-PT)	501.4	34.1
Others	78.6	5.4
Total	2,938.0	100.0
Alianza por el Cambio (PAN-PVEM)	886.6	30.2
PRI	891.4	30.3
Alianza por México (PRD-PT)	1,002.8	34.1
Others	157.2	5.4

Source: Reforma, July 17, 2000, and Presupuesto de Egresos de la Federación, 2000.
Note: Others are PCD, PARM, and DS.

Table 1.3 Airtime for the Presidential Candidates on Radio and TV (March 1–June 28, 2000)

	Paid Publicity (seconds)							
	Televisa	%	Azteca	%	Radio	%	Total	%
C. Cárdenas	14,611	27.0	6,354	27.2	13,200	9.7	34,165	16.0
V. Fox	10,810	20.0	4,340	18.5	44,400	32.8	59,550	28.0
F. Labastida	27,176	50.3	11,576	49.5	64,800	47.8	103,552	48.6
Others	1,476	2.7	1,130	4.8	13,140	9.7	15,746	7.4
Total	54,073	100.0	23,400	100.0	135,540	100.0	213,013	100.0
	Informative Coverage (seconds)							
	Televisa	%	Azteca	%	Radio	%	Total	%
C. Cárdenas	30,461	24.7	27,737	20.1	335,280	21.3	393,478	21.4
V. Fox	31,088	25.2	38,217	27.7	528,420	33.5	597,725	32.5
F. Labastida	29,822	24.2	37,877	27.5	435,420	27.6	503,119	27.4
Others	31,868	25.9	33,919	24.6	277,080	17.6	342,867	18.7
Total	123,239	100.0	137,750	100.0	1,576,200	100.0	1,837,189	100.0

Source: Reforma, June, 30, 2000.
Note: Others include Camacho, Rincón, and Muñoz Ledo.

Table 1.4 Opinion of Presidential Candidates on Radio and Television (from January 19–June 3, 2000)

	Informative Coverage (seconds)					
	Televisa			TVAzteca		
	% Neg.	% Neutral	% Pos.	% Neg.	% Neutral	% Pos.
C. Cárdenas	5	49	46	13	54	33
V. Fox	16	57	16	21	39	40
F. Labastida	9	50	41	11	36	53
Others	9	49	41	20	29	51

Source: Reforma, June 30, 2000.
Note: Others include Camacho, Rincón, and Muñoz Ledo.

Table 1.5 Trust in Elections Question: "If after the July 2 presidential elections your candidate would support a different result than the IFE, whom would you believe? IFE or your candidate?"

	% Total	Labastida Voters' %	Fox Voters' %	Cárdenas Voters' %
IFE	57	47	37	13
Candidate	29	33	46	18
None	4	31	35	26
Don´t know	10	51	32	12

Source: Reforma, June 22, 2000.

The money spent by the IFE to organize and control the elections, plus the public financing of political parties through the IFE, amounted to a significant expenditure of resources by the central government (see Table 1.6). However, it was money well spent. For the first time in history, it gave Mexico an unquestionably fair election and minimized the risk that private money of dubious origin would finance the campaigns. The risk of a fraudulent election carried a much greater cost.[1] And in the coming years, democracy should gradually become less expensive.

The gentle acceptance of Fox's victory by a PRI president, plus the recognition of Francisco Labastida's defeat, is the result of a long history of electoral reform. Although the PRI tried hard not to lose control over the process, an increasingly strong opposition forced Mexico's ruling party to yield enough ground through reforms to allow them a fair chance in the electoral game. The PRI slowly gave society more politi-

Table 1.6 Expenditure on the Federal Electoral System and Judicial Branch (% Central Government Budget)[a]

	Justice	Attorney General of the Republic (Procuraduría general de la Republica) PGR	Judicial Branch[b]	Federal Electoral Institute[c]
1991	0.69	0.29	0.41	0.85
1992	0.98	0.51	0.47	0.74
1993	0.95	0.47	0.48	1.06
1994	1.03	0.53	0.50	0.97
1995	1.02	0.50	0.52	0.46
1996	1.08	0.46	0.62	0.55
1997	1.24	0.49	0.74	1.00
1998	1.47	0.53	0.93	0.52
1999[d]	1.46	0.54	0.92	0.50
2000[e]	1.57	0.57	1.00	1.04

Sources: Web page of the Secretaria de Hacienda y Créditc Piblis, www.shcp.gob.mx; INEGI, "Cuaderna de infaración oportuna" (Aguascalientes, Mexico: INEGI, several years); *Presupuesto de Egresos,* 2000 (Mexico: Secretaría de Hacienda y Crédito Público, 2000); and *5 to Informelde Gobierno del Presidento Ernesto Zedillo* (Mexico: Presidencia, 1999).

Notes: a. In Spanish, "Gasto programable," which means the federal expenditure excluding debt service and grants to states and municipalities.

b. Includes only the application of Justice.

c. This includes the Federal Electoral Institute, the federal Electoral Tribunal, and the Federal Electoral Registry, which were established in 1991. From 1997 it includes only the IFE. From 1998 the recently created Tribunal Electoral del Poder Judicial is included in the figures for the Judicial Branch. For the year 2000, the budget rose to 1,352 million pesos (.17% of central government budget).

d. Estimate.

e. Forecast.

Table 1.7 Rural and Urban Votes for Presidential Candidates, 2000

	Labastida	Fox	Cárdenas	Others	Total	%
Total votes	13,576,385	15,988,740	6,259,048	957,455	36,781,628	100
	36.91%	43.47%	17.02%	2.60%	100.00%	
Rural	4,539,687	2,689,065	1,956,502	167,998	9,353,252	25.4
	48.5%	28.8%	20.9%	1.8%	100.0%	
Urban	9,036,698	13,299,675	4,302,546	789,457	27,428,376	74.6
	32.9%	48.5%	15.7%	2.9%	100.0%	

Source: IFE, www.ife.org.mx.
Note: Excludes blank votes.

cal space in order to avoid a radicalization of the opposition, which threatened to encourage extra-institutional political participation, such as blockades, strikes, and even guerrilla movements.

These electoral reforms allowed the opposition to gradually gain power at the municipal and state levels.[2] By 1996, the government was convinced that political pressures could only be dealt with by yielding control over the electoral process to a completely autonomous institution, the IFE, and by renouncing the most salient inequalities of the electoral process.[3]

More profound structural changes explain the change of electoral rules as well as the acceptance of defeat. After decades of modernization, by the end of the 1960s Mexico saw the emergence of a middle class that was increasingly difficult to accommodate within the corporatist structure of the PRI. After the deep crisis of 1982, a severe fiscal austerity weakened the patronage system used by the president to cement the alliance of diverse social groups behind the PRI. It is no coincidence that the first major electoral defeat of the PRI came in the local elections of 1983, when the PAN gained power in several major cities in the north.

An economy based on trade protection and regulation, both powerful tools to maintain political loyalties among businessmen and workers, was substituted first by adhesion to the General Agreement of Tariffs and Trade and then to the North American Free Trade Agreement (NAFTA). Deregulation in many areas further weakened the patronage capacity of the Mexican bureaucracy. Mexicans are now more dependent on the markets than on government subsidies and regulations. Businessmen who financed Fox since the beginning of his campaign are less prone to pressure the government than in the past.

Throughout his *sexenio* (six-year term), Zedillo made clear his intention of respecting the vote. The opposition increasingly won positions in local elections during Zedillo's administration. Zedillo also faced a major economic crisis in 1995, which damaged the credibility of his party and of his presidency. The crisis also demonstrated the need to maintain healthy public finances, as markets were aware of the cost of past imbalances. In the last year of his sexenio, the president had to be particularly cautious to ensure austere public finances, as he knew all too well the cost of another new end-of-sexenio crisis. Zedillo perceived that his most important legacy would be to leave the country in a situation of economic stability at the end of his sexenio.

Today, society is more open and better informed, and the capacity of the PRI machinery to mobilize people, even in rural areas, has been seriously challenged by the legislative changes as well as by international observers and stronger opposition parties in rural Mexico. Participation was lower in those states that have traditionally been strong supporters of the PRI and where Labastida performed better (see Figure 1.1). If the PRI had mobilized the same level of participation in these states as in the more urbanized states, the outcome might have been different. The greater capacity of the opposition to mobilize traditional PRI voters meant that the Alianza por el Cambio, Fox's PAN-led coalition, had more than half as many votes as the PRI in the rural areas and more support than Cuauhtémoc Cárdenas. Fox even won a majority of the rural votes in some of the states that the PAN already governed (see Figure 1.1 and Table 1.8).

With no end-of-sexenio crisis, Fox had the advantage of starting his government without needing to impose an austerity program to cope with an economic crisis. His political capital could have instead been used to promote new reforms, not wasted in confronting a deep recession. This is a luxury no Mexican president has had since 1970, when Luis Echeverria inherited an economy that had grown with stability for more than twelve years. Echeverria, however, still faced the profound political crisis resulting from the 1968 student movement that ended in bloodshed.

It can be argued that democracy does not necessarily imply that an opposition party reaches power. What matters is that there are civil liberties and fair conditions for competition and that the party in government can, in principle, be defeated. These three conditions currently exist in Mexico, as we now know, although the opposition was only able to accept this once the PRI was defeated.

Fox's victory makes the existence of democracy undeniable. As shown in Figure 1.2, most Mexicans now accept that their country is a democracy. Defeating the PRI in clean, peaceful, and fair elections gives Fox the legitimacy bonus that comes with a democratic government. He has started with strong authority, with the capacity to directly demand the support of his followers to promote reforms, even if they affect strong interest groups in the short run.[4] Coming from a different party allows him to deal more effectively with old complicities within the system and to inform society of the costs of policies devised to favor specific interest groups .

The United States and other world powers demonstrate greater confidence in a regime that more closely resembles the standard conception of democracy. If Carlos Salinas de Gortari created a honeymoon with world markets based on the idea that Mexico had finally become mar-

Figure 1.1 Fox/Labastida Ratio of Votes Versus Electoral Participation by State

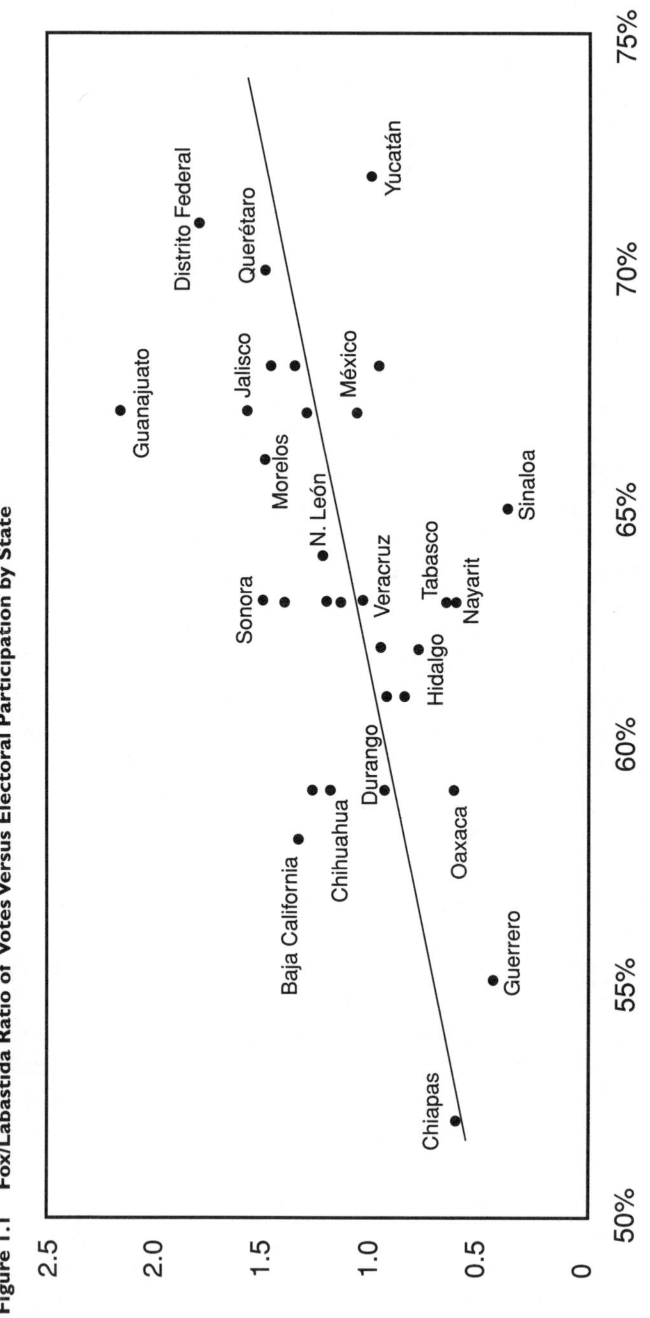

Source: Developed by author with data from the IFE.

Table 1.8 Distribution of Preferences According to Voters' Profiles, in % (July 2000)

	Labastida	Fox	Cárdenas	Others	% of the Sample
Total	36	45	17	2	100
Education level					
University	22	60	15	3	15
Baccalaureate	28	53	16	3	21
Secondary	34	49	15	2	22
Primary	46	35	18	1	34
None	46	30	21	3	8
Gender					
Male	32	47	20	1	52
Female	40	43	14	3	48
Age					
55 or older	42	34	23	1	13
45–55	38	45	16	1	14
35–45	36	44	16	4	24
25–35	34	48	15	3	31
18–24	32	50	17	1	18

Source: Exit poll, *Reforma,* July 3, 2000.

ket-oriented and by presenting leadership with a global vision rather than traditional *priista* nationalism, Fox can create a positive view of Mexico by underscoring his democratic and entrepreneurial credentials.

For the first time in many years, Mexico was on the front pages of major international newspapers and magazines not as a result of a major scandal, such as corruption, violence, or economic crisis, but with positive expectations for the future government. Even Jesse Helms, a conservative senator and long-time foe of Mexico, promoted an official congratulation of the U.S. Senate to Fox and Zedillo in the belief that the United States would finally have a partner that could be trusted.[5]

During the five-month transition period, President Fox faced the immediate challenge of quickly constructing links with high- and middle-level bureaucrats to ensure continuity of government functions. President Zedillo promised to collaborate in the transition between administrations, starting a more transparent process of relinquishing the administration and receiving praise from Fox for this democratic and nonpartisan approach. The transition between the administrations was one of the most professional and transparent in Mexican history.

The electorate did not deliver Fox a blank check. In both chambers

Figure 1.2 Do You Consider Mexico a Democracy?

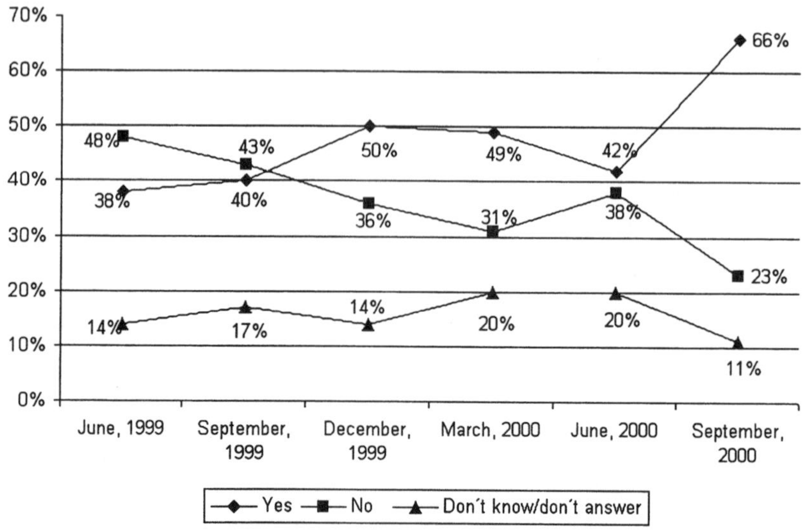

Source: Reforma, September 10, 2000.

of the legislature the PAN lacks a majority. In the Senate, where members are elected for a six-year period, the PRI is even a larger party. In order to legislate, Fox needs the cooperation of the PAN's partner in the Alianza por el Cambio, the Green Ecology Party of Mexico (Partido Verde Ecologista de México, or PVEM), and/or that of the PRI or the Democratic Revolutionary Party (PRD; see Table 1.9).

Structural Challenges

In this section I move to some of the more structural challenges facing the Fox administration. The Mexican political and economic system has undergone a profound transformation. The economy is now market-oriented and the political process democratic. Despite the absence of some sort of Moncloa Pact, as in Spain, or an electoral coalition of the opposition to defeat the tyrant, as occurred in Chile, the slow but incremental transition avoided a collapse of the entire system, as in some Eastern European and Latin American transitions.[6] There was no evacuation of a foreign army, as in East Germany or Czechoslovakia, or a military defeat, as in Argentina, that left the government helpless. On the morn-

Table 1.9 Senators and Deputies According to Party Affiliation

	Total Senators	% of Votes[a]	% of Seats	Distortion of Representation (%)
Alianza por el Cambio	50	38.99	39.06	0.07
PAN	45		35.16	
PVEM	5		3.91	
PRI	59	37.60	46.09	8.49
Alianza por México	19	19.29	14.84	–4.45
PRD	17		13.28	
PT	1		0.78	
PSN	0		0.00	
CD	1		0.78	
PAS	0		0.00	
Total	128		100	

	Total Deputies	% of Votes[a]	% of Seats	Distortion of Representation (%)
Alianza por el Cambio	224	39.14	44.80	5.66
PAN	207		41.40	
PVEM	17		3.40	
PRI	211	37.79	42.20	4.41
Alianza por México	65	19.14	13.00	–6.14
PRD	50		10.00	
PT	7		1.40	
PSN	3		0.60	
CD	3		0.60	
PAS	2		0.40	
Total	500		100	

Source: IFE.
Notes: a. Excludes null votes of total.

ing of July 3, 2000, Mexicans awoke in a democratic country. A silent transition from a peculiar authoritarian system had been completed.

However, throughout this long process of political and economic reform, the state's capacity to regulate conflict and promote welfare was seriously damaged. Salinas's state reform was meant to lead to a smaller, but stronger, state capable of ensuring propitious conditions for economic growth. This promise is still unfulfilled. The economy has been growing steadily since 1996, but only since the acute 1995 peso crisis. In fact, gross domestic product (GDP) per capita in 1999 was close to the same level as it was in 1981 (Figure 1.3).

Within the realm of the state, the government and its remaining public enterprises function with problems. Powerful trade unions and

Figure 1.3 GDP Per Capita (1993 pesos)

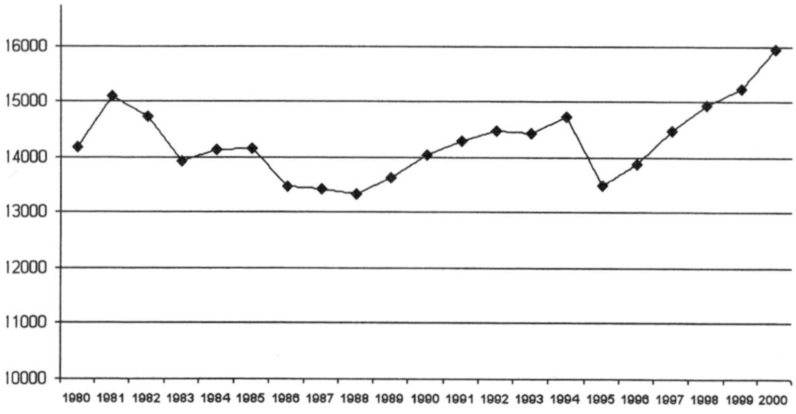

Source: Hugo Ortiz Diet, México, Banco de Datos, 1999, El Inversionista Mexicano, INEGI, and CONAPO. The 2000 data considers first-semester GDP and the estimated population by CONAPO, which is bigger than the one reported in the Censo de Población y Vivienda of INEGI 2000.

political considerations impede a more efficient administration. The middle- and lower-level bureaucracy is inefficient, is poorly paid, and suffers from systemic corruption in some areas. The prices of some goods provided by the public sector, such as domestic electricity and water supply, are lower than their costs, creating the potential for serious bottlenecks that can make sustainable growth difficult. The state has many debts, both financial and social, but has a weak capacity for tax collection.

Within society many people depend on the informal economy, and crime is widespread and growing, eroding the political system (see Figure 1.4).[7] Diverse social groups have their own privileges. The rich have bodyguards that carry illegal weapons, and they close the streets of their homes to public access. Some poor neighborhoods protect residents who rob or kill outside their community from being captured by the police, yet they can set fire to a person who is believed to have committed a crime within the community. Some parts of Mexico are modern and competitive, capable of exporting relatively sophisticated manufactured goods throughout the world; others survive by selling stolen goods or by growing insufficiently productive agriculture.

The challenges remaining are quite complex. The democratic institutions that are emerging in a peaceful way still have to show they are

Figure 1.4 Crimes Per 100,000 Citizens in Mexico, 1980–1997

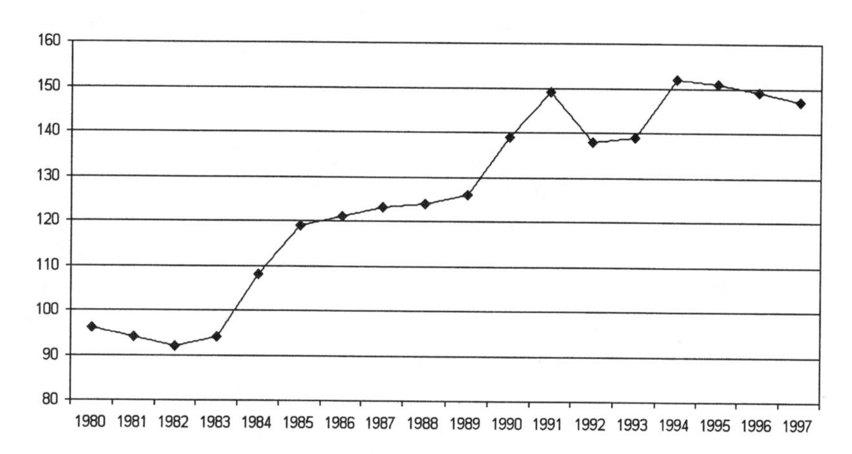

Source: Estadisticas Judiciales, INEGI.

capable of coping with the very serious demands of Mexican society. Power in a democracy is more dispersed and limited by social organizations, the media, and institutions such as IFE. This will fortunately make the misuse of power less likely. However, this now democratic and legitimate power has to be capable of delivering the public goods demanded by society and of imposing the costs of sustaining economic growth on some groups of society.

So far, the transformation of the Mexican political system has occurred within the limits imposed on the presidency by a new economic model—paradoxically imposed by the PRI presidency since 1985, though essential to avoiding a tax crisis—and a more plural distribution of political power with respect to Congress, federal entities, and municipalities, resulting from more just electoral laws and strengthened opposition parties. However, except for the electoral law and some changes in the judicial system, the institutions defining the responsibilities of the president have remained virtually untouched.

These institutions worked during the days of PRI dominance because the president controlled the PRI, and the PRI controlled the Congress, at least until 1997. The president was very strong, not because his legal attributions were larger than in other presidential systems but because the PRI dominated most of the country's political space.

In fact, in many areas, such as the process for approving the budget, the actual rules give more power than other constitutions to the lower chamber, the Chamber of Deputies, which is solely responsible for the budget. The president cannot veto the budget approved by the deputies, and there is no provision in the event that there is no agreement in the lower chamber by year's end. Neither is there any provision for what would happen if both chambers failed to approve a new tax law, which would impede the government from collecting income.

I will not discuss the details of the changes needed, but I do not think that these changes should be based only on the fashionable idea of enhancing the power of Congress or the states. The presidency should have veto power over the budget, perhaps even a line-item veto; both chambers should have a say on budget and taxes; and if an agreement cannot be reached, a mechanism to resolve the problem needs to be devised. For its part, Congress should develop greater technical capacity in this area, because the treasury dominates the timing, information, and analysis of budgetary discussions. Reelection should be considered as an option to increase the capacity and responsibility of Congress.

So far we have not faced a major budgetary crisis that could trigger volatility in the financial markets, since the PAN acted in a way that is consistent with its conservative constituency during the second half of the Zedillo administration, when the PRI lost control over the lower chamber. The lack of adequate rules in budgetary and tax issues is, however, important, as Fox's party did not gain control over Congress. Constitutional reforms to confront these uncertain rules are difficult to implement, precisely because no party has a majority even to enact normal laws. Prior to the election, when no one knew who would win, new rules would have been easier to implement, as the veil of ignorance over the future, to borrow John Rawls's metaphor, made just agreements easier to reach.[8] Now the PRI and PRD are likely to oppose any of the changes needed to decrease uncertainty, as these changes will diminish their legislative power at the end of the year when the budget and the tax law have to be approved by Congress.

Other rules that should be modified are those governing the fiscal relations between states and the federation as income and spending responsibilities are divorced, and the constitutional rules defining who succeeds the president if he dies, just to list some of the changes still needed.[9] I am sure many other articles could be improved, and many voices have quickly concluded that a new constitution should be written. The 1917 constitution, it is argued, was created and adapted through a series of reforms for an authoritarian world now dead. Few changes to adapt the constitution to the new situation of plurality have taken place, except for those dealing with elections and the integration of both chambers.

Some of Fox's allies have been vocal defenders of a major constitutional reform. Such a course of action is difficult to implement, as the PRI has more than the one-third of votes needed to block any reform of the constitution. Fox, however, could be tempted to seek a more grandiose route to reform, such as convening a constitutional convention, though such a decision, without the acceptance of Congress, would be illegal. Hopefully this will not happen, especially as Fox's victory was the result of strong electoral institutions; the cost of undermining them would be high.

However, it is a very common Mexican solution to radically transform the constitution when a new era begins and differences have become deeper. This is ironic due to the well-known difficulties of respecting a new constitution once it is enacted. Mexico's relationship with the rule of law is, to say the least, ambiguous. These difficulties in enforcing the law are in part the result of grandiose schemes that have usually accompanied constitutional reforms.

Once a constitutional assembly is formed, its members fight forcefully for approving very politically correct laws, such as giving more power to the Congress, to the states, to nongovernmental organizations, and granting more generous social rights to everyone. However, a new constitution is usually very difficult to adapt to the restrictions of governing a complex and unequal society such as Mexico.

In fact, more than new laws, the challenge is enforcing the ones already in place, and making the relevant reforms for improving the mechanics of the legal process, although what is wrong here has not been adequately studied. In the area of criminal law, the fashion in recent years has been to increase the punishment for serious offenses, but the problem is punishing serious criminals at all. Only a small fraction of the crimes reported by society to the authorities, already a small proportion of all crimes committed, are solved (see Figures 1.5 and 1.6).

This incapacity to impose the rule of law is a serious challenge due to the administrative weakness of the state, its feeble legitimacy, and the very lax attitude of Mexican society with respect to the law (see Figure 1.7).

The problem is not only to give more certainty to society so that the authorities will not abuse their powers, which is a serious problem in the more backward regions of Mexico; even more important is the need

Figure 1.5 Resolved Cases for Reported Crimes in Mexico City, 1990–1996 (percentage of total)

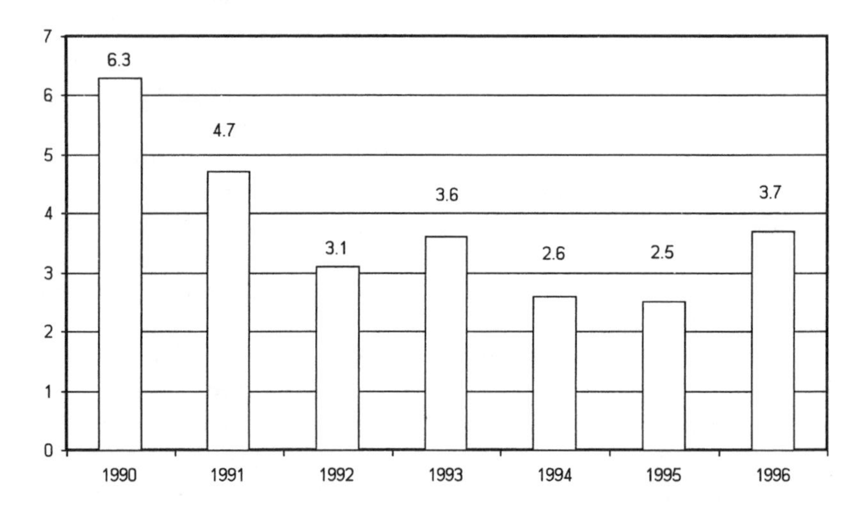

Source: Inge Lore Mascher, in *Este País*, no. 106 (January 2000).

Figure 1.6 Resolved Cases for Reported Crimes, 1994 (percentage of total)

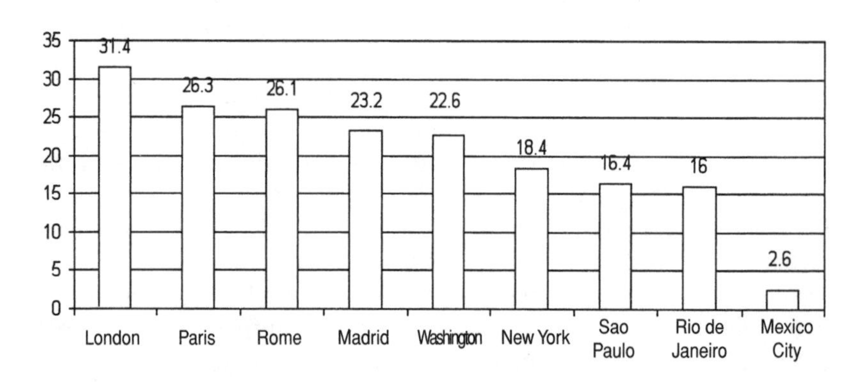

Source: Inge Lore Mascher, in *Este País*, no. 106 (January 2000).

to ensure society that impunity for criminal members of society will not be the norm.

The secular laxity with respect to enforcement of the rule of law is aggravated by the problems that come with drug trafficking. The Mexican mafias have the money and the coercive power to corrupt

Figure 1.7 Citizen Attitudes Toward the Law Question: "Which of the following statements do you agree with?"

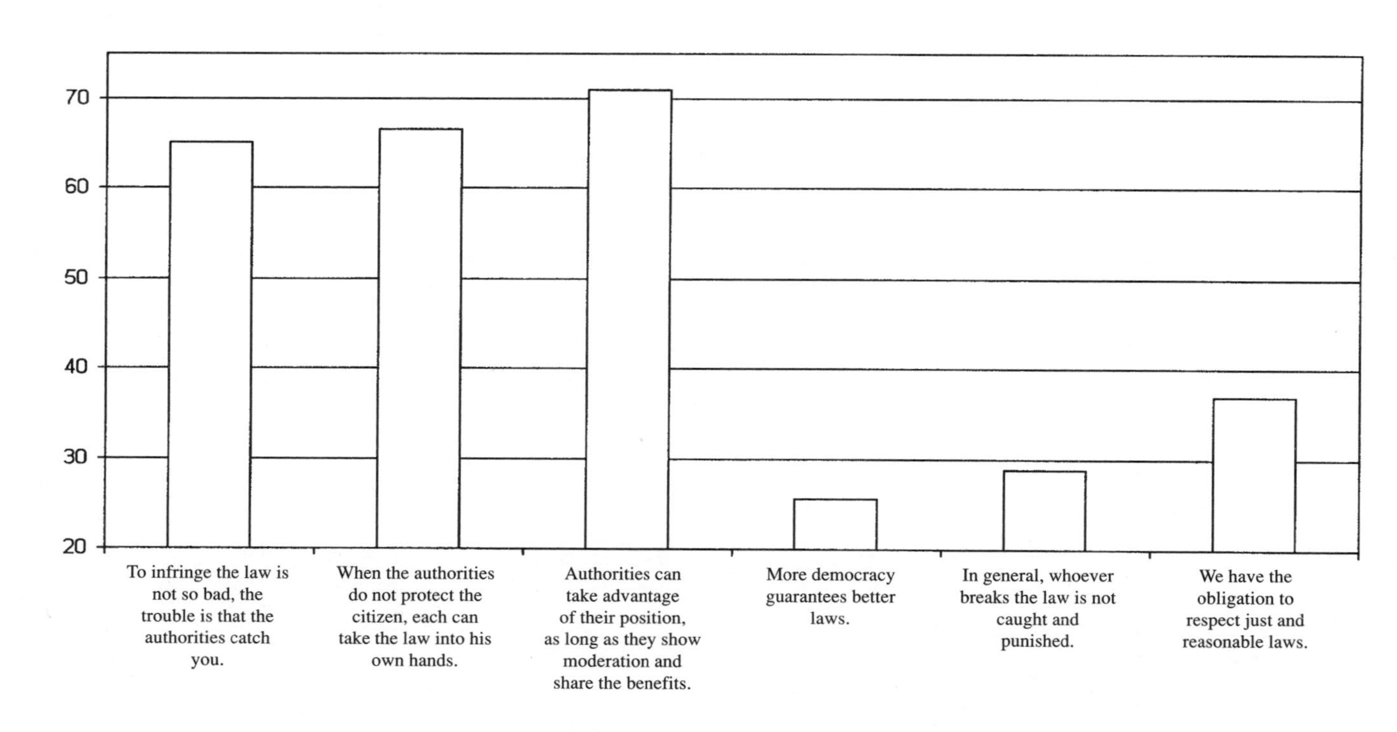

Source: Alduncin y Asociados, August 1995, in *Este País,* no. 80 (November 1997).

judges and policemen or to kill them if they refuse to be bought. Due to the addictions of U.S. citizens and the nonliberal institutions that regulate their decision to consume drugs, Mexican society confronts a challenge that seems to go beyond its institutional capacities. This can easily erode efforts to confront the very serious problems of public security that have appeared with the destruction of the authoritarian machinery that was also a mechanism of social control.

Finally, I address what I think is the most serious challenge confronting the Fox administration: very weak tax collection. Latin America has a very low rate of tax collection for its level of GDP per capita and its demographic, social, and political conditions. On average, the deficit is around 8 percent of GDP.[10] Within Latin America, Mexico's tax capacity is one of the lowest (see Figure 1.8). In spite of very serious efforts to create a more neutral tax law that will also increase revenue, since the early 1980s tax collection has remained virtually unchanged (see Figure 1.9).

Throughout Mexico's history, a weak tax base has been a difficult restriction. This has led to perennial public deficits that in the nineteenth century ended in coups (often led by unpaid soldiers) or, in the 1970s, ended in the debt moratorium. In these periods of long stability enjoyed by the country, fiscal weakness was compensated by controlled spending, leaving social demands unattended to later create serious political problems. The most extreme example of this was the Porfiriato. The budget was balanced for decades, but 70 percent of Mexicans were illiterate, just to mention one of the various social problems not confronted by the government. A balanced budget can create a politically unmanageable social deficit.

Since the spending excesses that led to the debt moratorium of August 1982, the government has once again controlled spending. However, even subtracting the income that comes from PEMEX, but excluding gasoline taxes so as to compare only income derived from society through taxes, there has been a primary surplus from 1987 to 1995. This means that the taxes collected from society, due to debt commitments that come from the past, are greater than public expenditures. But because the quality of expenditure is usually poor, the result is a very low provision of public goods when compared to the taxes collected (see Figure 1.10).

Raising taxes is therefore difficult, as taxpayers do not perceive the benefits of their taxes. Social spending in Mexico is around 4 percent of GDP lower than what would be expected for its income level.[11] Without more public resources, the inequalities of Mexican society, where a rel-

Figure 1.8 Tax Revenue and GDP Per Capita in Latin America and the Caribbean (average, 1994–1996)

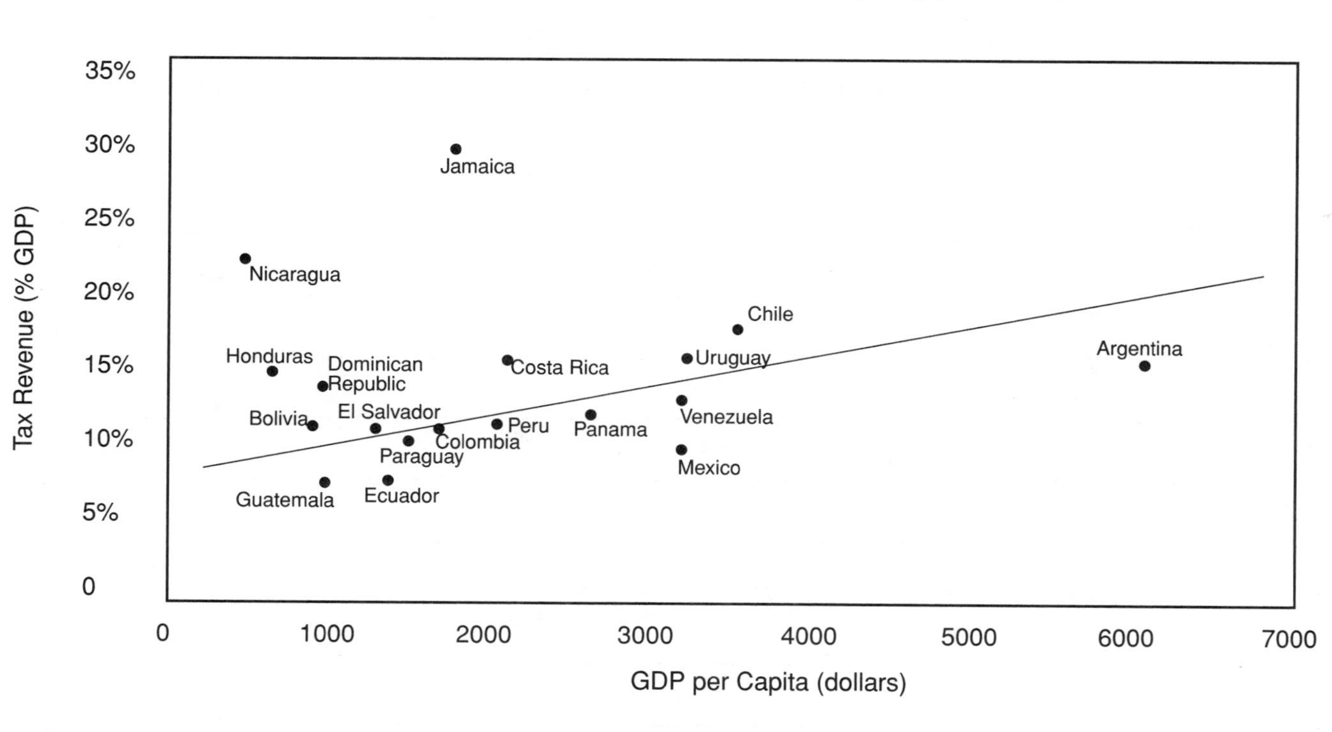

Source: América Latina frente a la desigualdad 1998–1999, International Development Bank.
Note: Excludes Social Security.

Figure 1.9 Federal Government's Revenues in Mexico, 1980–2000 (% GDP)

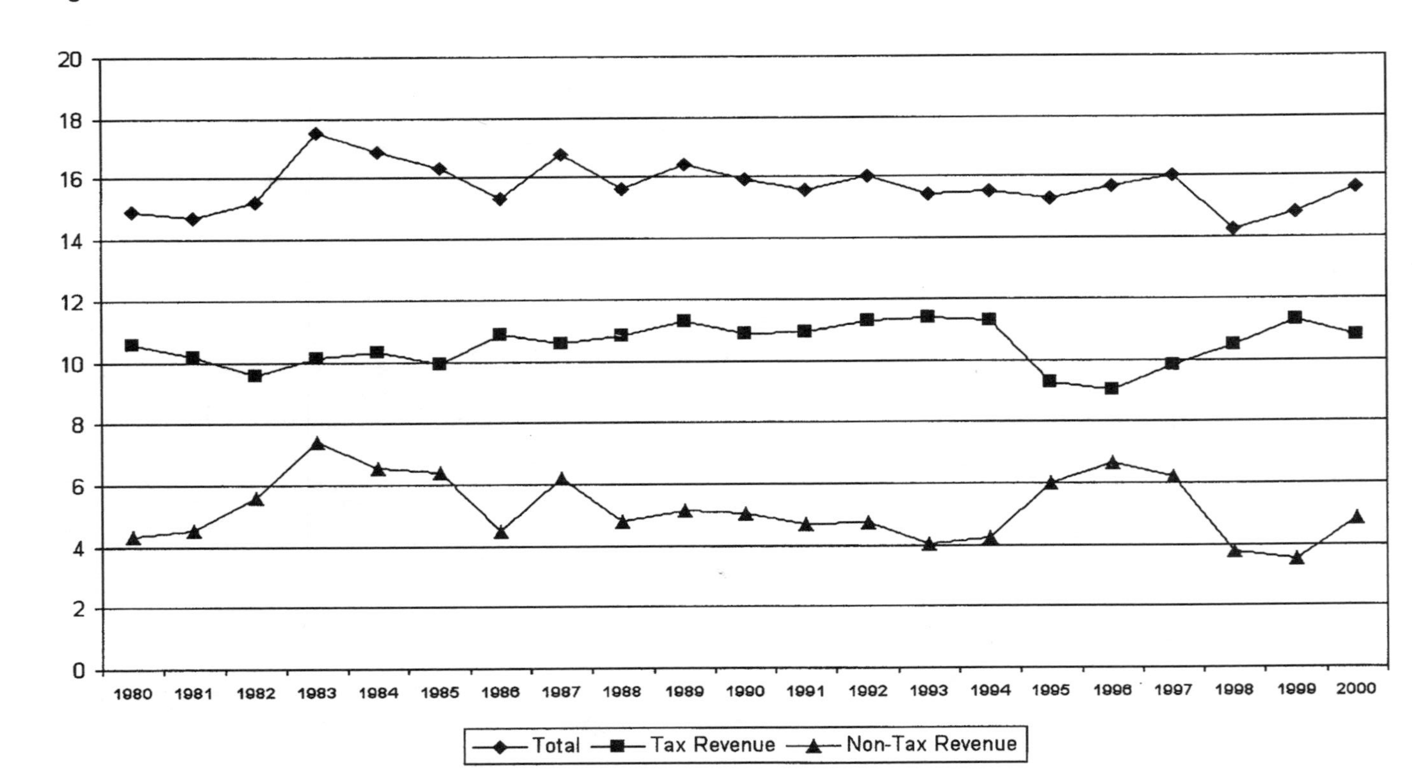

Source: Secretaria de Hancienda y Crédito Público, www.shcp.gob.mx.
Note: Data for 1999 are an estimation and 2000 data are forecast.

Figure 1.10 Primary Public Balance, 1977–1999 (% GDP)

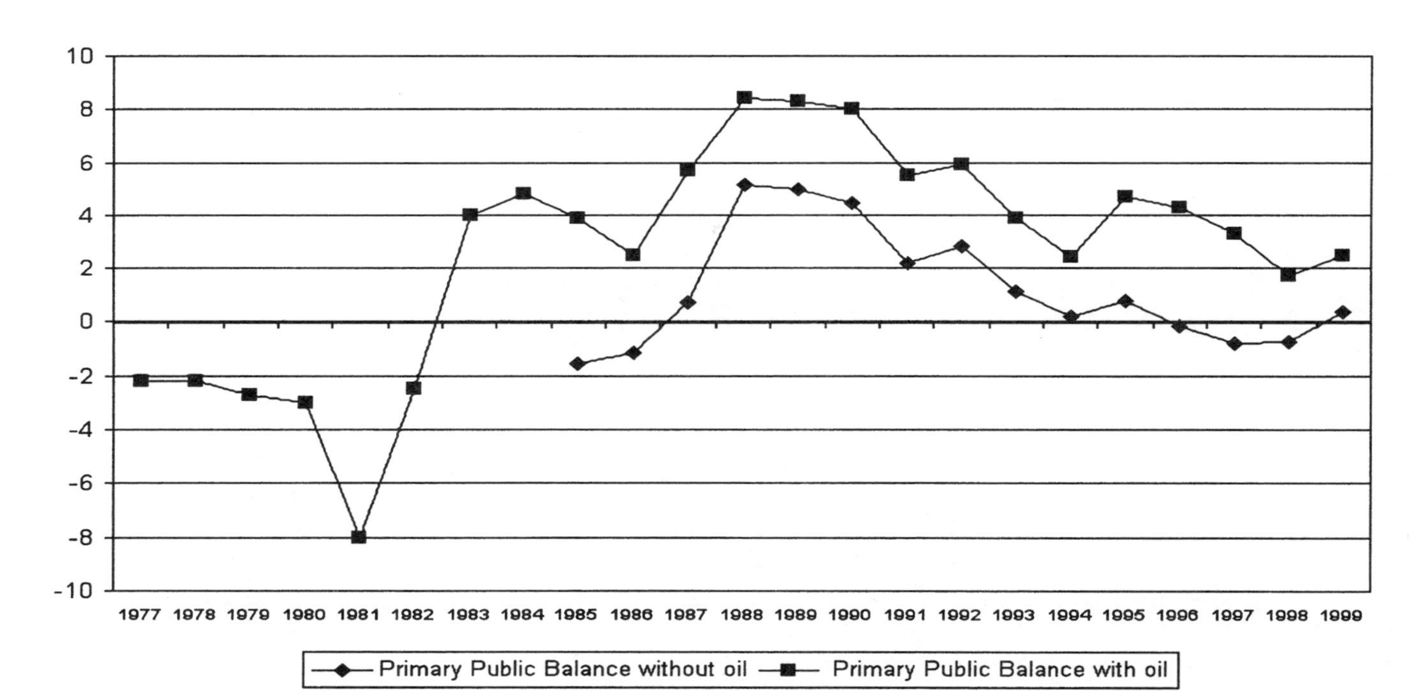

Source: Banco de México (*The Mexican Economy*) (Mexico: Banco de México, several years, and electronic database www.bancodemexico.gob.mx), Banamex (*Review of the Situation of Mexico*) (Mexico: Grupo Financiero Banamex-Accival, various months), and INEGI (electronic database, www.onigi.gob.mx).

Note: Oil revenues refer to rights paid by PEMEX and exclude gasoline tax and PEMEX VAT.

atively low GDP per capita implies that significant numbers of Mexicans live in poverty, will persist even under the most optimistic growth scenario.[12]

There is no easy answer to confronting the acute inequalities of Latin American societies. More public spending in itself is not a solution. In fact, a serious analysis is needed to determine where the state could give space to the private sector, such as in the electric sector, and to identify mechanisms that ensure social spending is progressive.[13] It is a challenge to break the inefficiencies that result from an administration that has worked with a political rather than a technical logic and where there are very strong trade unions in areas where the government will have to invest more resources, as in education.

More high-quality spending can make a difference. But even if the quality of spending improves, many obligations remain from the past, such as servicing the debt, including the banking rescue, as well as financing the old pension system and the public-sector pension, which is increasingly in the red. The resources left for investing more in people and in the public goods needed by a democracy and by a growing economy are insufficient. A democracy permits more actors to satisfy demands through political mobilization. Ideally this occurs inside the law, but that is not always the case. Every day, more actors will use blockades and other illegal tactics, and the government cannot do much except meet their demands in part, but it needs tax resources. This need for increased revenue can be met by introducing a tax-law reform while

Table 1.10 Public-Sector Liabilities (% of estimated GDP, 1999)

	%
Domestic debt	10.4
Foreign debt	19.3
Total debt	29.7
ISSSTE (Institute of Social Security and Services for Civil Servants)	15
IMSS (Mexican Institute of Social Security)	50
Infonavit	1.9
IPAB (Institute for the Protection of Bank Savings)	10.3
Trusts (Fideicomisos) and development funds	6.5
Pidiregas	2.5
State debt	3
Other liabilities	89.2
Total	118.9

Source: Informe Económico Grupo Financiero Bancomer (November–December 1999).
Note: These figures are estimates.

Figure 1.11 Income Concentration and Acceptance of Democracy

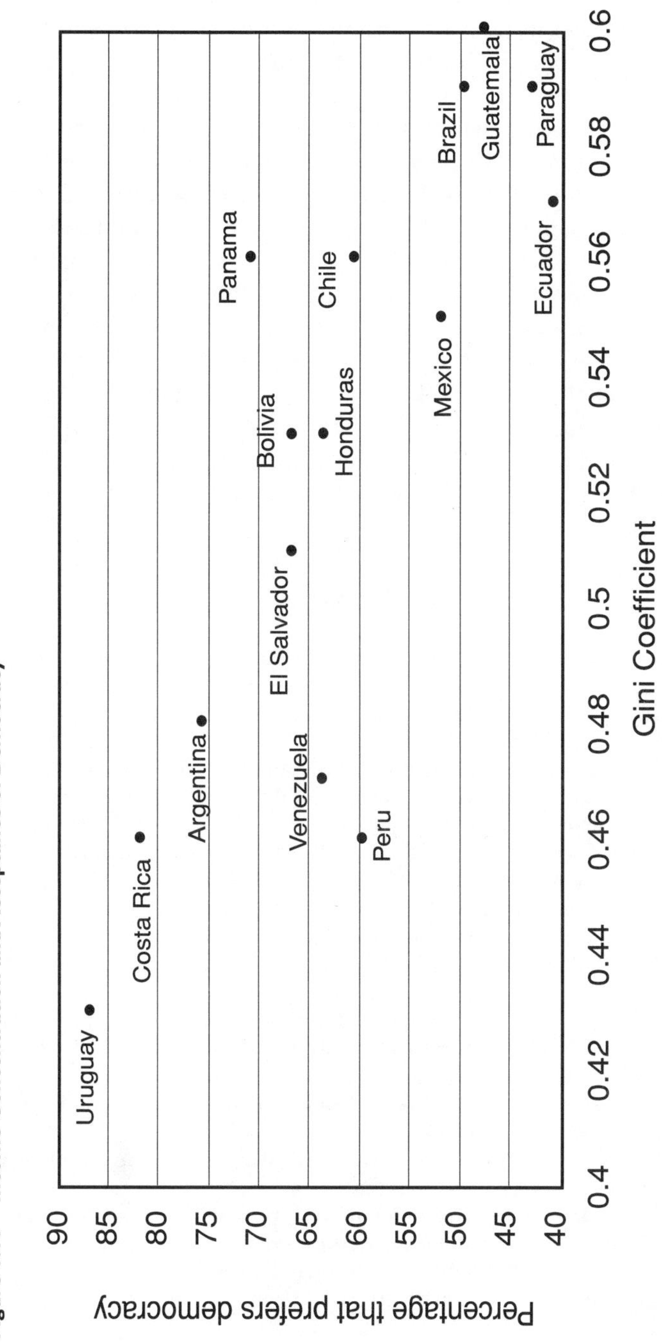

Source: Inter-American Development Bank, *Facing Up to Inequality in Latin America*, IADB Report 2000, figure 1.22 (Washington: IADB, 2000).

making public spending more efficient and transparent, or else the government will have to limit its capacity of responding to demands. The excess income from high-priced petroleum could help, but only in the short term.

Figure 1.11 shows that in highly unequal societies democratic values are weaker than in societies where resources are better distributed. The worst off see few benefits from democratic institutions that are based on the principle that all individuals are equal, a particularly hollow statement in societies where inequality is so great that most social goods are concentrated in the hands of the wealthy.

For the rich, democracy is a latent risk to their comfortable position. In order to construct a stable democracy, Mexico's government must confront this tension through an effective administration that avoids costly recessions and stimulates stable growth through further reforms while devising a fiscal policy that is capable of expanding the opportunities available to those who are worst off.

Notes

1. However, if the electorate had given Labastida a majority, most analysts and members of opposition parties would find insufficient evidence to conclude that Mexico is a democracy, even if the same institutions delivered the same quality elections.

2. Data from one study summarize the dramatic changes that took place over a twelve-year period. In 1988, the opposition governed thirty-nine municipalities, 1.84 percent of the total population of Mexico. In 1999, the opposition governed more than 500 municipalities, 24 percent of all municipalities, comprising slightly more than half of Mexico's population. See Alonso Lujambio, *El poder compartido* (México, D.F.: Oceano, 2000), pp. 83–84.

3. For a detailed account of the evolution of electoral law, see Ricardo Becerra, Pedro Salazar, and José Woldenberg, *La mecánica del cambio político en México* (México, D.F.: Cal y Arena, 2000), p. 491.

4. As there is no referendum in the Mexican constitution, Fox cannot give society direct input with respect to key issues. Therefore, he will have to negotiate with the Congress where his party does not enjoy a majority.

5. Jim Cason and David Brooks, "Helms, *entusiasmado*, con la elección del panista," *La Jornada*, July 14, 2000.

6. The Moncloa Pact, though, was basically an agreement around wage politics to avoid industrial confrontation.

7. The National Institute for Geographical Information Statistics (INEGI) affirms that the informal subsector represented 12.7 percent of GDP in 1998, growing that year at a rate of 7.1 percent, absorbing 28.5 percent of the employed population, equivalent to 10 million people. See *Reforma*, August 23, 2000.

8. John Rawls, *A Theory of Justice* (Cambridge: Belknap, Harvard University Press, 1971).

9. Mexico has no vice president. If the president dies, faces serious mental problems, or resigns, both houses have to elect the new president by a majority. This is a lengthy and uncertain process under current conditions of plurality. It is mere luck that since 1934 all presidents have finished their six-year term.

10. See Inter-American Development Bank (IADB), *Facing Up to Inequality in Latin America, 1998–1999 Report* (Washington, D.C.: IADB, 2000), p. 189.

11. Ibid., figure 8.4.

12. Nora Lustig and Miguel Székely say that even with an annual growth rate of 5 percent extreme poverty will not be completely eradicated until the year 2033. Eradication of moderate poverty will take seventeen additional years. See Nora Lustig and Miguel Székely, *México: Evolución económica, pobreza y desigualdad* (Washington, D.C.: Inter-American Development Bank, Economic Commission for Latin America and the Caribbean, and the UN Development Program, 1997), p. 78.

13. See John Scott, "Who Benefits from the State in High-Inequality, Middle-Income Countries? The Case of Mexico" (México, D.F.: CIDE, 2000, photocopy).

2

Security and Governance: The Urgent Need for State Reform

Raúl Benítez Manaut

A series of conditional variables, both external and internal, define the debate on security and civil-military relations in Mexico. The end of the Cold War has contributed to the consolidation of the democratization process, which began in the early 1990s. This took place parallel to the appearance of an active civil society, a new appreciation of human rights, a reduction in levels of impunity granted to police security forces and military personnel, and a construction of a modern system of political parties. In summary, a profound reform of the state has taken place, incrementally abolishing authoritarian forms of exercising power by controlling governmental corruption, reforming economic structures, and instituting political reform.[1]

The End of the Cold War in Mexico

In Mexico the democratization process that took place during the 1990s and the entrance of the country into new plans for economic and market integration, principally through the signing of the North American Free Trade Agreement (NAFTA) in 1994, have redefined the security threats coming from the political sphere.[2] New social conflicts and other phenomena, such as narcotrafficking, also strongly affect national security.

Since the political-electoral process of 1988, civil society, political parties, and the international community have increased pressure for democratization. The authoritarian political regime based on the hegemonic control of the Institutional Revolutionary Party (PRI) has eroded since 1988. However, since the transition to democracy in the 2000 elections, various phenomena that threaten the stability of the country, such as organized crime and narcotrafficking, have emerged, and social problems that have converted themselves into a challenge to the democratization process, such as the crisis in Chiapas, have appeared.

As a result, Mexico is experiencing a process of remilitarization in some regions of the country and within some state institutions, principally in those that enforce the law, apply justice, and oversee public security. This has become a national security problem. In the same manner, the appearance of radical social protest phenomena, such as the armed uprising in Chiapas, presents an important challenge to the democratization process. Therefore, a search for a peace accord, the demobilization of the Zapatista National Liberation Army (EZLN), the demilitarization of Chiapas, and the solution of the indigenous question have become issues of national security and a challenge for civil-military relations.[3]

The government has implemented a profound state reform in which two new concepts appear: democratic security and human security. However, the economic policies for combating poverty are not aimed at reducing social polarity.

At the beginning of the twenty-first century, the principal domestic security problems in Mexico are common delinquency, trafficking in drugs and arms, and the activities of organized crime such as kidnapping, extortion, and auto theft. In this context, the armed forces are slowly abandoning the administration of these problems, and police institutions under civilian control are confronting them instead.

All of this leads us to conclude that a direct relationship between democratization and subregional economic integration exists. This is true for Mexico in its relationships with the United States, Canada, and Europe.

The Historic Role of the Military and the Political System of the Revolution

Historically, because of the absence of a strong civil society and developed governmental institutions, the Mexican armed forces have carried out a key role in constructing the state apparatus and granting social cohesion and political leadership to the country. The armed forces, in particular the army, were important mechanisms for national integration. From them have come a significant portion of the projects that have supported the state.

In the nineteenth century, given the civil wars between the liberals and conservatives (1821–1846), the war with the United States (1846–1848), the liberal consolidation period (1848–1860), and the French intervention (1860–1865), the army was a principal state institution. The reconstruction of the state, begun at the end of the 1860s, was carried out using the foundation of the military, which had triumphed over the French.

The military was the fundamental institution to support the long regime of Porfirio Díaz, and his collapse in 1913 was what defined the beginning of the revolution between 1910 and 1913. The numerous revolutionary armies were the only forces that unified Mexico during the tragic decade of the revolution. The leaders were the mechanisms for political and social cohesion; at the same time, they were military, political, and social leaders. The vast majority of leaders were from the military, and they marked the path of revolution. In the same manner, when the process of rebuilding state structures began near the end of 1916, along with the writing and approval of the 1917 constitution, the ideological and political path of the revolution was defined by the military correlation of forces among the distinct groups of revolutionaries.

Once the military phase of the revolution was over, during the long period of reconstruction of the state and governmental apparatus (1917–1940), military leaders led the state. The armed forces decided upon and implemented the new mechanisms for social cohesion, such as the land distribution program, and the fundamental projects of the new revolutionary state needed to have military support. The principal political institutions of the country during the twentieth century, such as the National Revolutionary Party (PNR, founded in 1929) and its two successors, the Party of the Mexican Revolution (PRM, founded in 1938) and the PRI (founded in 1946), were creations of the armed forces. They were necessary and vital tools given the urgency of demilitarizing in an organized manner under the control of a new elite and given the new set of social and political relations.

Precisely because of the strength and influence of the armed forces in the constitutional and political design of the new state, they managed to maintain notable amounts of autonomy (real and legal), through which the armed forces granted, in return, their backing to the revolutionary elite. It was a harmonious relationship that was not altered even in moments of serious crisis, such as the repression exercised against the student movement in 1968.

In the 1990s, we witnessed the crisis in Chiapas, the war against narcotrafficking, and the appearance of armed guerrilla groups (such as the Popular Revolutionary Army and the Revolutionary Army of the Insurgent People). Simultaneously, we witnessed the increase in military forces and the military budget and the incorporation of army and navy officials in combating public insecurity. Both sets of events began to give new shape to the military institutions and their functions.

This internal challenge was accompanied, in an indirect form, by external pressures on the armed forces regarding the need to participate in, or integrate themselves into, the new international security structures. Thus, the globalization process also included challenges for the armed forces that questioned its essence, which is nationalist, defensive, and focused almost exclusively within national borders.

In Mexico there has been an active civil-military pact since the 1940s. This pact is based on the following rules: the first civilian president of the revolution, Miguel Alemán, accepted the sign of authority that the generals of the revolution gave him in 1946 in exchange for his absolute respect of the military institution. Correspondingly, they issued the second unwritten rule, agreed upon against all Mexican military traditions since the Republic was born at the beginning of the nineteenth century: the military forces would respect absolutely that civilian power.

The respect by both parties of this pact brought about the political leadership of the sons of the revolution when they came of age. These sons were principally the sons of Alvaro Obregón and Plutarco Elias Calles (who controlled the Mexican state in the 1920s) as well as Lázaro Cárdenas (highest leader of the revolution in the 1930s). These leaders developed with notable efficacy the party of the revolution. The PNR of 1929, transformed into the PRM in 1938, also matured and could walk on its own without the protection of its ancestors, the military leaders who founded the Mexican state.[4]

When the party in 1946 celebrated seventeen years, it was rebaptized, institutionalized, and from then on managed to successfully lead the revolutionary state. The PRI knew how to lubricate the political machinery. Its founders—the military leaders—helped it only when it truly found itself in difficulty, such as during the railroad strikes of 1958 and the student movement of 1968.[5] In the 1970s, its mission was the containment of the rural guerrillas, principally those established in the state of Guerrero, led by the Party of the Poor.[6] But the army intervened only temporarily to save the situation and rapidly withdrew to its barracks. In addition, the army acted upon request, thus never breaking or altering the pact.[7]

With regard to this, one can consider that the Mexican army never was autonomous from the political system (as was the case with the vast majority of Latin American armies); thus it never was a factor of instability. In other words, the army was subordinate to the president according to its supreme constitutional mandate. Analysts note that the armed forces, given the great capacity of the political system, came to carry out a "residual" role (used only in exceptional cases)[8] without abandoning its role as the "armed branch" of the PRI,[9] being one of the sources of stability of the political system.

The Armed Forces in the 1990s

In the 1990s, principally under the government of Carlos Salinas de Gortari (1988–1994), one observed a "remilitarization." This took place principally in the occupation of high offices in the public security bodies by active and retired officials from the army, air force, and navy, as well as in the overload of missions for the armed forces as public security entered into a serious crisis, narcotrafficking alarmingly increased, and armed movements reappeared.[10] The crisis in Chiapas, which began in January 1994, obligated the civil powers to resume using the armed forces to contain the EZLN.

The correlation between militarization and the crisis of governability is clear; when the country's institutions successfully and on their own channel and resolve political conflict without resorting to violence, these are moments of rest and professionalization for the armed forces. Stated differently, the political system demilitarizes itself. When the PRI, the offspring of revolution, began to grow old, the tendencies toward instability appeared in distinct segments and regions of the country, and the government resorted to the armed forces as a factor of contention (as they were used during 1968 and to confront the guerrillas in the 1970s), deterrence, and support for other security bodies (as during the 1990s).[11] After 1994, remilitarization occurred not only quantitatively but also qualitatively because of the specific weight of the armed forces.

The historical tendency of demilitarization-remilitarization is shown in Tables 2.1 and 2.2, through the analysis of the military budget as a percentage of government expenditures and gross domestic product (GDP).

In 1999, the armed forces had 232,000 active military personnel. At the budgetary level, at the beginning of the 1920s, the revolutionary armies demanded more than 50 percent of total government expenditures. This correlation decreased gradually until 1990, when one of the

Table 2.1 Military Expenditures as a Percentage of Government Expenditures, 1935–1994

1935–1940	Gen. Lázaro Cárdenas	22.03
1941–1946	Gen. Avila Camacho	18.85
1947–1952	Lic. Miguel Alemán	10.08
1953–1958	C. Adolfo Ruíz Cortines	7.87
1959–1964	Lic. Adolfo López Mateo	6.92
1965–1970	Lic. Gustavo Díaz Ordaz	2.63
1971–1976	Lic. Luis Echeverría A.	4.86
1977–1982	Lic. josé López Portillo	2.55
1983–1988	Lic. Miguel de la Madrid	2.33
1989–1994	Lic. Carlos Salinas de Gortari	3.08

Source: Guillermo Boils, *Los Militares y la política en México, 1915–1974* (Mexico: Ediciones El Caballito, 1975); SHCP (various years).

Table 2.2 Military Expenditures as a Percentage of Government Expenditures and of Gross Domestic Product, 1994–1999

	1994	1995	1996	1997	1998	1999
Government expenditure	3.93	3.60	3.68	3.50	3.60	3.34
GDP	0.57	0.68	0.56	0.58	0.58	0.60

Source: Presupuesto de Egresos 1999 (Mexico: Secretaria de Hacienda y Crédito Público, 1999).

lowest historical percentages was registered: only 0.48 percent of GDP and 1.96 percent of government expenditures went to defense. However, in the 1990s one observed an important exponential growth in this percentage. In 1992, the percentage rose to 0.52 percent of GDP and 2.55 percent of government expenditures; and in 1995, after the outbreak of the crisis in Chiapas, it rose to 0.68 percent of GDP and 3.9 percent of government expenditures in 1994 (see Table 2.2).[12]

The 1990s signified a challenge for the Mexican state structures on many levels. For the first time in the twentieth century, in 1997 the opposition had a majority within the legislative power. In addition, members of the two major opposition parties (the Party of the Democratic Revolution and the National Action Party) began to protest the role of oversight and control of many state apparatuses, including the armed forces. In political systems with consolidated democracies, such protests are called demands for accountability. Evident in the institutions of the Mexican state dedicated to national security and defense is that they have not passed through the reform-adaptation process necessary to confront the new circumstances. Thus, with the transition to democracy, the unwritten civil-military pact of the 1940s can no longer work; as a result, the civil-military relationship in Mexico will be redefined.

In the case of the armed forces, the army, air force, and navy have structures, rules, doctrines, and institutional practices whose foundations were laid in the 1930s. Although they have experienced transformations, these have not touched their essence; thus there are now frictions with parts of the state that have transformed themselves such as the legislature and, probably soon, the judiciary. One of the dilemmas of the Mexican political transition is that in Mexico, in contrast to the processes of political change that have taken place in South America (Argentina, Brazil, Chile, Uruguay, Paraguay, and Bolivia) and Central America (Guatemala, El Salvador, Nicaragua, and Honduras), where democratization has taken place alongside demilitarization, democratization—because of the phenomenon of ingovernability—is taking place with a militarization of rural areas and of some state structures that were not prepared for democracy and modernization.

Constitutionally, and in the laws that regulate the activity of the army, air force, and navy, three plans of war and doctrines to drive the deployment of the armed forces exist: DN-I, which is the preparation for external defense; DN-II, to guarantee internal security and social peace; and DN-III, to protect the population in the case of natural disasters.[13] These three doctrines have remained unchanged over time, but circumstances have resulted in the strengthening of some and the formal maintenance of others. As a product of the geopolitical location of the country, by the end of the twentieth century Mexico had no external enemies. Two neighboring countries, the United States and Cuba, have much larger and better-equipped armed forces than Mexico has. However, as a product of its diplomacy of lowering tensions, Mexico has excellent bilateral relations with them. Thus, they are not considered military threats. Neither is Guatemala a military threat, although it has a very powerful military, and Belize has never been a military threat. Finally, Honduras, which has a squadron of supersonic airplanes, would have a hard time using them against Mexico. Given these considerations, external warfare in reality is very far off as a scene of combat, as a result of which the DN-I is maintained only in the sphere of the hypothesis of war.

The DN-III, in force since the 1960s, is one of the military missions most appreciated by the population. They take advantage of the training, organization, and deployment of the three armed forces to support the population when hurricanes, floods, and earthquakes hit with unusual force. This armed forces capacity has been exported to Central America for years and lately with greater intensity. When Hurricane Mitch partially destroyed Honduras, Nicaragua, Guatemala, and El Salvador in November 1998, the Mexican air force, army, and navy arrived to support the rescue mission even before the U.S. Army arrived. In December 1999, a large contingent of the Mexican military participated in the rescue of the civilian population from the floods that took place in Venezuela.

For the deployment of troops for the Plan DN-III-E, the armed forces are subordinated to the National System for Civil Protection (SINAPROC) of the Interior Ministry.[14] The actions of the DN-III mission can be understood as "humanitarian action." With difficulty, one could question this military deployment of the Mexican army and navy.[15]

At the beginning of the twenty-first century, Mexican armed forces are facing a dilemma. They will support a state that cannot reestablish political stability, and thus their function will remain, in the sphere of Plan DN-II, overloaded with missions. Or on the contrary, the state will modernize itself and the political system, reconstruct mechanisms for and ways of achieving and maintaining stability, and the armed forces will be able to professionalize and modernize themselves.

The modernization and professionalization of the Mexican armed forces does not depend on the armed forces themselves. Their future is linked to the process of the transition to democracy (whether or not it is successful) and will depend on many of the conflicts (principally social) resolving themselves in the future with the help of other government entities (e.g., health and dental campaigns in essence are a mission of the health secretary). Another case is the war on narcotrafficking, which constitutionally is a mission of the attorney general of the Republic; therefore, this institution ought to professionalize the Federal Judicial Police, eliminating corruption and efficiently combating narcotrafficking. Only in that way will the army withdraw to its barracks. Or in the corresponding mission to confront armed groups, the state ought to eradicate endemic violence and bossism and make rural zones adhere to the law so that the army does not have to be responsible for citizen security.

In addition, to be able to transform rebel movements such as the EZLN into political forces with their own instruments and strategies for a modern and democratic state, the state ought to develop the capacity for political negotiation, as happened in Central America between 1990 and 1996, which effectively achieves the disarming of the people in insurrection without using repressive military violence. This advanced notably at the beginning of 2001 with the occurrence of the "Zapatour" and the presence of the EZLN in the Mexican Congress and, for the government's part, by seeking a renewal of dialogue with the EZLN and the approval of the new Indigenous Law in the Congress. At the same time, the government has begun the process of demilitarizing the state of Chiapas as a key element for bringing the government of President Fox and the EZLN closer together.

Given the preceding scenario, the dilemma that the Mexican armed forces face at the beginning of the twenty-first century depends on the successful transition to democracy and the reform of political, economic, and social structures. Only when those are achieved will the armed forces be able to concentrate on their fundamental constitutional missions and not continue centering their action, as it has historically been, on the maintenance of social peace and internal security.

The Mexican armed forces, in particular the army, are trapped in various contradictions. These are not defined by themselves; rather, the weaknesses of other structures of the Mexican state and the requirements of the federal government are what bring the armed forces to develop their corresponding missions to Plan DN-II and are a source of national and international questioning. The lack of solution to conflicts, such as that in Chiapas; the existence of semifeudal and backward power structures, generators of great political violence, principally in rural areas; and the slow transition to democracy invite the overburdening of the missions of the armed forces. This is the challenge of the Mexican armed forces: to advance toward the modernization of the state and modernize their forms of combat while respecting the human and political rights of the population.

In Mexico, the role of the armed forces does not depend on themselves alone. The armed forces do not define their missions; rather, this is in the hands of the distinct challenges that oblige the president to use them. The perverse cycle of the Mexican history of militarization-demilitarization-remilitarization should be broken, and if structural demilitarization takes place, the armed forces will be the first beneficiaries as an institution, since they would slowly abandon their commitments that are covered in Plan DN-II, thereby deepening their professionalization.

If this is to become possible, a democratization of the political system in the entire country (above all, bringing democratization to rural areas) would have to take place, and this would have to create stability and governability. At the same time, it would make it possible to resolve social inequality and modernize and make efficient the systems of justice and public security, in order to then abandon the missions that involve the armed forces because of the current weakness of police forces. That is to say, future missions of the armed forces depend on the success (or failure) of the state reform at the judicial level, in the political system, and in public security.

Another level of debate is whether or not the armed forces are carrying out a political role. In the discourse, they are professional institutions and take on missions "of the state," not "of the government." That is to say, according to their doctrine, they are disconnected from their connection at birth with the PRI. However, many critics note that the armed forces respond to the PRI's needs, principally in some rural regions of the country, such as Chiapas. With regard to this criticism, overcoming the missions contained in Plan DN-II and concentrating their activities on DN-I and DN-III would be key for their complete depoliticization in the future.

An element that has appeared on the scene of the Mexican armed forces is their probable participation in missions of international security. According to doctrine and tradition, in military terms the Mexican armed forces are defensive and are used as deterrents. However, pressures have appeared urging them to take on a more active role contributing to international security. With regard to this, Mexico refuses to participate in peacekeeping operations of the United Nations[16] and also opposes all efforts to militarize the hemispheric security system. However, unilateral participation in humanitarian operations to rescue populations from natural disasters has become a new area of action that notably improves the image of the armed forces.

This discussion opens a debate that starts as an ideological and doctrinal paradigm in the heart of the Mexican armed forces: the extremes of this debate oscillate between "nationalism" and "globalization" or, in operational terms, between Plans DN-I and DN-III versus Plan DN-II. In the same manner, the processes of regionalization (resulting from NAFTA coming into force) and globalization (a rising phenomenon since the fall of the Berlin Wall in 1989) are having a decisive impact on the doctrines, missions, and structures of the Mexican armed forces.

In Mexico there are tensions in the four levels of governability: economic, political, social, and cultural. In the first place, economic governability means harmonizing the strength of foreign capital with the national macroeconomy and making the microeconomy able to benefit through market mechanisms. In the second place is political governability. On the one hand, this means consolidating the democratic structures of the selection of political leaders. On the other hand, it means ensuring that the demands of the population to which the government has not attended do not create political pressure that can lead to anarchy or a lack of government and, in the end, oblige the armed forces to act in the case of a crisis beyond political control and the control of security forces. There is also a challenge confronting traditional conservative forces principally located in rural areas, which is where the armed forces concentrate their territorial deployment. In addition, added to political governability are respect for human rights and the ability to make effective the rule of law and resolve the problems of emerging minorities, such as demands for indigenous rights.

In the third place is social governability, which makes the new macroeconomy compatible with the microeconomy. It is that which creates social balance and is threatened by the exclusion, poverty, and marginalization of wide sectors of the population. Social governability is what connects the economy with politics. In the fourth place, cultural governability refers to how national and traditional cultures survive with the "American way of life" trying to transform into the "global way of life" through the process of globalization. In addition, the paradigm of cultural unity of citizens of a nation entered into crisis with the emergence of the theme of cultural diversity, even as an issue of "human rights." The case of the Zapatista rebellion in Mexico fits within this pattern. One must remember that Mexico is a culturally authoritarian country.

At the end of the regime of the revolution, determined by the triumph of Vicente Fox on July 2, 2000, many questions are raised about the role of the armed forces. One of the fundamental doctrines of the armed forces—loyalty to government institutions and the constitution—would result in a relation of subordination and respect. However, because of the magnitude of the transformations that are beginning to be seen in the process of state reform, which necessarily ought to modify military autonomy and open the armed forces to civil society (principally to academics and the media) and to other powers of the state that can question the current military structure. One ought to remember that the armed forces, in their theoretical sense, are the resource of last resort of the state and that, as such, they guarantee social and political cohesion against phenomena of ingovernability or if other security bodies, principally police, are overcome.

Final Reflections: The Armed Forces of Mexico at the Beginning of the Twenty-First Century

In spite of the professionalization process and the test of loyalty to civilian power that one observed in Mexico in the 1990s, principally with the change of government, the armed forces still continue to live in a contradiction that is very difficult to overcome between the old politicized missions guaranteeing internal order (police and political) and the new missions, such as the war against narcotrafficking and support for the civilian population in cases of natural disasters.

Modern armed forces are composed of soldiers with high levels of education, officials who are well paid and well trained, equipment that incorporates advanced technology for modern war, and reformulated doctrines for the defense of the country against new security threats. The armies at the end of the twentieth century were capable of collaborating in humanitarian missions based on rapid reaction and, in many countries today, are trained for missions that collaborate in international security (so-called peacekeeping operations).

In Mexico the globalization phenomenon is having a positive impact on the doctrine of the armed forces: they are respecting the new democratic political order. As a result, it would be very difficult to repeat the phenomenon of "repoliticization" of the armed forces, at least in the short term. Similarly, the appreciation of the rights of the population and the disappearance of military impunity are now a very advanced fact. One can even state as a hypothesis that in Mexico it would be almost impossible to try to stage a military takeover of the state.

There are transnational phenomena that little by little are influencing the missions, doctrine, and training of the armed forces in Mexico. An example is the war against narcotrafficking, being carried out in part because of the great pressure that the United States is putting on Mexico. Similarly, one observes a tendency in which the United States exercises great influence in the plans to create new mechanisms for collective security that substitute—or complement—existing mechanisms through the Inter-American Treaty of Mutual Assistance and the Inter-American Defense Committee.

Currently, national leaders in the heart of the Organization of American States are discussing the concept of hemispheric security. This tendency has been strengthened after the attacks of September 11, 2001, on the United States. Yet the tendency in Mexico, given its foreign policy, is to reject military participation in military intervention operations where there are serious conflicts of governability. Mexico sends troops outside of the country only on humanitarian missions to address natural catastrophes. This has taken place in Mexico's area of geopolitical influence in Central America and the Caribbean (including Colombia and Venezuela).

With regard to the construction of a new civil-military relationship, a slow creation of an elite of civilians specialized in issues of security and defense is taking place. Also, new parliamentary, budgetary, and political controls have appeared, given that the political parties have begun to concern themselves with the training of their leaders in this area. In civil society, especially in academia and the press, one also observes the appearance of specialized academics and journalists who did not exist in the past.

The missions of the Mexican armed forces, in forward-looking terms, oscillate between internal and external. In the near future, one cannot eliminate internal missions of the armed forces, given that the creation of civilian structures for civil protection, combating narcotrafficking, intelligence against organized crime, police who guarantee public order, and forces capable of confronting terrorism have been very slow to materialize. Professionalizing civilian structures that can substitute for the armed forces is an effort that began more than ten years ago in Mexico, but it has not had the necessary speed to allow military personnel to withdraw to their barracks.

There are no conventional threats of foreign war near Mexico, as a result of which the armed forces do not have a hypothesis of war with neighboring countries. As a result, the armed forces are demanding the increasing modernization of their equipment, according to new nonconventional threats, principally from narcotrafficking and terrorism.

The principal mission of the armed forces in Mexico in the 1990s, fighting narcotrafficking, will continue to be so in the future. Its prosecution demands multinational cooperation and an improvement in technical military equipment for detection. For example, detection equipment (satellites and radar) and interception equipment (airplane interceptors; high-speed boats; helicopters; rapid reaction forces; forces especially trained for air, sea, and land combat) are very costly. The new mission of the whole Mexican national security system, the war on terrorism, has just opened a debate regarding the armed forces. Since September 11, the Mexican armed forces have made themselves responsible for the protection of strategic installations.

In reference to the training of the Mexican armed forces, they are prepared for traditional land and sea warfare and to confront nonconventional enemies such as guerrilla groups. However, given the changing nature of the enemies that they must combat (such as narcotraffickers, organized criminals, and terrorists), they need to transform military training and military education systems. Surely, this change will take place in the future.

In Mexico, a debate is taking place regarding whether the doctrine of internal and external security ought to adjust itself to the new reality created by NAFTA (i.e., whether the accelerated process of integration with the United States will also present the armed forces with a process of increased exchange, cooperation, and joint efforts). The tendency toward military regionalization is observed to be advancing slowly, although the discourse of sovereignty continues to remain in place. At the level of doctrine, nationalism, as the element that creates cohesion for the Mexican armed forces, surely will continue to be present but at a specific level, above all in the training of special forces by the United States; the slow but sustained modernization of equipment, cooperation, and connections with the United States and Canada will continue to be strengthened.

As a product of the support that Mexico is granting to the United States to combat terrorism, the Mexican government is not contemplating the direct participation of the armed forces. However, it has talked about the creation of a trinational security doctrine. With regard to this, President Fox has noted:

> In the same way, we consider that the struggle against terrorism forms part of the commitment of Mexico to Canada and the United States, as a result of constructing in the framework of the North American Free Trade Agreement a shared space for development, well-being and integral security.
>
> The Government of Mexico also adheres to the struggle against terrorism as a mandate of international character, contracted through the multiple legal instruments signed with the member countries of the United Nations.
>
> At the hemispheric level, Mexico considers that the current struggle against terrorism is a basic component of our regional security that demands a redefinition of the doctrine of continental security and a redesign of the legal and diplomatic instruments for our legitimate defense.
>
> The terrorist acts carried out in the United States have seriously affected Mexican interests. Many Mexican citizens were direct victims of the attacks. To their memory and to their families, we owe a direct and energetic response. In addition, those acts have accented the recessive tendencies of the world economy, generated uncertainty

> with respect to the future of diverse industries, provoked unemployment, dislocated the financial and stock markets, and damaged the energy markets.[17]

With respect to the reform of the state, the tendency is toward the consolidation of the democratic civil-military relationship and armed forces that are subordinate to civilian power that depends, in addition to institutional and legal variables, on the ability to achieve political governability in a social and economic context threatened by poverty.

As a final reflection, parallel to and depending on the processes of consolidation of democracy in Mexico, the general tendency in the medium term is:

- A redefinition of the relationship between the armed forces and civilian authorities, strengthening the latter;
- The appearance of political-legislative control;
- The emergence of a civil society that increasingly influences security and defense policies;
- The more active participation of the armed forces in the international security system, principally through peacekeeping operations;
- The mechanisms of subregional integration and cooperation and mutual trust agreements;
- The change in the fundamental missions of the armed forces, where humanitarian action and aiding the civilian population are central;
- The slow change of recruitment with a tendency toward its disappearance, moving toward a system of professional enrollment;
- The elevation of the educational level of the members of the armed forces;
- The technological modernization of the army, air force, and navy;
- International military cooperation in the war against narcotrafficking;
- International military cooperation in the face of natural catastrophes;
- The change of the military intelligence system, now directed toward the war against organized crime, narcotrafficking, and terrorism;

- The tendency toward the disappearance of the hypothesis of war between bordering countries; and
- The slow substitution of the public security missions carried out by the armed forces or members of the armed forces by professional police forces.

Notes

1. This effort is still in its first phase, unable to completely reduce and control governmental corruption in Mexico, given that it is "structural" corruption, deeply rooted in governmental management mechanisms.

2. In the 1990s, Mexico signed nine market agreements with twenty-seven countries. Some of them are bilateral (Chile, Israel, Costa Rica, Nicaragua, Bolivia), others are trilateral (NAFTA and the agreement with Venezuela and Colombia), others are quartilateral (with the Triangle of the North: Guatemala, El Salvador and Honduras), and one is multilateral (with the European Union, ratified in 2000 and subject to a democratization clause until after Mexico's national elections on July 2, 2000).

3. On the peace accord, see Raúl Benítez Manaut, "Los debates sobre el conflicto en Chiapas y los retos de la negociación de paz," in Cynthia Arnson and Raúl Benítez, eds., *Chiapas: los desafíos de la paz* (Mexico: Miguel Angel Porrúa, 2000), pp. 13–25, 2000b.

4. In 1938, when Lázaro Cárdenas founded the PRM, in its corporative structure it even had a Military Sector, within which were all the officials, active and retired, of the armed forces.

5. Sergio Aguayo, *1968: Los Archivos de la Violencia* (México, D.F.: Grijalvo-Reforma, 1998); Julio Scherer and Carlos Monsivais, *Parte de Guerra: Tlatelolco 1968* (México, D.F.: Nuevo Siglo-Aguilar, 1999).

6. The capacities for the war of counterinsurgency and "civic action" in the 1970s are analyzed in José Luis Piñeyro, *Ejército y sociedad en México: pasado y presente* (México, D.F.: UAM, 1985).

7. For the bibliography on the historic aspects of the Mexican army and the relation with the political system, see SEDENA, *El Ejército y la fuerza aérea mexicanos*, 2nd ed., 2 vols. (México, D.F.: SEDENA, 1982); Roderic Camp, *Generals in the Palace: The Military in Modern Mexico* (New York: Oxford University Press, 1992); SEDENA, Escuela Superior de Guerra, LX Aniversario, Mexico, 1991; Edwin Liewen, *Mexican Militarism: The Political Rise and Fall of the Revolutionary Army, 1910–1940* (Albuquerque: University of New Mexico Press, 1968); Stephen Wager, *The Mexican Army, 1940–1982: The Country Comes First* (Ph.D. diss., Stanford University, 1992); Stetson Conn, Rose Engelman, and Byron Fairchild, *United States Army in World War II: The Western Hemisphere—Guarding the United States and Its Outposts* (Washington, D.C.: Office of the Chief of Military History, U.S. Army, 1964); Guillermo Boils, *Los militares y la política en México, 1915–1974* (IIS-UNAM, 1975); and Michael Dziedzic, *The Essence of Decision in Hegemonic*

Regime: The Case of Mexico's Acquisition of a Supersonic Fighter (Ph.D. thesis, University of Texas, 1986).

8. David Ronfeldt, "The Modern Mexican Military: An Overview," in David Ronfeldt, ed., *The Modern Mexican Military: An Assessment* (La Jolla: Center for U.S.-Mexican Studies, University of California–San Diego, 1984).

9. This hypothesis is supported in Adolfo Aguilar Zinzer, "Las relaciones cívico-militares en México," in Louis Goodman et al., eds., *Los militares y la democracia: El futuro de las relaciones civico-militares en America Latina* (Montevideo: PEITHO, 1990); and Arturo Sánchez, "El Estado y los militares en los años ochenta," in Jorge Alonso et al., *El nuevo estado Mexicano* (México, D.F.: Nueva Imagen CIESAS, 1992).

10. Graham Turbiville Jr., "Law Enforcement and the Mexican Armed Forces: New Internal Security Missions Challenge the Military," in *Low Intensity Conflict and Law Enforcement* 6, no. 2 (1997).

11. The vast majority of analysts agree that the period of "growing old" of the PRI, as an authoritarian-corporative political party, began in 1985.

12. My own work with information from the secretary of the treasury and public credit.

13. Raúl Benítez Manaut, "Fuerzas armadas mexicanas a fin de siglo: Misiones," in Rut Diamint, ed., *Control civil y fuerzas armadas en las nuevas democracias latinoamericanas* (Buenos Aires: Universidad Torcuato Di Tella, 1999), pp. 469–513; Jorge Luís Sierra, *El Ejército y la Constitución Mexicana: Combate al narcotráfico, paramilitarismo y contrainsurgencia* (México, D.F.: Plaza y Valdés, 1999).

14. See SEDENA, "Protección civil," in *Revista del Ejército y Fuerza Aérea Mexicanos*, Epoca III, Año 93 (January 1999): 40–47. The foundations of SINAPROC are contained in the Official Paper of the Federation on May 6, 1986. The juncture of chaos in the rescue of the population affected by the earthquakes of September 19 and 20 led to the creation of SINAPROC as an interinstitutional coordinating organism. At the same time, SINAPROC includes the National Center for Disaster Prevention (CENAPRED). To coordinate prevention and rescue efforts in support of the population whom the disaster has harmed, thirteen offices of the federal government participate in the National Council for Civil Protection, which was created in May 1990. To it, one must add the participation of other entities, such as the Mexican National Autonomous University (UNAM, to detect earthquakes and meteorological events) and state and municipal governments.

15. Benítez Manaut, "Fuerzas armadas," pp. 469–513; SEDENA, "El ejército y fuerza aérea mexicanos en la protección civil y ecológica," *Revista del Ejército y Fuerza Aérea Mexicanos*, Epoca III, Año 94 (January 2000).

16. Although a first step in that sense was taken in El Salvador between 1992 and 1994, nonetheless they were contingents of police (112 police from diverse entities), not military personnel.

17. Shorthand version of the words of President Vicente Fox Quesada at the end of the Meeting for the Evaluation of Coordinated Actions for Border and National Security, Tijuana, Mexico, October 3, 2001.

3

Mexican Labor at a Crossroads

Katrina Burgess

> [Our traditional alliance with the government] will not be reaffirmed [because] we know the origins of the [National Action Party] and the ideology that animates the candidate who won the Presidency.
>
> —*Leonardo Rodríguez Alcaine, secretary-general of the Confederation of Mexican Workers, July 2000*[1]

On July 2, 2000, the Mexican people dealt a serious blow to the sixty-four-year-old alliance between the Confederation of Mexican Workers (CTM) and the Mexican state. By electing Vicente Fox from the opposition National Action Party (PAN) as their next president, they severed the historic bond between the state and the Institutional Revolutionary Party (PRI), which had been in power since 1929. In the process, they uprooted a state-labor alliance that began with the CTM's creation in 1936, prospered during the "Mexican miracle" of the 1950s–1970s, and even survived the neoliberal reforms and democratizing pressures of the 1980s and 1990s. Although the CTM has expressed its intention to work with the Fox government, it will no longer be embedded in the network of institutionalized exchanges that characterized its alliance with the PRI-controlled state between 1936 and 2000.

The demise of the CTM-state alliance has implications that go far beyond the uncertain future of the CTM itself. Besides sustaining the CTM's own hegemony, the alliance served as a pillar of the postrevolutionary regime and shaped the structure and actions of the Mexican labor movement. In this chapter, I examine the evolution of this alliance, particularly during the difficult period of neoliberal reform and political opening in the 1980s and 1990s. I begin by disaggregating the labor movement, which has been dominated but not monopolized by the CTM. I then review the socioeconomic and political bargains that undergirded the state-labor alliance during the heyday of import substitution industrialization (ISI) and PRI hegemony. Finally, I turn to the impact of neoliberal reform and political opening on the alliance in the 1980s and 1990s. Whereas neoliberal reform depended quite heavily on the CTM's collaboration, political opening unleashed changes that promise to transform the Mexican labor movement and thereby end the CTM's long hegemony.

Disaggregating Mexican Labor

Despite its reputation as a paradigmatic case of corporatism, the Mexican labor movement has always been very divided. In part, this division can be attributed to Mexico's labor code. The 1931 Federal Labor Law (LFT) separated unions into two jurisdictions: federal and local. Although national confederations could incorporate unions from both jurisdictions, each had its own system of accounting and regulation. The LFT also permitted the formation of national autonomous unions (SNAs) on a sectoral basis. While encouraging encompassing unions in strategic sectors such as oil, mining, railroads, and telecommunications, this provision promoted competition among SNAs, as well as SNA resistance to the formation of a peak labor confederation. SNAs often affiliated with national confederations, particularly the CTM, but they retained their organizational autonomy. In addition, a 1960 constitutional amendment established separate rights and regulations for public employee unions (Apartado B), reinforcing a requirement that all public employees belong to a single but separate organization, the Federation of Public Service Workers (FSTSE).

An equally important source of fragmentation and division within the labor movement was the system of dominant-party hegemony established and maintained by the PRI for most of the twentieth century. This system encouraged a split between "official" unions affiliated with the PRI and "independent" unions either autonomous from any political grouping or, less often, affiliated with an opposition party. The official sector incorporated the vast majority of unionized workers, but independent unions always existed and were strong in key sectors such as the automobile industry.[2]

In addition, the PRI pursued a divide-and-conquer strategy within the official labor movement, thereby allowing the party to shift allegiances from one PRI-affiliated union to another as needed. While supporting the unification of industrial unions in the CTM in 1936,

President Lázaro Cárdenas created separate organizations for peasants and public employees. He reinforced these divisions when he restructured the official party in 1938 to include four mutually exclusive groupings: a Labor Sector, a Peasant Sector, a Military Sector, and a Popular Sector.[3] Both the FSTSE and the powerful National Teachers Union (Sindicato Nacional de Trabajadores de la Educación, or SNTE) were incorporated into the Popular Sector rather than the Labor Sector. This division split the labor movement into competing groups that sought to outbid each other for special privileges from the PRI.

Cárdenas's successors continued this divide-and-conquer strategy by encouraging the formation of rival organizations among PRI-affiliated workers. In 1952, President Miguel Alemán supported the creation of the Revolutionary Confederation of Workers and Peasants (CROC). Like several other confederations, the CROC attracted unions that belonged to the PRI but rejected CTM membership. When open rivalry between anti-CTM and pro-CTM factions threatened to undermine the effectiveness of the Labor Sector, President Gustavo Díaz Ordaz encouraged the two coalitions to unify under a single umbrella organization, leading to the formation of the Labor Congress (CT) in February 1966.[4]

The CT institutionalized a system in which the PRI could shift allegiances within the labor movement without encouraging dissidence or abandoning its overall commitment to labor. In 1979, the CT accounted for 73.5 percent of unions and 83.9 percent of unionized workers (see Table 3.1).[5] With the exception of unions in nuclear power and telecommunications, all CT affiliates formally required their members to belong to the PRI.[6] At the same time, these unions retained their organizational autonomy and continued to engage in direct negotiations with the party and the state, often in competition with one another. Although the CTM dominated the Labor Congress, accounting for 63.9 percent of CT unions and 32.6 percent of CT workers in 1979, it never achieved a monopoly of representation and often found itself vying with rival CT unions for privileges granted by the PRI.[7]

The Postrevolutionary Bargains

Keeping in mind the layered and competitive nature of the Mexican labor movement, the rest of this chapter will focus on the most significant of Mexico's unions, the CTM. Under the leadership of Fidel Velázquez, who led the confederation from 1940 until his death in 1997,

Table 3.1 Structure of the Mexican Labor Movement, 1979

Type of Organization	Number of Unions		Number of Workers	
	Absolute	% of Total	Absolute	% of Total
Labor Congress	7,801	73.5	2,238,287	83.9
CTM (Confederation of Mexican Workers)	4.987	47.0	731,015	27.4
Other national confederations	3,708	25.5	306,729	11.6
FSTSE (Federation of Public Service Workers)	68	0.7	835,534	31.3
Regional or craft unions	28	0.3	6,779	0.3
SNA	10	0.1	358,230	13.4
Independent unions	1,021	9.6	239,279	9.0
Other	1,788	16.9	189,492	7.1
Total	10,610	100.0	2,667,058	100.0

Source: Cesar Zazueta and Ricardo de la Péna, *La Estructura del Congress de Trabajo* (Mexico: Fondo de Cultura Económica, 1984), pp. 400, 404.

the CTM served as the central pillar of labor support for the PRI regime.[8] In return, the CTM received important benefits. This arrangement took the form of two bargains—one socioeconomic, one political—that required concessions but also brought benefits to both the PRI and the CTM. As long as the PRI pursued a development strategy of ISI and maintained its hegemony in the political system, the bargains were self-reinforcing. They entered into crisis, however, when these conditions evaporated in the 1980s and 1990s.

The Socioeconomic Bargain

The CTM played an important role in sustaining the PRI's economic project, particularly during hard times. First, the confederation contributed to labor peace by favoring conciliation and arbitration over mobilization. Besides discouraging strikes by its own affiliates, the CTM signed tripartite pacts to ensure labor peace and exercised a moderating influence through its control of the majority of labor seats on the special Juntas of Conciliation and Arbitration (JCAs).[9] Second, the CTM contributed to wage moderation through formal participation on the tripartite National Minimum Wage Commission (CNSM), informal agreements with the government, and influence over contracted wage bargaining by CTM affiliates at the plant level. Although the CTM preferred to use these channels to transmit real wage gains to its members, it was willing to negotiate wage austerity in periods of high inflation.

In return for its cooperation with the PRI's economic policies, the CTM received considerable material benefits. Many of these benefits were positive externalities of the PRI's successful implementation of noninflationary ISI. In the 1950s, the government launched a strategy of stabilizing development that combined conservative fiscal and monetary policies with protectionist trade policies, extensive state regulation, and high levels of public investment. After an initial period of austerity, this strategy unleashed the "Mexican miracle" of rapid growth with low inflation. Between 1950 and 1970, Mexico's economy grew at an average annual rate of 7.8 percent while annual inflation remained at around 3 percent.[10]

Stabilizing development brought both employment and wage gains to workers. First, it generated millions of jobs in industries with relatively high rates of unionization. Between 1940 and 1969, the number of workers employed in the secondary sector of the economy (mining, petroleum, manufacturing, construction, and public utilities) grew at an average annual rate of 5 percent, from 826,000 to 3.4 million.[11] Second, it contributed to a quadrupling of average real wages between 1952 and 1976.[12] In real terms, industrial workers saw their wages and benefits grow by an average of 85 percent between 1960 and 1975. During this same period, the real urban minimum wage grew by an average of 110 percent.[13]

Workers also profited from policies specifically designed to raise their living standards. In the mid-1950s, the PRI revived the practice of using the extensive powers of the Labor Ministry to pressure employers to increase wages and benefits in collective contracts negotiated with unions. In addition, wage increases negotiated by collective contract set the pace for increases in the minimum wage, which were determined every two years by the CNSM (established in 1962). As a result, some of the gains achieved by the unions reached nonunionized workers.

The PRI also provided nonwage gains to labor in the form of social security, health care, education, and subsidies on basic commodities and housing. Coverage by the Mexican Social Security Institute (IMSS) expanded from 4 percent of the workforce in 1952 to 25 percent in 1970, and most unions in nationalized sectors negotiated generous social security benefits in their collective contracts.[14] The PRI also fulfilled its constitutional mandate to require worker participation in company profits and to create a worker housing agency (INFONAVIT). Although some of these programs reached nonunionized workers, union members tended to have privileged access.

Besides distributing benefits directly to workers, the PRI guaranteed unions representation on government agencies with an impact on workers. Three agencies of particular importance to the CTM were the IMSS, the CNSM, and INFONAVIT. Although other official unions received seats on the governing boards of these agencies, the CTM tended to control the largest share. As of 1979, the CTM controlled one out of the four labor positions on the IMSS and 55.6 percent of the labor representatives on the CNSM, with the remaining 44.4 percent divided among four other organizations.[15]

The CTM had even greater success in dominating labor's participation in INFONAVIT. Although originally designed to grant financing to workers on the basis of technical criteria, INFONAVIT quickly evolved into a source of patronage resources for the CTM. Besides becoming directly involved in housing construction, it shifted from a computerized system for assigning housing to one of so-called external promotions, whereby groups of workers selected by the unions, the private sector, or the government would submit development plans (including their choice of a construction company) to the agency for approval.[16] Soon thereafter, the CTM gained control of labor's representative on the INFONAVIT board and took charge of the INFONAVIT union with the help of the Labor Ministry.[17]

Finally, the PRI contributed to the CTM's financial solvency. Besides receiving PRI subsidies to compensate for its lack of self-financing, the CTM built its national headquarters on expropriated land donated by the state, and staff members received two paychecks: one from the CTM, and another from the PRI. In addition, President José López Portillo created the Workers' Bank (Banco Obrero) in 1977. The Banco Obrero not only provided banking services to workers and their families but also extended low-interest loans to unions and confederations.[18] Although many unions were shareholders, the CTM dominated the bank's administration.[19]

The Political Bargain

The CTM played a crucial role in sustaining the PRI's long hold on the Mexican political system. Within the party, the CTM exercised a stabilizing influence during the transition from one administration to another. Because politicians are constitutionally prohibited from serving more than one term in Mexico, the PRI had to choose a new presidential candidate every six years (*sexenio*). Rather than leaving this critical decision in the hands of party factions, the outgoing president personally selected his own successor in a veiled process known as the *dedazo* (fingering). Party militants would then unite around his choice and mobilize the party's machinery to bring the PRI another victory in the presidential elections.

The CTM, and particularly Fidel Velázquez, took the lead in circling the wagons around the president's nominee. Following a pattern established in the late 1930s, the CTM would endorse (and sometimes announce) the new candidate and, in the process, undermine the candidate's intraparty rivals, particularly from the party's left wing. This contribution was vital to Mexico's dominant-party system, since the decisive moment in the transfer of power was "the selection and designation of the official candidate rather than the casting or counting of votes."[20] In a clear indication of the CTM's critical role in managing these transitions, Velázquez always assumed the presidency of the Labor Congress during the period of candidate selection.

The CTM also participated actively in PRI campaigns at the municipal, state, and national levels. In the months leading up to an election, the CTM distributed propaganda and organized mass demonstrations in favor of PRI candidates. Often the CTM enticed workers to gather in the town square by offering them transportation and food. CTM leaders also helped the PRI buy votes and lambasted the opposition as enemies of the Mexican Revolution. On election day, the CTM delivered the working-class vote—entire districts in some cases—to the party. Besides requiring CTM members and their families to vote for the PRI, the CTM frequently brought workers to the polls and, when necessary, helped local PRI officials doctor the results.

Finally, the CTM bolstered the PRI's hegemony by maintaining controls on dissidence in the workplace. Although the PRI occasionally used direct intervention to squash labor militancy, it preferred to delegate this task to the leaders of the CTM and other official unions. With the blessing of the PRI, the CTM centralized control in the hands of Velázquez and his cronies at the expense of more progressive leadership groups. In addition, the CTM took advantage of a provision of the LFT that allowed the creation of a closed shop through the incorporation of so-called exclusion clauses into collective contracts.[21] By linking union membership to employment, these clauses protected incumbent leaders from dissent from below and facilitated the imposition of pro-PRI policies. They also facilitated the negotiation of protection contracts with employers, contracts that the union usually sold to the employer unbeknownst to the workers, preventing organization of the workplace by a more militant union.[22]

In return for its support for PRI hegemony, the CTM received various political and organizational benefits. First, the party's system of sectoral representation guaranteed the CTM access to party posts and elected office at the local, state, and federal levels. While receiving a relatively small share of total PRI candidacies, the CTM dominated those allocated to the Labor Sector. Because the PRI won the vast majority of elections through the 1970s, these candidates were almost certain to take office. Second, the CTM received protection from serious challenges to its hegemony in the labor movement. On those rare occasions when regularized mechanisms of control proved inadequate, the PRI intervened directly to remove dissident leaders. These purges, which became known as *charrazos*, proved crucial to defeating challenges to the CTM and the PRI in the 1940s, 1950s, and 1970s.[23]

Bargains in Crisis

The socioeconomic and political bargains between the PRI and the CTM had a symbiotic relationship with the economic and political models that prevailed in Mexico from the 1940s until the early 1980s. This relationship proved unsustainable, however, in the face of growing pressures at home and abroad. Secular trends such as the exhaustion of ISI and growing public indebtedness combined with international price shocks in the 1970s and early 1980s to bring the Mexican economy to its knees.[24] At the same time, the increasing heterogeneity of Mexico's social structure and decades of top-down politics heightened demands for an opening of the Mexican political system. In response to these pressures, the Mexican government abandoned ISI in favor of market-opening and presided, albeit reluctantly, over a gradual democratization of the political process.

The impact of these changes on the Mexican labor movement has been devastating in economic terms but potentially promising in political terms. From 1982 to 1994, the bargains between the PRI and CTM suffered serious setbacks but continued to define the parameters for action both within the labor movement and between labor and the state. Beginning in 1995, however, Mexico's process of democratization showed signs of profoundly altering the key players and rules of the game in the labor movement. With the July 2000 victory of Vicente Fox, the presidential candidate for the PAN, these changes can be expected to accelerate.

Between Delinking and Dependency, 1982–1994

Between 1982 and 1994, the PRI radically altered its development model away from ISI and gradually conceded political space to opposition parties. In the process, its bargains with the CTM became a mixed blessing. On the one hand, the PRI no longer possessed the economic and political resources with which to meet the CTM's demands. In fact, close ties to the CTM were becoming costly for the PRI, particularly in political terms. On the other hand, the PRI continued to depend on the CTM to carry out the very reforms that threatened to render the old bargains obsolete, as well as to maintain its faltering hegemony while attempting a transition to an alternative support coalition. Thus, the PRI engaged in a balancing act between dismantling its old bargains with the CTM and offering CTM leaders enough goodies to keep them from withdrawing their support.

Dismantling the Old Bargains

In many respects, the CTM became more of a liability than an asset for the PRI in the 1980s and 1990s. The kinds of privileges to which the CTM had become accustomed were no longer readily accommodated in an environment of economic and political competition. In the economic arena, delivering real wage growth, stable employment, and generous social spending often clashed with controlling inflation and competing in the global marketplace. In the political arena, guaranteeing candidacies to CTM leaders often clashed with the requirement that candidates be electable. Relatedly, some of the CTM's contributions under the old bargains were losing value. In a labor market increasingly characterized by uncertainty, fragmentation, and informality, the PRI became less dependent on the CTM to hold down wages and suppress strikes. Moreover, the CTM lost much of its capacity to deliver large blocs of votes on election day, particularly when compared to the power of the media and other modern campaign tools to mobilize voters without the help of intermediary organizations such as unions.

In this context, the PRI had strong incentives to dismantle its old bargains with the CTM and restructure its support coalition to match Mexico's new economic model and increasingly heterogeneous social structure. During the administration of Miguel de la Madrid (1982–1988), the government focused primarily on limiting the CTM's influence over economic policy, particularly wage determination. The emphasis shifted during the administration of Carlos Salinas

(1988–1994) toward reducing the CTM's political and organizational prerogatives, partly in response to the PRI's poor showing among workers in the 1988 elections.

Restructuring the Wage Bargain

Upon taking office in December 1982, de la Madrid adopted an orthodox anti-inflation plan that consisted of unilateral wage restraints, drastic budget cuts, and trade liberalization. The CTM responded, particularly in 1983 and 1987, by filing thousands of strike petitions and warning that its collaboration with the regime was in jeopardy if the government did not grant higher wage increases.[25] In contrast to the 1950s and the 1970s, however, the CTM's actions brought almost no wage concessions from the government. Rather than taking on the risk of carrying out its threats, the CTM repeatedly acquiesced. In the process, real wages plummeted, and the CTM experienced a significant loss of decisionmaking authority.

This loss of authority took two forms. First, de la Madrid effectively transferred control over minimum-wage levels from the tripartite CNSM to the economic cabinet.[26] Second, he reversed a traditional pattern whereby wage increases negotiated in collective contracts set the pace for minimum-wage adjustments. With the brief exception of 1986 and 1987, minimum-wage adjustments served as caps for increases in contracted wages (see Figure 3.1).[27] Such policies "tended to erase . . . the boundary between unionized workers and non-unionized workers, eliminating or seeking to eliminate one of the central functions of the union and the collective contract: the negotiation of wages."[28] In the process, the CTM lost much of its ability to deliver real wage gains to its members.

Despite the drastic wage declines brought on by these policies, inflation continued to plague the Mexican economy. Increasingly convinced of the need for negotiated wage and price controls, a network of officials in the Ministry of Planning and Budget, the Bank of Mexico, and the Ministry of Finance persuaded representatives from government, business, labor, and the peasantry to sign the Pact of Economic Solidarity (Pacto) on December 15, 1987.[29] The Pacto mandated another devaluation of the peso, budget austerity measures, price and wage controls, and trade liberalization. Initially intended as a temporary measure to break the inflationary cycle, the Pacto was renegotiated periodically over the next decade.

Figure 3.1 Index of Real Daily Wages, 1980–1989 (1995 pesos; 1980=100)

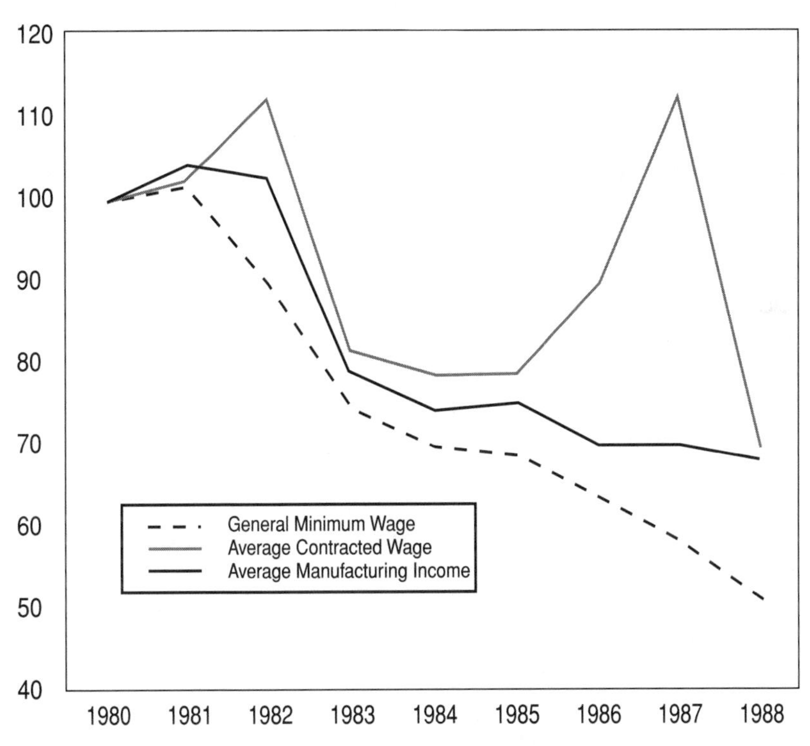

Source: Dávila Capalleja, "Mexico: The Evolution and Reform of the Labor Market," in Sebastian Edward and Nora Lustig, eds., *Labor Markets in Latin America* (Washington, D.C.: Brookings Institution Press, 1997), pp. 301–302.

While creating a new space for the CTM to participate in wage policy, the Pacto reinforced the centralization of wage bargaining in the hands of the economic cabinet. For one, the CNSM became further marginalized in the wage-setting process. Although the CNSM retained its formal authority to establish minimum wages, its business and labor delegates were obligated to follow the guidelines established by the Pacto.[30] These guidelines, in turn, were generally predetermined by the economic cabinet and then delivered to the Pacto signatories for their approval.

Second, the Pacto retained the practice of using minimum-wage adjustments as caps for wages negotiated in collective contracts.[31] After extending increases in the minimum wage to contracted wages in

December 1987 and March 1988, the Pacto froze all wages between April and December 1988.[32] As manufacturing wages began to diverge from the downward trend of the minimum wage (see Figure 3.1), the Pacto explicitly prohibited the extension of minimum-wage increases to contracted wages and, in 1993, explicitly required that collective wage bargaining "be resolved within the inflation rate guiding this Concertation."[33] Evidence suggests that these provisions caused earning differentials between unionized and nonunionized workers to narrow, particularly in the late 1980s.[34]

The Pacto essentially brought the CTM's combative response to national wage policy to an end, even after a drastic devaluation of the peso in 1994.[35] Rather than filing a rash of strike petitions, the CTM chose to pursue its wage demands through the Pacto, which was renewed in early 1995.[36] In part, this change resulted from the Pacto's success in controlling inflation and thereby improving the conditions for real wage growth. While the minimum wage continued its downward spiral in the 1990s, average manufacturing income began to recover, especially after the CTM abandoned its long-standing objection to linking salary increases to productivity gains.

But the CTM's less combative tactics cannot be explained entirely by improved economic conditions. As shown in Figure 3.2, contracted wages in federal jurisdiction activities continued to stagnate, and all wages fell after the peso devaluation in 1994. The CTM's tactical shift also signaled the institutionalization of a restructured wage bargain with the PRI. Although suffering a devaluation of its traditional mechanisms of wage determination, the CTM gained a formalized—and privileged—channel through which to engage in insider bargaining, which it always preferred to external pressure.[37] Moreover, the Pacto made the CTM an indispensable partner in the government's economic program, giving it valuable leverage in its overall relationship with the PRI. Given their extensive protections from dissent from below, CTM leaders could afford to accept this trade-off, however reluctantly.

Challenging the CTM's Prerogatives

Although de la Madrid engineered a permanent reduction in the CTM's real influence over wage levels, he did little to challenge the political and organizational prerogatives of CTM leaders. In fact, he created a new fiefdom for the CTM by giving constitutional status and government funding to the so-called social sector of worker-owned enterprises.[38] By contrast, Carlos Salinas led a direct assault on these preroga-

Figure 3.2 Index of Real Wages, 1989–1999 (1994 pesos, 1989=100)

Source: Ernesto Zedillo, *5°Informe de Gobierno,* Anexo Estadístico (Mexico, D.F.; Presidencia, 1999).

tives as part of an attempt to reconstruct the PRI's support coalition to match Mexico's new economic model and increasingly heterogeneous social structure.

First, Salinas cultivated new interlocutors in the labor movement. Calling for a "new unionism" to meet the demands of a modernized and market-oriented economy, he began wooing the support of "modern" union leaders in the public sector and in recently privatized sectors. With his implicit backing, several unions from the latter group formed the Federation of Public Goods and Services Unions (FESEBES) in April 1990 under the leadership of Francisco Hernández Juárez, the secretary-general of the Telephone Workers' Union (STRM). Although the Labor Ministry did not grant FESEBES's petition for registration until August 1992, Salinas sent signals that he was grooming Hernández Juárez and the FESEBES as an alternative to Velázquez and the CTM.

Second, Salinas enacted reforms to reduce union control over social programs. In 1989, he created a new program, PRONASOL, that bypassed traditional organizational and party channels to deliver benefits directly to poor consumers. This program received cabinet-level status with the creation of the Ministry of Social Development (SEDESOL) in March 1992. As part of PRONASOL, Salinas formed the National Solidarity Institute (INSOL), which organized training seminars for union cadres. Both agencies cultivated ties with FESEBES, which participated in the INSOL's creation and signed the Union Modernization Accord with Sedesol in February 1993.[39] Although CTM members participated in INSOL seminars, Velázquez became a vehement critic as part of his crusade against FESEBES.[40]

Salinas also challenged the CTM's control over pensions and worker housing. Although union opposition led government officials to withdraw an ambitious proposal to transform the IMSS in early 1991, the government officials went ahead with plans to create an individual pension fund administered by private banks to complement the existing financial structure of the IMSS. They also engineered a reform of the worker housing agency INFONAVIT to limit the role of the unions to "monitoring the global dynamic of the system, but without the power to intervene specifically in its regulation, administration, or direction."[41]

Under the regulations approved for INFONAVIT in September 1992, the unions lost their control over housing construction contracts, as well as their capacity to assign housing credits to union members.[42] Moreover, Salinas removed a close ally of Velázquez from the directorship of INFONAVIT and replaced him with a financial technocrat committed to rationalizing the agency's administration.[43]

Finally, Salinas sought to reconstruct the popular bases of the PRI at the expense of organized labor. This initiative was prompted by the CTM's failure to get out the vote for the 1988 elections, in which the PRI suffered record losses. Some of the worst hits came in districts with heavy concentrations of working-class voters, including traditional PRI strongholds in oil-producing regions.[44] In addition, union candidates suffered unprecedented defeats.[45] In response to this debacle, Salinas set out to reorganize the PRI. In November 1989, the PRI's president, Luis Donaldo Colosio, announced an initiative to restructure the party along territorial rather than sectoral lines, with an emphasis on building new constituencies in poor urban neighborhoods.

Despite vehement opposition by the CTM, the PRI's Fourteenth Assembly adopted several changes that undermined the CTM's influence. The new PRI statutes emphasized the importance of citizen activity and established equal representation for the sectors and the territorial structure in assemblies, councils, and conventions. They also restructured internal party organs at all levels to multiply the number of actors involved; eliminated the sectoral posts on the National Executive Committee (CEN); and added the category of "sympathizer" to the dual system of individual and collective affiliation.[46]

Keeping Fuel in the Old Jalopy

A decade after de la Madrid started Mexico down the path of neoliberal reform, the CTM found major facets of its socioeconomic and political bargains with the PRI in disarray. Not only did CTM leaders have significantly less to offer their members, but their own leadership privileges were under attack. At the same time, however, the PRI continued to rely on the CTM to perform a few key functions. In the words of Raúl Trejo Delarbre, the CTM "is like an automobile built in the 1930s; it keeps functioning, even if badly."[47] Until the PRI could build a new, more efficient car to match Mexico's changing terrain, it needed to keep fuel in the old jalopy.

The CTM performed three functions that were particularly important to the PRI in the context of neoliberal reform: (1) endorsing and enforcing the anti-inflation pacts; (2) backing the PRI's policies of industrial restructuring and global integration, particularly negotiation of the North American Free Trade Agreement (NAFTA); and (3) exercising a stabilizing influence on the presidential succession. In exchange for these services, the PRI respected some features of the old bargains and ultimately retreated from its attempts to undermine the CTM's organizational and political prerogatives.

Anti-inflation Pacts

As discussed above, the CTM played a key role in the PRI's anti-inflation strategy after 1987. Besides participating in periodic renegotiations of the Pacto, CTM officials were involved in weekly meetings of the Commission of Enforcement and Evaluation, which played "an extremely important" role in monitoring compliance.[48] Moreover, the CTM acted as "first among equals" within the labor delegation. According to Jaime Serra Puche, the secretary of commerce from 1988 to 1994, the Labor Congress was the formal representative of labor "but Fidel was the real leader."[49] Velázquez was the only union official to sign the original Pacto in 1987, and the Labor Congress extended his term as president until June 1988 to manage the sensitive negotiations regarding the Pacto's renewal.[50]

As long as the Pacto remained a priority for the government, the PRI had strong incentives to ensure the CTM's ongoing participation by respecting some features of the old bargains. Well aware of its leverage, the CTM did not hesitate to threaten defection from the Pacto to win concessions on other issues. Although these concessions tended to benefit CTM leaders rather than workers, the Pacto gave the PRI incentives to continue investing in its historic alliance with the CTM.

Industrial Restructuring and NAFTA

Ratification of the PRI's anti-inflation policy was not the only means by which the CTM facilitated neoliberal reform in the 1980s and 1990s. Although with less fanfare, the confederation also provided essential support for two related reforms: (1) industrial restructuring, and (2) NAFTA. The PRI's neoliberal technocrats viewed both reforms as crucial to their objective of making Mexican industry more competitive and export-oriented. Industrial restructuring involved introducing new technologies, raising productivity, shedding excess labor, and flexibilizing the workforce through "the elimination of legal, political, and social restrictions to carrying out changes in the enterprise."[51] The creation of a free trade zone in North America was intended to upgrade Mexican firms by exposing them to foreign competition while providing them with greater access to capital, technology, and markets.

Both reforms posed real challenges to Mexican unions. Industrial restructuring threatened not only immediate layoffs but also a permanent reduction in the collective and individual rights of workers. And even though NAFTA promised to bring new investment and higher salaries, it was likely to accelerate the painful process of restructuring as well as destroying those firms incapable of adapting to increased competition. Aware of these challenges, the government sought the CTM's cooperation to defuse labor opposition and provide an environment favorable to foreign investment. It won such cooperation by (1) retreating from any reform of the LFT, and (2) supporting the CTM in its struggles against rival unions.

De jure, Mexico did not undergo any flexibilization of the rules governing the individual or collective rights of workers. Despite congressional hearings on labor-law reform and repeated threats by President Carlos Salinas to rewrite the LFT, the PRI took no real action on this front for at least three reasons. First, Mexican unions were united in their virulent opposition to any devaluation of the legal rights of workers or unions. Thus, any serious attempt to reform the LFT would have elicited strong resistance by the labor movement. Second, the PRI discovered that the *threat* of labor-law reform was a valuable bargaining chip for extracting other concessions from the CTM. Third, the PRI was not especially interested in jeopardizing those provisions of the LFT that enabled the regime to protect itself and its labor allies against worker militancy, particularly the exclusion clauses and the state's authority to determine the legality of strikes and intervene in disputes between groups of workers vying for control of a collective contract.[52]

In fact, these provisions ended up facilitating de facto flexibilization, which was widespread in the 1980s and 1990s. Rather than taking place through legislation, this flexibilization occurred on a firm-by-firm basis through the revision of collective contracts. The changes sought by employers included (1) fewer rules regarding the hiring and firing of permanent workers; (2) more freedom to subcontract and hire temporary workers; (3) greater control over labor mobility, task assignment, pay scales, and promotion criteria within the workplace; and (4) the legal right to rescind contracts in the event of extreme economic necessity. Taken together, these changes represented a significant shift in the balance of power between capital and labor within the workplace.

As chronicled by several authors, such changes were written into collective contracts in a number of major enterprises in Mexico in the 1980s and 1990s.[53] The CTM collaborated in this process, especially when challenged by a rival confederation backed by workers opposed to the contract revisions. Rather than resisting contract flexibilization as a threat to worker rights, the CTM saw it as an opportunity to expand its presence in key economic sectors. Not surprisingly, the government used its extensive authority to support this trade-off.

The CTM pursued this strategy on two fronts. First, it capitalized on its reputation as an employer-friendly union to extend its influence in export-oriented growth sectors, particularly in transnational enterprises.[54] This trend was most pronounced in automobile manufacturing and the *maquiladoras*.[55] Having lost its hegemony to independent unions in the automobile industry in the 1970s, the CTM seized the chance to gain title to contracts in new plants constructed by companies such as Ford, Nissan, and General Motors in the 1980s. In the process, the CTM regained its hegemony but at the expense of contracts that were more flexible than the norm.[56] Likewise, the CTM accepted flexible provisions in return for control over new contracts in the fast-growing maquiladora industry.[57]

Second, the CTM used contract disputes to seize or regain control in plants that were already unionized but undergoing industrial restructuring. In several conflicts in major firms (e.g., Ford-Cuahtitlán, Modelo Brewery, Tornel Rubber Company), the government sided with the CTM against rival unions because of its greater willingness to support the negotiation of market-friendly contracts. In a style reminiscent of the charrazos of previous decades, the labor authorities backed the CTM by declaring strikes illegal, refusing to recognize surveys granting a majority to a rival union, and/or turning a blind eye to coercion by union thugs. In most cases, the outcome was the reestablishment of CTM control and a much more flexible contract.

In the midst of this process of de facto flexibilization, President Salinas proposed the negotiation of a free trade agreement with the United States in 1990.[58] The purpose of NAFTA was not so much to initiate neoliberal reforms as to deepen and formalize them. Nonetheless, Salinas viewed the successful conclusion of the NAFTA negotiations as crucial to his project of transforming Mexico into a market-driven, globally integrated economy attractive to foreign investors. Particularly given the strong anti-NAFTA stance of U.S. unions, his administration made a concerted effort to win the support of Mexican unions despite their long-standing nationalism and protectionist leanings.

According to one CTM official, a fierce debate took place within the CTM over whether or not to support NAFTA. In particular, the agreement's advocates had to work hard to convince Velázquez of its merits.[59] Ultimately, the nonagenarian leader decided in favor of the agreement, declaring in February 1991 that "the CTM unconditionally supports the FTA between Mexico and the United States, because the federal government will respect the rights of workers."[60] The price of the CTM's support was withdrawal by the government of its threat to modify existing labor laws.[61]

Another development that helps explain the CTM's support for NAFTA is the emergence of FESEBES as a potential rival. Velázquez and the CTM responded to FESEBES with hostility, threatening to expel the six unions in the federation from the Labor Congress[62] and supporting a dissident movement against Hernández Juárez in the STRM.[63] At the same time, the CTM adopted the more subtle tactic of trying to steal FESEBES's "new unionist" fire. Besides supporting NAFTA, the CTM signed the National Accord for the Elevation of Productivity and Quality in May 1992 and withdrew its opposition to the incorporation of productivity bonuses into contracted wage agreements during the renegotiation of the Pacto in October 1993.[64] This policy shift contributed to a recovery of the CTM position relative to FESEBES in 1993 as indicated by the CTM's success in blocking its bid for legislative candidacies for the 1994 elections.[65]

However, neither the CTM's support for NAFTA nor its embrace of increased productivity can entirely explain its improved relations with the PRI in the mid-1990s. With the approach of the presidential succession, Salinas largely abandoned the project of alliance restructuring to refurbish the old but reliable CTM jalopy. Although the CTM could no longer deliver as many votes as before, it continued to play a crucial role in preserving the fragile equilibrium that enabled the PRI to renew its power while changing its leader. Moreover, the PRI needed every vote it could get in the face of increased electoral competition. Thus, as in previous sexenios, time ran out on the president's attempt to shift the bases of the PRI's support coalition.

Managing the Presidential Succession

The CTM's traditional role of mobilizing support within the PRI for the president's chosen successor may have become even more important in the 1980s and 1990s because of discontent among party leftists with the neoliberal turn of the PRI leadership. During the 1988 succession, a group of PRI members led by Cuauhtémoc Cárdenas defected from the party to run against Salinas—with nearly disastrous results for the PRI. Moreover, the immediate reaction of Velázquez to the selection of Salinas suggested that the CTM's support for the dedazo could not be taken entirely for granted. Although the CTM quickly conformed to the ritual of throwing its full organizational and ideological weight behind the president's choice, Velázquez appeared less than enthusiastic during the traditional *abrazos* (greetings) with the candidate and walked out in the middle of Salinas's acceptance speech.[66]

To ensure the CTM's full cooperation with the dedazo in 1993–1994, Salinas retreated from his assault on the CTM's prerogatives toward the end of his sexenio. The retreat began at the PRI's Sixteenth Assembly in March 1993.[67] Despite initial plans "to citizenize" (*ciudadanizar*) the party, the PRI ended up reaffirming the role of the sectors and restoring some of the privileges denied to them in 1990. The assembly opened with the abrupt announcement by a CTM leader that the PRI's reformist president had been replaced. The CTM subsequently succeeded in defeating several proposals that would have diluted the Labor Sector's influence.[68] In addition, the PRI accepted a CTM proposal to reinstate the sectoral posts that had been eliminated from the CEN in 1990.[69] The CTM's secretary of social welfare, Abelardo Carrillo Zavala, concluded that "it is very heart-warming that when the time of the presidential succession approaches, the organic alliance between the sectors of the PRI and the government is reestablished."[70]

The CTM also enjoyed a revival of its privileges in INFONAVIT. In April 1993, a close friend of Velázquez, Francisco Ruiz Massieu, became president of the agency. After frequent meetings between the two leaders, INFONAVIT's administrative council restored the old system of union intermediation in October 1993.[71] Carrillo Zavala noted the benefits of the revised system: "INFONAVIT permits us to propose the construction of housing units, to present a list of those to whom we would like to provide housing and, in some way, to present a directory of builders who at the state, regional, and national level have the capacity to build where the unions would like, given the needs of their members."[72]

By early 1994, the basic contours of the political bargain between the CTM and the PRI had been restored. In return, the CTM closed ranks with the PRI during a succession marred by the Zapatista uprising in January 1994 and the brutal assassination in March 1994 of Colosio, who had been named the PRI's presidential candidate. Velázquez spoke out against destabilizing forces in the country, and the CTM made an exaggerated but symbolically important promise to deliver 5.5 million working-class votes to the party in August 1994.[73] In the days leading up to the elections, the CTM and its affiliates offered financial incentives for workers to attend PRI rallies, threatened CTM members with sanctions if they failed to vote, and published an advertisement in the national media urging workers to support the PRI's replacement candidate, Ernesto Zedillo.[74] Although Zedillo did not receive an absolute majority, he won by a sizable margin in a relatively clean election.

Radical Changes in Terrain, 1995–2000

Despite sharing the technocratic profile of his two predecessors, Zedillo held out the hope of better times, both economically and politically, for the Mexican labor movement. Campaigning with the slogan "For the Welfare of Your Family," he argued that the hard years of the transition from state-led to market-led development were over and that his administration could now turn to improving the living conditions of the majority of Mexicans. He also made an important gesture of conciliation toward the CTM that suggested that the confederation's influence might grow during his sexenio. Soon after taking office in December 1994, he appointed the CTM's secretary of education, Juan Millán, to the position of PRI secretary-general, the highest PRI position ever held by a labor leader.

These hopes were quickly dashed, however. Less than two weeks after Zedillo's inauguration, the Mexican peso crashed and the economy went into a deep recession. During 1995, economic output declined by more than 6 percent, nearly 1 million workers lost their jobs in the formal sector, and real manufacturing wages contracted by 13.5 percent.[75] Especially after so many promises by Salinas of a neoliberal Mexican miracle, the crisis fueled a wave of anti-PRI sentiment that translated into major victories for the opposition. Rather than standing in the way of these changes, Zedillo sought to accommodate them while reforming the PRI to make it more capable of competing in fair elections. In the process, he presided over changes in Mexico's political terrain that threatened to alter the parameters for action both within the labor movement and between labor and the state.

Zedillo's immediate response to the economic crisis was to reimpose austerity and accelerate structural reform. He agreed to the terms of an emergency bailout package set by the United States, imposed harsh austerity measures, and sought to extend privatization into sectors such as petrochemicals, social security, and electrical power. Although the austerity measures helped reverse the economy's free fall by 1996, they also contributed to electoral backlash against the PRI. In July 1997, the PRI suffered two defeats that profoundly altered the balance of power in the political system. First, Cuauhtémoc Cárdenas, the candidate for the Party of the Democratic Revolution (PRD), won the first election for the newly created governorship of the Federal District. Second, and more important, the PRI lost its majority in the Chamber of Deputies for the first time since 1929. This defeat transformed Congress from a rubber stamp into a real check on executive power.

In the meantime, dissidents within the PRI began to break the old rules regarding party discipline. At the party's national congress in September 1996, delegates defied the executive by rejecting Zedillo's proposal for privatizing the secondary petrochemical industry and dashing the presidential hopes of most members of Zedillo's cabinet by requiring that the nominee be a PRI member and have held elective office. A few PRI legislators also dared to violate the party line in Congress, which would have been unthinkable a few years earlier. Moreover, the PRI was wracked by increasingly high-level defections, especially when party officials imposed their candidates without consulting the bases. For example, the PRD won its first state governorship in 1998 when a PRI candidate rejected by the party hierarchy ran instead under the PRD banner.

By far the most deadly blow to the PRI came in the July 2000 presidential elections. Despite Zedillo's attempt to enhance the PRI's chances by replacing the dedazo with an open primary, the PRI finally lost its hold on the presidency. In the cleanest election in Mexico's history, the PAN candidate, Vicente Fox, won with 42.7 percent of the vote compared to 35.7 percent for the PRI candidate, Francisco Labastida. In addition, the PAN's coalition gained the largest share of seats in the Senate and the Chamber of Deputies as well as two governorships. The PRI's defeat unleashed a power struggle within the party, which scrambled to make the adjustments necessary to survive after Fox's inauguration in December 2000.

These developments contributed to the emergence of new players and rules in the Mexican labor movement. First, the combination of renewed economic hardship and loosened control by the PRI encouraged several organizational initiatives in the labor movement that threatened the CTM. Second, branches of government other than the PRI-controlled executive began, albeit in small ways, to reshape the rules of the game in the labor movement. Although these rule changes are still incipient, they may ultimately be more significant because of their potential effect on authority structures both within and among Mexican unions.

New Players

Although Zedillo and the PRI continued to pay homage to the CTM as a valiant defender of Mexican workers, the confederation found itself besieged from both within and without. Internally, the CTM was rocked in June 1997 by the death of Velázquez, who had been at the helm for more than forty years. His passing did not provoke the succession crisis or worker revolts that many predicted, but it did remove a critical source of the CTM's power. Eulogized by media commentators as a powerful figure who often rivaled the president himself, Velázquez had an impressive network of personal ties and loyalties that gave the CTM a degree of influence that went beyond its actual strength as an organization. His successor, Leonardo Rodríguez Alcaine, was another member of the old guard who shared many of Velázquez's ideas but lacked his personal authority. To the dismay of those who hoped for a new style of leadership in the CTM, Rodríguez Alcaine won unanimous reelection in 1998 to serve until 2004.

This internal blow was accompanied by external challenges to the CTM's hegemony, especially as exercised through the increasingly dysfunctional Labor Congress. In September 1995, a group of important unions, led by Hernández Juárez and the FESEBES, created the Forum of Unionism Before the Nation to discuss the problem of unemployment. Meanwhile, the National Social Security Workers' Union joined with more than a dozen other unions to form the Front in Defense of Social Security against the government's plan to privatize the IMSS.[76] Although neither movement succeeded in blocking Zedillo's reforms, their leaders were emboldened by Velázquez's death and the PRI's loss of its majority in the Chamber of Deputies to form a new umbrella organization to rival the CTM-dominated CT. In August 1997, more than 300 delegates from 132 unions claiming to represent more than 1 million workers agreed to create the National Union of Workers (UNT).[77]

The UNT was formally established at a convention in November 1997 with an estimated membership of 1.5 million workers.[78] The UNT's central objectives were (1) to challenge the economic policies imposed through elite pacts, and (2) to free labor organizations from the corporatist practices associated with the PRI.[79] In addition, the UNT made a commitment to union autonomy and political pluralism.[80] Although several of the UNT's key figures belonged to the PRI and/or held important posts in the party, one of its three presidents, Agustín Rodríguez Fuentes, openly sympathized with the PRD.[81]

In addition to mobilizing workers, the UNT sought to use the newly independent Congress as an avenue for demand-making. Soon after the organization's creation, the UNT executive expressed the expectation that the legislature "will be a new arena of action for independent unionism."[82] Hoping to capitalize on this opportunity, the UNT joined with other independent unions in 1999 to create the Social Workers' Movement (MST), which planned to register as a political organization and possibly run candidates for office. Although the MST's founding documents (and several informed observers) indicated that its true goal was to act as a pressure group on the major parties rather than as an alternative to them, the MST posed a symbolic challenge to the PRI's Labor Sector. In making the case for the MST, Hernández Juárez stated that "until now there has not been any national organization which reflects the interests of the workers themselves in the legislative arena."[83]

The UNT and the MST were not the only organizational innovations to threaten the CTM and the CT during this period. Zedillo sparked another one when he announced that he would seek a constitutional amendment to allow privatization of the electrical power industry. This proposal met with the fierce resistance of the powerful Mexican Electrical Workers (SME), which created the National Front of Resistance Against the Privatization of the Electrical Industry (FNRCPIE) in February 1999 with thirty other labor organizations, PRD legislators, a reform faction of the PRI, dissident members of the Sole Union of Electrical Workers of the Mexican Republic (SUTERM), and leaders of the Oilworkers' Union of the Mexican Republic (STPRM).[84] In March, the FNRCPIE organized a demonstration attended by an estimated 100,000 workers, and by April it had established a presence in more than half of Mexico's states.[85]

The FNRCPIE's antiprivatization crusade crystallized a wider opposition to the CT and the government's economic program. In April 1999, the SME announced that it was withdrawing from the CT because "we have not been treated with dignity by its leader [Rodríguez Alcaine], who has shown a lack of interest in taking an urgent stand regarding the privatization of the electrical power industry."[86] The following month, the most important independent unions, including the FNRCPIE, the SME, the UNT, FESEBES, the Mexican Union Front (FSM), and the May 1st Inter-Union Group, marched together on May Day for the first time in many years to protest neoliberal reform, antidemocratic labor structures, and privatization. According to one labor historian, "This is the first time that an independent demonstration has been larger than the official one."[87] Later that year, the UNT, the SME, and the FSM signed a unity pact pledging to work together to meet the challenges of globalization and modernization, fight for union autonomy and democracy, improve collective bargaining and the minimum wage, and inculcate class-consciousness in workers.[88]

This groundswell of unified opposition by independent unions threatened the CTM on several levels. First, it represented a clear and viable alternative to the CTM's strategy of currying favor with the PRI government. Besides winning the support of thousands of workers, the movement enjoyed uncharacteristic freedom to form a broad front against government policy. Although clearly irked by its direct challenge to his agenda, Zedillo no longer possessed a highly disciplined, hegemonic machine that could easily restore the primacy of the CTM and its collaborationist policies. Thus, he did not subject the movement's instigators to the charrazos of the past—despite the proximity of the presidential elections—and he retreated when the privatization plan was blocked in Congress.[89] This sequence of events reinforced the impression that new spaces had opened up for independent action in the Mexican labor movement.[90]

Second, the movement sparked dissidence within the CTM's own ranks. As noted above, the FNRCPIE included members of the STPRM (oil) and the SUTERM (electrical power), both of which were affiliated with the CTM and officially supported Zedillo's privatization policies. In fact, Rodríguez Alcaine was secretary-general of the SUTERM as well as secretary-general of the CTM and president of the CT.[91] Thus, internal opposition to the SUTERM's support for the reform translated into a direct challenge to the leadership of the CTM and the CT. In March 1999, some 2,000 workers from three SUTERM locals sent a document to the Senate expressing opposition "to dissolving our workplaces."[92] Two months later, more than 3,000 workers from forty SUTERM locals marched to oppose privatization and to demand the resignation of Rodríguez Alcaine as head of both the SUTERM and the CTM.[93] Aware that his leadership was in jeopardy, Rodríguez Alcaine reversed his position on privatization after thousands of SUTERM members participated in an antiprivatization demonstration in August 1999.[94]

New Rules

Besides having to compete with new players in the labor movement, the CTM found its privileged position threatened by several initiatives by branches of government other than the PRI-controlled executive to change the rules of the game. In the second half of the 1990s, the PAN and the PRD sparked a critical debate regarding the future of Mexican labor by introducing two proposals for labor-law reform in the Mexican Congress. Although differing in important ways, both proposals called for changes that would enhance union autonomy, encourage union democracy, and transfer control of labor justice from the executive to the judiciary.[95] Either proposal, if passed into law, would have dismantled the institutional foundations of the CTM's power, especially in light of its failure to deliver socioeconomic benefits to its members since the early 1980s.

The PAN proposal, presented to the Congress in 1995, was the most far-reaching of the two. Besides calling for a prohibition against exclusion clauses, the elimination of all registration requirements, transparent electoral procedures within unions, and the creation of special judges to replace the tripartite JCA, the PAN proposal drew explicitly on the Spanish Workers' Statute to advocate the creation of "factory councils" to represent workers on the shopfloor.[96] Although unions could still have a presence in the workplace, they would no longer have the right to bargain collectively except insofar as workers elected their militants to serve on the factory councils. As clearly illustrated in the Spanish case, this system would radically diminish the protections from worker dissent enjoyed by the CTM and other official unions.[97]

The PRD proposal, presented to the Congress in 1998, stopped short of prohibiting exclusion clauses and preserved a central role for unions in representing workers.[98] Nonetheless, the proposal called for an end to government intervention in union affairs (e.g., registration, strikes, wage bargaining), the removal of labor justice from the hands of the tripartite JCA, and a prohibition against the collective affiliation of unions to parties.[99] All three reforms would prevent business-as-usual by the CTM. Besides requiring its members to belong to the PRI, the CTM continues to depend heavily on state intervention and its dominance of the labor seats on the JCA to squelch dissent from within and outside the CTM. Without such protections, the CTM would be highly vulnerable to backlash for its collaboration with policies that have brought far more pain than prosperity to organized workers.

Although neither of these proposals reached the floor of Congress during the Zedillo administration, President Fox has called for a "national dialogue" on labor-law reform and indicated his support for controls on union corruption as well as measures to enhance employment, training, productivity, and competitiveness.[100] Thus, although the factory council system proposed by the PAN in 1995 has few prospects given strong union opposition, the anticorporatist provisions supported by both the PAN and the PRD could prosper under a Fox administration with an opposition-controlled Congress and an increasingly independent labor movement.

Even if labor-law reform remains a dead letter, other rule changes have been enacted with the same result of weakening the corporatist protections long enjoyed by the CTM and other official unions. One potentially threatening initiative came out of Mexico City's PRD-controlled government after July 1997. In 1999, the city's labor department created a public registry of labor unions in cooperation with the Local Conciliation and Arbitration Board (JLCA).[101] This decision, which reflected a generalized demand for greater transparency in government, put a dent in a long-standing policy by labor authorities of guarding union data like a state secret.[102] In the process, it threatened to expose the thousands of protection contracts that existed in the Federal District, often under the control of the CTM. According to one estimate, protection contracts accounted for nearly 75 percent of the labor contracts in the Federal District in the early 1990s.[103]

The most far-reaching initiatives, however, came not from the legislature or opposition-controlled executives but from the Mexican Supreme Court (SCJM). In early 1996, the SCJM ruled that public employees have the right to affiliate freely with unions of their choice or to create new unions. This ruling overturned a provision of the LFT that required public employees to belong to the FSTSE. A subsequent ruling by the SCJM in May 1999 made its decision regarding union freedom for public employees binding on all lower courts.[104] These rulings prompted the defection of dozens of public employee unions from the FSTSE, which had been closely affiliated with the PRI since its foundation in 1937.[105]

These two rulings did not directly threaten the CTM—and could even have been seen as an opportunity for the CTM to recruit public employees—but they put yet another dent in the top-down, PRI-dominated structure on which the CTM had long depended to maintain its power. Moreover, the court's willingness to challenge one of the corporatist tenets of the LFT suggested that others of more direct relevance to the CTM could also be vulnerable.

This possibility became a reality after the PRI lost the presidential elections in July 2000. The following September, the SCJM issued an unprecedented decision in favor of 400 SUTERM members who claimed that Rodríguez Alcaine had embezzled their savings and ordered the labor leader to return the equivalent of $20 million to the union's mutual fund.[106] Seven months later, in April 2001, the SCJM delivered the greatest blow of all to the CTM when it declared the LFT's exclusion clauses unconstitutional. Although it must rule similarly in four more cases before its decision becomes binding on the lower courts, its finding is consistent with prior decisions in favor of freedom of association and is likely to end one of the key mechanisms by which CTM leaders have protected themselves against dissent from below.[107]

Conclusion

The momentous changes in Mexico's political system are likely to continue reshaping the structure of authority in the labor movement in favor of looser political ties, more union autonomy, and possibly more union democracy. Where such a transformation will leave the CTM remains unclear. Throughout the Zedillo administration, the CTM clung to its old ways rather than trying to adapt to changing circumstances. While other members of the Labor Congress forged a more independent path from the PRI and its policies (often leading to their defection from the CT), the CTM continued to participate in the Pacto, cancelled its traditional May Day celebrations in 1995 and 1996 to avoid protests against the government, lambasted the destabilizing influence of opposition parties, rhetorically reaffirmed its historic alliance with the PRI, and engaged in its usual tactics to get out the vote for the PRI in local, state, and federal elections.

The CTM's continued loyalty to the PRI, especially in the context of redoubled worker hardship and declining PRI hegemony, reflects the meager options of its leaders. After years of sacrificing the interests of workers to safeguard their alliance with the PRI, the leaders had so little legitimacy that they could not afford to abandon even a sinking ship. Their best hope was to fight to the death for the PRI as the only party willing and able to offer them leadership privileges and protections. But now that the ship has sunk, the CTM is likely to need new leadership and/or strategies to survive. It does have a few younger, reformist leaders who might be able to lead a major restructuring of the confederation, which continues to represent the largest share of Mexico's industrial workers. An equally likely possibility, however, is that the old guard will block any changes that threaten its power, even if it results in massive defections by member unions.[108]

In either event, the CTM is no longer likely to set the parameters for action in the Mexican labor movement. In contrast to the pattern that prevailed between 1936 and 2000, state-labor relations appear to be moving in the direction of more contingent, fragmented, and loosely institutionalized interactions between relatively autonomous actors. Although this trend will only accelerate if the corporatist provisions of the Federal Labor Law continue to be dismantled, it has already been set in motion by the pressures of a globalized economy and the PRI's loss of political hegemony. The CTM will either adapt to this paradigmatic shift or be left behind.

This trend has positive as well as negative implications for Mexican workers. On the positive side, unions promise to be more responsive to their bases in a context of greater autonomy from the state, increased union competition, and enhanced access by workers to mechanisms for holding their leaders accountable. On the negative side, autonomy and responsiveness may come at the expense of policymaking influence.

Unless Mexico's unions can find ways to broaden their membership and/or build alliances with other popular organizations, they are unlikely to regain the policymaking influence once enjoyed by the CTM and may face even greater obstacles to engaging in collective action, particularly in an environment of deindustrialization, labor-market fragmentation, and informality. Thus, the challenge for Mexico's unions is to find a workable balance between autonomy and influence in a world of market uncertainty.

Notes

1. *La Jornada*, July 8, 2000.

2. César Zazueta and Ricardo de la Peña, *La estructura del Congreso de Trabajo* (México, D.F.: FCE, 1984), p. 35; Ian Roxborough, *Unions and Politics in Mexico* (Cambridge, UK: Cambridge University Press, 1984).

3. The party eliminated the Military Sector in 1940. The Popular Sector was a catch-all grouping that came to include public employees, small entrepreneurs, middle-class professionals, and popular organizations.

4. Victor Manuel Durand Ponte, "The Confederation of Mexican Workers, the Labor Congress, and the Crisis of Mexico's Social Pact," in Kevin Middlebrook, ed., *Unions, Workers, and the State in Mexico* (La Jolla: University of California–San Diego, Center for U.S.-Mexican Studies, 1991), p. 89.

5. Zazueta and de la Peña, *La estructura del Congreso de Trabajo*, p. 400.

6. Durand Ponte, "The Confederation of Mexican Workers," p. 89, n. 4.

7. Zazueta and de la Peña, *La estructura del Congreso de Trabajo*, p. 456.

8. For a brief interlude (1947–1950), Velázquez relinquished his formal position as secretary-general to a close associate, Fernando Amilpa.

9. Among other things, these juntas resolved individual and collective labor disputes and ruled on the legality of strike petitions. Kevin Middlebrook, *The Paradox of Revolution* (Baltimore: Johns Hopkins University Press, 1995), p. 61. In 1979, the CTM controlled 78 percent of the labor representatives on the special juntas. Zazueta and de la Peña, *La estructura del Congreso de Trabajo*, pp. 379–380.

10. Nora Lustig, *Mexico: The Remaking of an Economy*, 2nd ed. (Washington, D.C.: Brookings Institution, 1998), pp. 14–15.

11. Peter Gregory, *The Myth of Market Failure* (Washington, D.C.: World Bank, 1986), p. 30.

12. Miguel Basañez, *El pulso de los sexenios* (México, D.F.: Siglo Veintiuno Editores, 1990), p. 171.

13. Gregory, *The Myth of Market Failure*, p. 232.

14. Carmelo Mesa-Lago, *Social Security in Latin America* (Pittsburgh: University of Pittsburgh Press, 1978), pp. 216–219.

15. Zazueta and de la Peña, *La estructura del Congreso de Trabajo*, pp. 381–382. In the first IMSS General Assembly, created in 1945, the CTM received seven out of the ten labor positions. Richard R. Wilson, "The Corporatist Welfare State: Social Security and Development in Mexico" (Ph.D. diss., Department of Political Science, Yale University, 1981), pp. 208–226.

16. The participation of unionized workers in external promotions increased from 32 percent in 1975 to 60 percent in 1976, and the share of housing assignments made on the basis of external promotions increased from 27 percent in 1976 to 100 percent in 1980. José A. Aldrete-Haas, *La deconstrucción del Estado Mexicano* (México, D.F.: Alianza Editorial, 1991), pp. 93–94, n. 9; p. 109, n. 36.

17. Ibid., p. 112.

18. George Grayson, *The Mexican Labor Machine* (Washington, D.C.: Center for Strategic and International Studies, 1989), pp. 51, 55.

19. Middlebrook, *The Paradox of Revolution*, p. 222. In 1979, the CTM controlled the presidency of the bank's administrative council, along with 75 percent of its members. Zazueta and de la Peña, *La estructura del Congreso de Trabajo*, p. 384. When López Portillo nationalized Mexico's banking system in September 1982, he spared the Banco Obrero, which remained in the hands of the unions.

20. Gabriel Corona Armenta, "La burocracia sindical mexicana ante la sucesión presidencial: los procesos recientes," *Estudios Políticos*, No. 8 (Nueva Época, 1995): 128.

21. An "entry clause" made membership in the union holding the collective contract a prerequisite to employment, thereby eliminating the possibility of defection to a competing union (or no union). A "separation clause" required the employer to dismiss any worker who lost his or her union membership, thereby exposing troublesome workers to the threat of unemployment if kicked out of the union.

22. Most prevalent in small and medium-sized unions, protection contracts were estimated in the early 1990s to account for the majority of labor contracts in the Federal District. Dan La Botz, *Mask of Democracy* (Boston: South End, 1992), p. 55. They were also common in the maquiladora plants along the U.S.-Mexico border.

23. The term *charrazo* derives from the PRI's intervention in the late 1940s to replace a dissident leader in the railroad workers' union with a rival who was nicknamed *el charro* for his cowboy attire.

24. Among the most important international shocks were the collapse of the Bretton Woods international monetary system, the global spread of inflation (linked to the two oil crises), and a dramatic increase in U.S. interest rates.

25. The LFT requires that unions file strike petitions (*emplazamientos*) before holding a legal strike. The CTM frequently engaged in this practice to pressure the government during difficult wage negotiations.

26. A constitutional reform in December 1986 further centralized the process of wage determination by eliminating regional minimum-wage commissions. G. S. Franco and J. Fernando, "Labor Law and the Labor Movement in Mexico," in Middlebrook, ed., *Unions, Workers, and the State in Mexico*, p. 113.

27. Moreover, the government did not extend a shift from annual to need-based adjustments of the minimum wage to contracted wages, which continued to be limited to annual revisions. Franco and Fernando, "Labor Law," p. 113.

28. Max Ortega and Ana Alicia Solís, "Estado, capital y sindicatos," in Esthela Gutiérrez Garza, coord., *Los saldos del sexenio* (México, D.F.: Siglo Veintiuno Editores, 1990), p. 225.

29. Robert R. Kaufman, Carlos Bazdresch, and Blanca Heredia, "Mexico: Radical Reform in a Dominant Party System," in Stephan Haggard and Steven B. Webb, eds., *Voting for Reform* (New York: Oxford University Press, 1994), p. 377.

30. Author interview with Javier Bonilla, Secretary of Labor, Mexico City, June 18, 1996.

31. Christopher Woodruff, "Inflation Stabilization and the Vanishing Size-Wage Effect" (unpublished paper, 1997), pp. 5–6.

32. CSE (Comisión de Seguimiento y Evaluación del Pacto para el Bienestar, la Estabilidad y el Crecimiento), *Pacto para el bienestar, la estabilidad y el crecimiento y sus antecedentes, 1987–1994* (México, D.F.: CSE, 1994), pp. 285–290.

33. Ibid., p. 297.

34. Woodruff, "Inflation Stabilization," p. 24.

35. The CTM continued to file strike petitions after 1987, but these petitions were overwhelmingly motivated by collective contract disputes. Out of the strike petitions filed by all unions in federal jurisdiction activities, the share motivated by "other" concerns, including salary adjustments and emergency raises, declined from 52 percent in 1987 to less than 2 percent each year through 1996. Ernesto Zedillo, *3rd Informe de Gobierno, Anexo Estadístico* (Mexico, D.F.: Presidencia, 1997).

36. George Grayson, *From Corporatism to Pluralism* (Fort Worth, TX: Harcourt Brace Publishers, 1998), p. 114.

37. Even after rejecting wage and price controls in the late 1990s, the signatories renewed the institutional form of the Pacto. In February 1998, they negotiated the Accord of Cooperation and Consultation of the Productive Sectors (ACCSP) to "conserve a permanent space for dialogue in which to monitor the evolution of the principal economic variables at home and abroad." *La Jornada*, February 25, 1998. Like the Pacto, the ACCSP privileged the CT and the CTM over its rivals in the labor movement. *La Jornada*, March 20, 1998.

38. Katrina Burgess, "Alliances Under Stress: Economic Reform and Party-Union Relations in Mexico, Spain, and Venezuela" (Ph.D. diss., Department of Politics, Princeton University, 1998), pp. 126–127.

39. *El Financiero*, March 5, 1993.

40. Author interview with Pedro Zepeda Martínez, INSOL's Director General of Research and Development, Mexico City, December 2, 1994. According to one CTM official, Salinas was using INSOL and the FESEBES to put external pressure on the CTM. Confidential author interview, Mexico City, November 23, 1994.

41. Julian Bertranou, "Decisiones públicas y formulación de políticas en el México contemporaneo" (Master's thesis, Social Sciences, FLACSO, 1994), p. 256.

42. *El Financiero*, February 17, 1993.

43. Author interview with José Landa, a former consultant to the INFONAVIT, Mexico City, December 9, 1994.

44. Alejandro Alvarez Béjar, "Economic Crisis and the Labor Movement in Mexico," in Middlebrook, ed., *Unions, Workers, and the State in Mexico*, p. 48. In a sample based on official figures for seven cities with a high concentration of working-class voters, Cárdenas won an average of 51.4 percent of the vote, compared to only 30.3 percent for Salinas. Raúl Trejo Delarbre, "Sexenio de cambios aplazados," in Carlos Bazdresch et al., comps., *México: Auge, crisis y ajuste* (México, D.F.: Fondo de Cultura Económica, 1992), p. 288, n. 9.

45. Of the 101 candidates for the Chamber of Deputies presented by the Labor Congress, thirty lost. The CTM was particularly hard hit, with only thirty-four of its fifty-one candidates winning seats. Juan Reyes del Campillo, "El movimiento obrero en la Cámara de Diputados (1979–1988)," *Revista Mexicana de Sociología* 52, no. 3 (1990): 157–158. The CTM also failed to win a Senate seat in the Federal District for the first time since 1940. Election losers included prominent members of the CTM's executive committee and secretary-generals of CTM-affiliated unions and federations.

46. Rogelio Hernández Rodríguez, "La reforma interna y los conflictos en el PRI," *Foro Internacional* 32, no. 2 (1991): 242; Leonel Pereznieto Castro, "Algunos cambios probables en los estatutos del PRI, de acuerdo a las resoluciones de la XIV Asamblea Nacional," in *El partido en el poder: seis ensayos* (México, D.F.: Instituto de Estudios Políticos, Económicos, y Sociales, PRI, 1990), p. 297.

47. Author interview, Mexico City, December 5, 1994.

48. Author interview with Javier Bonilla; José Cordoba, "Mexico," in John Williamson, ed., *The Political Economy of Policy Reform* (Washington, D.C.: Institute for International Economics, 1994), p. 241.

49. Author interview, Princeton, NJ, May 29, 1996.

50. Grayson, *The Mexican Labor Machine*, p. 46.

51. Pablo Pascual Moncayo and Raúl Trejo Delarbre, *Los sindicatos mexicanos ante el TLC* (México, D.F.: SNTE, Instituto para el Estudios para la Transición Democrática, 1993), p. 47.

52. Workers had the right to ask the labor authorities to conduct a survey to determine which group was supported by the majority of workers and thereby had the title to the contract. Although in theory the outcome depended on the opinion of workers, in practice it often reflected the whims of labor authorities, who not only had the power to decide whether a survey would be taken but controlled the process by which the responses were collected and counted. Ilán Bizberg, *Estado y sindicalismo en México* (México, D.F.: El Colegio de México, 1990), p. 124; La Botz, *Mask of Democracy*, p. 47.

53. See, e.g., Pascual Moncayo and Trejo Delarbre, *Los sindicatos mexicanos;* Enrique de la Garza Toledo, *Reestructuración productiva y respuesta sindical en México* (Mexico, D.F.: Universidad Nacional Autónoma de México, 1993); and Graciela Bensusán and Samuel León, eds., *Negociación y conflicto laboral en México* (Mexico, D.F.: Fundación Friedrich Ebert, 1991).

54. Confidential author interview with former high-ranking PRI official, Mexico City, December 6, 1994.

55. Graciela Bensusán, "Estrategias sindicales y relaciones laborales frente al TLC: el caso de México," paper delivered at the Latin American Studies Association, Nineteenth International Conference, Guadalajara, Mexico, April 1997, p. 15.

56. Marisa Von Bülow, "Reeestructuración productiva y estrategias sindicales: El caso de la Ford en Cuautitlán, 1987–1993" (Master's thesis, FLACSO, Mexico, D.F., 1994), pp. 28–30.

57. De la Garza Toledo, *Reestructuración productiva*, p. 155. The CTM was unable to extend its dominance west of the Texas border, where the majority of plants were nonunionized or had protection contracts with other confederations. Moreover, President Salinas used charges of corruption to depose Agapito González, the legendary leader of the CTM's Day Laborers' and Industrial Workers' Union in Matamoros, when he made the mistake of challenging U.S. management in the midst of the NAFTA negotiations. *Washington Post*, February 28, 1992.

58. Salinas officially requested the negotiation of a free-trade agreement with the United States in August 1990, and Canada joined the negotiations in February 1991. Lustig, *Mexico: The Remaking of an Economy*, p. 132. The agreement went into effect in January 1994.

59. Confidential author interview, Mexico City, December 7, 1994.

60. Pascual Moncayo and Trejo Delarbre, *Los sindicatos mexicanos*, p. 20.

61. Confidential author interview with a CTM official, Mexico City, November 23, 1994. The CTM also received official backing for the creation of a CTM-affiliated union in the auto parts sector in return for its support for NAFTA. *El Financiero*, August 18, 1992.

62. María Xelhuantzi López, "Reforma del Estado Mexicano y sindicalismo" (Master's thesis, Political Science, UNAM, 1992), pp. 425–429.

63. *El Financiero*, February 26, 1993.

64. *El Financiero*, October 7, 1993. Author interview with Enrique de la Garza Toledo, professor at the Universidad Autónoma de México, Mexico City, November 16, 1994.

65. Confidential author interview with a CTM official, Mexico City, November 23, 1994. It is interesting to note that the Labor Ministry initially rejected FESEBES's petition for registration in December 1990 and did not reverse its decision after the conclusion of the NAFTA negotiations.

66. *Proceso*, October 12, 1987, and November 9, 1987.

67. The CTM also negotiated an accord with the president's office just weeks before the assembly to appoint a close associate of Velázquez as the gubernatorial candidate in Nayarit, thereby restoring the CTM's quota of three governorships per sexenio. *El Financiero*, April 4, 1993.

68. Specifically, the CTM (1) defeated a previously negotiated proposal to incorporate the Labor and Peasant Sectors into a territorial movement; (2) blocked the organizational cells (social base committees) of Pronasol from becoming part of the party's territorial structure; and (3) reduced a worker-peasant alliance from a "structure" to a "strategy." *El Financiero*, March 30, 1993, and April 4, 1993.

69. Luis Mendez Berrueta and José Othón Quiroz, eds., *Modernización estatal y respuesta obrera: historia de una derrota* (Azcapotzalco: Universidad Autónoma Metropolitana, 1993), p. 17.

70. *El Financiero*, May 7, 1993.

71. *El Financiero*, October 29, 1993. Author interview with José Landa.

72. *El Financiero*, October 29, 1993.

73. *El Financiero*, June 9, 1993.

74. *La Jornada*, August 12, 1994. Confidential author interview with a CTM official, Mexico City, November 23, 1994.

75. Lustig, *Mexico: The Remaking of an Economy*, pp. 190, 211.

76. Raúl Madrid, "Laboring Against Neoliberalism: Unions and Patterns of Reform in Latin America," paper delivered at the Annual Meeting of the American Political Science Association, Washington, D.C., August 30–September 3, 2000, p. 22.

77. Several important unions withdrew from the assembly, but sixty other worker and peasant organizations indicated their desire to join the UNT in the following weeks. *Mexico Labor News and Analysis* (hereafter *MLNA*), September 1997.

78. *La Jornada*, November 28, 1997.

79. *La Jornada*, November 26, 1997.

80. In a less momentous but similar development, eight federations claiming to represent 350 unions and 500,000 workers formed the National Alliance for Democratic Unionism (ANSD) in August 1998 to represent workers from small and medium-sized firms. Like the UNT, the ANSD committed itself to operating in a horizontal, democratic, and participatory fashion. *MLNA*, August 1998.

81. Hernández Juárez belonged to the PRI, but he increasingly distanced himself from the party's policies, particularly after 1995. In August 1999, he was dropped from the PRI's National Political Council, perhaps for stating in a newspaper interview that "only if the PRI loses the next election will there be real change within the labor movement." *MLNA*, September 1999.

82. *La Jornada*, November 28, 1997.

83. *MLNA*, February 1999.

84. *La Jornada*, February 12, 1999.

85. *La Jornada*, April 6, 1999, and April 27, 1999.

86. *La Jornada*, April 6, 1999.

87. *La Jornada*, May 2, 1999. The same unions organized another large demonstration against privatization of the electrical power industry in Mexico City in August 1999.

88. *MLNA*, October 1999.

89. *MLNA*, September 1999.

90. The success of the FNRCPIE's campaign and the election of Vicente Fox to the presidency inspired several major unions, including the SME, the STPRM, and the SNTE to propose the creation of a new labor confederation to act as a counterweight to both the CT and the UNT. *MLNA*, September 2000.

91. Whereas the SME represents workers at Light and Power, which serves Mexico City and central Mexico, SUTERM represents workers at the Federal Electrical Commission, which serves the rest of the country.

92. *MLNA*, February 1999.

93. *MLNA*, June 1999.

94. *MLNA*, September 1999. It should be noted, however, that this rever-

sal was somewhat disingenuous, as Rodríguez Alcaine subsequently argued that he opposed "privatization" but supported "private participation" in the electrical power industry. *MLNA*, November 2000.

95. Maria Lorena Cook, "The Politics of Labor Law Reform: Comparative Perspectives on the Mexican Case," paper delivered to the International Congress of the Latin American Studies Association, Chicago, Illinois, September 24–26, 1998, p. 17.

96. Ibid., p. 15; PAN (Partido de Acción Nacional), Iniciativa de Decreto que Reforma la Ley Federal del Trabajo, 1995.

97. For a detailed comparison of how the systems of industrial relations in Mexico and Spain shape relations between union leaders and workers, see Katrina Burgess, "Loyalty Dilemmas and Market Reform," *World Politics* 52 (1999): 105–134.

98. While allowing for the exclusion clauses in collective contracts, the PRD proposal would require that union members vote to authorize their leaders to negotiate them. Cook, "The Politics of Labor Law Reform," p. 16, n. 27.

99. Ibid., p. 17.

100. *La Jornada*, November 2, 2000.

101. *Informe de política laboral*, no. 12 (July 1999).

102. For example, during an interview with an official in the technical office of the Labor Ministry in 1994, this author was informed that basic data on union membership were not public information. Similar concerns with transparency prompted a group of PRD and PAN legislators, labor lawyers, and independent unions to issue a document in June 2000 calling for "the installation of a public and transparent system of registration for labor unions and for collective bargaining agreements" and measures "against deceitful registration and administration of contracts that protect employers." Both the PRI and the PAN presidential candidates agreed to meet their demands if elected. *MLNA*, July 2000.

103. La Botz, *Mask of Democracy*, p. 54. The registry indicated that there were 95,000 contracts on deposit with the JLCA and that the CTM accounted for 45 percent of the unions and 70 percent of unionized workers in local jurisdiction activities in the Federal District. *MLNA*, October 1999.

104. *MLNA*, June 1996 and June 1999.

105. A report issued by the Labor Ministry several months after the May 1999 ruling indicated that 108 new unions had been registered in the public sector, with fifty-six belonging to the old labor federations and fifty-two registered as independent. *MLNA*, September 1999.

106. *MLNA*, November 2000.

107. *MLNA*, June 2001. In a move that was unrelated to the labor movement but further indicated the growing independence of the Mexican judiciary, the SCJM took the unprecedented step in August 2000 of issuing a constitutional ruling in favor of opposition legislators against the executive. The ruling supported the legislators' position that the executive was required to release information to Congress regarding possible links between a bank bailout and donations to Zedillo's 1994 campaign. *New York Times*, August 25, 2000.

108. The CTM's relationship with the PRI is likely to depend, in part, on the outcome of an ongoing battle between different factions of the party.

4

Mexico's Unfinished Symphony: The Zapatista Movement

Rodolfo Stavenhagen

The administration of President Ernesto Zedillo that took office in December 1994 inherited from its predecessor, Carlos Salinas de Gortari, the unresolved issue of an armed antigovernment uprising in the state of Chiapas. After the shock waves of the political transition—including a financial crisis and the severe devaluation of the Mexican peso—had more or less dissipated, public opinion expected the new administration to address this conflict responsibly and competently, as had been promised during the presidential campaign. Indeed, shortly after the handing over of power, contacts between the federal government and the rebels were renewed, leading eventually to the initiation of a formal peace dialogue and later a signed accord between the parties in 1996. But thereafter negotiations stalled, new tensions arose, and the dialogue between the Zapatista National Liberation Army (EZLN) and the federal government broke off. The Zedillo administration came to its end in 2000 without having accomplished its aim of solving the armed conflict in Chiapas or, for that matter, any of the major issues that provoked the uprising in the first place. In a larger perspective, this lack of progress on the Chiapas conflict must be considered a major failure of the Zedillo presidency.

During the waning years of the administration, officials stated frequently that the violent conflict in Mexico, in contrast to the civil wars in Colombia, El Salvador, and Guatemala, was quite short-lived, whereas the peace process was dragging on. It is not clear whether this assessment gives more credit to the government than to the Zapatistas, but in my opinion the emphasis is misplaced. The Chiapas uprising is essentially an expression of a deeply rooted social and political conflict, and the violent or military aspect of the rebellion is not its most essential feature, much less the cause of it. The failure of the Zedillo administration to solve this confrontation during his *sexenio* (six-year term) resulted from the fact that the government was mainly concerned with the overtly military aspect of the encounter—a group of poorly armed Indian peasants declaring war on the powerful centralized Mexican state—and was much less interested in dealing with the underlying roots of the rebellion. It is likely that if these social causes are not addressed by the new administration of Vicente Fox in a sensible and coherent manner, then the conflict will simmer for a time, making its outcome by no means predetermined.

The origins and background of the Zapatista rebellion are well known.[1] Briefly, a highly stratified and hierarchical political and social structure of colonial vintage succeeded in keeping the Indian peasantry in Chiapas marginalized and socially excluded well into the second half of the twentieth century.[2] Demographic pressure and soil erosion pushed a growing population out of the traditional Indian highlands to join an increasing flow of poor peasants claiming land in the tropical lowlands—the Lacandon Forest area next to the Guatemalan border. Here they encountered other settlers seeking subsistence and struggled against the interests of non-Indian cattle-ranchers and *latifundistas* (large landholders) who were logging the tropical forest and appropriating what used to be considered nationally owned lands. Land conflicts, peasant organization, and periodic violence marked the opening-up of Mexico's last frontier for several decades during the second half of the twentieth century. The development of infrastructure, the construction of several multipurpose dams, and the opening-up of vast new oil fields offered seasonal nonagricultural employment to Indian peasants and contributed to the weakening of communal bonds and solidarity. Government agrarian and social policies were unable to provide adequate solutions to these growing problems, even as radical political organizations increasingly challenged the traditional corporate patron-client relationship that was supported by the official ruling Institutional Revolutionary Party (PRI) and often exercised in autocratic manner by the local governors. While Samuel Ruiz, the Catholic bishop of San Cristóbal de las Casas (the state capital and regional hub city in the Indian highlands), promoted his version of Indian theology (a variant of liberation theology), to which numerous highland communities adhered, a number of Protestant denominations made spectacular inroads among the traditionally Catholic population, particularly in small urban centers and in the shantytowns growing up around larger cities, notably San Cristóbal de las Casas, Tuxtla Gutiérrez, Ocosingo, and Comitán.[3] In the early 1980s, another ingredient was added to this bubbling cauldron of rival and often conflicting interests: the arrival of a group of radical left-wing militants from northern Mexico who intended to organize revolutionary activity along the lines of movements that had taken hold in other Latin American countries in the 1960s and 1970s. Simultaneously, during the 1980s the border region became a haven for tens of thousands of Maya peasant refugees fleeing repression and counterinsurgency in Guatemala. The stage was set for the Zapatista uprising in 1994, although the public in Mexico was generally unaware of the heightening tensions and growing unrest among the Indian peasantry in Chiapas. The better-informed federal-level government, however, chose to ignore the problem while Mexico was negotiating the North American Free Trade Agreement (NAFTA) with the United States.

Rather than face the basic issues raised by the rebellion directly—the various demands put forth by peasant and Indian organizations as well as the EZLN—the government adopted the position that the underlying cause of the rebellion was the "poverty" of the Indians and that development aid and investments would easily turn the situation around. To be sure, Chiapas occupied one of the lowest rungs of all Mexican states on any economic or social development scale. The 1993 United Nations Human Development Report mentioned Chiapas as an extreme case of deprivation on the Human Development Index, a measure of well-being based on numerous social and economic indicators. Less than 40 percent of the population of Chiapas is classified as Indian, but indigenous Indians are systematically placed lower on any development scale compared to non-Indian populations, as elsewhere in Latin America.[4]

During the Zedillo years, the government was able to mobilize international resources for projects in Chiapas. In one of his reports to the nation, President Zedillo stated that during his administration U.S.$76 million was destined for Chiapas. It is not clear whether this figure included the expenditures of the regular state budget or whether it referred to new resources specifically negotiated for development in the state or to public and private investment. At any rate, no independent objective evaluation of the impact of investments and development aid in Chiapas during the period 1994–2000 is available; neither is it known where these funds ended up and who benefited from them or even if they have been disbursed at all. Scholars and specialists agree, however, that throwing money at Chiapas does not provide a solution to the conflict and will not make the problem go away. Increased spending in the region, if not accompanied by a democratic consensus, will probably lead to greater inequities and social tensions.

Before looking at the possibility of a lasting solution, let us recall the main highlights of the process of war and peace in Chiapas. The country was taken by surprise on January 1, 1994, when a group of armed and masked guerrillas briefly occupied several towns in central Chiapas and their spokesman, identified as "Subcomandante Marcos," stated that the EZLN, by declaring "war" on the Salinas government, was fighting against 500 years of oppression and injustice. *Basta!* (Enough!) they cried and in their first public document laid out the objectives of their armed struggle: work, land, housing, food, education, independence, liberty, democracy, justice, and peace.[5]

These demands were formulated the same day that NAFTA entered into force and at the beginning of the presidential election year. No doubt the significance of the timing of the uprising was not lost on the Zapatistas—it certainly spoiled the triumphalism with which the Salinas administration entered its final year in office.[6]

Over the next few days, several small battles were fought. The federal army overcame its initial surprise and retook the initiative. The Zapatistas withdrew their forces and retreated to the rural *municipios* in the region known as Las Cañadas (The Canyons) from whence they had emerged. Informed estimates place the number of victims killed in the fighting at around 150—not many by the current standards of mass killing and ethnic cleansing but enough to alert Mexican public opinion to the seriousness of the situation and the intentions of the revolutionaries.

The Salinas administration was split between hawks and doves. The former demanded massive and quick military action to liquidate the Zapatista movement at once, arguing that their very presence was, if not threatening the stability of the country militarily (no other expression of Zapatista military activity occurred in the rest of the country), then at least politically destabilizing. The doves, however, recognized the social background of the uprising and advised prudence and negotiations. It is to the credit of the Salinas administration that it decided to listen to the doves and within twelve days proposed a cease-fire and the beginning of a dialogue with the EZLN. President Salinas named one of his cabinet ministers (Manuel Camacho Solis, an outspoken dove and a frustrated aspirant to succeed Salinas in the presidency) as his personal envoy and negotiator.[7] The Zapatistas accepted the truce, and conditions were ripe for a first encounter between the two sides.

The next six and a half years consisted of a series of false starts, mutual misunderstandings, betrayals, and disappointments. The full and detailed history of what really happened remains to be written but will probably never be completely disentangled.[8] Let me briefly recount what I feel to be the major milestones in this process:

1. The Zapatista uprising immediately received national and international media coverage—unlike guerrilla exploits in other countries and in Mexico during the 1970s. Within days a host of human rights organizations and assorted associations descended upon San Cristóbal to establish a "peace cordon" around the Zapatista strongholds and monitor possible human rights abuses by the federal army and other authorities. The Mexican National Commission on Human Rights sent observers into the area. Press reports and live TV coverage were widely disseminated, and during the first few days of the rebellion, Subcomandante Marcos, a literate and articulate spokesman, gave interviews, made statements, and established contacts with what was to become a vast world network of sympathizers and solidarity with the Zapatista movement. The skillful use of the mass media became a landmark of the Zapatistas—again in contrast to other similar movements—to such an extent that people began to talk about an "Internet war."[9] The Mexican government was increasingly irked by the attention given the Zapatista movement worldwide and willingly adopted the idea of a "virtual" war rather than a real one. This cavalier attitude was to guide its involvement in the peace dialogue that followed and probably contributed to its failure.

2. Even though they withdrew from the urban centers they had occupied for a few days, the Zapatistas continued to build up contacts and reach out to civil society in Mexico and abroad; this vision has certainly been one of their strengths. Official public media at first labeled the Zapatista movement as manipulated by foreign and antinational interests, made up of "subversives" and "bandits," a band of spoilers at a time when Mexico had become a first world country.[10] However, the mass media in general painted a favorable picture of the movement, underlining its indigenous membership—despite the fact that Marcos was not an Indian—and the legitimate grievances and demands that fueled the uprising. Opinion polls in Mexico during the first few months after the uprising showed a generally favorable attitude toward the Zapatistas among the Mexican people. The EZLN, in turn, has continued to court public opinion and in 2002 still counts on significant, though fragmented and diminished, support among key sectors of the population.[11]

3. How indigenous was this Indian uprising in southeast Mexico? Critics, to disqualify the movement as a whole, pointed to the fact that Marcos was not an Indian. But it soon became apparent that the Zapatista army was indeed made up essentially of Maya Indians, and so were its other leaders. Another debate centered on the Zapatistas' first public proclamations, which dealt with general social and economic issues and did not specifically concern Indian peoples. Marcos later explained to French anthropologist Yvon LeBot that in order to gain recognition the Zapatistas wanted to be seen as a force for change at the national level and therefore had to deal with larger issues. Marcos learned much from the Indian peoples with whom he identified and became conscious of the fact that indigenous issues were indeed of primary importance. This change of heart—or tactics—became apparent in later developments within the Zapatista movement. It is clear that worldwide support for the movement continued—and continues today—precisely because of its indigenous nature.

4. Peace talks began in the months after the initial uprising, but they did not prosper despite the mediation efforts of Bishop Ruiz. Tensions increased in February 1995 when the federal army suddenly advanced from its cease-fire line and, without firing a shot, occupied positions that had been tacitly accorded the Zapatistas. Simultaneously, the government announced it had discovered the true identity of Marcos and issued orders for his arrest and of some of his putative coconspirators. It was widely believed that the army's February offensive was a failed attempt to capture Marcos, but the government stated that it was no more than an effort to bring the Zapatistas back to the negotiating table.

5. The deteriorating situation finally shook the Congress into action. Responding to a proposal submitted by the executive, the Congress enacted the Law for Dialogue and Peace in Chiapas, in which it recognized the EZLN as an armed party to the conflict and established the mechanisms to be implemented for the peace dialogue. With the active participation of the now formally established National Mediation Commission (CONAI), headed by Bishop Ruiz, serious talks between the two parties began in September 1995. Five months later, in February 1996, they signed the San Andrés Accord on Indigenous Culture and Rights, the only negotiated agreement so far between the federal government and the EZLN.

6. The San Andrés process was tumultuous and complex. The Zapatistas invited a host of advisers from all sectors of Mexican society, whereas the government had difficulty in even putting together a small group of independent experts, who, as it turned out, were more sympa-

thetic to the Zapatista positions. The agreement on indigenous culture and rights was the first of seven topics that the parties agreed to put on the agenda. The second topic, democracy and justice, never got off the ground, and the rest were not even broached.

7. Among other points, the accord underlines the need for a new legislative framework to regulate relations between indigenous peoples and the state; the right to self-determination of indigenous peoples as expressed through territorial autonomy within the national state; and the recognition of indigenous customary law. It was agreed that a proposal to this effect was to be presented jointly by the signatories (the federal government and the EZLN) to the national Congress, but this was not to be.

8. Once the accord had been signed and further dialogue on the other topics did not prosper, little happened in the way of implementation, even as local conditions in Chiapas deteriorated with the appearance of paramilitary groups, factional strife within indigenous communities, and sporadic violence. The government did not appear to be overeager to act on its agreement, and the Zapatistas lost faith in the process. In September 1996, the Commission of Concordance and Peace (COCOPA), a congressional commission of delegates of every represented political party, decided to embark on a parallel track to rescue the peace dialogue. It negotiated discreetly and separately with both parties and in December came up with a draft proposal to be submitted jointly to the Congress that included the essential points of the previous accord. Whereas the Zapatistas agreed to the draft, the government after a few weeks of procrastination decided to propose amendments, which were rejected by the Zapatistas in January 1997. COCOPA's efforts to bring the sides together failed, and the peace dialogue was brusquely interrupted.

9. The government's rejection of a proposal to which it had agreed to earlier surprised many observers and exposed the internal contradictions among the country's governing elite. Official statements argued that indigenous autonomy and recognition of customary law were unacceptable and represented a grave danger to national sovereignty. As these were obviously points of importance to the Zapatistas (as they were, indeed, to numerous indigenous organizations and their advocates), the EZLN felt betrayed once more and withdrew from any further open dialogue with the government, which in turn leveled accusations of intransigence and unwillingness to negotiate. In 1997 it became clear that the peace dialogue was going nowhere and that neither the government nor the Zapatistas were willing to retreat from their posi-

tions. The Zapatistas accused the government of not wanting to comply with the San Andrés Accord it had signed, whereas the government implied that the Zapatistas never wanted to reach an agreement in the first place. The storm broke dramatically in December 1997, when a paramilitary group of local highland Indians massacred forty-seven unarmed pro-Zapatista internal refugees—including men, women, and children—at a prayer meeting. This was no military encounter between the federal army and the forces of the EZLN, who were holed up several hundred miles away; rather, it was a settling of the score between highland factions that had become involved in the struggles over resources and power that were dividing well-integrated Indian societies. The massacre, which drew international condemnation by human rights groups, also exposed a darker side of the conflict: the arming of paramilitary groups by government authorities to divide Indian communities and weaken support for the Zapatistas in the region, as well as the murkier power politics of local political bosses and caciques. Human rights organizations spoke of the government's low-intensity warfare and time-tested counterinsurgency actions against the Zapatistas, who in turn denounced the government's "genocidal" intentions. A war of reciprocal accusations supplemented the "netwar," but there was no denying the violence, the fear, and the atmosphere of repression that hung over the Indian communities.

10. By 1998, the peace process was moribund, at least as far as the Zedillo administration was concerned. Though the president shuffled around his cabinet ministers and peace negotiators and publicly invited the Zapatistas at least twice to come back to the negotiating table (in early 1998 and in mid-1999), observers did not see any significant change in the federal government's position on the San Andrés Accord. The Zapatistas, in turn, insisted that they would resume dialogue only if previously set conditions were met, including a partial withdrawal of the federal army to positions held before the February 1995 offensive, the dismantling of the flourishing paramilitary groups (the attorney general's office had identified at least eighteen such groups), and strict adherence to the signed accord. To make matters worse, in 1998 Bishop Ruiz's CONAI dissolved itself because it felt it no longer had a constructive role to play. COCOPA was internally divided along party lines and thus was effectively neutralized. This was the legacy that President Vicente Fox faced upon his election in July 2000.

Beyond the details of a tortuous process that led nowhere, several issues are at stake that need to be considered. The Zapatistas insist that their fundamental demands be addressed by concrete government actions—that is, the implementation of the San Andrés Accord. The government, however, is more concerned with ending the state of war and returning to normalcy—a normalcy that the Zapatistas and many others in Mexico consider a return to the status quo ante, that is, to the situation that provoked the Zapatista rebellion in the first place. The Zapatista movement now represents more than a *foco* (origin, source) of guerrillas threatening the stability of a democratic state (a view derived from earlier guerrilla experiences in other Latin American countries). It challenges the international system (globalization and neoliberalism) on which the Mexican national state nowadays attempts to base its legitimacy. Thus, the Zapatista movement has been labeled an antisystemic movement, in contrast to other military-political uprisings that intended to overthrow existing governments. Whereas Mexico's Octavio Paz at first decried the Zapatista movement as a return to a "premodern" form of struggle, Carlos Fuentes greeted it as the first "postmodern" conflict. In fact, however, it is neither and can best be described as a fully modern type of social movement because the demands it raises are based on the modern—and eternal—principles of justice, equality, dignity, liberty, and human rights. By wishing to deny the Zapatistas any kind of political legitimacy, which explains the de facto rejection of the San Andrés Accord, the Mexican government not only deprives the movement of a role in national politics but also effectively denies indigenous peoples meaningful participation in national affairs (official rhetoric to the contrary notwithstanding).[12]

The EZLN craves a national role beyond institutionalized political party and electoral mechanisms. Numerous indigenous organizations, even if they do not support the EZLN's choice of violent action to achieve its ends, have acknowledged that the position of the EZLN has strengthened *their* hands in negotiating an effective space for political action on the national scene. There is no doubt that indigenous peoples, thanks to the Zapatistas, now command more respect in the country than ever before. Therefore, many reject the government's efforts to reduce the Zapatista movement to mere local insignificance, to reduce the various expressions of violence (paramilitary groups, repressive measures) to "intra- or intercommunal rivalry" (as official documents label it), and to deal with indigenous demands as nothing that cannot be processed through traditional clientelistic channels.

As the Zedillo presidency drew to an end, there was much speculation in Mexico as to why his administration had been unable (or unwilling) to solve the conflict in Chiapas. A few months before leaving office, while on one of his trips abroad, President Zedillo declared that the Zapatista rebellion was a mere incident in Mexico's history, of no great import to the country. On other occasions he said it was a light guerrilla rebellion (presumably in contrast to the heavy rebellions and civil wars that decimated other Latin American countries during several decades in the twentieth century). Perhaps his outspokenness expressed a much deeper misunderstanding among the governing elites as to what the Zapatista movement is all about, a misunderstanding that is likely to be shared by the Fox administration.

As with all social conflicts, the Zapatista conflict has a number of underlying causes, plots and subplots, and several possible solutions. But there is no easy way out, for in reality this one conflict subsumes several other conflicts. Moreover, as in Akira Kurosawa's famous film *Rashomon*, various narratives have been woven about this conflict, narratives that confound not only public opinion but also specialists and perhaps even the players themselves. The conflict is constantly being redefined by participants and the observers, and it is unlikely to be resolved unless the quarrel over definitions and narratives of the conflict is decided. These issues might be looked at from three different perspectives:

1. We must notice the structural conflict that occurs not only in Chiapas but also in other parts of the country in which there are indigenous peoples and communities. This structural conflict is as old as the social and economic system that produced the great inequalities in economic welfare, social status, and political power between the Indian peasantry and the non-Indian population. The internal colonialism that prevailed for centuries has been replaced by a postcolonial situation that is more flexible and fluid, and Indian communities have become more divided and polarized in the roiling waters of modernization. The vision of integrated, harmonious communities—as described by anthropologists a few decades ago—no longer holds. Yet indigenous organizations, conscious of this multifaceted social disintegration, are pleading for strategies to "recompose" their communities, and they see the implementation of the San Andrés Accord as one way to achieve that objective. Contrary to some currently fashionable assessments, NAFTA and neoliberal globalization have not led to an across-the-board improvement of living conditions for Indians in Chiapas or elsewhere in the country.[13] Rather, these changes have generated growing socioeconomic inequalities, the disappearance of solidarity networks in rural villages and townships, the weakening of social compensatory institutions, and

the growth of not only poverty but also pauperism. Although this is not a new phenomenon in world capitalism—once labeled the "development of underdevelopment"—it is still a major cause of tension and structural conflict.

There are several actors in this conflict, most notably the indigenous peasantry, who have always been the historical victims of this situation. But there are others: local and regional interest groups—landowners, cattle ranchers, large and small merchants, and intermediaries; as well as government bureaucrats and indigenous power brokers who now have a stake in the system.

Structural conflict is not only a class struggle in the traditional sense of the haves and the have-nots, the privileged and the deprived. In Chiapas, it is also an ethnic confrontation between Indians and mestizos, a confrontation deeply rooted in the history of internal colonialism. Whereas some commentators on Chiapas have blamed anthropologists for inventing ethnic differences—suggesting that if only academics would stop concerning themselves with these topics people would easily learn to get along together—the fact is that ethnic distinctions are deeply rooted in the local imagery as a result of the asymmetrical power relations in the economic and social arenas since colonial times. Local people distinguish clearly between Indians, *caxlanes*, *gente de razón*, and *ladinos*, which are not only descriptive labels in everyday discourse but concepts used in social and cultural mapping. They refer to different social status, systems of interpersonal relations, and types of discrimination and exclusion. This is all part of the structural conflict in Chiapas, as elsewhere in the country, and it should not be forgotten that the situation has led to persistent human rights abuses of Indians and peasants, social activists, women, children, migrant workers and settlers, and entire communities. It has also led to violations that have been assiduously documented by human rights organizations and that surely may be considered as one of the triggering factors of the 1994 uprising.

The structural conflict cannot be solved in the short term; the San Andrés Accord, or any other negotiated agreement, will not do away with it. The social, economic, and political structures of inequality will change only by means of a long-term process and persistent social and economic policies that directly benefit indigenous peoples and communities through redistribution of power and wealth. Mere legislative changes at the local state or national levels will be necessary but not sufficient to effect such transformations.

2. The second perspective must focus on the political conflict between a political-military organization, the EZLN, its nonmilitary

members (known as *bases de apoyo*), other supporters in specific areas of the region, and a wide array of peasant and popular organizations, and, on the other side, the local power structure concentrated around the ruling elite of the state of Chiapas. This has traditionally been an autocratic, authoritarian, centralized, and antidemocratic structure that at times may appear to be legal and institutional. Although some observers accuse the EZLN of being authoritarian (and like all tightly knit revolutionary organizations, it may certainly have an authoritarian streak), the real authoritarianism is represented by those who have wielded power against the interests and well-being of the peasants and the Indians.

The main actors in this political conflict, which now has also become a military or pseudomilitary one, are the peasant and indigenous organizations that have addressed their grievances and demands to the government since their emergence in the 1950s after the Instituto Nacional Indigenista (INI, a federal government agency) established a base of operation in San Cristóbal las Casas. These various organizations, which multiplied and grew during the following decades, are the principal contenders in the political conflict that erupted in the 1970s. Besides the peasant and workers' unions, mention must be made of the role of religious groups, including both the Indian Theology, promoted by Bishop Ruiz in the San Cristóbal diocese since the 1960s, and the various Protestant denominations. An important ingredient was added by the arrival of small organizations of militant leftists, representing different tendencies and often at loggerheads with each other, which joined and occasionally managed to lead the struggles of the Indian peasant associations in a pattern of changing alliances. Out of one of these groups came the EZLN, which decided on armed struggle.[14] On the opposite side, we find the business and landowners' associations, the *auténticos coletos* (local aristocracy) of San Cristóbal las Casas, as well as the municipal *caciques* (political bosses) who are the backbone of the national PRI at the local level. In earlier years, members of some of these sectors fostered the creation of small, private armed bands in the service of certain *guardias blancas* (landowners), who used violence and the threat of violence against the leadership and members of popular organizations, often in connivance with government authorities. The picture became more complex in the 1980s when new political parties challenged the traditional control of the PRI through electoral contests at the municipal and state levels. Inasmuch as the EZLN "declared war" on the Mexican state, which led to a massive increase of military presence in the area (some estimates place the number of federal troops in the state at 40,000), it is also necessary to take into consideration the various vested interests in the conflict that the military itself has acquired. Finally, one can only speculate about the influence—often mentioned in the media—of drug trafficking on the political balance in the state.

As can be seen, there are numerous different actors with special interests in this political-military conflict, a result of the structural tensions mentioned earlier. What solutions might there be to this problem? The government has often suggested, but has been slow in promoting, the need for modernization and democratization. The traditional power structures in Chiapas are arrayed against the modernization and democratization of political life. This may finally have changed in August 2000, when an alliance of opposition parties was able to defeat the PRI's government-supported candidate for governor of Chiapas. The new governor, Pablo Salazar, formerly a member of the PRI, was a member of the federal legislative commission dealing with the peace process (COCOPA). With two opposition candidates winning the national presidency and the local governor's office, things may finally begin to change in Chiapas.

3. There is a third perspective that can be brought to bear on the problem, and this is the fact that since 1994 there has been an armed conflict between the EZLN and the national and state governments. The former has its bases de apoyo and supporters and sympathizers in the country and abroad. The government controls resources, military power, public administration, and political institutions. Let us recall that in 1995 the national Congress adopted a law for dialogue and peace in Chiapas in which it legally recognized a "group of dissatisfied, mainly indigenous Mexicans." In other words, it recognized the EZLN as a de facto, if not de jure, belligerent in this war.

Although the duration of open armed conflict was truly short, the period of negotiations has been unduly long. And whereas the number of direct casualties is relatively small, the situation has become more complex due to the presence of a number of paramilitary outfits (which the government prefers to call "armed civilian groups"). As in other areas, the danger these units represent is that in time they may escape from the control of their masters who armed and financed them. However, it is not publicly known who in fact is behind these groups, and the federal army vehemently denies any involvement. Nevertheless, they are responsible for numerous instances of violence, including murder, torture, and abduction of Zapatista sympathizers and presumed members of the EZLN. Their existence and relative freedom of action is an additional factor that makes the resumption of peace talks difficult.

Again, the principal actors in this military conflict are the EZLN; local army and police units; the political supporters of the Zapatistas, such as the autonomous municipalities established in defiance of local legislation; the different levels of public administration; and both COCOPA and CONAI (despite the fact that the latter has been formally disbanded). The solution to this conflict can only come through continued dialogue and negotiation, though events since the signing of the accord hardly lead to optimism.

From the vantage point of this third perspective, there has been an overlap of timing and strategies between the structural conflict and its underlying causes, the political conflict due to incomplete democratization, and the armed conflict since January 1994 and everything that occurred thereafter. The three perspectives are linked but must be kept separate.

The Mexican government has occasionally announced major new investments in Chiapas provided by multilateral agencies and transnational corporations. These are intended to create jobs and improve living standards of the local population, thus helping solve the "structural" causes of the uprising. Where are these resources and what have they accomplished? A recent study finds that between 1994 and 2000 direct foreign investment in Chiapas (on which current development policies rely heavily) amounted to $5.4 million, less than $1 million per year. Most of these enterprises are registered in the major cities, so it is not known what effect they may have had on income in rural areas, but probably their overall impact is slight.[15]

Nevertheless, it has often been said that the EZLN does not trust the political party system and does not believe that democratic elections will alter the system, a belief held by many observers. The Zapatistas have announced repeatedly that they will submit to the larger organization of civil society. But where is this organization? Not much has resulted from the numerous conclaves that the Zapatistas have sponsored in their territory. The Party of the Democratic Revolution, the party sometimes believed to be closest to the EZLN, came in third place in the 2000 presidential elections at the national level, having lost electoral support since 1988. The historical alternative for the country, which the Zapatistas have promised, has not been spelled out clearly and is not reflected in any of the major political platforms. Civil society, despite its diverse manifestations and its strong commitment to human rights, has not proven adept or organized enough to impose peace on the two contenders, and in the meantime, social and economic conditions continue to deteriorate in the area. The real victims of the struggle are the Indian and peasant communities whose situation has deteriorated over the last six years. The government has promised more democracy and development while it has been unable to negotiate a solution to the armed conflict. Between 1994 and 1999, the state of Chiapas had five governors, none of whom was elected democratically. Perhaps the election of an opposition candidate in 2000 has opened a window of opportunity. (See Postscript.)

Chiapas represents Mexico's biggest and most important unfinished business. It expresses the deep social contradictions that national development policies have generated since the middle of the twentieth century (aggravated enormously by neoliberal globalization). Indians (15 percent of the Mexican population) have been historically shortchanged. Economic development has passed them by. Despite official rhetoric to the contrary, Indians are eternally excluded in social, economic, and political terms. The Zedillo administration dismissed the Chiapas conflict as a minor "historical incident" and was unable to offer a satisfactory solution. Hopefully, the Fox administration will do better.

But the Zapatistas have not provided a clear alternative political strategy that may find large-scale appeal within civil society; rather, they appear to be carving out a niche for themselves (with difficulty), preparing for a "long march" in political terms. They have not publicly commented on Mexico's political transition, but perhaps they are willing to give the Fox administration more opportunity to negotiate a peace agreement than the previous one, providing, of course, that the new administration will do the same.

There are many points on the agenda for peace, including new legislation concerning the status of indigenous peoples, their territories, the use of natural resources, the legal recognition of customary law, their rights to political representation, access to the media, and, of course, the question of self-determination and autonomy—all of which was negotiated and agreed to in the San Andrés Accord.

Beyond the still-to-be-debated issues of democratization, justice, and economic and social development for indigenous peoples, there are significant unfinished themes that exist beneath the current dialogue: human dignity, collective identity, political recognition, social equality, and human rights. Mexico's process of democratization is surely incomplete without the participation of the Zapatistas and, more inclusively, of the country's indigenous peoples. Mexico can continue to ignore indigenous demands as it has over the decades, but it cannot claim to be a truly democratic society until Indian peoples are included in the political and social agenda of the twenty-first century. And this means, first of all, making peace in Chiapas.

Postscript

In December 2000, Vicente Fox took over as first popularly elected opposition president in Mexico. Many observers greeted this political change as Mexico's graduation into a true democracy. Trying to make good on his campaign promise that if elected he would solve the Chiapas problem quickly, President Fox dusted off the COCOPA bill of 1995 (which the previous administration had reneged on) and sent it to the Senate to be passed into law. He also named a new government negotiator. The Zapatistas took the cue and organized a march on Mexico City to support this new development. On their way to the capital, they visited numerous towns and staged rallies in many places. Hopes were high that a breakthrough was finally at hand.

After much haggling, the Senate decided to invite the EZLN and hear what its leaders had to say. Comandante Esther, a small, frail indigenous woman, presented the Zapatista case to the Congress in broken Spanish, in full view of the national media. For a few days, public hearings were held, but in the end the political pros of all parties struck a backroom deal and adopted a constitutional amendment (a new article 2 of the constitution of Mexico) on the basis of the bill sent by the president. Although recognizing, for the first time, the rights of indigenous peoples in the country, the text is weak on some basic issues that the Zapatistas thought they had achieved in the San Andrés negotiations, notably, autonomy, collective land rights, control of natural resources, access to media in native languages, customary law, and the legal recognition of indigenous "peoples" (rather than communities) as subjects of domestic law.

The government hailed the constitutional amendment as a progressive step forward and thought this meant it had kept its campaign promise. The Zapatistas, however, felt cheated once again and decided to return to Chiapas and keep their silence. The amendment was passed by the Senate and the House; it was later ratified by a number of states and came into force in August 2001. Dissatisfied indigenous organizations, jurists, and politicians immediately began agitating for repeal, and in a first-ever development in Mexico, numerous municipal governments and some state legislatures that had rejected the amendment took their constitutional case to the Supreme Court to have the amendment overturned, arguing procedural irregularities and violation of Convention 169 of the International Labour Organization, which had been ratified by Mexico and indicates that any decision affecting indigenous peoples must be widely and legitimately consulted with those peoples themselves, something that did not occur at the time of the congressional hearings on the constitutional amendment. At the time of this writing in 2002, the Supreme Court was expected to rule on the cases some time in 2002

During President Fox's second year in office, the outlook for peace in Chiapas was not good. All contact between the parties had broken off; Fox's indigenous policy was basically no different from that of his predecessors, and not even the new governor of Chiapas, elected on an opposition ticket, had been able to move closer to the Zapatista communities. The world changed after September 2001, and it is possible that the new government will choose a hard-line approach if the situation becomes embarrassing. Otherwise, the latent conflict will be a reminder that all is not well in the country.

Notes

1. George Collier with Elizabeth Lowery Quaratiello, *Basta!: Land and the Zapatista Rebellion in Chiapas* (Oakland, CA: Food First Books, 1999); Carmen Díaz Legorreta, *Religión, política y guerrilla en las Cañadas de la Selva Lacandona* (México, D.F.: Cal y Arena, 1998); Neil Harvey, *The Chiapas Rebellion: The Struggle for Land and Democracy* (Durham, NC: Duke University Press, 1998); Yvon Le Bot, *Subcomandante Marcos: El sueño zapatista* (México, D.F.: Plaza and Janes, 1997); Carlos Tello Diaz, *La rebelión de las Cañadas* (Mexico, D.F.: Cal y Arena, 1995); John Womack Jr., ed., *Rebellion in Chiapas: An Historical Reader* (New York: New Press, 1999).

2. Emilio Zebadúa, *Breve historia de Chiapas* (México, D.F.: Colegio de Mexico and Fondo de Cultura Economica, 1999). *Marginalization* and *social exclusion* are used here as code words to refer to a heavy-handed and persistent system of discrimination, exploitation, and oppression that has characterized the world of the indigenous in Chiapas for several centuries. Evon Z. Vogt, *Zinacantan: A Maya Community in the Highlands of Chiapas* (Cambridge: Harvard University Press, 1969); Robert Wasserstrom, *Class and Society in Central Chiapas* (Berkeley: University of California Press, 1983).

3. Evangelical Protestantism has made numerous converts in Latin America in recent decades. David Stoll, *Is Latin America Turning Protestant? The Politics of Evangelical Growth* (Berkeley: University of California Press, 1990).

4. George Psacharopoulos and Harry Anthony Patrinos, eds., *Indigenous*

People and Poverty in Latin America: An Empirical Analysis (Washington, D.C.: World Bank, 1994).

5. "Primera Declaración de la Selva Lacandona, Declaración de Guerra del Ejército Zapatista en Chiapas, January 1, 1994.

6. Salinas's handpicked successor, PRI presidential candidate Luis Donaldo Colosio, was murdered in March. Presidential elections were held in July, and in December Salinas handed over power to Ernesto Zedillo.

7. Camacho Solís resigned as negotiator in March following the murder of Colosio. He later broke with the PRI and became an independent contender for the presidency in 2000.

8. As is so often the case, many people know parts of the story, and only a few people may think they know the whole story, but they probably do not.

9. David Ronfeldt et al., *The Zapatista "Social Netwar" in Mexico* (Santa Monica, CA: RAND, 1998).

10. After a strenuous public relations campaign by the Salinas government, Mexico was accepted as a member of the Organization for Economic Cooperation and Development, a club of industrial states, the first "developing" nation to have achieved this status.

11. The EZLN organized a "Democratic Convention" in their jungle stronghold in August 1994, just after the presidential election, which was attended by several thousand participants from all over the country and abroad. In the following years they organized other similar international gatherings, maintaining a constant flow of visitors to their base communities. Although the Mexican government has been accused of selectively and illegally harassing numerous "observers" from different countries—including arbitrary detentions and deportations—considering the fact that a "war" had been declared in the country, it was surprisingly willing to allow these contacts to continue and the meetings to take place in rebel territory, thinking perhaps to improve its international image and to coax the peace process along.

12. Official opinion holds that the Zapatistas should lay down their arms, take off their masks, and transform themselves into a political party. The Zapatistas, however, insist that they will do this only after the peace agreement has been fully implemented. In other words, they feel that only by obtaining the government's compliance to the agreement will they be able to achieve the political legitimacy needed to become an alternative political force in Mexico. For this they count on the continued support of the Mexican civil society—which the government considers a useless distraction to any future peace negotiations.

13. A recent study by the UN Food and Agriculture Organization (FAO) reports that 40 percent of Mexico's population is undernourished. FAO, *The State of Food Insecurity in the World* (Rome: FAO, 2000).

14. See Harvey, *The Chiapas Rebellion,* and Carmen Legorreta Díaz, *Religión, política y guerrilla* (México, D.F.: Cal y Arena, 1998).

15. CIEPAC, *Boletín "Chiapas al día,"* No. 216 (September 29, 2000), ciepac@laneta.apc.org.

5

The Role of Women in the New Mexico

Marta Lamas

It is impossible to speak of Mexican women as a homogeneous entity, even though all women in the country bear the weight of different forms of machismo, from the most blatant to the most subtle. Regional heterogeneity, economic differences, rural or urban residence, age, and ethnic identity shape the various ways in which women experience being a woman, have access to education and paid employment, and engage in politics. However, for the purposes of this chapter I will make some necessary generalizations that serve to show how women have played, and are playing, an important role in the changes Mexico is currently experiencing.[1]

The lives of Mexican women must be understood within the context of a history that has been influenced by two cultures—indigenous and Spanish—and by the impact of the Mexican Revolution at the beginning of the twentieth century. Gender inequality permeates the entire Mexican society, and the concept of womanhood is structured around extremely patriarchal conceptions, strongly influenced by Catholicism. Mexican culture venerates motherhood and celebrates traditional feminine qualities—submissiveness, beauty, domesticity—while it belittles and disapproves of women's independence, education, and work as a means of achieving autonomy and self-esteem.

In most parts of the country women's sexuality is directly tied to procreation, virginity continues to be highly valued, the sexual double standard is rampant and far from being a matter of choice, and childbirth is considered to be a woman's destiny. However, because the only consistent public policy aimed toward women in the last twenty-five years has been family planning, one of the most important changes to occur has been women's increased control over their own fertility.[2]

Although access to birth control has given Mexican women the possibility of more control over their bodies and their lives, sexual repression still dominates the mentality of large sectors of the female population, and sexually active women are still considered to be immoral.

Although changes have taken place in the sexual behavior of young women who leave their home communities, the AIDS epidemic has cast a shadow over the possibility of new sexual freedom. In Mexico, most women are unaware of the extent of men's sexual activity, and thus a significant number of women have been infected by partners who engage in risky sexual practices while they (i.e., women) remain monogamous. In general, women are oblivious to the danger they are in, and their vulnerability is reinforced by the traditional dominant discourse, which values and promotes women's sexual ignorance. The sexual double standard makes it difficult for women to be assertive, and they are unable to demand that their partners use condoms. So, as in other parts of the world, there is a constant increase in the number of women who become infected with HIV. Social inequality further complicates the problem, as those with fewest resources are also the least informed.

Despite its interest in diminishing the country's birthrate, the Mexican government has taken no steps to extend the legal boundaries that define the practice of abortion as a punishable offense. The penal codes of all thirty-one Mexican states and the Federal District define abortion as a crime, with only one exception nationally: when the pregnancy is the result of rape.[3] Other exceptions to illegal abortion include when a woman miscarries due to an accident (twenty-nine states) and when abortion is necessary to save the life of the woman (twenty-eight states). In eleven states abortion is permitted in the case of fetal impairment and, in another eight, when the woman's health is at risk. Legislation penalizing abortion has created high costs in terms of women's lives and health, in addition to hospital expenses to care for the victims of back-alley abortions. Estimates of the number of women who abort annually vary between 220,000 and 850,000.[4] Deaths caused by illegal abortions rank as the third most common cause of maternal mortality. Thousands of public hospital beds are filled due to complications resulting from unsafe abortions.

The greatest obstacle to changing Mexican abortion legislation has been the persistent opposition from Catholic Church officials. According to nationwide Gallup polls, more than three-fourths of the Mexican population believes that the decision to abort should be made only by women or the couple; nevertheless, social pressure to overcome the Church's opposition has been insufficient.

The fact that women now have fewer children has produced an increase in the number of nuclear families. Nevertheless, the extended family persists in most of Mexico, especially among the poor. The structure of the extended family allows for the diversification of economic strategies, family cooperation, and distribution of responsibility for child care and housework, thus facilitating women's entrance into the paid workforce.

The number of women who have entered the workforce has increased so dramatically that by 1995 women represented 32 percent of the labor force.[5] The distribution of women within the workforce reflects gender inequality, as women's representation in public and private management and directive positions is minimal. Traditional wage discrimination spans the job spectrum, and the ingrained attitudes that overvalue women's traditional role continue to be very critical, casting blame on women in need of salaries. The scarcity of child-care centers, the incompatibility of school and job schedules, and the high cultural value placed on motherhood all have a negative effect on working women. Because femininity is defined by maternity, it comes as no surprise that women, if they can afford it, tend to leave their jobs when they marry and have children.

The profile of women with paying jobs has changed: in the 1970s, a high proportion of the female workforce consisted of young single women, but currently the presence of older women is becoming more notable. Married women and women with small children need salaried work for family survival or to maintain their standard of living. Also, more and more women are the heads of households.

In large cities, women have found jobs mainly in manufacturing or in self-employed commercial activities such as selling small items, most typically food, in markets or on the street. Migration from rural areas to larger cities continues but has changed slightly. Some women take the traditional path to domestic work in the cities, but many others establish themselves in the most developed and productive rural areas in Mexico and across the border. There is also a constant flow toward the *maquiladora* industries (plants using imported parts for assembly into items for export), transforming the migrants from peasants to industrial laborers. The maquiladoras, at first located mainly on Mexico's border with the United States, currently extend to the central and southern regions of Mexico where they have become the main source of employment for women. This has resulted in increased migration of young women, with older women staying behind to tend to the family plot of land and care for smaller children, who may be their own or their grandchildren.

All of this has led to a notable increase in the number of female industrial workers, but the effects of paid work on daily life and on the values and habits of thousands of poor and peasant women from various regions of Mexico are still ambiguous. To understand these effects we must take into account the economic independence women receive from salaried work in addition to the contrast between their new lifestyles and certain constrictive aspects of their previous lives: they are able to escape the limitations of provincial life and the constant vigilance of patriarchal families and neighbors. Women's appreciation of freedom from such oppressive situations explains in part the paradox of their apparent satisfaction with poorly paid jobs and less than desirable working conditions, exacerbated by the impossibility of organizing themselves into unions and, in some cases, such as in the maquiladoras, the implications of serious health risks. However, on the whole the experience of working outside the home has shown positive social and psychological consequences for women from the lower income sectors.

In Mexico, a salaried job does not assure a woman's independence because of profound economic and gender inequalities: nearly half of all women workers, compared to only one-fifth of all male workers, earn less than the official minimum wage. Only a few women with educational resources and professional training are in the best position to join the workforce. These women tend to pay other women to do their housework and to take care of their children. Although paid domestic work continues to be an important source of jobs for many women, especially for those from rural areas and from the poorest areas of the cities, there has been a noticeable decline in the total percent of women working in the service sector. Although in 1970 domestic workers were the largest group represented in the statistics of women's annual economic activity, since the 1990s statistics show that office workers are now the predominant group.

The inequality of Mexico's social structure makes it possible for a broad sector of Mexican women to hire domestic help. For this reason, and in contrast to the experience of North American and European feminists, Mexican feminism has not emphasized the oppression of housework, the role of the housewife, and the responsibilities associated with motherhood. Also because domestic workers serve as a buffer, there has been no organized demand for formal child-care centers.[6] It is ironic that women from the middle and upper classes blindly impose on other women the situations they are trying to escape.

The traditional division of labor according to gender is still perpetuated, with men supporting the family economically and women being mothers. The domestic sphere continues to be the domain of women, and domestic violence is a constitutive aspect of the scene. Sexist violence has two paths: symbolic and physical. Symbolic violence is enacted basically through the sexual double standard, whereas physical violence takes a high toll as domestic battering, which occurs within all social classes. Rape is also a danger for every woman, but women from lower classes, who walk or take public transportation instead of driving or being driven by a chauffeur, are at a higher risk. The murders of young maquiladora workers in Ciudad Juárez have become a symbol of the little importance given to women's lives and are a sign of the lack of interest on the part of the local *panista* government to investigate the chain of murders. Up to now, 187 women have been tortured and raped before being brutally killed.

Thus, at the start of a new century, the situation in Mexico is not equally promising for all women, since the distribution of resources and information is more unequal than ever. The majority of women find it very difficult to improve their situation because they cannot reap the benefits of modernization. Nevertheless, Mexican women's desire for change is obvious and accelerates the speed with which they have been able to define their interests as women and their demands for changes in the country's political life.

In spite of the restrictive socioeconomic context that conditions women's integration into or exclusion from Mexico's political and industrial development, its technological advances and modernization have led to great changes and new opportunities for women. But in comparison with the advances achieved in other areas, Mexican women's participation in positions of political power has been minimal. It is still exceptional for a woman to be named as head of a government department or elected as governor of a state; and even when they are nominated, they are used like interchangeable tokens. Women are found in greater numbers at midlevel positions within public administration, but they tend to hold more positions in the cultural and social areas and fewer in the purely political areas.

Although political party leaders tend to be men, women are now presidents of the Institutional Revolutionary Party (PRI) and the Party of the Democratic Revolution (PRD), albeit with restricted power.

Political parties continue to pay lip service to the women's agenda, and their interest in women's issues has been limited to electoral promises. They have not considered gender issues in designing their political platforms, and they have not further developed quota strategies; the two parties that have a 30 percent quota for women (PRD and PRI) have, for the most part, appointed them to lower positions, as *suplentes* (replacements for elected officials). The idea and the practice of political correctness do not exist in Mexico. Quotas and tokenism are just beginning to emerge, and there is no tradition of affirmative action whatsoever.

Nevertheless, women within the parties are making their way into positions of power and are posing gender-related demands. New issues such as women's role in the state, sexual and reproductive rights, and quotas for women in government and party structures have recently been addressed in internal debates. With the election of Cuauhtémoc Cárdenas as mayor of Mexico City, some feminist initiatives were taken up by the government: the creation of the Centers for the Integral Attention of Women, as well as a health project funded by Novib of the Netherlands. With a feminist succeeding Cárdenas as interim mayor the commitment grew, and Mayor Rosario Robles installed policies for equal pay and labor conditions for policewomen and introduced a proposal to the legislative assembly of the Federal District to increase access to safe abortions in cases of fetal impairment and when the health of the woman is threatened.[7] However, there is still much ground to be covered before a basic democratic partnership between the women's movement and the government can positively advance the women's agenda.

Women's political experience has been formed in the specific context of economic inequality and a *machista* cultural tradition. This has shaped women's activities and their individual and collective identities. Young, urban, middle-class women today are questioning the generally accepted concepts of power and politics, and this transformation is reflected in a growing self-awareness; women see themselves as experiencing various forms of cultural and social oppression, and they are beginning to realize the value of political participation. Formulating their desires and needs from a political perspective, women have become more insistent on being part of the debate concerning national development. Also, women are taking the idea of democracy beyond the concept of a representational political system, asking for "*Democracia en el país y en la casa*" (Democracy in the country and at home).[8]

The absence of an organized political force of women also explains the persistence of many negative situations, such as the lack of equal labor opportunities, the risks of penalization for abortion, and devastating sexist violence. Women do not lobby politicians as "women" but on behalf of wider, mixed interests. The natural bases or foundations of the movement are the women in popular sectors who, in turn, respond to the interests of political parties.[9] The problem of women's minimal representation in the political system is also linked to the lack of mass pressure from women. The movement has been unable to energize common women around crucial issues. Furthermore, there is a paradoxical situation in the movement; notwithstanding the absence of victims' voices (there are no common women questioning the meaning and practice of sexism), feminist activists within the movement continue to use an irritating victimist discourse. This attitude of victimization has driven away younger women. Today there is a generational crisis in traditional feminist groups: most of its militants are women in their forties and fifties. The notable absence of younger women can be interpreted as their resistance to join organizations that they do not consider to be their own or that they view as their mother's. The sectarianism of some of those feminist groups also does not encourage the participation of young women.

It was not until the 1990s that feminists became convinced of the need to act within the political system. No longer idealizing feminist politics, many reoriented their radicalism toward civic practices. Some still persist in a revolutionary nostalgia, trapped by absurd rivalries because they belong to different networks or groups. The absurd competitiveness within the same political currents, a consequence of the so-called politics of identity favored by these groups, has led to political uneasiness and persistent discrepancies, but the general objectives of the movement are slowly finding acceptance within Mexico. Although there are still activists taking refuge within small, sectarian groups, and although there are members of successful nongovernmental organizations (NGOs) who still use womanist and identitarian frameworks, the political impact of the feminist movement is visible in the lives of many women.[10]

In the 1990s, many feminists joined mixed-sex NGOs that encouraged civic participation, and this, along with the impact of the Zapatista National Liberation Army (EZLN) in Chiapas since 1994, repositioned feminism within the national political dynamic. These two paths—the civic and the pro-Zapatista—channeled the main political interests and developments of feminism. Perhaps the most notable transformation that occurred during that decade is that feminists articulated antisexist behavior in a different way: as "institutionalized" feminists working to reconcile their private motivations with public necessities.[11] However, the growing specialization and professionalization in NGOs also introduced competitive elements that were previously unknown, giving rise to populist and anti-intellectual expressions, such as criticisms of elitism referring to the privileges of a university education.

The big change in the 1990s was that much of the feminist political practice responded to political realities rather than ideological postures. The political interventions of many feminists have thus taken on a pragmatic dimension. The desire for democracy has fostered an internal reformulation, where womanist demands are slowly being displaced. Tired of merely expressing feminist values rather than acting on them, many feminists recognized that the advancement of the movement was also dependent on greater political participation and gaining positions within party and governmental structures. Simultaneously, the appearance of new political contexts, with friends and allies in power, enriched politics and created a complex panorama.[12]

Positioning themselves as politically republican and democratic subjects, rather than as victims or oppressed women, has led many feminists to discover a different way of thinking that includes men not only discursively but also concretely. The search for a different kind of politics implies something more than pushing for demands related to gender issues. It also means fully accepting gender within political institutions. While recognizing gender differences, one cannot think only of women, or even direct oneself toward women only, to modify the distribution of work, time, and social assignments: one must rethink every circumstance and situation in terms of its implications for women and for men.

It is thus not surprising that in 1996 a group of feminists decided to create DIVERSA, a political association of feminist women and men. A feminist organization that includes men overturns the traditional concept of the feminist movement and poses a threat, especially when large sectors of women who suffer from machismo have already decided to act based on their discovery of the benefits of womanism. Those who have recently positioned themselves as women (politically speaking) have yet to experience the limitations of politics rooted in identity. DIVERSA gained federal recognition as a legal political association in 1999.[13] It proposed to abandon the politics of identity for a broader, more citizen-oriented focus to carry out the democratic transition. DIVERSA seeks to redefine the frontiers of citizens' agency and to create an exercise of citizenship that could open politics to new identities as well as new political practices. This has required building a collective praxis that—while recognizing particular identities—outlines a larger goal capable of exceeding those same identities. It is, without a doubt, the most interesting political proposal today.

As Jean Franco states, although Mexican revolutionary ideology permitted a high degree of secularization in public life, it absorbed machismo in its national imagery. Due to the dramatic cultural oppression of machismo, there has been significant progress for feminism in the cultural sphere. On the one hand, the feminist discourse on women's rights has been popularized, with the image (whether it is admired or reviled) of a new, liberated woman. The symbol of the liberated woman has become part of the country's cultural iconography and has entered the popular imagination: it is a point of reference, a model, or a warning. On the other hand, there are new cultural expressions that question the traditional machista representation of women's experience. Women have found writing and communication to be an effective outlet for many of their ideas. In addition to creative works (literature, theater, music), a body of feminist criticism is developing.

The existence of a number of feminist and gender-oriented academic centers has stimulated the publication of research and has been particularly important in helping to give permanence to educational programs on women.[14] Although their influence in the country's intellectual debate is still limited, these centers provide opportunities for academic exchange and also serve to form the next generation of feminist academics. Unfortunately, among Mexico's intellectuals there does not yet exist a serious debate with feminist thought, due in part to the absence of a rigorous intellectual discussion within the feminist movement itself. Nevertheless, feminist theory influences research in many academic centers, and some respected intellectuals view it as a legitimate perspective.[15]

In contrast to the shortfalls in the political arena, there has been significant progress for women in the educational sphere. Although the main educational deficiency continues to be found among young peasant and indigenous women, as well as among older women, the entry of more women into higher education has been a determining factor in the changes occurring in birthrates, family life, and opportunities for paid employment. Statistics regarding literacy are deceptive, for a high percentage of those who have received formal schooling are functionally illiterate, incapable of reading a newspaper. There are more illiterate women than illiterate men, the highest rates of illiteracy being found among peasants and indigenous Mexicans. In addition, the rising presence of the TV culture has discouraged the habit of reading. Obviously, lower literacy is detrimental to women's access to better jobs and educational possibilities.

It is known that educational processes, under conditions of modernity and economic development, tend toward equity between the sexes; this is now happening with Mexico's urban youth. Male and female enrollment in primary and secondary schools is approximately equal. The equality of the sexes at these levels coincides with the expansion of the educational system. One apparently constant phenomenon is the attrition rate at the end of each unit of schooling: at the end of primary school, girls tend to redirect their studies toward vocational training; upon finishing secondary school, many young women leave school in order to join the workforce or begin a family. These trends illustrate the influence of traditional cultural patterns on the lives of young women.

In recent years, women's enrollment in universities has increased exponentially. However, there is still a significant difference favoring male university students that increases with scholastic level: for every six male students enrolled at the undergraduate level, there are four female students, whereas there are seven male graduate students for every three female graduate students. Women students tend to enter fields traditionally considered to be feminine, although they are beginning to major in fields such as engineering, agricultural sciences, and physics.

Placing other considerations to the side, the strength of Mexican feminism lies more in its activist element than in the intellectual. Carlos Monsiváis states that there is no true political change if it is not accompanied by cultural transformation. The scarce number of women participating in the feminist movement contrasts with the symbolic presence of feminism. With great political effectiveness, feminism has mobilized a number of outstanding women writers, artists, government officials, and politicians. For example, the 1997 campaign for the liberation of Claudia Rodríguez, a woman who injured a man who tried to rape her, demonstrates the capacity for feminist coordination. Rodríguez's attacker died a few hours after the incident due to lack of medical attention, and Rodríguez was arrested and imprisoned. A combination of feminists, women politicians, writers, and artists challenged the judicial decision, stating that Rodríguez had acted in self-defense and that the authorities' neglect led to the victim's death. Due to this active coalition of women coordinated by feminists, Rodríguez was liberated after a year in prison.[16]

Feminism has grounded its presence in three noteworthy ways: (1)

professionalization, through the financing of organized groups that work on specific themes (health, education, violence) and have the ability to make effective political demands; (2) academic and political legitimization of the gender perspective, with proliferation of academic programs, courses, conferences, publications, forums, and research; and (3) consolidation, in the public arena, of a womanist discussion that combines, in spite of everything, many feminist doubts and aspirations. In Mexico, the political achievement of feminism lies precisely in this cultural discourse, which has fueled the demand for the rights of every woman. To confront sexism, the knowledge that women have rights has been very effective.

Thus, the role of women in public life today has changed some cultural patterns, thereby generating new forms of family life, neighborhood sociability, workers' consciousness, and political identity. More women have higher self-esteem, a greater capacity for self-expression, a better ability to manage political resources, and a more clear commitment to other organized groups. This has fueled the creation of multiple support networks and relations with other women fighting for social justice, including academics and government and party officials. The struggle to find a niche and recognition in the realpolitik has been exhausting, and DIVERSA offers an attractive means for political participation for many women. In the July 2000 presidential elections, DIVERSA had several candidates running for parliament and office through external candidacies with three different parties: PRD, PRI, and Democracia Social. Undoubtedly, it is a feminist triumph that DIVERSA's candidates were elected.[17]

In spite of the fact that many public figures and political organizations have embraced feminist ideas, there is still much resistance to a movement that is publicly identified with abortion and lesbianism. Those who support these ideas in private are unwilling to do so publicly. Pro-choice positions and gay rights disturb the current paradigm of what is "natural" for women and clash with the dogma of the Catholic Church. Although the pro-choice struggle has been supported by noteworthy intellectuals, scientists, and artists, Mexican politicians resist supporting positions that are stigmatized by the hegemonic Catholic ideology. No party wishes to confront the enormous power of the Catholic Church by legitimizing these crucial demands.

Notwithstanding cultural and economic obstacles, the general objectives of the movement are slowly finding acceptance within Mexico. Increasing numbers of individuals and organizations are incorporating the idea of diversity into their work, which is indispensable for embracing democratic politics. Many women have assumed a pragmatic dimension in their political discourse and action and show a passion for negotiating conflicts. Thus, after thirty years, a substantial part of the feminist movement is leaving behind the activist model of ideological feminism, moving away from the passionate identification with sectarian points of view, and overcoming the reticence to collaborate with those who have different ideas.[18] Today many groups are beginning to follow the model of interest groups, which emphasize equal rights before the law and work politically as pressure groups.

This is, perhaps, the most notable change that is currently under way: women are working to acquire basic political skills and develop a less dogmatic practice. Three new political dimensions form the core of women's new role. First, to fight gender inequality, women are integrating themselves into the country's political dynamic. Although women have yet to become prominent in the world of politics, the great success of Mexican feminism is the fact that its ideas have influenced the conduct of women because it offers a kind of emotional, political, and intellectual training that compels women to stop being victims. During the recent presidential campaigns, women were active, asking the candidates about their position on gender issues, and they made one thing clear: more women are needed in public positions.

Second, Mexican women are participating in the international political arena. In spite of having ratified international conventions mandating the elimination of discrimination against women, the Mexican government has not implemented actions to carry out this commitment. This has led women to a greater awareness of the need to influence the government by participating in international conferences, like the two held by the United Nations in Cairo (1994) and in Beijing (1995). International conferences oblige the government to take a position on subjects that are silenced in Mexico, such as sexual and reproductive rights. Due to this international pressure, a state office for women—the National Program for Women—was created in 1996.

The third dimension is the "mixed" reorientation of feminist activism, of which the most interesting example is DIVERSA. DIVERSA subverts the traditional concept of the feminist organization, creating a political constituency of feminist people, both women and men, along with the strong participation of young people.

Perhaps the principal lesson to be learned is that there is not a natural unity among women; unity must be built politically. This knowledge has forced new political configurations: there are more women activists working within society, establishing alliances, and dedicated to gaining public spaces. While also attempting to influence electoral issues, it is evident that feminists throughout Mexico have an extraordinary interest in building a common agenda.[19]

This offers an interesting goal for women: to improve their position in the existing political order while attempting to transform this order. Creating unifying processes and achieving shared objectives for Mexican women could alter the machista bias within institutional power.

In 2002, Mexico faces a number of challenges. One that is especially crucial for women is to sustain the advances they have achieved in face of the new government under the National Action Party (PAN). The desire for change in government blinded Mexicans to the point that they voted for Vicente Fox, unconcerned with the consequences of his true political stance, as long as the PRI lost. The task for women will be to defend the set of rights they have acquired. Scarcely a month after the elections, the PAN-dominated state congress in Guanajuato (Fox's home state, where he was still serving as governor on leave of absence) tried to change abortion laws, banning a woman's right to terminate a pregnancy caused by rape. The motion caused a national upheaval, and it was vetoed a month later by the state governor after a heated debate in which many of the intellectuals who formerly had pronounced themselves for the "useful vote" (i.e., against the PRI and for Fox) criticized the PAN.

This is not a lone incident. On the contrary, it represents a signal of what is to come. It will be hard to carry out democratic change with a party in power like the PAN, whose positions on gender issues represent a terrible reversal of many of the advances women have made in recent years.

Thus, Mexican women face the challenge of developing a better-organized political structure able to influence a number of areas: the government in its definition of public policy; the political parties so that they incorporate a gender perspective into their platforms and sponsor more women as candidates; the public to raise awareness of gender issues; critics and intellectuals so that their work deals with sexism; and finally, the large numbers of women who are not politically active and who, in their isolation, suffer silently from machismo, so as to bring them to discover that collective action offers a way to address the problems of their daily lives.

In a sense, fully accepting the idea of diversity and understanding that a gender perspective is radical by nature in a machista society, the women's movement will have to mobilize to ensure that sexual difference is not used as a justification for inequality. Seen in this light, in a country where independence is considered totally unfeminine, and in some cases even immoral, the role of feminism is both key and imperative.

Notes

1. A longer, more detailed account of women's transformation in Mexico, of which I take some parts, can be found in Marta Lamas, A. Martínez, M. L. Tarrés, and E. Tuñón, "Building Bridges: The Growth of Popular Feminism in Mexico," in Amrita Basu, ed., *The Challenge of Local Feminisms: Women's Movements in Global Perspective* (Boulder: Westview, 1995).

2. The official program of "family planning" was started by President Luis Echeverría in 1974.

3. In August 2000 in the state of Guanajuato, the home state of President Vicente Fox, the conservative National Action Party (PAN) passed a bill to ban the rape clause. A tremendous scandal followed that led the governor of Guanajuato to veto the law reform. Society's prochoice position was so evident that a liberal reaction followed: the PRD reformed Mexico City's legislation to allow legal abortion for fetal impairment and risk to the woman's health, and the PRI similarly modified the law in Morelos.

4. The first figure comes from the National Council on Population (CONAPO), the second from Dr. Raúl López García, medical subdirector of the Instituto Nacional de Perinatología.

5. The figures vary depending on the source. This percentage is from the national population and housing document of the National Institute of Statistics and Geographical Information (INEGI), *Censo general de población y vivienda* (Aguascalientes: INEGI, 1995).

6. Rosario Castellanos said in 1971 that when the last domestic worker disappears, the first radical feminists will appear. Rosario Castellanos, "La liberación de la mujer, aquí," *Excélsior*, September 5, 1970; reproduced in *El uso de la palabra* (México, D.F.: Ediciones de Excélsior, 1974).

7. This bill passed in the legislative assembly on August 18, 2000. The PRI also supported this bill.

8. The slogan was first used by Chilean feminists.

9. See Esperanza Tuñón, *Mujeres en escena: de la tramoya al protagonismo (1982–1994)* (México, D.F.: Miguel Angel Porrúa, PUEG, Ecosur, 1997); Maria Luisa Tarrés, "Hacia un equilibrio de la ética y la negociación," *Debate Feminista*, no. 7 (March 1993).

10. Womanism is a perspective that idealizes the "natural" conditions of women and mystifies the relationships among women. A typical womanist attitude is to speak in the name of women, as if they have a uniform position in society.

11. The idea of multiple feminist identities created an internal crisis at the end of the 1980s. Since then, the differences in the field of collective identifications have grown deeper between two strong paradigms, fueling a contraposi-

tion between the "feminists of utopia" and the "feminists of what is possible" (this categorization was created during the Sixth Feminist Congress in El Salvador, 1993). This has led to another manichean characterization of two types of feminists: autonomous and institutionalized. See Ximena Bedregal, "Ruptura de acuerdos de feministas autónomas," *Triple Jornada*, no. 3 (November 1998); Haydée Birgin et al., "Del amor a la necesidad," *fem.*, vol. 11, no. 60 (December 1987); Haydée Birgin, "Vivencias del encuentro de Chile: lo personal y lo político," *Debate Feminista*, núm. 15 (April 1997).

12. The new political context, with the triumph of the PRD in Mexico City, and with Rosario Robles as head of the Mexico City government, has strengthened the feminist agenda.

13. The Agrupación Política Nacional (National Political Association) requires 15,000 affiliates in all the country for an association to qualify as a precursor to a political party and to be recognized by the Federal Electoral Institute.

14. Mexico's principal universities have either gender studies or women's studies programs.

15. Carlos Monsiváis has been the most constant in his critical support of feminism.

16. Her case catalyzed feminists from all viewpoints, and famous women from all sectors were involved. See Marta Victoria Lamas and Claudia Rodríguez Ferrando, *Claudia: Una liberación* (México, D.F.: Plaza y Janés, 1998).

17. A lesbian was elected for Democracia Social, with a gay man as her alternate; a teacher was elected from the National Union of Teachers for the PRI and a well-known feminist for the PRD.

18. On the activist model of ideological feminism, see Joyce Gelb, "Feminismo y acción política," in Russell J. Dalton and Manfred Kuechler, eds., *Los nuevos movimientos sociales* (Generalitat Valenciana, Spain: Edicions Alfons El Magnánim, 1992).

19. This is the case of the Congreso Nacional de Mujeres, held in September 2000.

6

Transition or Restructuring of Society?

Ilán Bizberg

The groundbreaking study of the transition school defined citizenship as the right to be treated equally by other fellow human beings with respect to collective decisionmaking processes, the right to demand accountability from those who implement those decisions, as well as the right of government officials to act with authority to promote the efficacy of such decisions and protect society from threats to its capacity to survive. Yet this definition is a procedural minimum of democracy, consisting of periodic elections through secret ballots, universal adult suffrage, party concurrence and recognition, and free access to all associations and to all executive posts of responsibility.[1]

Two Distinct Paradigms

Although the theoretical choice made by the transition school correctly implies that there are no prerequisites of democracy and that there is not a unique model of democracy, there is an epistemological leap from the minimal definition of democracy to the concept of citizenship. Although they both seem to be merely formal, the definition of citizenship implies a principle of equality. This means that the minimal definition of democracy cannot assure that individuals be treated as equals and that deliberation between equals really exists. This latter requires that the individual be not only a formal citizen but also an active one, that is, able to exert his rights. This capacity is linked to the political, social, and even economic conditions that lead to the autonomy of the individual, which allows individuals to attain the subjective and fully conscious value of citizenship.[2] Yet accountability cannot be assured through mere legal means; it needs the organizational capacity of citizens to demand it from their governments and thus the sufficient density of civil society to allow citizens to exert their rights. Finally, formal democracy is not sufficient to ensure that those governed accept the legitimacy of power. Legitimacy exists where there is an explicit or (usually) implicit pact between the social sectors that constitute a society, which leads the individuals pertaining to these sectors and their organizations to accept the authority of institutions. This requires the "feeling" on behalf of citizens and their organizations that through their accepting the rules of the game they are actually enforcing the pact that founds their society. Legitimacy also implies that they are able to change the rules of the game, the institutions, and even the terms of the pact in order to defend their identities, interests, and projects.

It is true that there are laws that can help ensure equality and accountability, but they are not sufficient to ensure their application; there has to exist the individual and social capacity to demand both principles, something mere procedural forms cannot do. We thus need a more analytic and substantive definition of democracy, a definition that overrides another major characteristic of the transition school of thought, which is its emphasis on a purely contingent and decisionmaking theory of democracy, that focuses upon elites and neglects the action of collective actors.[3] The few transition-school studies that analyze popular action, as, for example, that of Valenzuela, do not analyze the contributions of the labor movement toward democracy but rather the manner in which its action has an influence on the strategic clash between the two sectors in which both the governing and the opposition elite are divided.[4] A more moderate example of this position is that of Juan Linz and Alfred Stepan, where civil society is supposed to have the capacity to *help* the transition, the consolidation, and deepening of democracy but does not really constitute an integral part of the definition of democracy.[5]

This interpretation arises from a partial interpretation of Alexis de Tocqueville, meaning that civil society is basically a limit to state power, an idea that was first posed by John Stuart Mill. Nevertheless, according to de Tocqueville, democracy has clear social roots: in its origins, it depended on the original homogeneity of American society, due to the absence of a hierarchy linked to birth; in synthesis, on social equality. Although this basic social situation enhances individuality, in America it did not result in anomie, because it was counterbalanced by a deeply entrenched idea of the collective good, derived both from religion and from the belief that the immigrants to America were to fulfill a special mission in the new homeland. This led to strong associationism and to the construction of democracy from below. The way civil society is conceived by de Tocqueville is far from being a mere guarantee or help for democracy; it constitutes its foundation.

If we accept this premise, we would have to put civil society at the center of any study on democracy. Rueschemeyer poses a definite relationship between democracy and civil society, which varies according to the type of association:

> While civic associations increase the power of civic society, without doing much to increase political participation and even less for class organization, the League of Women Voters and the ecological organizations empower civic society and political participation, while class-oriented organizations such as labor unions and agrarian leagues empower civic society, political participation and class organizations.[6]

For Touraine, and Cohen and Arato, it is social movements that are crucial for deepening democracy, as they have the merit of reminding society of the necessity of giving free institutions the basis of representativity that they frequently lack.[7] But social movements also "propose to modify the social utilization of resources in the name of cultural orientations accepted in any society";[8] they thus go beyond the institutionalized treatment of conflicts of a determined society and "serve as the principle of a reflexive, discussed, and decided reconstruction of a society."[9] In this way, social movements expand rights and deepen democracy, and keep a democratic political culture alive.[10] This does not mean that direct participation through social movements will supplant formal democracy, defined by institutions of representative democracy. It only means that when movements go beyond the institutions and manners of treating conflicts in a determined society, their action invents and helps organize social groups and institutionalize new political forms of solving conflicting identities, interests, and projects.

What Arato calls a culture of interaction and a civil society–based politics can be assimilated to what H. Arendt considers to be the basis of power, and thus of politics, when she states that "power corresponds to that human capacity to act in common."[11] Another concept that supposes this principle is what Charles Sabel[12] calls constitutional orders, which are not preestablished but constructed through the capacity that society[13] or social actors[14] have to construct the social institutions in which they live. Sabel defines *constitutional orders* as "trust-based coordination mechanisms," in contrast to both markets and hierarchies.

Arendt and Sabel help us to understand what allows for Arato's self-restriction of social movements, as well as for Touraine's conception of social movements that do not contest the general cultural orientation of society or destroy the institutional order, only the manner in which resources are used socially. Civil society is thus necessary both to found and to keep alive a society based upon the peaceful resolution of conflict, where there are not metapolitical conditions to ensure social order, such as religion, charisma, tradition, violence, or terror. In this situation, only an agreement upon the fundamental orientations of society, a social contract, and its crystallization in a social order renew the institutions that are capable of peacefully solving problems and bind people together democratically.

What all this discussion shows us are the limits that the concept of transition encounters in trying to encompass such a variety of questions. We have to adopt the much more open concept of reconstruction of society: that means the capacity of society to work on its conflicts, its differences, to permanently invent new forms of processing them without canceling identities and projects.

We will now go on to analyze the Mexican case, as an example of these ideas. Our discussion will focus on the capacity to reconstruct society given the forces behind the Mexican process of transition. We will, nevertheless, begin by a discussion of the characteristics of the old regime and of the way in which it gradually decomposed.

The Decomposition of the Old Mexican Political Regime

In order to analyze the Mexican transition, one has to begin by describing how the Mexican political authoritarian regime had a different origin from that of the other countries that have been considered by the transition literature. In contrast to most authoritarian regimes in Latin America, which were basically military, antipopular, and established through a coup d'etat that overthrew a national-popular regime such as those existing in Argentina and Brazil (established in the 1930s, about the same time as in Mexico), the Mexican regime had enough legitimacy to endure until 2000. Nevertheless, its legitimacy quickly evaporated when the economic model was changed as a result of the 1982 economic crisis.

The Mexican political regime drew its legitimacy from its revolutionary (nationalist and popular) origins. Its institutionalization was achieved at two different moments: the first in 1929, when the party that was to rule for the next seventy-one years was created; the second in 1938, when the elite party was transformed into a mass party. The precursor of the Institutional Revolutionary Party (PRI) was conceived as a mechanism to allow ruling elites to negotiate and solve their differences institutionally rather than through the violence that had characterized prior power transmissions. The founding of the National Revolutionary Party institutionalized the power struggle. In 1938, during the presidency of Lázaro Cárdenas, a mass party that regrouped the popular sectors—trade unions, peasant organizations, and other popular groups—was substituted for this elite organization.

Seen from the perspective of a founding pact, this party sealed an alliance between the popular sectors and the state. In the new pact, the social organizations (partly autonomous, partly promoted by the state) would support the regime, and in exchange the state would become the main agent of development and pursue an economic and social project designed to develop the country and distribute wealth as it was created. The main goal was to integrate the mass of the population that had been left out by the old economic model of the Porfiriato.[15] Although this pact endured important changes during the more than seventy years that it lasted, it never changed its fundamental nature, as did the national-popular pacts in Argentina and Brazil, which were overthrown by the military. Yet it was never identified with a non-national elite or power, such as the regimes of Eastern Europe. It always maintained a reserve of legitimacy and showed a capacity both to refurbish its legitimacy through specific measures and programs such as job creation, land distribution, and extended educational and health services, and to control the social actors through clientelism, co-optation, and repression.

The fact that in the old regime the state was the main agent of development, paired with the way the regime was basically institutionalized from above, left society in a subordinate position. The government spoke in the name of the people and accumulated attributions that allowed it to control the different social organizations that were part of the pact. It had the capacity to intervene in the activities and internal affairs of trade unions and peasant organizations. It could accept or deny the registry of a specific union or peasant organization, its leadership, and the legality of strikes and collective negotiations between employers and workers. The pact also created an institutional framework that allowed the regime to continue through clientelism, the co-optation of independent organizations and leadership, and through selective repression of the more radical elements.

Accumulated capacity for control allowed the regime to eventually become more exclusive and diverge from its inclusive character, as was the case during the Miguel Alemán period (1946–1952). It also allowed it to go through less paternalistic and clientelistic and more authoritarian periods (again the Alemán and in addition the Díaz Ordaz period [1964–1970]) without abandoning its nature as a national-popular regime and falling prey to a military coup, something that the Argentine and Brazilian regimes were not capable of doing when they lost control over popular organizations. Just as with Eastern Europe and Russia, the Mexican regime also passed from a strict to a more lenient regime and again to a more authoritarian one.

Based on its revolutionary ideology and origins, the Mexican authoritarian regime had the capacity to change its character without modifying its nature. After the end of World War II, when tight control of worker demands was needed in order to ensure the expansion of Mexican industry, the government of Miguel Alemán adopted an authoritarian stand toward workers' unions. He purged unions and peasant organizations of their communist and Cardenist leadership in order to impose a decrease of real wages and halt land distribution. This was in accordance with an economic policy intended to favor the interests of capital and to create wealth before it was distributed. This marked the end of the "authentic" stage of the national-popular regime, when the popular organizations supported the government because they agreed with its economic and social project. The governments of Alemán, as well as that of Adolfo Ruíz Cortines (1952–1958), were characterized by the subordination of the social organizations to the state and the creation of the control mechanisms that allowed it. This was possible to do without changing the character of the regime, something that was not achieved by the national-popular regimes of Argentina (where Juan Perón was forced to resign by the military in 1955) and Brazil (where Joao Goulart was ousted by the military in 1964).

In 1958–1959, when the workers and peasants reacted to twelve years of antipopular economic policies with strikes and massive land invasions, the Mexican political regime once again showed its capacity to adapt. The government of Adolfo López Mateos (1958–1964) went back to revolutionary rhetoric and again changed the character of the regime. It pretended to maintain the pact established in the 1930s, although its action was oriented by a strategic logic aimed to diffuse social discontent. It targeted its resources toward the best-organized and more strategic social sectors that were also most active. Of the peasant groups, these sectors included the northeastern part of the country that had experienced the highest rate of investment during the previous twelve years, as well as the old Zapatista regions of Morelos and Guerrero. Of worker and employee groups, the teachers', railroad, and petroleum workers' unions were favored. The government created the Institute of Social Services for Federal State Employees, considerably improved the wage and labor conditions of the railroad, petroleum, and electric workers, and distributed massive amounts of land in the regions of the country that had seen the largest number of mobilizations.

The government of López Mateos was successful in rescuing the revolutionary authoritarian regime, substituting the ample national pact of the 1930s with a more corporate one that greatly favored certain specific groups and sectors of society while maintaining the facade of the most inclusive alliance. There were also changes on the part of the popular organizations, in that they gave up their conviction in a common project in order to obtain economic and social benefits that came with their political support of the regime.

The corporate pact that included part of the popular sectors and excluded the majority (something that was especially true when there were economic hardships, as in 1976 and 1982) survived until the 1982 crisis, when the economic capacity of the state was dramatically reduced. From that time on, the state was obliged to give up its role as agent of development, something that implied the reduction of its investments and eventually forced the opening of the Mexican economy. This situation had as its consequence a radical decrease in the capacity of the corporate regime to continue giving privileges and subsidies to its base: the workers of the most strategic economic sectors (most of them owned by the state) and the social agricultural sector (*ejidos*).

This situation eventually led the government of Miguel de la Madrid (1982–1988) to altogether abandon the nationalist and popular project. Although this eroded the legitimacy of the state and the regime, as well as that of the popular organizations they were based on, it did not radically change the control faculties of the state upon the social organizations that constituted the PRI. Although the retreat of the state profoundly reduced the capacity of the PRI organizations to control their membership in clientelistic terms, the state maintained allegiance and tight administrative controls over most of the official leadership established during the fifty-plus years that the regime had been in place.

This allowed the government to impose drastic austerity measures and restructure the economy with little resistance on the part of the popular sectors.

During the presidency of de la Madrid, the Mexican government once again modified the character of the political regime without changing its nature. It again changed the alliance to include entrepreneurs, who would benefit from a more productive and internationally competitive Mexican economy. The same strategy was followed by Carlos Salinas de Gortari, who had success in abandoning not only the popular character of the original alliance but also the national one as well. With the signing of the North American Free Trade Agreement (NAFTA), the government sought the North American capitalists as partners in order to incorporate the Mexican economy into the international arena rather than rely on national entrepreneurs.

There was, nonetheless, a crucial difference between both presidencies. At the beginning of his presidency, de la Madrid thought that the PRI would be able to appeal to the urban and middle classes in order to win elections by advocating a realistic and technically correct management of the crisis instead of depending on clientelism and popular support for the regime. The first sign indicating that this strategy was a failure was Chihuahua's 1983 local elections, in which the PRI lost in practically all of the major cities—precisely where this more urban and middle-class population lived. As a result, the government had to abandon that strategy and once again rely on traditional corporate-style leadership and electoral fraud, such as in the 1985 elections in Chihuahua and the national elections in 1988.

When Salinas took office after the contested elections of 1988, the governmental strategy radically changed. He discarded the idea that the PRI would be able to stay in power based upon a more solid experience of government while its traditional bases were left behind. Yet the possibility of continuing to win elections through fraud was drastically reduced because the government had to face a more conscious and better-organized civil society and greater vigilance from the international scene. Salinas's government intended to maintain the support of the traditional corporate apparatus, although it functioned less and less effectively, until it was ready to substitute it with other organized social forces and eventually establish a new party apparatus.

Because most of the legitimacy of the original alliance was extinguished, and both the state and popular organizations were showing a lessened capacity to deliver privileges to the most strategic popular groups upon which the corporate pact was based, the government of

Salinas again changed the character of the regime in order to convert it into an essentially clientelistic pact targeted at the poorest sectors of society. The government established the Solidaridad program in order to substitute a clientelistic structure mediated through corporate organizations, with a clientelistic system linked to the presidency, that would directly relate the "agency" that controlled economic resources in Mexico to "organizations" based upon a primary identity, defined by their living quarters and their immediate needs.[16]

Nevertheless, this project of constituting a clientelistic state to substitute the corporate one was condemned to fail in the medium term, as it further weakened the organizations and institutions of the national-popular pact. Although this clientelistic state functioned conjuncturally, it was not capable of generating a durable new alliance between the state and society; neither was it capable of refurbishing the regime with legitimacy.[17] This was not possible because the clientelistic pact was built upon conjunctural and immediate needs and not upon longer-lasting interests or projects.

This attempt to constitute a clientelistic pact independent of the organizations of the national-popular pact not only failed to establish solid popular organizations but also actually worked to sap the former of the legitimacy they still had and greatly affected their efficacy. It also contributed to eventually weaken the presidency, as was evidenced during the administration of Ernesto Zedillo (1994–2000).

The political and economic crisis of 1994 made it clear that the intent to constitute a clientelistic pact had failed. The region where the indigenous Zapatista National Liberation Army (EZLN) appeared had received the most resources from Solidaridad. In addition, the presidential candidate of the PRI, who had been the director of the program, was assassinated in March. His substitute, Ernesto Zedillo, an economist who had been the secretary of education, reduced the Solidaridad program to a minimum, abandoning the political project of the previous administration. At the same time, the remaining institutions of the national-popular regime, such as the Mexican Institute of Social Security and the CONASUPO—an agency that subsidized the prices of agricultural products both to producers and consumers—started being dismantled. All of this continued to sap the regime of its content, further weakening the traditional clientelistic instruments, and made the Mexican state less and less capable of controlling the process of political liberalization.

The 1994 crisis and the pressure of opposition parties that had strongly contested the elections of 1988 weakened the position of the

Salinas government. An agreement was reached among the three major parties to create an autonomous institution to organize the elections previously organized by the government itself. However, it should be noted that the Federal Electoral Institute (IFE) still had the secretary of the interior as its president during the 1994 elections. This was changed in 1996, when the current IFE was created with complete independence from the government. The new IFE has nine counselors, recommended by the major political parties and elected by Congress with a two-thirds majority. All this amounted to the fact that the PRI was not able to control the outcome of the election in 2000 and had reduced capacity to influence the people's votes by offering permanent clientelistic advantages.

In this manner, the principal factor of power of the Mexican political regime—the presidency—was being strongly eroded.[18] The Mexican constitution had given the Mexican president an ample array of instruments of power. But even more important, during the more than seventy years that had elapsed since the centralization of power in the 1920s, the presidency had been able to co-opt an enormous number of metaconstitutional attributions that in other political systems are in the hands of other institutions. The incumbent president could choose his successor, act as an arbiter in political disputes among members of his party, decide most public policies, initiate most of the lawmaking procedures, name Supreme Court judges, and act as the main distributor of benefits. When all the governors and a majority of members of the federal and state assemblies came from the PRI, the president could thus easily control the whole political scenario. He could threaten the governors with a censorship motion in the Senate and force their resignation. He could absolutely control the legislative process and the judiciary system by nominating Supreme Court and other high-ranking judges. In addition, the head of the Bank of Mexico was part of the presidential cabinet, so it was not an independent body as it is today.

Since the second half of the 1980s, but especially during the last PRI presidency (Zedillo, 1994–2000), these extraordinary faculties became dispersed.[19] Some of them went to the Chamber of Deputies, to the PRI itself, to the governors of the PRI, and to opposition parties. Even before the PRI lost the presidential elections in 2000, it had already lost control of more than ten states to opposition parties. One of the regions lost was Mexico City, Mexico's largest city, where 25 percent of the population lives or works. In addition, although the PRI still controlled the executives in many states, it no longer controlled the local legislatures, and many municipalities were in the hands of opposition parties. In the 1997 elections, the PRI lost the majority of the Chamber of Deputies, which meant that the president could no longer modify the constitution as he had done so often before. This change also meant that Congress would no longer limit itself to simply passing the initiatives that came from the executive.

With the weakening of the PRI at the national and local levels, the president lost his grip on his own party. The governors who belonged to the PRI gained increasing autonomy from the presidency. At the beginning of the Zedillo presidency, PRI members in Tabasco rebelled against the federal government in support of its governor (obviously controlled and manipulated by him). They stood up against the comprehensive political agreement that the Zedillo administration had reached with the opposition parties that included the deposition of the governor of Tabasco (who gained the governorship after a dubious campaign and election) and made it fail. It is this same governor, Roberto Madrazo, who in the year 2000 forced Zedillo to hold a primary election for the first time in the history of the PRI and ran against the "official" presidential candidate, Francisco Labastida. Madrazo also succeeded in having his local candidate elected in similarly dubious elections in August 2000, imposed an interim governor when the Federal Electoral Court annulled the former election, and eventually succeeded in having his original candidate elected to the governorship at the end of 2001.

This rebellion by the governor of Tabasco was not isolated; other governors of the PRI followed. The governor of Yucatán, Victor Cervera Pacheco, succeeded in getting himself reelected in elections marked by many irregularities, the primary one being that he had already served as interim governor during the previous four years, something that legally impeded him from running again. This same governor was, already under Fox's administration, the main protagonist of a serious electoral conflict, which involved the rejection of a decision made by the Federal Electoral Court. It was not only the governors who showed their autonomy from a weaker presidency but also other organizations that had been easily controlled by the presidency and the PRI in the past. After the death of the secretary-general of the largest trade union confederation of the country, the Confederation of Mexican Workers (CTM), the government of Zedillo failed to impose their choice of a modernizer as the new head, and one of the most traditional leaders was elected.

As long as this means that the power formerly concentrated in the presidency has diminished and counterweights to the executive have been created, it is a positive evolution. Nevertheless, this also means that we are living through a process of feudalization of political power in Mexico. This dispersion of power is leading to the consequence that in some regions (Yucatán, Tabasco, and Campeche, among others) and organizations (the CTM, the Revolutionary Confederation of Workers and Peasants, and the Regional Confederation of Mexican Workers) political power is falling into the hands of more traditional leaders who have been active in resisting the process of democratization.[20] Although the democratization of the country started in certain localities and regions, mainly in the northern and northeastern parts of the country, the local level began serving as the refuge for the traditional politicians who waged war against the more reformist ones under the PRI administrations and are now trying to offer resistance to Fox's government. The technocrats of the PRI, who presented themselves as the only ones capable of solving the economic crisis, had the capacity to control the party apparatus and the traditional politicians until the presidency of Salinas. They were able to do this partly because they had the support of the international financial agencies that were to help allocate the enormous amounts of loans the country needed. With the weakening of the PRI at the national level (especially now that it has lost the presidency), the strongholds of traditional politicians are these local governments and organizations, from where they try to regain not only the national PRI but also the presidency.

In addition to the dispersion of power once concentrated in the presidency, popular organizations have weakened under the control of the PRI. The labor, peasant, and other popular movements depended on a corporate relationship with the state, through which political support and control of the demands of the popular sectors were exchanged for economic and political privileges for the leadership and clientelistic benefits for workers and peasants. From 1982 on, this situation had to be reversed, first because the intervention of the state receded, then because the Mexican economy opened when the country entered the General Agreement on Tariffs and Trade in 1986 and imposed an increased international concurrence on the Mexican companies and the countryside.

Corporate organizations that mediated between the state and the social sectors weakened because the state-PRI maintained its administrative and political control mechanisms almost untouched and continued exerting hegemony over the (reduced) resources to distribute goods (public works, living quarters, drainage, water, electricity, etc.).[21] This fact did not result in the decreased legitimacy and profile of these organizations translating into massive popular opposition. This means that the power vacuum left by the corporate regime's decomposition is not being filled by the emergence of independent popular or civic organizations but rather by the *caciques* (local authoritarian leaders) who either rise out of the feudalization of the PRI or by the strengthening of openly illegal forces (trafficking in drugs, migrants, and stolen cars; smuggling; kidnapping; etc.).

Civil Society and the Mexican Transition

Some transitions have seen massive social movements against the old regime, such as Poland's experience with Solidarity and, to a lesser degree, Brazil's experience with the organized entrepreneurs and workers. Other transitions have been the consequence of a massive organization of civic associations, as in Hungary, or of the spontaneous emergence of civil society, as in Czechoslovakia and East Germany. Still others have resulted from the decomposition of the old regime, as in the former Soviet Union. Although the Mexican transition has also been dominated by the decomposition of the ancien régime, this decay has partly resulted from the pressure of political and social forces that questioned its legitimacy. In order to evaluate the capacity of Mexican society to reconstruct a political regime after the former regime has decomposed for thirty years, we will have to review the capacity of civil society to organize itself and struggle against the previous regime.

Labor and Peasant Organizations

As discussed above, the regime was based upon an alliance with the popular sectors that eventually subordinated these sectors and their organizations to the state. Nonetheless, the dependence of labor and peasant organizations on the state was also characterized by periodic outbursts of discontent. One significant mass movement was the upsurge of independent trade unions and peasant organizations during the early 1970s. Although this movement was short-lived and did not contribute much to actively dismantle the old regime, it was crucial because it showed the limits of the capacity of independent movements to organize in Mexico, as well as the difficulties faced by the regime in refurbishing its legitimacy and renewing its control over these social groups after the 1968 conflict.

These movements were also very important in questioning the subordination of unions to the state and the existence of a leadership that responded more to the directives of the government than to the demands of the workers. They also questioned the lack of democracy within the unions, as well as in other popular organizations, which served as the main support for the existence of this type of leadership. The fact that these structural and social issues, and not economic issues, were the main reasons for the emergence of this broad movement of union independence is proven by the fact that when these gained force during the presidency of Luis Echeverría, not only had wages reached a historic high in 1976 but also the government had established various institutions directed at subsidizing housing and furniture for the workers and distributing large amounts of good, arable land.

The independence movement started in the economic sectors that had gone through a process of modernization, had the most complex production and organization processes, and correspondingly required more qualified, better-schooled, and younger workers.[22] Among these sectors were the automobile and auto parts, electronic, airline, telephone, and electricity industries and education services. In the countryside, the movement began in the regions that had experienced the fastest development, such as the extensively irrigated and high-exporting regions of the northeastern part of Mexico.

This pressure for change in some popular sectors coincided with the will on the part of Echeverría's government to accept and even encourage it. This attitude of the government was crucial because the Ministry of Labor had great capacity to intervene in the internal questions of union and peasant organizations, especially regarding the decision to accept or reject the results of an internal election favoring autonomous leadership or the decision made by a union to leave an official confederation. In fact, the government of Echeverría actually induced the liberalization of the popular organizations. A few months after taking office, the president affirmed that workers' assemblies had the right to freely choose their own leadership and to decide which confederation they wanted to join.

This attitude on the part of the Echeverría government came out of its diagnosis of the causes of the student movement and of the incapacity of the Mexican state to respond in any terms other than repression. According to its diagnosis, the main cause of the crisis had been the lack of representative organizations through which the students, and in general the middle classes, could express their demands. There was no solid student organization to channel the demands; neither was there an interlocutor with whom the government could negotiate. The leadership and its organization (the General Strike Council) had emerged spontaneously in the heat of the movement and for this reason had soon radicalized. In order to prevent something similar from happening in other sectors of the political system, the government had to make sure that the popular organizations, which were the backbone of the regime, had enough legitimacy and representation. It had to accept and even encourage these organizations to put their old leadership on trial and renew them if that was the will of the workers, even if that meant risking its control over the movement. It was obvious that in this strategy the government of Echeverria had its own candidates for a more representative leadership capable of replacing the old leaders, with whom it hoped to be able to renew the alliance according to the traditional terms.

The close link of the more salient and active leaders in the movement to the government made the *insurgencia obrera* (workers' insurgency movement) more and more dependent upon the attitude of the government toward it.[23] A consequence was that as soon as this latter changed its attitude the movement lost its impetus. This occurred when, nearing the end of his term, President Echeverria was forced to increasingly rely on the same traditional leaders to both face the economic crisis that occurred in 1976 and have the capacity to impose the choice of his candidate on the presidency (as was the tradition in the PRI governments). The government had to stop supporting the independence movement in order to regain the support of the traditional popular leadership. And as soon as it did so, the movement stopped short. The next government, that of José López Portillo (1976–1982), decided to focus on regaining the confidence of Mexican and foreign entrepreneurs and helped the official union movement to co-opt the still-existing independent unions.

Although the movement was stopped short at its peak in June 1976 when the army prevented a strike of its main actor, the "democratic current" of SUTERM (the electrical workers' union), the prestige of the official popular organizations was gravely wounded, something that further eroded the legitimacy of the corporate organizations. Their legitimacy further declined due to their unconditional acceptance of the austerity measures and the retreat of the state beginning in 1982 that hit the workers and the popular classes hard. It was incapable of defending the workers from the consequences of the decision to open the Mexican economy, which gave way to a profound process of enterprise restructuring.

The independent peasant movement was much more easily defused due to its great autonomy.[24] Each of the organizations was founded to represent a group of peasants and usually fought on an individual basis to get land. Then, once the goal was obtained, usually via invading a terrain, claiming the property, and forcing the authorities to expropriate the land, it subsided. During the government of Portillo, the financial resources coming from the petroleum exports decreased the pressure of independent organizations that had received land during the previous presidency, which were now demanding resources to sow and commercialize their product. Still, the government repressed or was successful in marginalizing organizations that had united in the Plan de Ayala National Confederation, which countered the intent of Portillo to put an end to agrarian reform.

During the Salinas administration, UNORCA, the main independent peasant organization, was finally co-opted by the government when it backed its leader in his effort to gain the leadership of the National Peasant Confederation (CNC).[25] This apparent triumph of an independent group against the official leadership ended the autonomy of the most important independent peasant movement of the 1970s and 1980s. This organization was completely discredited by its leadership, which not only did not oppose but also backed the 1992 constitutional changes that ended agrarian reforms and gave peasants the possibility of selling their ejido lands. It was further weakened when it was time to contest the opening of the country to imports of maize and beans, as laid out in NAFTA.

For the last thirty years, the successive PRI governments have used administrative and legal mechanisms, co-optation, and repression to revert the impact of the upsurge of the independent unions and peasant organizations. At the same time, the capacity of the state to maneuver and fill the organizational space with its own organizations has led social movements to rely on elite agreements with the Mexican presidency, agreements that have always turned against and delegitimized them. Both of these situations have produced short-lived alternative social movements and organizations, even though the legitimacy and pretensions of representation of official organizations have been continuously worn out.

Nevertheless, we may currently be seeing a germ of change in this relatively closed situation. The creation of the National Union of Workers (UNT) in 1997 has been a qualitatively fundamental event in the history of the workers' movement in Mexico, as it is the first confederation created independently of the state. This organization grouped some of the most active unions in the country—among others the telephone workers' union, the union of the Volkswagen plant in Puebla, and the airline workers' unions. They have managed to exert pressure on their own enterprises and have much higher wages and benefits than the rest of the trade union movement. However, they appear to have limited their organization to defend exclusive and corporate interests, because their action has been restricted to their own enterprises. This impression has been reinforced by the fact that they have not led an important movement opposing the neoliberal measures taken by the last three PRI governments or against the authoritarian political regime led by the PRI. In fact, the leader of one of the most important unions, the telephone workers' union, is a member of the PRI and had an explicit alliance with former President Salinas, which led many observers to think that he was trying to emulate what the UNORCA did in the CNC and conquer the presidency of the CTM through an agreement with the government. The fact is that the UNT has not been able to alter the correlation of forces in the trade union movement.

Thus, in contrast to other transitions in Latin America and Eastern Europe, where an organized labor movement was crucial to the democratization of the regime and society, organized workers and peasants in Mexico have expressed their opposition to the regime only on some rare occasions and almost always under government control. On the one hand, the PRI has managed to occupy most of the political space and preserve the loyalty of the popular organizations to their regime. On the other hand, independent organizations either fell into the trap of trying to ally with the government in order to achieve power from above or have adopted a critical but corporate position. This prevented the appearance of a strong organized opposition against the regime, allowing the PRI to control the rate of political liberalization and make the Mexican transition one of the longest in the world.

In fact, most of the worker, peasant, and popular organizations (taxi drivers, street vendors, etc.) have remained loyal to the PRI even after it lost the presidency. The big question is whether these organizations will continue to be affiliated to the PRI or if they will start experiencing a growing discontent from their bases against their traditional leadership, which may eventually lead them to abandon this party. Nevertheless, our main question deals with the fact that if we accept that there is more to a transition than mere elections, and that democracy means the capacity to reconstruct society in terms that habituate and allow society to solve conflicts peacefully while respecting differences, then the control of the social space by the state is a great obstacle.

Civic and Social Movements

The most influential civic movement in Mexico in the last thirty years has surely been the 1968 student movement. More than in any other country in the world, the student movement in Mexico was more political than cultural. Although the movement had salient cultural traits, it soon became fundamentally political, because it encountered the authoritarian regime at the peak of its consolidation.[26] Adopting a political character and demanding the democratization of the Mexican regime consequentially put it in direct confrontation with the government. The result of this situation was the well-known massacre of students in Tlaltelolco in October 1968.

Although this movement constitutes a crucial moment in the history of Mexico—and has a very strong symbolic significance and a durable impact on the political culture of the political and cultural elite—it was weakly organized. This characteristic meant that after the repression it not only failed to institutionalize but also practically disappeared as a movement. It was only seven years later, in 1975, that some of the leaders participated in the creation of the professors' union at the National University. Then, in 1977, the Mexican Communist Party was legalized as part of the political reform of López Portillo's administration. These two events were in many ways influenced by that movement. Nevertheless, the more immediate result of the way the state responded to the students was the expansion of the guerrilla movement, which had emerged in the early 1960s in the northern state of Chihuahua and in the southern state of Guerrero.

Other successors of this movement were the ample array of nongovernmental organizations (NGOs) that emerged in the 1990s and met together in Mexico City in the National Citizen Organizations Encounter of 1995. The 568 organizations that attended that reunion were dedicated to varied endeavors: women's issues, human rights, electoral observation, services to the handicapped, gay and lesbian rights, support of prostitutes and AIDS patients, rural development, ecology, and others.[27] Their contribution to the organization of civil society is more than evident. Moreover, most observers also agree that they greatly contributed to the defeat of the PRI at the 2000 elections.

The organizations devoted to electoral observation at the local level between 1991 and 1994 finally worked together and convinced other NGOs dedicated to other questions that it was critical that they unite their efforts in order to observe the federal elections of 1994. These presidential elections were to take place in very critical conditions: after the Zapatista rebellion and the assassination of the PRI presidential candidate. This scenario seemed to forebode an extremely complicated and perhaps dangerous outcome if the elections were not completely transparent. This is what convinced a considerable number of NGOs to organize a civic alliance (Alianza Cívica) to observe them.

The Alianza Cívica was an important step in creating a network of NGOs capable of influencing Mexican politics. In fact, it was their pressure that achieved the creation of a totally independent electoral institution, the Federal Electoral Institute. Alianza Cívica's other important contributions to the democratization of the country were helping to increase the population's awareness of the importance of elections, implementing the first experiences concerning direct democracy in Mexico (it organized the first independent citizen consultations and referendums), and beginning a campaign to demand accountability from government functionaries, including the president.[28]

Nevertheless, this NGO movement did not try to lead the opposition struggle against the old regime, as it did in other countries such as Hungary and East Germany and, partly, in Czechoslovakia and Brazil. In Mexico, the Alianza Cívica decided that it would maintain its neutrality with regard to the political scenario. It intended to be an organization dedicated to observing elections and eventually organizing citizen consultations on topics of national interest without taking sides. This neutrality became most apparent when the Alianza Cívica rejected an appeal by the Zapatista rebellion in 1994, which demanded that civil society takes sides with it against the regime.

The neutral stand of Alianza determined that this NGO network did not institutionalize into a permanent organization, which would have allowed it to have an influence in the aftermath of the elections. This was evident from declarations by some of its leaders expressing that once the elections were organized by an independent and citizen-controlled institution the civic alliance had practically lost its raison d'être. At this point, it was more important to act at the political level in order to press for laws to ensure human rights and limits to state action.[29]

In this manner, although the Mexican NGOs were very active and achieved a degree of organization that was crucial in order to focus attention on the elections (which finally decided the defeat of the PRI), the fact that they never adopted an open opposition stand to the authoritarian regime made them lose momentum in the aftermath of the July 2000 elections. They thus contributed to making the transition possible without ever acting directly against the former regime. They did, however, contribute to the increase in the density of civic society.

Another important civic movement was the Barzón, which was originally organized by medium agricultural producers in defense of their property, which was threatened by their financial situation in the mid-1990s.[30] At that moment, conjunctural and structural events coincided to make it impossible for them to pay their debts. This movement started in 1993 with tractors blocking downtown Guadalajara and the international bridge linking Ciudad Juárez, Chihuahua, with El Paso, Texas. Up until the end of 1994, the Barzón maintained its fundamentally agrarian identity. But the financial crisis in December of that year and the increase of interest rates to more than 100 percent in 1995 led thousands of middle-class debtors (whether from credit cards, automobile loans, or housing) to join the movement.

With its expansion into the urban middle class, the Barzón managed to continue throughout the Zedillo administration, continuously contesting the financial policy of the government and obliging it to decree three different plans intended to reduce and restructure their debts. The movement also managed to prevent massive expropriation of debtor property by the banks. But the most important accomplishment of the movement was that although it did not explicitly demand the democratization of the regime it clearly contested its technocratic and authoritarian character. In this respect, the pressure it exerted throughout Zedillo's administration led Congress to radically modify the law sent by the executive in order to convert the FOBAPROA (the former insurance fund; the Mexican version of FDIC) into public debt.[31] The Barzón exerted enough pressure on the legislators to force them to proclaim a law that would allow Congress to investigate some of the larger debts to inquire if a fraud was committed. It also achieved substantial discounts for small and medium-sized debtors, which the government programs had not included.

In this manner, this movement questioned one of the most important policy measures of the Zedillo government—the banking system bailout—contributing to further wear out the legitimacy of the regime and to increase the prestige of the opposition parties. Nevertheless, as many of the middle-class members of the Barzón and some of the peasants saw their economic expectations turn brighter with the final financial plan and economic growth of the last years of the Zedillo administration, the movement lost its momentum.

The most important social movement of this period, and probably since 1968, was surely the Zapatista rebellion of 1994.[32] This movement has both a social and a cultural element. It also has a special ethical character in representing the demands of the most marginalized sector of Mexican society, rather than the defense of corporate privileges that are being retrieved, as most other popular movements do. Although the indigenous population was supposed to be integrated into the national-popular project, after the presidency of Cárdenas it was permanently marginalized with regard to other sectors like labor or the rest of the peasantry. In fact, in order to get what was promised and never delivered to them, the indigenous population had to fuse into peasant organizations, adopt a generic peasant identity, and abandon their cultural specificity.

The Zapatista movement does not arise from a sector of society relegated by the new economic project or that lost the support of the Mexican state. Rather, it is a sector of society hurt by erratic public policies that have rendered difficult its modernization efforts. The Zapatista rebellion does not come from the poorest and most marginalized of the indigenous population but from a sector that has tried to organize and modernize itself in economic terms. It represents those that tried to modernize the culture and commercialization of coffee in the Lacandon Forest but failed due to the indiscriminate opening of the Mexican economy and of the complete lack of governmental regulation.

This movement also arises from the frustration that has resulted from the systematic repression of the independent peasant associations by the government of Chiapas and from the co-optation of the most important regional organization: the Unión de Uniones de Chiapas. This situation has systematically blocked all legal channels of representation and implies the destruction of the legal organization efforts on the part of the population of the region rather than a desperate position.[33]

The reform of article 27 of the constitution by the Salinas government, with the acceptance of the national peasant organizations that signified the end of agrarian reform and allows for the dismantling of the existing ejidos, has endangered not only the basis of the efforts of economic modernization of the indigenous population but also the material basis of their identity. It thus marked the end of their willingness to bury their differences in order to fight for their rights as peasants through agrarian organizations and renewed their will to fight for their economic and social demands through an affirmation of their native identity.

In contrast to other Mexican and Latin American guerrillas, from the very beginning the Zapatistas did not orient themselves to take over power but rather to oust the Salinas government and allow the national

Congress to define a new government and modify the economic model. But their concept of identity, differences, and democracy are not determined in exclusive terms. They pose an inclusive rather than an exclusive concept of identity, which is dominant in other contexts such as that of Eastern and Central Europe and the Middle East. The EZLN holds a concept of democracy that goes beyond elections and implies the capacity of society to accept all the existing identities and projects without assuming the disappearance of the differences. It does not oppose indigenous identity to national identity but supposes that the existence of the nation—like that of democracy—depends on the acceptance of all the existing different identities. This point is especially pertinent in an international context where national identities tend to be erased in order to impose a globalized cultural homogeneity and has been the fact determining the ample international impact of this movement.

Although this movement is the most comprehensive social movement in decades, its violent origin and its reduction to a military character (by its encirclement by the federal army) dramatically reduced its capacity to extend to civic society and become an open social and political movement.[34] It was nevertheless crucial as a catalyst of the electoral reform of 1994 that created the Federal Electoral Institute and thus greatly contributed to the democratization of the country.

The Entrepreneurs

Although popular and social movements prepared the ground for the transition, they did not play a central role as in the Brazilian and the Eastern European transitions (Poland, Czechoslovakia, and Hungary). The central role was in many senses limited to entrepreneurs.[35] To understand their intervention it is necessary to go back a few decades, to the beginning of the 1970s. The government of Echeverría liberalized the relationship between the state and the popular organizations that were its social basis and in so doing, it alienated one of its main economic allies: the entrepreneurs. The attitude of the Echeverría government toward the popular organizations and the aggressive rhetoric against private capital opened a new front against the old regime, which in retrospect had a decisive result.

The Mexican entrepreneurs had been traditionally subordinated to the authoritarian political regime and to the economic project. They were economically dependent on a state that acted as the main agent of development for almost fifty years (from 1936 to 1982), stimulating economic growth and closing the economy from international concurrence. Politically, the Mexican regime assured social peace by controlling the popular sectors per se (necessary to ensure their investments and interests) and by preventing labor from exerting excessive pressure on their benefits when demanding better salaries and working conditions.

Both dimensions of the relation between the state and entrepreneurs began to change at the beginning of the 1970s. A more mature entrepreneurial class, which had expanded significantly during almost thirty years of continuous economic growth, began to contest the economic terrain occupied by the state. This conflict became most acute during the presidency of Echeverría, when the state significantly increased its investment and regulation of the economy. One of their first battles was fought against the government's effort to enact significant tax reform, which they managed to abort.

The basic political warranty the regime gave the entrepreneurs also began to fade away during the same period. As part of Echeverria's strategy to reaffirm the popular basis of the Mexican political regime, the president began rhetorically attacking the entrepreneurs. In addition, the support given to independent unions and peasant organizations resulted in waves of significant strikes and land invasions that were seen as a threat by Mexican entrepreneurs. This led to open recriminations against the government, which reached a high point in 1973 when a guerrilla assassinated one of the most prominent entrepreneurs in the country, Eugenio Garza Sada, leader of the Monterrey group. At his burial, the Garza family openly accused the president of having created an environment that was hostile toward entrepreneurs and had shaken social peace in Mexico.

The clash between the entrepreneurs and the state did not subside after this event. On the contrary, it increased and forced employers to imitate labor and peasant organizations by transforming their organizations (which were subordinate to the state) into closer representations of their interests. An important development was the creation of the Employers Coordinating Council in 1975, a centralized organ representing all the entrepreneurs, who were usually divided among sectors. The clash reached a new high when Echeverria, the day before leaving office, expropriated a large tract of some of the country's best lands in eastern-northeastern Mexico in order to create one of the largest conglomerates of collective farms (or one of the largest ejidos).

From this moment on, the entrepreneurs' perception of the Mexican regime changed. And as in other transitions, the entrepreneurs (in this case mostly small and midsized businesspeople) adopted a definite opposition stand against the authoritarian regime. They realized that although the regime had been an essential factor of political stability that had perfectly suited their interests, it could quickly turn against them. This feeling was increased tenfold when the government of López Portillo nationalized the banking system three months before leaving office in September 1982. His government had succeeded in regaining its confidence by dismantling the independent unions, putting an end to land invasions, generously compensating for expropriated lands, and pursuing an economic policy favorable to their interests.

At this point, entrepreneurs realized that it would not be enough to exert pressure on the government through their organizations in order to gain better treatment. During the administration of López Portillo, everything they had achieved had been reversed. The entrepreneurs decided to revert not only to their corporate organizations but also to direct participation in politics in order to struggle for the transformation of the regime.

The participation of the entrepreneurs was mainly achieved through the National Action Party (PAN), which eventually won the presidential elections that culminated the electoral dimension of the transition. In fact, from 1982 onward the entrepreneurs contributed to creating a new current inside the PAN that distinguished them from the traditional members of this party in that they were more pragmatic, less dogmatic, and prone to negotiate with the government in order to gain power positions rather than conceiving their activity as an example to politically educate the Mexican population.[36]

Although the intervention of Mexican entrepreneurs in the transition process was partly to fight against the intervention of the Mexican state in the economy, which was seen as competing with their interests, its main rationale was political. The impulse to directly enter politics was in order to defeat an authoritarian regime that had gone from protecting the interests of Mexican entrepreneurs to attacking them through arbitrary measures. In fact, the entrepreneurs basically responded under a political rationale, resulting in greatly strengthening the PAN to the extent that it eventually won the elections against the PRI. The entrepreneurs became the "winners" of the transition and the main resource for functionaries in the new government of Vicente Fox.

Conclusion

This chapter began with the idea that democracy is more than a transition from an authoritarian regime that does not hold elections to another regime that guarantees a free and competitive electoral system. Transition to democracy is a broader process of restructuring society in the sense of establishing social relations (through the action of social associations, organizations, and movements) and increasing the capacity of society to work on the conflicts that social life inevitably generates. Democracy also implies that social conflicts are solved in institutional and peaceful terms, respecting identities and differences. This means that one of the indicators of democracy is the existence of a dense civic society, whether organized through civic associations, class organizations, or social movements. Both class and social movements have to be capable of self-restraint in order to allow their institutionalization. Finally, institutionalization does not mean to solve conflicts by way of dissolving social differences but to construct socially accepted ways of working on differences by constituting "constitutional orders."[37]

The main characteristic of the Mexican transition is that although some important autonomous organizations and movements emerged that eroded the legitimacy and stability of the older regime, they were not decisive in bringing it down. Although other Latin American and the Eastern European transitions were not revolutions, there was a decisive movement that toppled the regimes. In contrast, the former regime in Mexico did not confront a social movement such as Solidarity, or the insurgence of civil society, as in Hungary, Czechoslovakia, and East Germany, or the combined action of the entrepreneurs, the union movement, and the NGOs, as in Brazil.

In consequence, the Mexican transition seems to lack the social forces necessary to attain its completion. The Mexican situation differs from the Latin American cases, where the civilians dismantled the old institutions once the military left government and went back to the barracks. It also differs from some Central European cases, where the absolute lack of market and political institutions forced the new social and political organizations to construct the economic and political institutions at the roundtables and through the elaboration of new constitutions. Moreover, although the Mexican regime was profoundly worn out, it did not collapse like the communist regime of the Soviet Union.

We have seen that most of the organized social forces—unions and peasant and other popular organizations—have been effectively controlled by the state until the present. As a matter of fact, although the organization of civil society has advanced considerably (as witnessed by the hundreds of NGOs created and the success of Alianza Cívica), the alternative unions have managed to create a new confederation (the UNT), and two very important social movements have recently emerged (the Barzón and the EZLN), for different reasons no one social movement has been able to take the lead in the struggle against the old order. This means that no one social movement has been able to capitalize upon the defeat of the PRI with the necessary impetus to dismantle the old regime.

The demise of the old regime in Mexico was basically the consequence of the development of the electoral system. What actually happened is that the electoral-political balance tipped against the PRI regime. The fact that the electoral victory was the result of a diffuse rejection of the old regime and of a very loose and unorganized alliance of electoral attitudes is a sign that there is no sufficiently strong social power or coalition to force the necessary dismantling of the institutions of the former regime and the construction of new ones. The fact that the popular classes are still basically under the control of the PRI, or are collectively too weak to have a real impact on the reconstruction of civil society, means that a restoration is one of the possible scenarios. This will continue to be the case unless the current government and the real opposition (other than the PRI) can find the social basis needed to demolish the institutions and organizations this party still controls and to develop something to occupy the spaces vacated by the PRI.

Nevertheless, the capacity of the PRI to continue controlling the popular organizations may change with the electoral alterations. The great question is if, notwithstanding the loss of the presidency, the PRI will manage to maintain popular organizations under its control without the aid of the state or, alternatively, if we will see the dispersion of these forces and their passing to the opposition. This question hinges not only upon the existence of an opposition to the PRI inside PRI-controlled popular organizations but also the manner in which the Vicente Fox government will or will not continue using the mechanisms of popular organization control in the hands of the state, tools that the PRI governments used exhaustively. In the case of labor, for example, Fox's government may be tempted to make use of the ample faculties of the Ministry of Labor in order to control the trade unions and favor economic stability, sacrificing their democratization.

Restoration would be clearly impossible in other Latin American or

Eastern European countries without a complete regime reversal; this would mean a military or a civic coup (as in Peru) in the case of the former. But it can be a real possibility in Mexico if Fox's government does not proceed to dismantle the institutions and organizations created by the PRI when they were in power in order to allow the emergence of independent organizations to oppose them. The fact that Fox and his cabinet come from the entrepreneurial world may mean that it will be incapable of realizing the importance of the emergence of the independent popular organizations and also that the legitimacy of the PRI may be refurbished if the government continues to apply neoliberal measures without an effective social policy. We have witnessed how this evolution led to the return of the Communist Party into power in some countries of Eastern Europe. The aggravator in the Mexican case is the fact that most of the institutions of the former regime are still practically intact.

Nevertheless, the power that is still in the hands of the Mexican presidency may shield us from this scenario—notwithstanding the process of decentralization the country has undergone since the early 1980s. The alternative may be a consequence of the fact that the transition has been basically electoral and that a center-right party has dominated it. This probably means that the government will not be interested in stimulating the organization of society and the establishment of institutions oriented to solving conflicts collectively. Mexico will thus most probably lack a crucial element of the Central European transitions. For example, a paternalistic approach to labor conflicts would be used rather than an establishment of tripartite institutions (state, entrepreneurs, trade unions) to solve industrial conflicts and define in a negotiated manner certain aspects of economic policy.[38] The most probable scenario is the application of neoliberal measures, accompanied by obstacles to social organization, something that will further weaken civic society. To summarize, the new government will probably not be able to recognize that what is at stake in a political transition is not merely electoral change but the reconstitution of society.

The fact that the main actor of the Mexican transition is the entrepreneurial current of the PAN will probably have further consequences. It should be kept in mind that the entrepreneurs used politics to pressure the government. We should also note that the workers' unions were maintained subordinate to the state through all those years when the new economic model was implemented, which contributed to maintaining employers and their organizations as paternalistic and as opposed to workers' unions as ever. This situation is aggravated by the fact that the main economic positions of Fox's government are occupied by entrepreneurs and also that the Ministry of Labor is headed by the former president of the COPARMEX, the most conservative of the employer organizations. This seems to augur the continuation of the paternalistic position toward workers and an offensive against trade unions. They will probably extend this attitude to the rest of society.

In contrast, although in Brazil the entrepreneurs were also very active in setting the transition in motion, their rationale was basically economic. The main entrepreneurial organization, the FIESP of São Paulo, started acting against the military when it realized that the administration of General Ernesto Geisel proposed to continue the development of Brazil with a model of accumulation based on capital goods, which in its turn meant the expansion of state-owned enterprises.[39] The fact that the workers' unions also had the capacity to organize and oppose the military in an objective alliance with the entrepreneurs can help us understand why, in Brazil, the clash against the authoritarian regime helped modernize both the entrepreneurs' and the workers' organizations.[40]

We have been discussing the situation of industrial relations because they point to the general relationship between government and society. The conception that entrepreneurs in government will have of the latter will surely be individual rather than collective and electoral rather than social. This coincides with the way in which the PAN has governed in the states in which it has won elections. Society is seen as a conglomerate of individuals who have to invest themselves individually in order to progress. Government has to be organized so as to deliver services efficiently to this society of individuals and to paternalistically help those who cannot be considered citizens (due to poverty, lack of education, health, etc.) and eventually educate them in order to realize what their real interest is. This means that they consider citizenship in purely individual terms—as the right that people (conceived as clients of government services) have to complain against, or change, the functionaries in charge of these service-rendering institutions.

In this perspective, conflict is not an inherent part of social life, and it requires neither collective solutions nor social organization. It is conceived as a default, a sign of inefficiency on the part of government. Social conflicts are also seen as ways through which political forces turn individuals into instruments. They are thus conceived as a disruption of normal social life.

This posture toward society may mean that the deterioration of the authoritarian and corporate regime that has dominated the Mexican transition may continue and that during Fox's presidency the central power factor of the old regime, the presidency, will continue losing its grip on the political system and the social organizations and go on being substituted by the process of power dispersion. Without an impulse toward the reconstruction of society through a propositive attitude on the part of Fox's government or by the existence of social forces that may impose themselves, the process of the feudalization of power will surely continue.

In this scenario, the presidency will have to increasingly deal with the more conservative forces entrenched at the local space. We have already seen this happening in the state of Tabasco, where the local PRI contested the decision of the country's highest electoral authority, the Federal Electoral Tribunal (TRIFE), to annul the October 2000 election for governor and elected an interim governor under very questionable circumstances. Although this developed into an open rebellion against the tribunal, the president did not intervene, as he would have surely done before. Rather, he waited for the opposition and the local PRI to negotiate a political solution.[41]

A similar situation happened in Yucatán, where the governor and the local PRI chose the electoral officials to organize the local April 2001 elections without seeking the consensus of the opposition parties, as the law requires. The opposition complained to the TRIFE, which resolved that the local congress should repeat the election of the electoral officials. For a couple of tense months, the local congress rejected the tribunal's resolution. This was an intervention of the federal authorities and the beginning of a campaign of local nationalism in a state with a strong separate identity. Nevertheless, in the end the local authorities accepted the resolution of the TRIFE, and the PAN won the governorship.

Although the cases in Tabasco and Yucatán finally reached a negotiated settlement, they are examples of how local caciques are responding to the weakening of the central power of the presidency. Another more disturbing example is the expansion of illegal forces in many regions of Mexico. Although one may suppose that the centralization of resources that exists in Mexico could impose a degree of control upon the evolution of this dispersion, the Mexican state has been abandoning many of its former functions of coordination and of its financial programs through both decentralization and reduction of state spending, which means that the state has significantly reduced its leverage capacity in this respect.

Finally, there may be a more positive evolution. It could be that the first democratic government in seventy-one years will try to impose the rule of law and stimulate the construction of democratic institutions and organizations. Nevertheless, the ideology of the group in power and the weakness of civil society may well mean that despite all the good intentions of the government it may simply not have sufficient leverage to impose the rule of law and democratic institutions in the country.

Notes

1. Guillermo O'Donnell and Philippe Schmitter, *Transitions from Authoritarian Rule: Tentative Conclusions About Uncertain Democracies* (Baltimore and London: Johns Hopkins University Press, 1986), p. 8.

2. Autonomy in the sense of Pierre Rosanvallon; for example, see J. P. Fitoussi and Pierre Rosanvallon, *Le nouvel âge des inégalités* (Paris: Seuil, 1996).

3. Ruth Berins Collier, *Paths Toward Democracy* (Cambridge, UK: Cambridge University Press, 1999), p. 8.

4. J. S. Valenzuela, "Labor Movements in Transitions to Democracy: A Framework for Analysis," *Comparative Politics* 21, no. 4 (1989): 445–472.

5. Juan Linz and Alfred Stepan, *Problems of Democratic Transition and Consolidation* (Baltimore and London: Johns Hopkins University Press, 1996), p. 9.

6. Evelyn Huber, Dietrich Rueschemeyer, and John D. Stephens, "The Paradoxes of Contemporary Democracy: Formal, Participatory, and Social Dimensions," *Comparative Politics* 29, no. 3 (1997): 323–342.

7. Jean L. Cohen and Andrew Arato, *Civil Society and the Political Theory* (Cambridge and London: MIT, 1997); A. Touraine, *Qu'est-ce que la Démocratie?* (Paris: Fayard, 1994).

8. Touraine, *Qu'est-ce que la Démocratie?* p. 99.

9. Ibid., pp. 99–101.

10. Ibid., p. 20.

11. Hannah Arendt, *On Violence* (1969), reprinted in Steven Lukes, ed., *Power* (New York: New York University Press, 1977), p. 64.

12. Charles Sabel, "Constitutional Orders: Trust Building and Response to Change," in J. Rogers Hollingsworth and Robert Boyer, eds., *Contemporary Capitalism: The Embeddedness of Institutions* (Cambridge, UK: Cambridge University Press, 1997), pp. 157–187.

13. Peter L. Berger and Thomas Luckmann, *The Social Construction of Reality* (New York: Anchor Books, 1967).

14. Alain Touraine, *La production de la Societe* (Paris: Seuil, 1972).

15. The old regime, destroyed by the revolution, had developed the country by using economic enclaves that basically benefited foreign capital and labor and had a very weak connection to the rest of the Mexican economy and society. The Porfiriato refers to the period from 1877 to 1911 when Porfirio Díaz served as president.

16. Sergio Zermeño, "Estado y sociedad en el neoliberalismo dependiente," *Revista mexicana de sociología* LVI, no. 4 (1994): 109–132.

17. It had assured Salinas the majority of the legislative body in the midterm elections of 1991, which permitted him to reform the constitution in order to reaffirm his economic project.

18. On the power of the presidency, see Daniel Cosio Villegas, *El sistema político mexicano* (México, D.F.: Joaquín Mortiz, 1972); Pablo González Casanova, *La democracia en México* (México, D.F.: Era, 1965).

19. Lorenzo Meyer, "La crisis del presidencialismo mexicano: Recuperación espectacular y recaída estructural, 1982–1996," *Foro Internacional* 36, nos. 1–2 (1996): 11–30.

20. Ilán Bizberg, "Les transformations du pouvoir politique au Mexique," *Cahiers Internationaux de Sociologie* 107 (1999): 429–455.

21. Neither federal labor nor agrarian laws have been changed. In addition, the government continued to maintain its control over most of the urban popular organizations, although this was the sector where other parties like the PRD (with the Asamblea de Barrios in Mexico City) and the PT (in cities in the north of Mexico) more efficiently contested its hegemony.

22. On the labor independence movement of 1970–1976, see Javier Aguilar García, *La política sindical en México: industria del automóvil* (México, D.F.: Ediciones Era, 1982); Jorge Basurto, *La clase obrera en la historia de México: en el régimen de Echeverría: rebelión e independencia* (México, D.F.: Siglo XXI-IIS-UNAM, 1983); Manuel Camacho Solís, "La huelga de Saltillo: un intento de regeneración obrera," *Foro Internacional* 15, no. 3 (1975): 414–451; Silvia Gómez Tagle, *Insurgencia y democracia en los sindicatos electricistas* (México, D.F.: El Colegio de México, 1980); Kevin J. Middlebrook, "Union Democratization in the Mexican Automobile Industry: A Reappraisal," *Latin American Research Review* 24, no. 2 (1989): 69–94.

23. Examples are the electrical workers union—the SUTERM—and the Union Obrera Independiente that organized most of the automobile unions that had left the CTM.

24. On the peasant movement, see Gustavo Gordillo, *Campesinos al asalto del cielo: una reforma con autonomía* (México, D.F.: Siglo XXI Editores, 1989), and *Estado mercados y movimiento campesino* (México, D.F.: Plaza and Janés, 1989); Clarisa Hardy, *El estado y los campesinos: La Confederación Nacional Campesina* (México, D.F.: Ceestem-Nueva Imagen, 1984); Neil Harvey, "Nuevas formas de Representación en el Campo Mexicano: la UNORCA, 1985–1993," in Hubert C. de Grammont, ed., *Neoliberalismo y Organización Social en el Campo Mexicano* (México: UNAM-Plaza y Valdez, 1996); Gerardo Otero, "The New Agrarian Movement Self-Managed, Democratic Production," *Latin American Perspectives* 16, no. 4 (1989): 28–59; Luisa Paré, "Algunas reflexiones metodológicas sobre el análisis de los movimientos sociales en el campo," *Revista mexicana de sociología* Vol. LVI, no. 2 (1994): 15–31; Rosario Robles and Julio Moguel, "Los nuevos movimientos rurales por la tierra y por la apropiación del ciclo productivo," in *Historia de la cuestión agraria mexicana. Los tiempos de la crisis 1970–1982,* vol. 9, part 2, ed. Julio Moguel, (México, D.F.: Siglo XXI-CEHAM, 1989), 377–450; Steven E. Sanderson, *Agrarian Populism and the Mexican State: The Struggle for Land in Sonora* (Berkeley: University of California, 1981).

25. UNORCA emerged during the government of President Miguel de la Madrid from the unification of the independent organizations that received land

during the Echeverria government and that were now fighting for better economic conditions for their products, as a reaction to the drastic reduction of subsidies for the peasantry after the 1982 crisis.

26. Sergio Zermeño, *México, una democracia utópica: El movimiento estudiantil del 68* (México, D.F.: Siglo XXI, 1978).

27. Carlos San Juan Victoria, "Tendencia de la sociedad civil en México: la puja del poder y la sociedad a fin de siglo," in Alberto J. Olvera, ed., *La sociedad civil: De la teoría a la realidad* (México, D.F.: El Colegio de México, 1999), p. 157.

28. J. M. Ramirez Sáis, "Contribuciones democráticas de Alianza Cívica," in J. M. Ramírez Saíz, ed., *El debate nacional: Nuevos actores sociales* (México, D.F.: Ediciones Diana, 1997), pp. 341–364.

29. Author interview with Sergio Aguayo, March 2000.

30. On the Barzón, see Gabriel Torres, "El Derecho de 'Barzonear' y sus efectos políticos," in Jorge Alonso and Juan Manuel Ramírez Sáiz, eds., *La democracia de los de abajo en México* (México, D.F.: UNAM–Siglo XXI, 1997), pp. 265–291, and "Las siete vidas de el Barzón: tensiones en la construcción de una fuerza política nacional," in Saíz, ed., *El debate nacional*, pp. 315–340; Heather L. Williams, *Planting Trouble: The Barzón Debtors' Movement in Mexico*, Current Issue Brief Series, no. 6 (La Jolla: University of California–San Diego, Center for U.S.-Mexican Studies, 1996); Horacio MacKinlay, *Crisis y transformación de las relaciones corporativas tradicionales: Las organizaciones de productores rurales y el Estado en México* (México, D.F.: UAM, forthcoming); Guadalupe Rodríguez Gómez and Gabriel Torres, "Los agroproductores frente a las políticas neoliberales: El Barzón y Comagro," *Espiral* 1, no. 1 (1994): 130–176.

31. The Fund for the Protection of Bank Savings is the program established to save Mexican banks after the debt crisis of 1995.

32. On the Zapatista movement, see Neil Harvey, *Rebellion in Chiapas: Rural Reforms, Campesino Radicalism, and the Limits to Salinismo*, Transformation of Rural Mexico, no. 5 (La Jolla: University of California–San Diego, Center for U.S.-Mexican Studies, 1994), pp. 1–43, and "Peasant Strategies and Corporatism in Chiapas," in Joe Foweraker and Anne Craig, eds., *Popular Movements and Political Change in Mexico* (Boulder: Lynne Rienner Publishers, 1990), pp. 183–198; Yvon Le Bot and Subcomandante Marcos, *El sueño zapatista* (México, D.F.: Plaza and Janés, 1999); Xochitl Leyva Solano, "Militancia político-religiosa e identidad en la Lacandona," *Espiral* 1, no. 2 (1995): 59–88; Adriana López Monjardin, "Los acuerdos de San Andrés y los gobiernos autónomos en Chiapas," *Espiral* 5, no. 14 (1999): 127–145; Sergio Sarmiento Silva, "Movimiento indio, autonomía, y agenda nacional," in Hubert C. De Gramont, ed., *Neoliberalismo y organización social en el campo mexicano* (México, D.F.: Plaza y Valdez, 1996); Lynn Stephen, "The Zapatista Army of National Liberation and the National Democratic Convention," *Latin American Perspectives* 22, no. 4 (1995): 88–99.

33. Le Bot and Marcos, *El sueño zapatista*.

34. This situation is dramatically changing at the present time, with the willingness shown by Fox's government to dialogue with the Zapatistas, and the arrival of its leaders in Mexico City. We are thus probably on the verge of

seeing the EZLN becoming a political movement, which would represent the indigenous population, and maybe other marginalized groups, with large support in civic society.

35. On the intervention of entrepreneurs in politics, see Carlos Alba Vega, "Las relaciones entre los empresarios y el Estado a finales del Siglo XX," in Ilán Bizberg and Lorenzo Meyer, eds., *Cambio y resistencia: treinta años de política en México* (México, D.F.: Oceano, 2002); Ricardo Tirado and Maltilde Luna, "El Consejo Coordinador Empresarial de México: De la unidad contra el reformismo a la unidad para el TLC (1975–1993)," *Revista Mexicana de Sociología* LVII, no. 4 (1995): 27–59; Puga, *México: Empresarios y Poder* (México, D.F.: UNAM/Miguel Angel Porrúa, 1993); E. J. Molina, "La crisis de un pacto: las relaciones estado-empresarios en la coyuntura actual," in R. Pozas and Matilde Luna, eds., *Las empresas y los empresarios en el México contemporáneo* (México, D.F.: Grijalbo, 1989), pp. 151–171; Matilde Luna, Ricardo Tirado, and Francisco Valdés, "Los empresarios y la política en México, 1982–1986," in Pozas and Luna, eds., *Las empresas*, pp. 21–88.

36. L. Barraza and Ilán Bizberg, "El Partido Acción Nacional y el régimen político mexicano," in J. Alonso, A. Asís, and J. Tamayo, eds., *El nuevo estado mexicano II: Estado y política* (México, D.F.: Nueva Imagen, 1992).

37. Sabel, "Constitutional Orders."

38. Ilán Bizberg, "Las relaciones industriales en Europa Central," in Ilán Bizberg and M. Frybes, eds., *Las transiciones tras el muro: Lecciones para México* (México, D.F.: Cal y Arena, 2000).

39. Fernando Enrique Cardoso, "Entrepreneurs and the Transition Process: The Brazilian Case," in Guillermo O'Donnell, Philippe C. Schmitter, and Laurence Whitehead, eds., *Transitions from Authoritarian Rule: Comparative Perspectives* (Baltimore and London: Johns Hopkins University Press, 1988), p. 145.

40. A measure of the modernization by Brazilian entrepreneurs of their organizations is the fact that they had the will and that they actually managed to negotiate with the trade unions at the beginning of the 1990s.

41. It was accepted that the interim governor chosen by the former legislature (obviously manipulated by the former governor) would stay in charge until the election in November 2001.

PART 2

The Economics of Change and the Challenge of Development

7

A Long View of Mexico's Political Economy: What's Changed? What Are the Challenges?

Manuel Pastor and Carol Wise

In the short period between the end of the Institutional Revolutionary Party's (PRI's) seventy-year reign over the presidency and the election of President Vicente Fox on the National Action Party (PAN) ticket in July 2000, an increasingly rich literature has emerged with regard to Mexico's political opening.[1] The most convincing explanations for the PRI's long secular decline at the ballot box—which saw the party's share of the presidential vote erode from 77.4 percent in 1982 to just 36.1 percent in 2000—have centered on the interplay between electoral reforms, the internationalization of Mexican politics in the North American Free Trade Agreement (NAFTA) era, and economic performance. Our purpose in this chapter is to identify the longer-term economic trends that have accompanied Mexico's political transition. Whereas many analysts have focused on the pressure wrought by external shocks and financial disruptions, numerous cases in the region confirm that this does not automatically lead to the degree of reform and liberalization witnessed in Mexico. And whereas some might suggest that the dramatic liberalization strategy adopted by the government laid the groundwork for political change, the record turns out to be more mixed than thought by either the advocates or critics of Mexico's economic reforms.

For example, on the one hand, long-term economic growth has been quite mediocre, the distribution of income has been skewed further by cumulative distortions in domestic policy, and the growing dependence on the U.S. market has left Mexico more vulnerable than ever to recessionary trends in that market. On the other hand, the economy has shown significant resilience in recent years, and the fundamentals for solid economic and wage growth finally seem to be in place. This is a more complex story than commonly thought—and it is complicated further by the fact that at the very moment when economic recovery was solidified voters turned the ruling party out in favor of an untested alternative. To explore these topics, we begin with a review of economic transformation in Mexico since the onset of reforms in the early 1980s, focusing on patterns of macroeconomic stabilization, the shift to trade-led development, and the resulting adjustment stress on both small business and low-income households. We then turn to the challenges facing the Fox administration and, in particular, the need to spur higher growth rates, ameliorate distributional inequities, and engage in further political reform. We conclude with an assessment of what this complex historical pattern, as well as the emerging issues, mean for Mexico's future.

The Politics of Economic Transformation in Mexico: The Big Shift?

Like much of Latin America, Mexico's embrace of import substitution industrialization (ISI) had been intended to promote development. The initial record in the post–World War II period was promising: the 1950s and 1960s brought growth rates of 7 percent and 8.6 percent, respectively.[2] Even the increasingly volatile 1970s saw per annum growth of around 7 percent, partly because emerging problems of inefficiency and macroeconomic imbalance were papered over by rising oil revenues and an international financial market pumping loans into the developing world.[3] However, as the debt crisis broke in 1982 and oil prices tumbled through the ensuing decade, it became clear that Mexico's debt-backed, state-led growth could simply not be sustained. Both a new stabilization program and a markedly different development model were needed. Three main themes have characterized Mexico's economic reform strategy since 1982: (1) the ongoing effort to maintain macroeconomic stabilization in the context of market reforms; (2) the shift to a trade-led development model, including tighter integration into the North American market; and (3) a continuing failure to adequately address the distributional fallout from the macro, micro, and trade policies that have been implemented.

Macroeconomic Stabilization and Market Reforms

The key turning points in Mexico's ongoing macroeconomic stabilization effort are the period around the 1982 debt shocks, the 1987 implementation of the Economic Solidarity Stabilization Pact (which was renewed twelve times between December 1987 and November 1994), and the new challenges to stabilization that emerged in the wake of the December 1994 peso crisis. These macroeconomic stabilization efforts were implemented in tandem with ambitious structural reforms in the areas of liberalization, privatization, and deregulation. Although research suggests that a stabilization program can be derailed by an ill-timed introduction of deep structural reforms, particularly the liberalization of trade and capital accounts before export competitiveness is assured, the administration of Miguel de la Madrid (1982–1988) had little of the economic breathing space needed to heed this advice.[4]

The dire stabilization challenges inherited by this incoming team persisted through the entire *sexenio* (six-year term), regardless of the consecutive reform packages that sought to tackle inflation and reactivate the economy (see Table 7.1). Indeed, the record between 1982 and 1987—an erratic and often negative growth rate, stagnant exports, a burgeoning external debt, and a failure to halt a worrisome pace of price inflation—prompted Mexican policymakers to depart in 1987 from the strict orthodox stabilization strategy—consisting mainly of currency depreciation and fiscal discipline—that had prevailed since 1982.

By regional standards at the time, Mexico's 1987 inflation rate of nearly 160 percent was mild. Yet its strong trade and investment ties with the United States meant that the North American market was the more appropriate reference point, and by U.S. standards as well as Mexico's own history, inflation was running rampant. The December 1987 Economic Solidarity Pact was meant to address this problem head-on, and it did help to reduce inflation to just 12 percent by 1992. Although the pact included the usual orthodox strategy to curtail fiscal deficits, a key element was the setting of wage and price guidelines based on periodic tripartite consultations between government, business, and labor. Although the multilateral institutions were appalled at Mexico's "heterodox" adoption of a system of administered prices, the pact did conquer inflation. It also promoted dialogue between different economic sectors, and this helped win over business and even labor leaders who had resisted de la Madrid's market orientation.

The reliance on wage and price controls was crucial, but the real success of the pact lay in anchoring the peso to the U.S. dollar, liberalizing import controls, and dropping trade tariffs to an all-time low. Fortunately, both import compression and the depreciation strategy of the early to mid-1980s had allowed for a significant accumulation of international reserves in terms of monthly coverage, and thus policy-

Table 7.1 Macroeconomic Performance in Mexico, 1980–2000

	1980	1981	1982	1983	1984	1985	1986	1987	1988	1989	1990	1991	1992	1993	1994	1995	1996	1997	1998	1999	2000
Real GDP growth (%)	11.8	8.1	–5.9	–3.2	2.8	4.2	–6.8	3.3	2.8	4.2	5.1	4.2	3.6	2.0	4.4	–6.2	5.2	6.8	4.9	3.7	6.9
Real GNP growth per capita (%)	6.7	5.7	–6.0	–6.1	1.9	1.5	–6.5	0.8	0.4	2.5	3.5	2.9	1.8	–0.1	2.3	–9.2	4.0	6.3	3.5	2.6	5.0
Inflation (Dec.–Dec.)	29.8	28.7	98.9	80.8	59.2	63.7	105.7	159.2	51.7	19.7	29.9	18.8	11.9	8.0	7.1	52.0	27.7	15.7	18.6	12.3	8.9
Exports (billions U.S.$)	$18.0	$23.3	$24.1	$26.0	$29.1	$26.8	$21.8	$27.6	$30.7	$35.2	$40.7	$42.7	$46.2	$51.9	$60.9	$79.5	$96.0	$110.4	$117.5	$136.4	$166.4
Imports (billions U.S.$)	$21.1	$27.2	$17.0	$11.8	$15.9	$18.4	$16.8	$18.8	$28.1	$34.8	$41.6	$50.0	$62.1	$65.4	$79.3	$72.5	$89.5	$109.8	$125.4	$142.0	$174.5
Trade balance (billions U.S.$)	–$3.1	–$3.9	$7.0	$14.1	$13.2	$8.4	$5.0	$8.8	$2.6	$0.4	–$0.9	–$7.3	–$15.9	–$13.5	–$18.5	$7.1	$6.5	$0.6	–$7.9	–$5.6	–$8.0
Current account (billions U.S.$)	–$10.4	–$16.2	–$5.9	$5.9	$4.2	$0.8	–$1.4	$4.2	–$2.4	–$5.8	–$7.5	–$14.9	–$24.4	–$23.4	–$29.7	–$1.6	–$2.3	–$7.5	–$15.7	–$14.2	–$17.7
Current account (% of GDP)	–4.7	–5.3	–3.0	3.9	2.4	-.4	–1.1	3.0	–1.3	–2.6	–2.8	–4.7	–6.7	–5.8	–7.0	–0.6	–0.7	–1.9	–3.8	–2.9	–3.1
Debt (billions U.S.$)	$57.4	$78.2	$86.1	$93.0	$94.8	$96.9	$200.9	$10.95	$99.2	$93.8	$104.4	$114.1	$112.3	$131.7	$140.2	$166.9	$157.5	$148.7	$159.8	$167.0	$171.5
Debt (% of GDP)	25.7	25.5	43.9	62.4	54.0	52.5	77.9	78.0	54.2	42.1	39.8	36.3	30.9	32.7	33.3	58.3	47.4	37.1	38.4	34.5	30.5
Debt service ratio	44.4	46.4	51.0	45.3	45.1	43.7	43.7	32.7	37.1	32.6	20.7	23.6	33.8	35.8	28.1	27.8	35.6	33.2	20.0	25.1	23.0

makers finally had the leeway to shore up and sustain the macroeconomic stabilization plan. This was especially crucial given the impending 1988 presidential election and an electorate irate over depressed purchasing power and the slow pace of adjustment.

With the advent of the administration of Carlos Salinas de Gortari (1988–1994), the reform tasks shifted from the urgencies of macroeconomic stabilization to the completion of deep structural reforms. For example, the financial sector was more fully liberalized and deregulated, and eighteen domestic banks that had been nationalized by the outgoing administration of José López Portillo (1976–1982) were sold off to the private sector, as were the state airline, steel, and telephone companies. The agricultural sector was similarly liberalized, and the state's longstanding *ejido* system of communal rural landholdings was dismantled. The public sector itself was streamlined, and even the sacrosanct petroleum industry saw some privatization around the fringes, in processing and related services.

Apart from the Salinas team's ideological zeal for the market, these structural reforms obviously had a practical side: to entice foreign investment back into Mexico after the severe capital drought of the 1980s. Although the longer-term rationale for this revolved around the need to modernize the productive structure of the economy, the Mexican government was also desperate to increase inflows of capital in order to prop up the peso and maintain the macroeconomic stabilization victory. Thus, there was a worried haste to privatize state assets and to more fully open the stock market, the consequences of which would soon come home to roost.

The most immediate impacts were seen in the financial crash that beset the Mexican economy in 1994–1995. The real exchange rate became increasingly overvalued during the course of the Salinas sexenio as inflation reduction lagged behind the United States while the peso remained pegged (with only modest slippage) to the dollar (see Figure 7.1). The impacts on the trade balance were straightforward, with imports swelling well beyond export capacity (see Table 7.1). Mexican policymakers talked a brave game at the time, pointing to the balanced fiscal accounts, suggesting that the real appreciation of the peso was due to confidence in the Mexican economy, and emphasizing that private financing via portfolio investment was sufficient to cover the trade imbalance.[5] Behind the scenes, however, some economic policymakers, including incoming President Ernesto Zedillo (1994–2000), pressed for an orderly devaluation in late 1994.

The devaluation came, but orderly would hardly be the proper

Figure 7.1 Real Exchange Rate (value of imports)

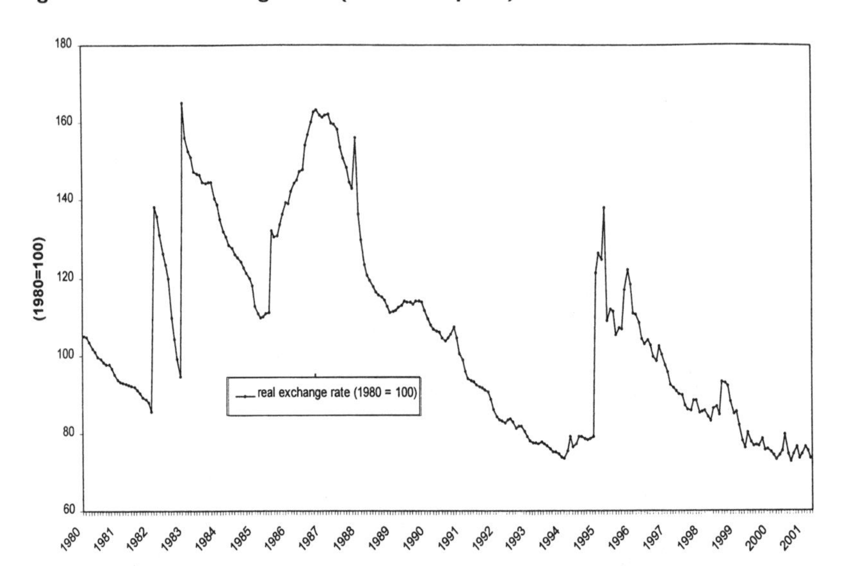

description.[6] An initial attempt at a step devaluation led to the peso's free fall, and the financial house of cards came tumbling down. Privatized banks were shown to have made a huge number of bad loans, hardly a testament to the virtues of liberalization, and the government was forced to step in, shoring up the banking system with loan purchases that would eventually cost nearly 20 percent of gross domestic product (GDP). To the shock of its international creditors, Mexico was once again begging for financial relief, and a $50 billion multilateral bailout package was duly assembled by February 1995. Stripped of any pretensions about a new and creative macroeconomic strategy, the government resorted to the old policies of depreciation to restore competitiveness, as well as financial discipline to balance budgets.

The surprising thing—and in stark contrast to the dismal results from a very similar strategy undertaken during the de la Madrid era in the early 1980s—is that the 1995 adjustment program worked. After a sharp recession, the economy rebounded in mid-1996, led largely by an export boom. Having sworn off exchange rate fixes and tripartite pacts, the government nonetheless managed to reduce inflation below double digits by the year 2000 (see Table 7.1). Private investment staged a rebound after a natural decline during the 1995 downturn, and by 1999–2000 it had reached nearly 19 percent of GDP, the highest over the entire twenty-year period. This private investment recovery occurred despite the fact that public investment hit an all-time low of around 2 percent of GDP, a somewhat surprising development given that public investment usually "crowds in" private spending in the developing world by offering complementary infrastructure.

What had happened to transform Mexico from stubborn adjuster to nimble adapter? Much of the story is due to the fundamental transformations in the external sector, a topic to which we now turn.

Trade-Led Development in Mexico: A Macro-Level Success Story

Although the desire for foreign investment flows reflected macroeconomic imperatives, the hunger for capital also responded to a longer-term project of economic restructuring. Recognizing that international patterns of trade and investment had become intricately linked through intraindustry trade and cross-border production, particularly with U.S. producers and markets, both de la Madrid and Salinas had pursued a series of bilateral accords with the United States in the late 1980s.[7] These followed on the heels of Mexico's 1986 accession to the General Agreement on Tariffs and Trade, which had seemed to signal the country's intentions to seek stronger multilateral economic ties and to diversify away from its strong historical dependence on the U.S. market.

As it turned out, the realistic prospects for significantly diversifying Mexico's trade and investment relations were not very auspicious at this time. With new competition from a liberalizing bloc of capital-starved countries in Eastern Europe, and a world recession triggered by the unexpectedly high costs of Germany's unification, Mexico quickly found itself back in the arms of U.S. investors. In 1990, the Salinas administration admitted as much by successfully petitioning the U.S. and Canadian governments for negotiated entry into the 1989 Canada-U.S. Free Trade Agreement; these negotiations were completed in 1992, and the North American Free Trade Agreement was launched on January 1, 1994.

As many observers noted at the time, NAFTA's most advanced chapters were those on the treatment of foreign investment.[8] This was expected to produce an inflow of capital, building on the increase in the 1990–1994 period that had followed Mexico's financial market opening and the 1989 Brady debt restructuring. Of course, most of this 1990–1994 inflow was portfolio investment—that is, the purchase of bonds, stocks, and equities—and was as likely to leave as to stay and, if it left, to do either with particularly rapid abandon. Such flight occurred in the wake of the peso crash, and the erratic stop-go pattern in the ensuing years was dizzying (see Figure 7.2).

But a key part of the story is the steady increase in foreign direct investment (FDI) into Mexico. As Figure 7.2 shows, FDI flows barely fell in the wake of the 1994 crisis and have risen significantly since. All available evidence suggests that much of this new investment has been attracted to those export sectors that have been liberalized and modernized, especially within the *maquila* (or in-bond) industries.[9]

Yet there is an interesting contradiction to Mexico's apparent success at economic transformation: the healthy expansion of exports under the impetus of greater and more dynamic inflows of FDI was not just the result of Salinas's commitment to liberalization. After averaging just 12.4 percent of GDP between 1980 and 1984, exports remained a lackluster 13.8 percent of GDP from 1990 to 1994. With Salinas gone and under the combined impetus of NAFTA-inspired investment flows and a competitive exchange rate, exports grew to a startling 28.1 percent of GDP in the 1995–1999 period.[10]

Perhaps more significant was the changing composition of Mexican exports, and we offer a breakdown of this shift in composition over the twenty-year period (see Figure 7.3).[11] As can be seen in the figure, manufacturing's share of exports has risen steadily and strongly, particularly after 1986. Although the timing suggests that liberalization may have played an indirect role by persuading firms to move away from traditional products and take their chance on manufactures, one of the striking features of Mexico's indisputable export success is that it is concentrated in those sectors that were fostered by earlier ISI policies and are now well-positioned for external sales: autos, electronics, and petrochemicals come immediately to mind.[12]

In this sense, industrial policy, which was anathema to liberal-minded Mexican technocrats in the 1980s and 1990s, played as important a role as pure market opening; both were necessary elements in the story, with the final trigger being the application of a competitive exchange rate to these restructured sectors. For example, the most dynamic sector, the maquilas, is a result of what some would call heavy-handed interventions, measures that date back to the 1960s: special tax incentives, exemptions, and infrastructure to promote border development and employment. Although the non-maquila balance has been volatile—and the rapid adjustment in the non-maquila sector largely responsible for the quick swing to an overall trade surplus in 1995—maquila trade balances have been positive and rising over time,

Figure 7.2 Foreign Investment Flows in Mexico, 1980–2000

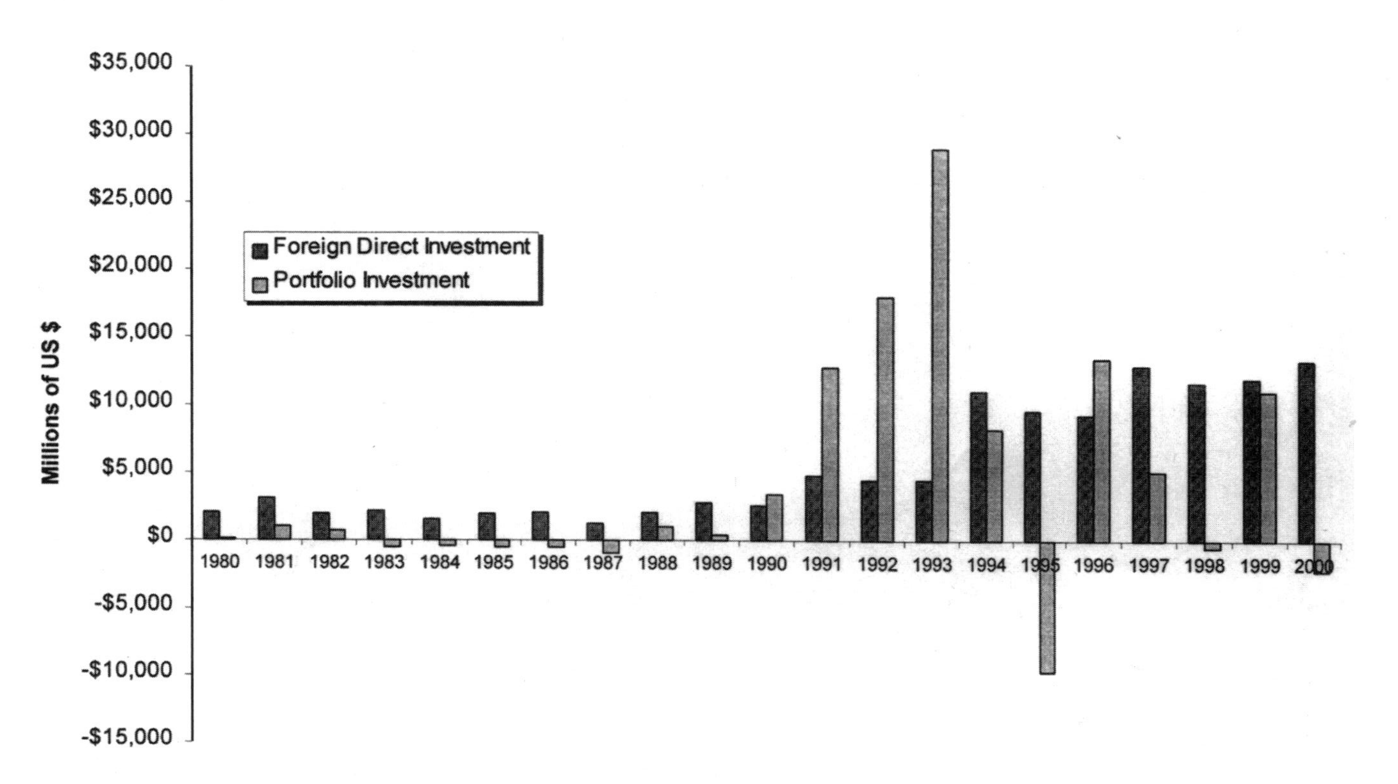

Figure 7.3 Changing Composition of Mexican Exports, 1980–2001

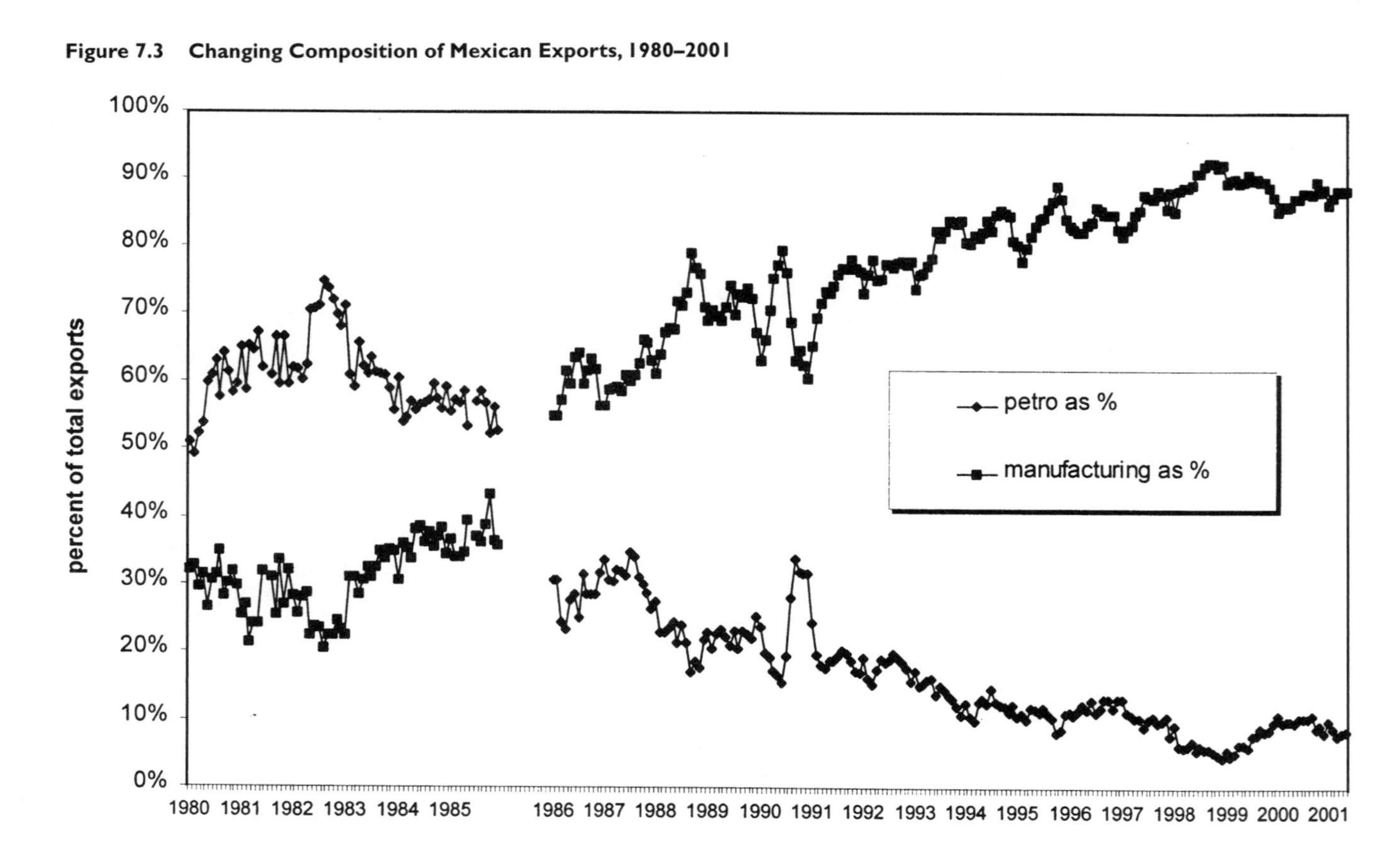

and gross fixed investment in the maquilas grew by 30 percent a year from 1993 to 1997 (see Figure 7.4).[13]

It is also possible to speak of a third generation of maquilas that now operate in more technologically advanced and higher valued-added sectors (e.g., autos, computers, electronics) and that coexist with first- and second-generation plants involved in assembly operations and industrial processing, respectively.[14] Although these higher-tech maquila firms still lack sufficient forward and backward linkages with the rest of the Mexican economy, they are becoming more geographically dispersed and not just clustered along the U.S.-Mexico border. Such companies have become a main impetus for job creation and wage gains.

This is not a set of facts that squares well with either neoliberal or neoradical accounts of Mexican development. Those within the antiglobalization camp that saw the peso crash of 1994–1995 as the harbinger of another "lost decade" overlooked the significant market restructuring and sweeping institutional reform undertaken during the previous decade. After the acute retrenchment of 1995, the Mexican economy began a dynamic export-led recovery that persisted through 2000. The exchange rate has appreciated, but a look at the underlying patterns of FDI and the clear evidence of enhanced trade capacity suggest a level of sustainability not characteristic of the earlier period. Indeed, growth rates have done anything but slow: the 5.5 percent annual average rate for 1995–2000 represents the best performance over a five-year period during the two decades (1980–2000) that we consider in this chapter.

Yet avid supporters of market reform, and Mexico's neoliberal reformers in particular, should be equally circumspect. After all, an exchange rate targeting experiment rewarded by capital inflows from supposedly rational international investors led to a precarious financial buildup and then a collapse—hardly an unequivocal recommendation for a strictly market-based adjustment. Moreover, despite market restructuring, the overall economy has not done as well on the trade side as the maquila sector; this hints at the importance of coupling commercial opening with appropriate public policies, including the targeting of higher value-added exports and selective incentives for companies restructuring toward tradable goods. Finally, diehard supporters of Mexico's market reforms should be chagrined, if not downright embarrassed, that the promise of growth and recovery has taken so long to trickle down to those laboring at the bottom of the income pyramid.

Figure 7.4 Trade Balance in Mexico by Month, 1980–2000

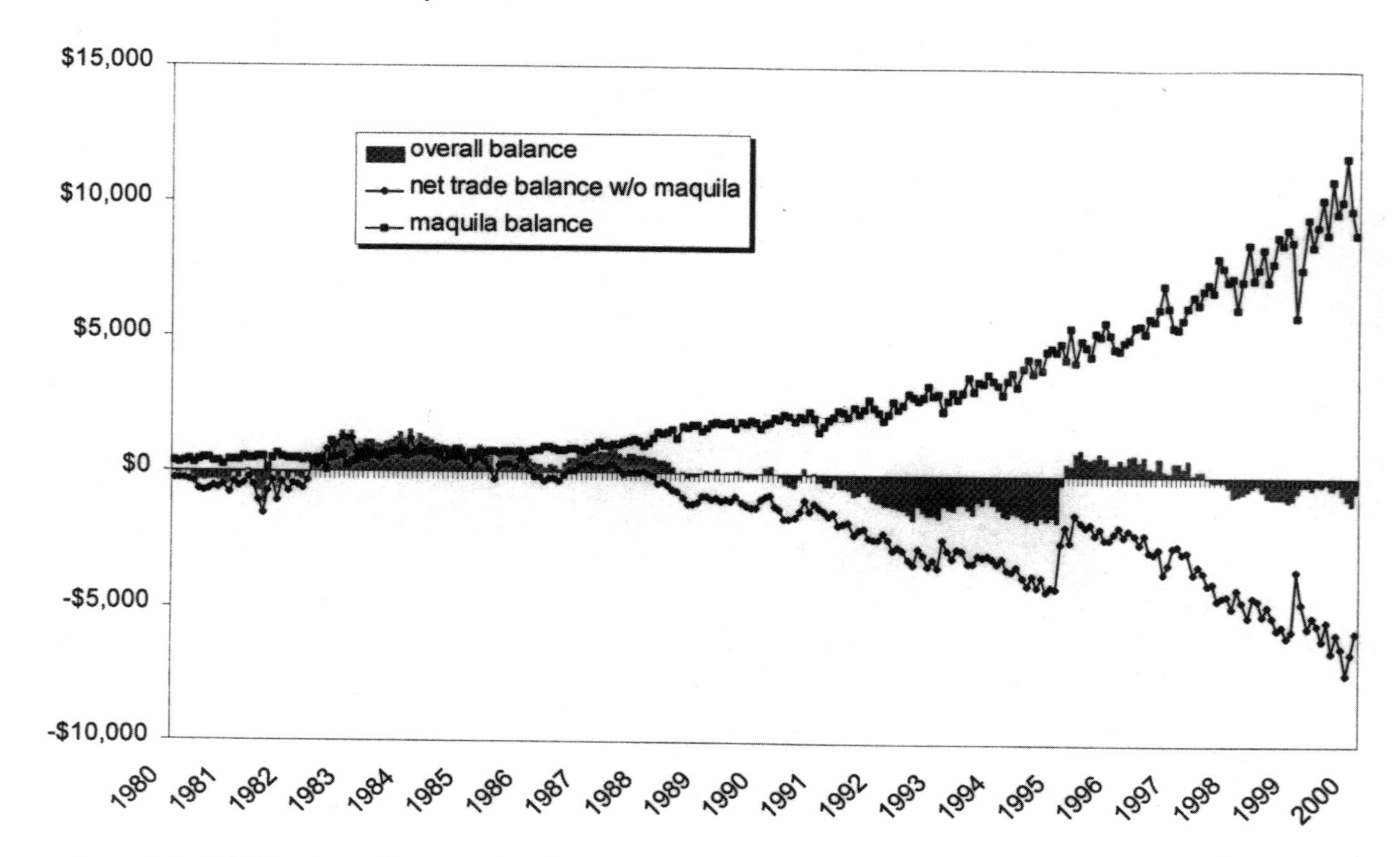

A Skewed Pattern of Gains from Trade: Export Orientation and Business Concentration

The impact of Mexico's liberal trade strategy has been especially negative for those smaller firms and their employees, both of whom are still struggling to adjust to the much higher levels of international competition. Figure 7.5 shows the initial sharp decline in manufacturing employment in the wake of the 1982 debt shocks and then a longer and more consistent slide during the Salinas sexenio. There was a recovery after the peso depreciation began to work its magic with manufacturing exports, but a detailed employment breakdown from 1994 on shows that nonmaquila employment has been flat, and thus virtually all of Mexico's job growth has stemmed from the maquila sector.[15]

Within the nonmaquila sector, large exporting firms with ready access to affordable credit and strong ties to the U.S. market now tower over their smaller and less competitive counterparts who produce for the domestic market. Growing market segmentation, in terms of credit access and foreign-versus-domestic orientation, has simultaneously fostered a virtuous cycle of capital accumulation at the top and a vicious circle of stagnation throughout the rest of the economy. As small and medium-sized enterprises (SMEs) currently represent approximately 99 percent of the Mexican private sector and account for 80 percent of

Figure 7.5 Index of Manufacturing Employment, 1980–2001

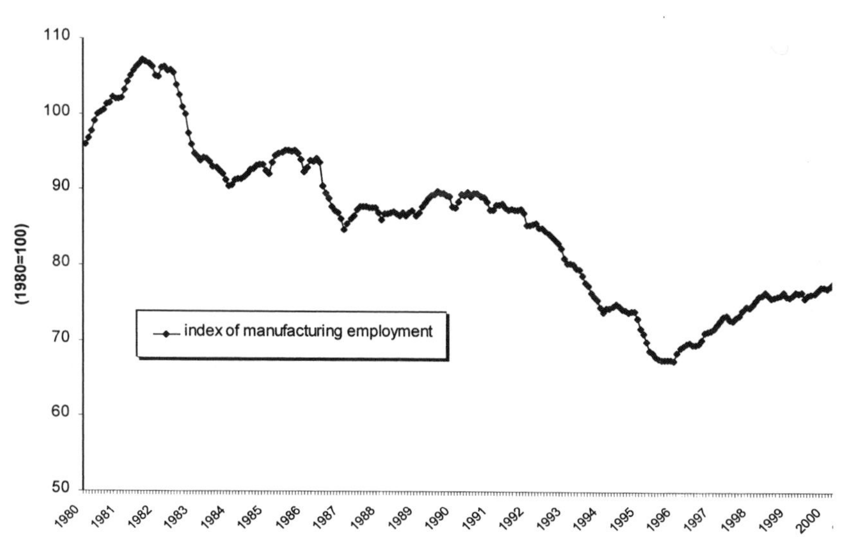

employment and 50 percent of GDP, this plight of the bulk of the country's private-sector firms is no small matter.[16]

There are, of course, some instances of successful adjustment within the SME sector during the 1990s. By 1999, domestic companies accounted for half of all exports, and more than 35,000 of these firms were classified as SMEs. Thus, some of these smaller enterprises have survived by becoming exporters and by restructuring in ways that allow for better market adaptation (e.g., greater managerial flexibility, lower overhead expenses, use of the Internet, and strategic alliances with other firms). But the more common story is one of SMEs battered by the unprecedented competition and struggling with the basics: market research, product upgrading, quality control, customer service, the application of technology, and access to affordable credit. Credit access, in particular, has been a sore spot for SMEs across the region in the 1990s; for smaller Mexican producers, the problem has been more severe due to the crash of the banking system in 1995 and the exorbitant interest rates and increased segmentation of credit markets that have persisted since.[17]

Government policies since 1996 have sought to more explicitly address the needs of vulnerable domestic firms, including the SMEs. For example, hoping to both spread the benefits from growth and gather support from the business class at large, the 1994–2000 Zedillo administration departed from the strict hands-off market strategy that had dominated policymaking pre-1994 and put forth the new Program for Industrial and Foreign Trade Policy (PROPICE). PROPICE offers information services for the production and marketing of exports; encouragement of export-oriented manufacturing clusters, as well as the closer integration of SMEs into these networks; assistance in building stronger supply and production ties between the country's diverse regions; and consultation on industrial policy needs from the numerous chambers of business and commerce that represent the bulk of the Mexican private sector.[18]

The fact that these policies are still led primarily by the market has drawn some cynical predictions as to their efficacy. However, it helps to recall that Chile's successful shift toward an outward model based on higher value-added exports and strong productivity gains was prompted by a similar set of policies.[19] Moreover, we should recall that Jaime Serra Puche, the trade minister under Salinas, repeatedly stated during his tenure that "the best industrial policy is no industrial policy." In this light, it is significant that any sort of industrial policy has been tried at all.

Distributional Policy and Poverty Alleviation: A Micro-Level Backlog

As Gustav Ranis points out in Chapter 10 of this volume, Mexico has long been characterized as one of the most unequal countries in Latin America. Economic and political reform held out the promise that the country would move up the ranks toward greater equality. Market reform, in particular, was supposed to better reward skill and initiative; reduce corruption, increase transparency, and thus eliminate the incentives and opportunities for rent-seeking; and liberalized trade was supposed to raise the demand for unskilled labor and thereby benefit the poor more rapidly than the wealthy. The evidence of actual Mexican progress in the distributional arena is, however, quite mixed.

The overall pattern is shown in Table 7.2, which offers the aggregate results for all of the household surveys taken over the period of restructuring. As can be seen, there is a sizable relative gain for those at the top over the time period considered. Distribution worsened for the

Table 7.2 Distribution of Current Monetary Income by Household Deciles

	Percentage of Total Income to Household Decile						
Household Deciles[a]	1984	1989	1992	1994	1996	1998	2000
Total	100.00	100.00	100.00	100.00	100.00	100.00	100.00
I	1.19	1.14	1.00	1.01	1.24	0.92	1.11
II	2.66	2.48	2.27	2.27	2.56	2.22	2.40
III	3.86	3.52	3.36	3.27	3.56	3.24	3.33
IV	5.01	4.56	4.38	4.26	4.60	4.33	4.32
V	6.26	5.76	5.45	5.35	5.67	5.47	5.47
VI	7.66	7.21	6.77	6.67	6.99	6.86	6.92
VII	9.68	9.02	8.62	8.43	8.78	8.76	8.65
VIII	12.42	11.42	11.22	11.19	11.38	11.59	11.29
IX	17.00	15.92	16.09	16.30	16.15	16.42	16.47
X	34.26	38.97	40.84	41.24	39.07	39.07	40.29
Gini coefficient[b]	0.46	0.49	0.51	0.51	0.49	0.51	0.50

Source: Instituto Nacional de Estadística, Georgrafía e Informatica, Encuesta Nacional de Ingresos y Gastos de los Hogares, Third Quarter, 1984, 1989, and 1992 (CD-ROM). Third Quarter, 1994, 1996, and 1998 (1998 CD-ROM). Third Quarter, 2000 (www.inegi.gov.mx).

Notes: a. Households are ordered in terms of income (the first decile includes the poorest, the last deciles the richest).

b. The Gini coefficient is an aggregate measure of income inequality that ranges from zero in a completely equal society to one in a completely unequal society.

bottom 40 percent of households—but contrary to common wisdom, the largest relative losers have been those in the middle of the distributional pyramid. Of the increase of 5.25 percentage points in the share of national income accruing to the richest 20 percent of Mexican households over the entire time period, 3.7 percentage points came from the middle 40 percent. This is partly because the poor were already scratching out a truly Dickensian existence, and hence the middle classes had more to give up. This pattern helps to explain the exodus of middle-class Mexicans from the PRI, while the party was able to retain some support from loyalists among the urban and rural poor.

Some defenders of reform have suggested that there should actually be little concern about distribution per se: slipping behind is relatively less painful if one is earning and eating more. In fact, distribution matters a great deal in Mexico. Between 1980 and 1999, the last year for which we have reliable figures, real per capita gross national income had posted a pathetic 4 percent increase over the entire twenty-year period, making for an average yearly per capita growth rate of 0.2 percent. This stagnation suggests that Mexico is light years away from reaping East Asian–style income gains based on an export-led orientation. When the pie is expanding so slowly, the size of the slice matters a great deal.

Not all of the news on the distributional front has been bad. As can be seen in Table 7.2, the 1996 survey suggests there was a brief and somewhat surprising relative gain during—or perhaps, better put, a smaller relative hit from—the 1995 recession. This quickly gave rise to a new cottage industry of explanations that basically argued that the 1994 peso crisis caused a loss in capital and interest income that most affected those at the top. More careful scrutiny suggests that this explains only a small portion of the pattern. As it turns out, those in the top 20 percent of the economic hierarchy saw their own labor incomes dwindle substantially, as they were disproportionately involved in domestic finance and other high-end nontradable goods.[20] Conversely, those working in the lower-wage export industries saw their incomes improve due to the postdevaluation takeoff in that sector.

Of course, the long-term performance of average wages could hardly be called strong (see Figure 7.6). Wages were sharply slashed in the early period of stabilization during the 1980s, then staged a recovery after 1989 under Salinas. Yet judging from the 1989–1994 distributional figures, the sharp run-up in average wages during the Salinas sexenio seems to have had little impact on the poorest Mexicans. The peso

Figure 7.6 Real Wage in Manufacturing, 1980–2000

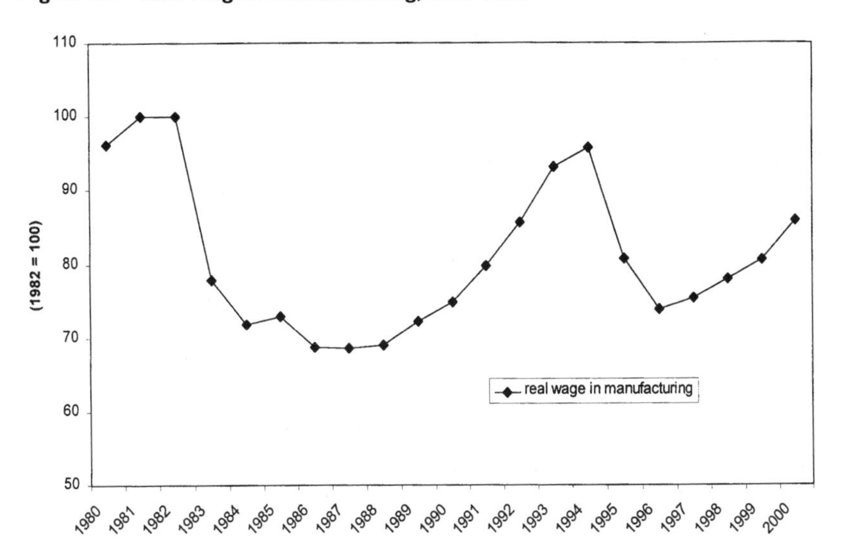

devaluation of 1994 had a negative impact on the manufacturing wage in 1995 and 1996, much as in the early 1980s. The household survey information on distribution suggests that the damage to the poorest was more limited in this period, perhaps because the decline in the overall average wage may have been driven more by falls at the top and middle of the wage-labor spectrum, a fact that squares with the redistribution from the middle class discussed earlier. Both 1999 and 2000 were better years for wage growth, and the dynamism was apparently concentrated in the lower-skill export sector. However, even if export-led recovery has finally begun to help the poor, the lagging and erratic income trends at the bottom do cast doubt on the neoliberal promise that the aggressive opening of the Mexican economy would quickly increase the demand for unskilled labor and produce a redistribution of income and wealth downward.

As shifting incomes fed back into domestic politics, paralleling and sometimes driving the PRI's electoral decline over the past two decades, the government sought to respond. After the benign neglect under de la Madrid, the Salinas administration tried to revamp poverty-alleviation policies as well as the PRI's traditional patronage machine with a social safety net program called PRONASOL. This involved the concentration of adjustment support in the office of the executive, which then determined spending priorities in response to community concerns and projects.[21] The underlying social-policy model of PRONASOL was attractive in its local and participatory character, but analysts readily pointed out that this sort of demand-driven model—in which the government funds local officials and organizations who clamor for support—does not necessarily make for effective targeting in terms of poverty reduction.[22] Under such a scheme, only the most vocal and cohesive sectors are able to obtain resources, creating a bias in favor of the more organized and away from the poorest. Such an approach also raises the potential for a program to be used simply as a tool of patronage and co-optation, particularly given the concentration of authority in the office of the executive. Such were the accusations against PRONASOL by opposition parties and independent analysts, partly based on the high correlation between PRONASOL spending and areas where the PRI needed to shore up support.[23] Indeed, this political logic may help to explain the relatively high spending on the program; PRONASOL had the highest dollar payout per capita of any of the social funds created in other developing countries for which they could collect data.[24]

The Zedillo administration, anxious to distinguish itself from the Salinas era, transformed PRONASOL into a more targeted program. Implemented in 1997, the Program of Education, Health, and Nutrition (PROGRESA) represented a shift in Mexican thinking about social spending—from compensation to productive investments in human capital—and the program attempted a number of innovative strategies in the areas of health, education, and nutrition.[25] For one thing, aid was delivered to families through mothers, with the explicit aim of ensuring that funds would be spent on children and improving women's say over the use of household income. Aid was also contingent on children attending school and regular family visits to local health clinics.

Although it is still too soon to speak definitively about PROGRESA's full impacts, careful internal studies suggest that it is making a significant difference in the lives of participants.[26] At the end of 1999, at least according to the government, PROGRESA was covering 2.6 million families, representing almost 40 percent of rural families.[27] For this group, school attendance was up, with researchers estimating around a 1 percent gain in elementary school attendance and a very significant gain of almost 6 percent for female high school students. The potential impact on human capital formation is straightforward: researchers estimate that if these attendance increases persist, the program would add 0.7 years of schooling for each participant, which, given the low levels of academic achievement in rural areas, represents an increase in the average educational level for eighteen-year-olds of almost 10 percent.

Of course, PROGRESA also has a direct effect on income: according to the government's own estimates, the program has lowered poverty by nearly 8 percent in the areas where it operates and has reduced one government measure of the severity of poverty (which takes into account not simply whether one is below the poverty line but how far below it, then gives disproportionate weight to the poorest of the poor) by a startling 45 percent.[28] The macro-level evidence from the 2000 distributional survey may also reflect this gain—although the portion due to larger macroeconomic and labor market dynamics or to the more successful targeting by government authorities should be the subject of future analysis. One preliminary indicator suggests that the broader macro recovery has been the driving force: PROGRESA's spending up through the Zedillo sexenio amounted to only 0.2 percent of GDP, including administrative costs.

Clearly, the underlying causes of Mexico's income disparities need to be more aggressively tackled. In particular, the differences in educational opportunities, inequalities in asset acquisition (land, capital, and access to credit), and the country's need to continue refining social policy are all imperatives.[29] A key factor—all the more important as liberalization attracted more sophisticated kinds of foreign direct investment in the 1990s—has been the increasing disparities in the return to education.[30] This is why PROGRESA's effort to tie compensation to enhanced school participation is so appropriate. Still, the country's skill deficit is not just limited to the poorest 40 percent of workers; there also remains a dire education/skills gap for the middle 40 percent of income-earners, and government policy has largely eluded this group.

Reconciling Democratic Politics with Economic Change: The Challenges Ahead

By 1997 the Mexican economy had finally begun to show signs of the takeoff that had been expected from the combination of NAFTA entry and the implementation of deep market reforms. A 30 percent real devaluation of the exchange rate unleashed the productive potential within the export sector, and even real wages turned upward. Poverty policy, though inadequate to the task, finally began to move in a direction that held the promise of long-term development for the country's poor. Despite controversies over the absorption of bad loans by the general public, banking reform was achieved and the financial system shored up. And in one of history's ironies, at the very point when the PRI had actually begun to deliver on its time-worn promises of future prosperity, voters opted to throw the rascals out.

Though spared the usual economic blowup that had long marked Mexico's passing of the presidential torch every six years, the Fox administration still inherited a bundle of unresolved issues that quickly became part of its own programmatic agenda.[31] On the economic side was the long overdue need for a tax reform bill, as tax revenues continued to stagnate at just 11 percent of GDP (compared to 25 percent for the United States and 30 percent for most European countries); the need to forge ahead with privatization and/or the introduction of competitive measures in the electricity, transportation, and energy sectors; and the urgent need to advance more quickly in rectifying income inequalities (see Table 7.2). On the political side were the unresolved challenges of the Chiapas guerrilla campaign, as well as the broader need to tighten campaign finance rules and create an orderly alternative to the highly conflicted process still surrounding elections at the state and municipal levels.[32]

Although the electorate expressed high hopes for democratic change and Fox has retained political goodwill (with, for example, a steady 70 percent approval rating in public opinion polls), the challenges are still significant—and the expectations for success extraordinarily high.[33] In our view, there are three main issues confronting the current administration: spurring higher levels of economic growth and employment expansion; reducing the income differentials by class and region that have plagued Mexico for decades; and persevering in the pursuit of political reforms that ensure a greater degree of transparency, accountability, and fairness.

Spurring Higher Economic Growth and Employment Expansion

The ability of the Fox administration to make good on its goal of achieving 7 percent annual growth rates and the creation of 1.4 million jobs each year goes to the very heart of Mexico's economic transformation. Despite a commitment to liberalization and modernization, policymakers have yet to hit anywhere near these targets in the two decades covered in this chapter. Still, the Fox team ushered in a high level of optimism, partly because the economic indicators inherited from the outgoing Zedillo team—including an average annual growth rate of 6 percent since 1997, a moderate fiscal deficit, the highest levels of FDI in the country's history, and a long-awaited recovery of real wages—suggested that Mexico was finally about to realize its tremendous postreform potential for high growth.

The abrupt slowdown of the U.S. economy in mid-2000 caused Mexico's own growth projections to plummet, and some estimate that the employment base may have already slipped by as much as a half-million jobs.[34] Meanwhile, the underlying dynamism and full potential of a radically reformed Mexican economy remain the subject of much debate. Economic growth is no longer driven by debt-backed state intervention but rather by trade and private investment against a backdrop of sustained macroeconomic stabilization. Critics, however, have rightfully questioned whether there are sufficient domestic linkages from the more dynamic export and maquila sectors where the bulk of private investment has been concentrated. Yet the transformation of Mexican exports has been substantial, as the line of tradable goods has moved up the value-added chain from basic commodities to electrical machinery, road vehicles, and telecommunications equipment, for example, and there are increasing supply links between Mexican and foreign (mostly U.S.) firms.[35]

How will the Fox team ensure that technological upgrading is more widespread? On the productive side, the basically laissez-faire industrial policy inherited from the previous administration will remain in place, but with greater resources and a more explicit emphasis on SME development.[36] At the level of symbolism, the president has affectionately referred to micro enterprises by their colloquial term, *changaros*, and consistently identified them as the country's engine of growth. As one high-ranking official put it, the thinking now is not so much what Mexico will do for small business but that a prosperous small business sector is essential for the country to achieve higher growth and employment rates.[37]

In terms of concrete policy, the government says that it will play a more active role in targeting resources toward firms with strong potential to participate in those higher value-added export activities that we mentioned above. For example, the various SME promotion efforts discussed earlier (e.g., PROPICE) are now being consolidated under one main office (CIPI) in the Ministry of Economy (formerly SECOFI), which itself has been assigned an unprecedented mandate to focus on microeconomic restructuring—including a doubling of its share of the federal budget.[38] The goal now is to reach at least 10 percent of those firms in need of support by the end of the Fox term. Apart from offering assistance in such areas as technology upgrading, skills training, and diagnoses for improving efficiency, the Fox microstrategy also commits to greater accountability in the allocation of credit to SMEs. In particular, the current reform package demands much higher levels of transparency from those development banks that are the main conduits for credit access by smaller firms.[39]

The need to invest more vigorously in education, skills, and human capital, partly to position Mexico higher up on the value-added hierarchy, was a vocal theme in the 2000 Fox campaign. Thus far, the most concrete plans to boost human capital include a pledge to raise the average level of schooling from seven to ten years and to do so by deepening the inroads made by the Zedillo administration in shifting a greater share of the education budget toward basic education. Whereas this crucial category captured about 58 percent of the education budget in 1990, it now accounts for about 66 percent and is slated to go higher under Fox.[40]

With regard to reforming domestic labor markets to encourage employment, Fox is stepping gingerly toward breaking the hold of those unions with long ties to the traditional wing of the PRI, some of which still control entire sectors through a web of corruption and coercion. One strategy to weaken union power involves moving toward plant-level negotiations, mostly to avoid the sectorwide rules that can block labor market mobility. Although this would supposedly serve the cause of creating employment, it also holds the potential to significantly lower wages; given the administration's distributional goals and the lingering power of the country's labor bosses, this presents both a contradiction and a political challenge.

The Fox administration has also put the question of migration firmly on the agenda—key since escape to U.S. labor markets has been a safety valve for Mexican workers and the issue of migration will increase in importance if current employment growth remains slow. Although Fox has backed down on his bold campaign calls for the free movement of labor within the NAFTA bloc, he launched discussions with U.S. president George W. Bush regarding an "orderly framework for migration" between Mexico and the United States. However, with recession in the United States looming indefinitely and public concerns about immigrants and security on the upswing, it is doubtful that discussions between Bush and Fox concerning, for example, a new guest-worker program for Mexicans in the United States, an increase in legal immigration from Mexico, and/or an amnesty bill for undocumented Mexicans now residing in the United States will amount to much. Still, by raising the issue of increased border flows, and by directly addressing the often poor treatment of Mexican workers in the United States—topics regarded as taboo under Salinas and Zedillo—Fox has been able to reap a political dividend at home while likely creating a safer environment for Mexican laborers to work abroad and send remittances to those family members that will need them to survive the coming slowdown.

Reducing Income Inequality

Although Mexico's regressive trends were most pronounced in the 1980s, policymakers did not get serious about redistributing income until the launching of the PROGRESA program midway through the Zedillo administration. Perhaps it was too little, too late, but even in the short time that the more targeted distributional approach has been in effect there is evidence that PROGRESA is having a positive impact on the bottom 40 percent of income-earners in Mexico. Of course, as we argued earlier, these improvements occurred against a synergistic backdrop of strong growth since 1997 and the heightened export demand for unskilled labor under NAFTA. There is no guarantee that these favorable macro trends will continue, especially in light of the severe market dislocations related to the September 2001 terrorist attacks on New York and Washington, D.C. Thus, the Fox administration must pledge all the more to promote distributional improvements, including the design of new strategies to meet his campaign vow to reduce poverty by 30 percent.

Raising productivity is also important, and Mexican policymakers will need to adhere closely to those research findings on the crucial role of asset accumulation (human, physical, productive) in promoting greater equality.[41] The PROGRESA program has nudged Mexican social policy in the right direction, and the government is under significant pressure to expand to urban areas the so-called *cinturones de miseria* (misery belts), with some of the rationale stemming from the need to deliver benefits to opposition-dominated metropolitan areas around Mexico City.[42] Apart from these political considerations, frontline social policy administrators now readily concede that the introduction of the free market was extremely fast. There is, in other words, a huge need to catch up and rectify past policy oversights in this area.

In terms of broader investments in human capital, even though total programmable public spending has been reduced by about 5 percent since 1994, social spending per capita was 19 percent higher in 2001 than it was in 1994.[43] But reversing the regressive trends reflected in Table 7.2 will require an even greater allocation of scarce public resources. As Figure 7.7 shows, public-sector income has been declining steadily as a share of GDP since the mid-1980s. With receipts from public firms dwindling due to past privatization, the Fox government must raise tax receipts as a share of GDP. The country's low level of tax incidence stems from a combination of granting too many exemptions to big business and from the fact that at least 40–50 percent of the workforce is operating in the informal economy. By definition, fiscal reform implies the drawing of yet another set of lines between winners and losers, and this has rendered the domestic debate especially contentious.

The difficulty of getting down to serious business with a fiscal reform bill in the national Congress was reflected in the mid-2001 decision to postpone the vote on the tax package until year's end. In principle, all of the major political parties in Congress are in agreement as to the urgency of passing a sound package of fiscal reforms. However, the opposition parties seem determined to stack the debate such that they can take credit for breaking the country's long-standing tax logjam while the PAN takes the blame for the less appealing trade-off that fiscal reform inevitably engenders. The challenges of reconciling Mexico's new competitive politics with this particular set of economic

Figure 7.7 Public Sector Income in Mexico, 1980–2000

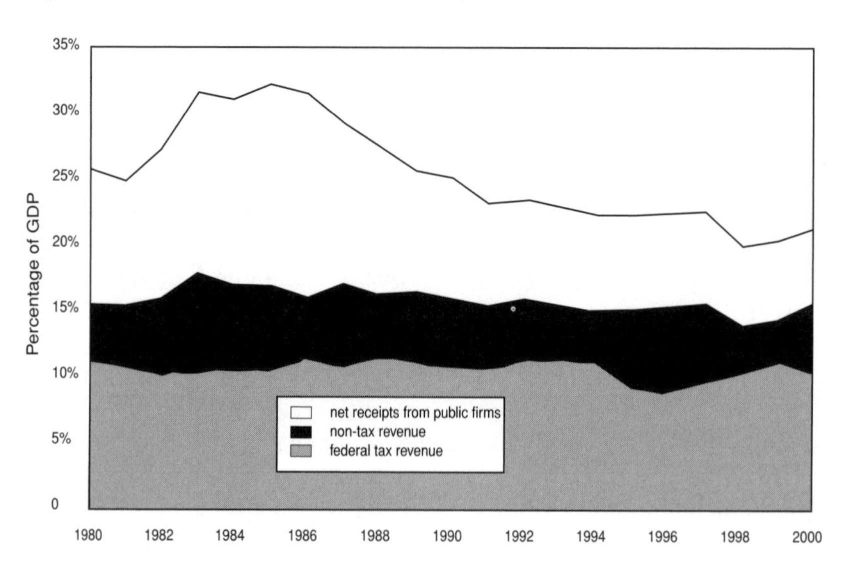

reforms has been compounded by the efforts of even some PAN deputies to distance themselves from their own party's proposals.

The stated fiscal reform goals are to increase the government's revenue intake by 2 percent of GDP in 2002 and by at least 4 percent a year thereafter.[44] When combined with public spending cuts, it is expected that the budget deficit will be reduced to less than 1 percent of GDP. Privatization revenues will be low: Zedillo helped give that strategy a bad name by rescuing the state banking system after a disastrous privatization under Salinas, thus draining scarce government resources through the acquisition of bad bank debt. As a result, the Fox team has targeted a rather low-profile group of assets for sale, including the state's remaining shares in an airline holding company, in a public insurance company, in partially privatized railway companies, and in the BBVA-Bancomer financial group.

Fox has identified the realistic options for raising revenue as widening the tax base and eliminating exemptions on the payment of a 15 percent value-added tax (VAT) for food, medicine, books, and educational fees. Not surprisingly, the administration's proposals concerning the extension of the VAT, a prima facie regressive tax, have provoked the most furor in Congress. With the legislative stalling of the tax bill, the Fox government quickly circulated a study that suggested that those in the top income decile were paying nearly 90 percent of the country's taxes and receiving only 7 percent of government spending, whereas those in the bottom 60 percent were paying no taxes and receiving nearly 75 percent of government spending. This assessment did not square with the public's sense of the tax burden and spending benefits, particularly in light of the bank bailout for billionaires, and the release of these figures did not lead to great public confidence in the government's distributional methodology.

Moreover, many poor and middle-class Mexicans are reluctant to support increased taxes, mainly because past experience does not lead them to believe that there will be any direct connection to the level of services. Although the Fox team has gone to great lengths to argue that those in the lower-income deciles will be compensated for the VAT increases through direct relief, there is also little confidence that a regressively collected tax will be spent in a progressive way. Despite these public doubts, fiscal pressure will mount, and the most likely outcome of the tax battle will be a VAT extension to previously exempt goods and services, albeit at a much lower rate than originally proposed.

Assuming that tax reform does occur, distributional policy in

Mexico holds the promise of moving in the Chilean direction: raising public revenues to target distributional needs, as well as broadening the social safety net in ways that encourage worker productivity versus the old-style compensation.[45] In the short run, however, projected revenues are dropping due to the onset of recession, and additional spending cuts will be needed. The new competitive political environment will make such cuts challenging, as incumbents no longer have the luxury of inflicting indefinite economic pain with promises of prosperity in the distant future. To succeed, the Fox administration will have to keep its eye on the distributional prize and follow through with social investments that clearly offset the regressive tax measures now on the drawing board.

Political Reform

The Fox government has wasted no time in advancing political reforms that uphold earlier campaign promises to combat crime and corruption and instill much greater levels of transparency and accountability into everyday political and economic life. Most prominent among these initiatives has been the creation of the new Ministry of Security, which took over the policing duties of the Interior Ministry.[46] Other measures, such as the Law of People's Savings and Credit, will regulate financial intermediaries that focus on low-income groups, and the new Stock Market Law will similarly protect small investors and seek to limit insider trading. Even though some of these gestures contain as much symbol as substance, it is noteworthy that political symbolism is being employed to deepen, rather than derail and distract from, the democratization process.

As with the fiscal reform package, those political reforms that dig into much deeper tissue with regard to Mexico's democratic transition—including the highly contested indigenous rights bill and the need for yet another generation of electoral reforms—will take longer to hammer out in Congress. On the indigenous rights bill, Fox has been plagued by an audacious campaign comment where he claimed that, in contrast to the PRI's bungling of this issue, he could resolve it in "fifteen minutes." Although it appears that Zedillo's negotiators could have done much more to avoid the acrimonious stalemate that developed between the Zapatista National Liberation Army (EZLN) and the government in 1997, Fox has not done all that much better to rekindle good-faith peace negotiations. The EZLN has demanded that the following conditions must first be met: the Fox administration must close most of the military bases in Chiapas; it must release those guerrillas still being held as political prisoners; and the Congress must pass an indigenous rights bill generated in 1996 by the multiparty congressional Commission of Concordance and Peace (COCOPA).

The COCOPA indigenous rights bill was indeed the first piece of legislation that the Fox administration sent to the Congress, and the president's strategy has been to basically concede to the EZLN's demands. The problem is that Fox alone cannot seal this deal, and his gestures of collegiality toward the Zapatistas are not shared by the more conservative elements within his own party. An indigenous rights bill was passed by Congress on April 28, 2001, but the content did not meet the desire of indigenous groups to establish autonomy in local political matters, including justice, land, and natural resource rights, and any autonomy was undercut by congressional insistence that it could be usurped when it conflicts with federal law. As a result, there is a lack of buy-in by affected groups and continuing discord among the major parties over how to make peace and achieve reform. In short, the time frame is longer than fifteen minutes, and for Fox this has become yet another thorn in his legislative agenda.

As fiscal reform and the unexpected gridlock on indigenous rights have consumed the bulk of the new administration's time and energy, it is worth noting that any of the preelection discussions among the major parties about the need for another wave of electoral reforms have yet to be resumed. Especially since the PRI's widespread losses in 1997, virtually every state-level gubernatorial contest involving a possible PRI defeat has erupted into the equivalent of a miniature civil war, the long saga over the PRI's highly disputed victory in the Gulf Coast state of Tabasco being yet another example. In particular, the need "not only to eliminate lingering inequalities . . . but also to adjust the electoral system to propagate greater electoral competition, power distribution, party checks and balances, and citizen mobilization" serves as another example.[47] On this point there appears to be some rest for the politically weary: no state-level elections were slated for 2002, which means that at least some political capital should be freed up for advancing on these crucial issues.

Conclusion

In looking at the last twenty years of Mexico's economic transformation, most analysts have focused on the liberalization effort per se, seeking to confirm their own point of view regarding the positive or negative nature of market reforms. As we have argued, the evidence here is mixed: the Mexican economy is far more dynamic than critics acknowledge; there has been much greater adjustment pain than market enthusiasts care to admit; and the future for Mexico's new president is full of challenges that will likely require him to think outside the ideological box. Having said this, we conclude by focusing instead on a different kind of cleavage that has accompanied the restructuring of the Mexican political economy: the division between policy efficacy, on the one hand, and what might be termed "policy opportunism" on the other hand.

At the macroeconomic level, policy efficacy shines due to the impressive track record in stabilizing inflation, attracting high levels of fixed investment, and the crafting of a more dynamic and competitive trade-led development model. At the microeconomic level, the same can be said for the massive restructuring that has occurred within Mexico's large and some medium-sized firms, which has contributed mightily to the shift away from commodity exports and toward the trade of much higher value-added goods. Clear gains have also been made since the mid-1990s in poverty alleviation (PROGRESA) and the more careful and aggressive targeting of social resources toward enhancing the productive potential of those most vulnerable to the whims of the market.

As indisputable as these advances are, instances of policy opportunism—that is, reforms made merely to appease constituencies and to create an aura of success for the sake of political survival—have repeatedly occurred as well. After the PRI's near loss of the presidency in 1988, PRI technocrats launched a politically motivated social safety net program (PRONASOL) and allowed the exchange rate to appreciate in order to superficially pump up consumer purchasing power. Meanwhile, Salinas privatized the country's banking system, enticing business leaders to support the PRI more strongly than ever before. The haphazard devaluation of December 1994 pulled the mask off this charade: the exchange rate was exposed as unsustainable, the resulting recession stripped away resources for any safety net, and the government was forced to launch a bank bailout that would eventually impose the costs of lenders' profligate mistakes on average citizens.

What is hopeful in the Mexican case is the increasing movement, over time, away from policy opportunism and uncompromising ideologies. Despite the pressures of the 2000 presidential election and the temptation to increase political spending, the Zedillo administration resisted excessive fiscal expansion and handed over the economy without provoking the usual fiscal or exchange rate crisis. The new administration has tended to lean heavily toward policy efficacy, keeping what worked from (and often who worked in) the previous government and directly raising uncomfortable issues like the need for new fiscal revenues. The president himself enjoys unprecedented popularity, goodwill, and, it seems, popular patience. He is likely to need it. All three of the major parties have been wrought with internal strife since the 2000 transition, and the lack of a working majority bloc in Congress is one manifestation of this political maelstrom. Because of this, much of the Fox policy agenda has either been stalled (e.g., fiscal reform) or watered down (e.g., the indigenous rights bill, privatization of the electricity and transport sectors) as it wends its way through a Congress that has ceased to be a mere rubber stamp.

Despite the obvious economic and political challenges, the analysis in this chapter suggests that Mexico's economic restructuring and political transition may now be more complementary than conflictual. Many of the economic fundamentals are sound, and nearly all political actors now concur on the need to seriously address distributional issues. It will be hard political work forging a new consensus on Mexico's future, but if it can be accomplished, the last twenty years of struggle and slow growth may eventually give way to an economy and democracy that can match the aspirations of Mexico's citizens.

Data Appendix

The data in this chapter have been gathered from many sources and include a series of estimates, particularly for the year 2000.

GDP growth is taken from the World Bank's World Development Indicators, 2001 (WDI 2001 on CD-ROM) with the 2000 figure taken from the Economic Commission on Latin America and the Caribbean (ECLAC). GNP per capita is from WDI 2001 with the 2000 figure estimated. Inflation is taken from monthly series available from the International Monetary Fund's International Financial Statistics, June 2001 (IFS 06/01). Exports, imports, trade balance, and the current account are from IFS 06/01, with the 2000 figures from the Economist Intelligence Unit (EIU). Current account as a percent of GPD is calculated using current dollar figures from WDI 2001; the 2000 estimate is from EIU. Debt and debt service numbers are from WDI 2001, with the debt as a percent of GDP derived using the dollar GDP figures; the 2000 figures are from EIU with an authors' estimate of dollar GDP for that year.

The distributional figures come from Mexico's Instituto Nacional de Estadística, Geografía, y Informática (INEGI). We relied on two CD-ROM databases: the Ingreso-Gasto de Los Hogares two-set CD that covers 1984, 1989, and 1992, and the Encuesta Nacional de Ingresos y Gastos de Los Hogares-98 that covers the 1992, 1994, 1996, and 1998 surveys. The 2000 distribution figures were downloaded from preliminary results available on the INEGI website, www.inegi.gob.mx but are less reliable than the other figures. We concentrate on monetary rather than total income; total income includes nonmonetary flows, such as imputed rent, and we have argued earlier that the characterizations are potentially too arbitrary.[48]

To calculate the changes in real monetary income, we attempted first to use the original databases, but the initial results seemed to overstate the distributional shifts because of the uncertainties of the survey approach. We chose instead to proxy the shifts by allocating the aggregate performance for real per capita income (taken from WDI 2001 and estimated for 2000) to each decile and estimating the change. The numbers for 1984–1989 for this indirect technique are remarkably similar to those obtained for the same period by Alarcon, who used the original data with corrections to square with the national accounts.[49] The difference is that we tend to estimate higher gains at the top; our estimates for deciles I–VIII are nearly identical to those of others.

The real exchange rate is calculated as the period average dollar exchange rate multiplied by the ratio of the U.S. wholesale price index to the Mexican consumer price index; a similar calculation using the Mexico wholesale price index produces roughly the same result, but the former measure has been more standard in the literature. The resulting measure is normalized at 100 for the year 1980. All data come from IFS 06/01.

Private and public investment as a share of GDP come from the International Financial Corporation (www.ifc.org) as part of Stephen Everhart and Mariusz A. Sumlinski, *Trends in Private Investment in Developing Countries: Statistics for 1970–2000* (forthcoming); the actual database can be downloaded at www.ifc.org/economics/data/dataset.htm.

The 1980–1996 figures on foreign direct and portfolio investment flows come from IFS 06/01; from 1997 on, they are from the Banco de México, with the series checked on overlap for consistency. The changing composition of Mexican exports comes from the Banco de México's balance of payments series. There is a break between December 1985 and January 1986 because of a shift in the methodology employed; the break is shown in the 1980–2001 figures; in addition, the July 1981 and June 1985 observations have been omitted from the series because they exhibit irregularities. Because of the methodology break, we begin the detailed composition breakdowns in January 1986; because that month has irregularities, as it was the first under the new system, we arbitrarily use the February 1986 data for January as well.

As for the long-term real wage in manufacturing, 1980–2000, it is assembled from data available in Edwards,[50] from ECLAC, and INEGI; care is taken to overlap these series to check for consistency when moving between one source and another. Gross per capita national income in local real and dollar terms is calculated from data in WDI 2001; the normalization is our own.

Notes

The research and writing of this chapter was supported by the John D. and Catherine T. MacArthur Foundation, the North-South Center, the U.S. Institute of Peace, the William and Flora Hewlett Foundation, and the Rockefeller Foundation's Bellagio Center.

1. Vikram Chand, *Mexico's Political Awakening* (Notre Dame, IN: University of Notre Dame Press, 2001); Daniel Levy and Kathleen Bruhn, *Mexico: The Struggle for Democratic Development* (Berkeley and Los Angeles: University of California Press, 2001); Joseph Klesner,"Electoral Competition and the New Party System in Mexico," paper presented at the Annual Meeting of the American Political Science Association, San Francisco, August 30–September 2, 2001.

2. Nora Lustig, *Mexico: The Remaking of an Economy*, 2nd ed. (Washington, D.C.: Brookings Institution, 1998), p. 5.

3. These data are drawn from the World Bank's *World Development Indicators, 2001;* see the data appendix for detailed discussions of sources for the tables, figures, and trends sited in this chapter.

4. Sebastian Edwards, "The Order of Liberalization of the External Sector in Developing Countries" (Princeton, NJ: International Finance Section, Department of Economics, Princeton University, 1984).

5. For early critiques of Mexican bravado prior to the 1994 peso crash, see Manuel Pastor, "Mexican Trade Liberalization and NAFTA," *Latin American Research Review* 29, no. 3 (1994): 153–173; and Rudiger Dornbusch and Alejandro Werner, "Mexico: Stabilization, Reform, and No Growth," Brookings Papers on Economic Activity, no. 1 (1994); for the *tecnicos*' defense of their strategy, even after it failed, see Francisco Gil Diaz and Agustin Carstens, "Pride and Prejudice: The Economics Profession and Mexico's Financial Crisis," in Sebastian Edwards and Moises Naim, eds., *Anatomy of an*

Emerging Market Crash: Mexico 1994 (Washington, D.C.: Carnegie Endowment for International Peace, 1997), pp. 165–200.

6. Elsewhere (see Manuel Pastor, "Pesos, Policies, and Predictions: Why the Crisis? Why the Surprise? Why the Recovery?" in Carol Wise, ed., *The Post-NAFTA Economy: Mexico and the Western Hemisphere* [University Park: Pennsylvania State University Press, 1998]), we have explored why the inevitable adjustment was so stubbornly postponed. Although economic factors played a role, politics and policy were also critical: in delaying the necessary currency adjustments, the Salinas administration secured the passage of NAFTA by the U.S. Congress in late 1993. By the time devaluation was a potential policy consideration, the Chiapas rebellion, the assassination of PRI presidential candidate Luis Donaldo Colosio in March 1994, and the subsequent mid-1994 presidential elections all intervened to make devaluation look like too much of a political risk.

7. Carol Wise, "Latin American Trade Strategy at Century's End," *Business and Politics* 1, no. 2 (1999): 117–153.

8. For example, see Gary Clyde Hufbauer and Jeffrey J. Schott, *NAFTA: An Assessment* (Washington, D.C.: Institute for International Economics, 1993).

9. Originally launched in 1965, Mexico's *maquila* program allows duty-free imports of capital equipment for use in manufacturing and assembly, with the stipulation that investors pay duty only on the value added within Mexico and that 80 percent of a plant's output must be exported. Leslie Sklair, *Assembling for Development: The Maquila Industry in Mexico and the United States* (La Jolla: Center for U.S.-Mexican Studies, University of California–San Diego, 1993). Once restricted to the states along the U.S.-Mexico border, foreign investors (80 percent of whom are U.S.-based) can now establish a maquila anywhere within Mexico, can own up to a 100 percent share, and can sell an increasing share of production to the local market. Hufbauer and Schott, *NAFTA: An Assessment;* Jorge Mattar, Juan Carlos Moreno-Brid, and Wilson Peres, "Foreign Investment in Mexico After Economic Reform," in Kevin Middlebrook and Eduardo Zepeda, eds., *Confronting Development: Assessing Mexico's Economic and Social Policy Challenges* (Palo Alto: Stanford University Press, 2002).

10. Some of this increase was admittedly a result of accounting pressures from the devaluation, as local GDP became worth significantly less when the peso declined. Yet the high values have persisted even as the peso again appreciated through the latter half of the 1990s (see Figure 7.2).

11. The figure shows a break in the series in 1986 because of a change in Mexico's accounting procedures.

12. Moreover, protection was not limited to domestic firms: sectors with a higher percentage of foreign direct investment enjoyed, or were attracted, by higher tariffs. Jean-Marie Grether, Jaime de Melo, and Marcelo Olarreaga, "Who Determines Mexican Trade Policy?" *Journal of Development Economics* 64, no. 2 (2001): 343–370. These once-protected sectors and the multinational firms operating within them have contributed to the evolution of manufacturing exports, for example, in auto parts.

13. Despite the prediction that NAFTA would wipe away the sector's

unique advantages, these export-processing firms have continued to draw strength from close proximity to the U.S. market and the wide gap between U.S. and Mexican wages.

14. Mattar, Moreno-Brid, and Peres, "Foreign Investment."

15. This growth began to slow in late 2000, and maquila employment actually declined steadily through April 2001, the last date for which we have data.

16. Unless otherwise noted, the data cited on the SME sector derive from Jerry Haar, "Globalization and Mexico's Small Business Sector," *North-South Center Update*, June 22, 2000. We also draw on our fieldwork interviews with SME representatives and government and development bank officials in Mexico over the past decade.

17. Celso Garrido, "Mexico's Financial System and Economic Development: Current Crisis and Future Prospects," in Middlebrook and Zepeda, eds., *Confronting Development.*

18. Enrique Dussel Peters, "Industrial Policy, Regional Trends, and Structural Change in Mexico's Manufacturing Sector," in Middlebrook and Zepeda, eds., *Confronting Development*, pp. 9–10. Smaller spin-off programs, like the National Committee for Productivity and Technological Innovation (COMPITE) and the network of the Regional Center for Business Competitiveness, have also been created to facilitate this adjustment effort. COMPITE even offers assembly line–level assistance, including the provision of subsidized consulting services from engineers. Authors' interviews, Ministry of Economy, Mexico City, March 22–23, 2001.

19. Rachel Schurman, "Chile's New Entrepreneurs and the 'Economic Miracle': Invisible Hand or a Hand from the State?" *Studies in Comparative International Development* 31, no. 2 (1996): 83–109.

20. Gladys Lopez-Acevedo and Angel Salinas, "The Distribution of Mexico's Public Spending on Education." Working Paper no. 2404, prepared for the Earnings Inequality After Mexico's Economic and Educational Reforms project of the World Bank (Washington, D.C.: World Bank, 2000); see http://econ.worldbank.org/docs/1159.pdf.

21. Li He, "Political Economy of Income Distribution: A Comparative Study of Taiwan and Mexico," *Policy Studies Journal* 28, no. 2 (2000).

22. Nora Lustig, *Mexico: The Remaking of an Economy.*

23. Denise Dresser, *Neopopulist Solutions to Neoliberal Problems: Mexico's National Solidarity Program* (La Jolla: University of California–San Diego, Center for U.S.-Mexican Studies, 1991).

24. Andrea Giovanni Cornia and Sanjay Reddy, "The Impact of Adjustment-Related Social Funds on Income Distribution and Poverty," World Institute for Development Economics Research, United Nations University, Discussion Paper no. 2001/1 (May 2001), p. 15.

25. Some high-level officials have confessed that another reason to introduce PROGRESA as a way of reaching parents, children, and schools was to bypass the Secretariat of Education, where obstructionist unions held so much sway.

26. Secretaria de Desarrollo Social (SEDESOL), *¿Está dando buenos resultados Progresa? Informe del los resultados obtenidoes de una evaluación*

realizada por el IFPRI (International Food Policy Research Institute) (Mexico City: SEDESOL, 2000).

27. According to Nora Lustig, "Life Is Not Easy: Mexico's Quest for Stability and Growth," *Journal of Economic Perspectives* 15, no. 1 (2001): 85–106, 80 percent of the families reached by PROGRESA by mid-2000 had been living in extreme poverty.

28. Ibid., p. 16.

29. Manuel Pastor and Carol Wise, "State Policy, Distribution, and Neoliberal Reform in Mexico," *Journal of Latin American Studies* 29, no. 2 (1997): 419–456.

30. Gladys Lopez-Acevedo and Angel Salinas, "How Mexico's Financial Crisis Affected Income Distribution," Working Paper no. 2406, prepared for the Earnings Inequality After Mexico's Economic and Educational Reforms project of the World Bank (Washington, D.C.: World Bank, 2000), pp. 9, 12; see http://econ.worldbank.org/docs/1161.pdf. Michael I. Cragg and Mario Epelbaum, "Why Has Wage Dispersion Grown in Mexico? Is It the Incidence of Reforms or Growing Demand for Skills?" *Journal of Development Economics* 51, no. 1 (1996): 99–117.

31. Jonathan Heath, *Mexico and the Sexenio Curse: Presidential Successions and Economic Crises in Modern Mexico* (Washington, D.C.: Center for Strategic and International Studies, 1999).

32. Jose Antonio Crespo, "Raising the Bar: The Next Generation of Electoral Reforms in Mexico," Policy Papers on the Americas (Washington, D.C.: Center for Strategic and International Studies, 2000).

33. "Fox's First Year: Still Popular," *Latin American Regional Reports*, July 10, 2001, p. 3.

34. See Tim Weiner, "Slump in U.S. Drags Mexico, and Fox's Agenda, Down," *New York Times*, August 21, 2001.

35. Gary Gereffi, "Mexico's Industrial Development: Climbing Ahead or Falling Behind in the World Economy?" in Middlebrook and Zepeda, eds., *Confronting Development*.

36. "Fox's Trade Plan to Focus on Smaller Firms," *Latin American Regional Reports*, December 12, 2000, p. 1.

37. Authors' interview with Luis de la Calle, Sub-Secretary for International Trade Negotiations, Ministry of Economy, Mexico City, March 22, 2001.

38. Authors' interview with CIPI Director, Luis Melgar, Ministry of Economy, Mexico City, March 22, 2001.

39. "Country Report: Mexico," *EIU Country Report*, April 2001, p. 17. The government also intends to offer tax incentives to encourage SME export activities outside of the maquila sector and to more vigorously enforce antitrust policies already on the books, but it remains to be seen whether these goals will be pursued in the event that the Congress remains difficult to traverse.

40. Authors' interview with Ignacio Chavez, Office of Health, Education, and Labor, Ministry of Finance ("Hacienda"), Mexico City, March 23, 2001.

41. For example, according to one public official, only 27 percent of Mexicans are part of the formal banking system.

42. Vicente Arredondo, National Coordinator of PROGRESA, has indicated that he hopes to start with smaller cities—the justification is logistics but the

pattern could also benefit the PAN politically. Authors' interview, Mexico City, March 22, 2001.

43. Santiago Levy, "Reorienting Mexico's Social Policy," in Andrew Selee, ed., *Mexico in Transition,* Woodrow Wilson Center Reports on the Americas no. 1 (Washington, D.C.: Woodrow Wilson Center Press, 2001).

44. "Budget Sent to Congress," *Latin American, Mexico, and NAFTA Report*, December 12, 2000, pp. 6–7.

45. To ensure that increases in education and other social spending actually translate into improved outcomes, there is also a need to improve administrative capacity. In the words of one public official, under Zedillo "you pitched and there was no catcher"—that is, at a local level, the capacity to absorb spending and use it productively has been limited. Partly as a result, SEDESOL has been putting more funds and energy into capacity-building.

46. This section draws on various issues of "Country Report: Mexico," *EIU Country Report*, July 2000 to July 2001.

47. Crespo, "Raising the Bar," p. 27.

48. Pastor and Wise, "State Policy."

49. Diana Alarcón, *Income Distribution and Poverty Alleviation in Mexico from a Comparative Perspective* (Palo Alto: Stanford University Press, 2003).

50. Sebastian Edwards, *Crisis and Reform in Latin America: From Despair to Hope* (Oxford, U.K.: Oxford University Press, 1995).

8

NAFTA and the WTO in the Transformation of Mexico's Economic System

Stephen Clarkson

In years past, one standard way to dichotomize the causes of economic or political change was to distinguish forces that worked from above—typically elite-driven measures—from pressures that came from below—which characteristically took the form of social movements or revolutionary uprisings. In more normal processes of incremental change, the two directions of transformatory pressure would often combine when, for instance, political parties included in their programs leader-inspired initiatives as well as member-voiced demands.

New forms of global governance now require us to add a horizontal dimension to this vertical image of change.[1] Given the intrusive role played by continental institutions such as the European Union and the unprecedented authoritative powers invested in the globally mandated World Trade Organization (WTO), we now need to distinguish between change from without and change from within the political economy. Of course, any Latin Americanist worth her salt will immediately point out that change from without is not new: every state south of the Rio Grande has experienced the heavy hand of Uncle Sam requiring that its political system make changes, often at the barrel of a gun.

The policy framework for guiding the Mexican economy provides a fascinating example of pressure for change from within acting in parallel with pressure for change from without, as a neoliberal domestic program to cut back the state's entrepreneurial role (instigated by the PRI) and a trade liberalization agreement at the continental and global levels (in the form of the North Aemrican Free Trade Agreement [NAFTA] and the WTO) were signed almost simultaneously. (The fact that the internal forces of change in Mexico were manifestly driven not from below but from above is for our purposes largely irrelevant.)

The aim of this chapter is not to offer a mechanistic exercise in identifying which cause led to what effect. Rather, it is to provide some greater analytical clarity to a debate that has become muddied by the quite understandable emotions dramatically voiced on the streets of Seattle in late 1999. Demonstrators against the WTO were expressing the view—from below—that a malevolent, corporation-led globalization was causing damage to the social, environmental, and human fabric of their national or community lives. There can be little dispute that the WTO and NAFTA are decidedly more powerful new legal orders that reach deep inside their members' societies to effect important changes in national systems of law and regulation. There can be legitimate disagreement about what exactly this impact has been on member states and how significant it is.

Introduction: Why Mexico Interests Non-Mexicans

Mexicans may not have been much in evidence during the battle of Seattle, but Mexico's role in the development of a new trade order over the past decade has provided a dramatic case study of how countries are being changed by trade liberalization.

- Some have argued that the adhesion of Mexico, as a third world economy, to NAFTA, as a first world trade bloc, played a pioneering role and paved the way for other countries of the South to rally behind the new WTO.[2] It provided a demonstration effect, showing it was possible for less developed countries to deregulate their systems, renounce import substitution strategies, and play by rules that were "made in the U.S.A."
- One of the political economies most closed to foreign trade and investment, Mexico transformed itself over a short decade into one of the most open.
- A country whose legal system is based on the European civil code is engaging in a process of deep integration with two states whose legal orders at the federal level derive from the common law tradition.
- A state whose political economy was run on dirigiste lines with an import substitution economic development strategy has

become one of the hemisphere's most radically neoliberal governments with an export promotion philosophy.
- Beyond simply attracting globe-watchers, Mexico's relationships with its continental partners attract comparativists for other reasons as well.
- Students of North American integration will find that Mexico's participation with Canada in forming a continental free trade area provides material for comparing how the two U.S. neighbors relate to their continental hegemon, which happens also to be the global hegemon.
- Students of comparative continentalism can compare Mexico's experience in joining NAFTA by having to accept the basic principles and processes enshrined in the Canada–United States Free Trade Agreement (CUFTA) with countries in Central and Eastern Europe that are proposing to join the European Union by internalizing in their legal systems the thousands of provisions of its *acquis communautaire* (community accession).
- Students of global governance can find Mexico's experiences help them understand better the dynamic process through which participation in external trade regimes at the continental and global levels affects countries' internally driven processes of deregulation.

This chapter proposes to address this last issue by looking at the most radical and surgical example of change (the implant of a domestic trade law system into Mexico) and by reviewing some of the other changes brought about by the mix of global opening and internal restructuring that has characterized the Mexican experiment. Before launching into the analysis, we need to provide a conceptual framework that will allow us to encompass this material.

NAFTA's and the WTO's Relationship to Mexico's Political Order

If it is true that states need markets and that markets also need states, then we cannot analyze Mexico's economic system without comprehending its political context. To analyze the impact of globalization on the Mexican political system, it will help to distinguish among five of the basic component notions of a political order: constitutional, legal, administrative, judicial, and coercive.

A constitutional order frames the basic principles establishing the institutions that a political system needs to function. These are typically:

1. an executive whose personnel provide leadership and decision-making;
2. a legislative capacity, that is, the ability to make new laws and amend old ones;
3. an administrative order to apply these rules by decree and regulation;
4. a judicial system that interprets these rules, generally when conflict arising from differing claims based on them needs to be resolved; and
5. a coercive capacity to enforce the law and maintain order in society.

In establishing the executive, legislative, administrative, judicial, and coercive institutions that a particular system needs if it is to cope with change, a constitution both invests them with powers and sets limits to these powers. Constitutions can be amended, but only according to specific conditions, which are typically much more difficult to achieve than simply passing a law. Normatively, a constitution may articulate general principles that are considered inviolate by the community and beyond the power of the legislature or the judiciary to nullify. It generally establishes specific rights for its members.

In popular discourse a constitution and its component elements are thought of in hermetic and permanent terms. Because the nation-state is sovereign, it follows in common-sense thinking that constitutions are self-contained constructs only amendable from within by processes that are themselves defined in a country's founding law. But such a view is too historically simplistic. Constitutionally defined states are a phenomenon only of the last 250 years. Far from being hermetic, they were written as part of an international, if not at first global, process in which, for example, the founders of the United States relied heavily on political theories generated in Europe and those of Mexico borrowed openly from the text of the U.S. Constitution.[3]

Even in the world of nations as we have known it in recent decades, there is an interaction between the legal order of one country and the outside world. When a state signs international treaties, it typically commits itself to internalizing their norms within its legal order. When it joins international organizations, it commits itself to certain obligations that constrain its autonomy in exchange for the advantages accrued from membership in them. Admittedly, signatory states do not always act in conformity to the conventions they have signed, whether they guarantee rights to children or promise specific reductions of polluting activities. (But then the practice of sovereign states does not always correspond to the text of their constitutions, either. The Soviet Union offers a dramatic, if distant, example. Closer to home, the living conditions of native peoples on many Canadian reserves have been censured as a violation of the United Nations [UN] Declaration of Human Rights; sweatshop workers and farmworkers have been famously abused in the United States; and the violation of the right to organize in many *maquiladoras* has little apparent connection with the labor rights guaranteed by the lofty prose of the Mexican constitution.)

NAFTA and the WTO are different from previous international agreements because of the breadth and intrusiveness of the signatories' commitments, which cover many areas of public policy and penetrate deep into the member states' legal and even administrative orders. They also innovate in the authoritative quality of judicial processes that discipline, with unprecedented effectiveness, member states that are judged to have broken the new rules.

NAFTA and the WTO have three kinds of impact on national members: direct, contingent, and supranational.

1. *Direct.* For Mexico, whose constitution (article 133) establishes that any properly negotiated and signed international treaty becomes part of the "supreme law" of the land, much of the NAFTA and the WTO provisions have direct effect. This means that if any Mexican law contradicts a NAFTA or WTO obligation, it is invalid. In practice, many Mexican laws may still run counter to the sense of its international treaty obligations. The dissonance between the international and the national can be resolved preemptively by statute and regulation or, subsequently, by judgment when some conflict between members of civil society is brought before judges, who must then reconcile national law with international obligations.

2. *Contingent.* Some of the NAFTA and WTO rules have a contingent effect. Much of the turmoil in member states during the initial phase of membership in these new continental and global regimes has been caused by the need to give specific meaning to ambiguously phrased rules. They define practices—such as the criteria stipulating what subsidies are acceptable—that a country may not knowingly be disobeying until some foreign complainant starts an intergovernmental

dispute process and a ruling is made through the appropriate multilateral dispute mechanism about the validity of that practice.

3. *Supranational.* As regimes with their own institutional structures, NAFTA and the WTO can also generate new rules that affect their members. Generally such new norms are negotiated intergovernmentally, which makes them the equivalent of amendments to the original treaties. But in some cases these institutions may actually create new norms through their own internal functioning. This happens, for instance, when a working group established by NAFTA issues some common standard for cross-border transport of dangerous chemicals that the three members have agreed in advance to accept or when the WTO's council or executive makes an "interpretation" that clarifies some hitherto ambiguous wording in the treaty. In this respect, then, Mexico's membership in NAFTA and the WTO can be considered to be participation in two external constitutional orders.

There is another way in which NAFTA and the WTO constitute external constitutions of loose confederations at the continental and global levels. NAFTA and the WTO enable their member states to exercise powers over their fellow signatories within these continental and global orders. NAFTA contains rules that bind not only Mexico but also the United States and Canada. Mexico can use these rules to enforce its rights in the United States and Canada (e.g., to sell its broomcorn brooms in those markets at specified tariff rates or to have its trucks deliver loads of Mexican goods to Florida). Whether these rights are respected by Mexico's partner states is an open question. If they are violated, NAFTA's juridical order gives Mexico a means for enforcing its rights on the nonconforming partner state. Similarly, the WTO's rules bind not only Mexico but also each of the other signatory states (144 as of 2002). So when Mexico thinks that the actions of some WTO member are violating its rights (e.g., when Guatemala imposes antidumping duties on cement imported from Mexico), it can launch an action against Guatemala to the WTO's dispute settlement body. If its case is sound, it is likely to win (as the panel did in fact rule in this example). But if its legal homework had been poorly executed, it can also lose the case (as the appellate body ultimately decided when Guatemala appealed the panel's ruling).

In discussing the relationships between NAFTA and the WTO, on the one hand, and Mexico's constitutional, legal, judicial, and administrative orders, on the other hand, there are two additional sets of issues to bear in mind: one pertaining to the country's political culture, the other relating to its geopolitical context.

Political Culture

Mexicans have had a conflicted historical relationship with their constitution that has been an instrument both of revolutionary emancipation from foreign control and political repression by national autocrats. As a result, it enjoys an ambivalent legitimacy. In some respects, such as the nationalization of the petroleum industry, its provisions are virtually sacrosanct. In other respects, the ease with which the ruling PRI was once able to make constitutional changes because of its command of the necessary two-thirds majorities in both houses of the federal Congress turned constitutional amendments into actions with little more significance than enacting new legislation. In addition, the frequency of constitutional amendments detracts from their supralegislative gravitas. Changing the constitution in order to nationalize the banks one year (in response to the 1982 crisis brought on by the devastating combination of falling commodity prices, rising interest rates, and high levels of external debt, the state under President José López Portillo took over almost the entire banking system) and changing it back in order to privatize them less than a decade later (as part of a general program of economic liberalization, put into process by President Carlos Salinas de Gortari in 1990) only served to undermine the overall legitimacy of the document itself.[4]

Geopolitical Vulnerability

A state's political order also needs to be understood within its geopolitical context. Its permeability (or, conversely, its ability to resist change) in the face of external pressures is related to three factors: the country's overall strength in the global balance of forces; the degree of its integration in the international system; and the distance separating the values that it expresses from those of the international community.

Mexico, being a midsized power with a weak economy, can be considered much more permeable to outside influence than, say, China. When it was a closed system, it was impermeable even to U.S. pressure to change, but as soon as it broke out of legal isolation it became vulnerable to influence.

Once Mexico opened itself to normative intercourse with international and continental players, then the large gap between the values embedded in its political order and those of the global community made them subject to massive change. Having been rigid for decades, the Mexican political order became flexible, if not completely pliable. At least this is the story of Mexico's adoption of an international trade-law regime, to which we will now turn.

Implanting International Trade Law

In reflecting on how Mexico came to adopt international practices in the arcane field of antidumping and countervailing duties, we need to remember that this was a specific case of a general problem: the country's breaking free from a decades-old stance of legal autarchy.

"For over half a century, Mexico's absolute territorialism led to the virtual exclusion of foreign law from that country's court system"; between 1932 and 1988, when it was isolated from the practice of private international law, "no foreign judgments were enforced in Mexico."[5] This was understandable, for the government had signed none of the relevant international agreements, whether that of Montevideo in 1889, of Bustamente in 1928, or any of the Hague conventions. As a result, Mexican courts applied only Mexican law to foreigners, whether tourists or corporate investors.

It was only in 1971 that Mexico adhered to the 1958 UN Convention on the Recognition and Enforcement of Foreign Arbitral Awards. Then in 1975 it adopted six Inter-American Conventions.

These steps were only a beginning. We need to remember that just because the constitution declares international norms to be the supreme law of the land does not make them necessarily part of the judicial order. However good their quality, Mexican judges at the federal level (and the legal practitioners who interacted with them) were unfamiliar with these conventions and with the notion of applying foreign law in Mexico. As for the quality of judicial practice at the state level, it seems that the less said the better.

In the particular domain of trade law, Mexico had not needed any. Foreign trade was completely managed through a burdensome and mysterious system of import licenses, official prices, and export subsidies administered case by case at the discretion of bureaucrats who were subject to corporate pressure, political influence, and, of course, corruption.[6] The system was highly protectionist and had no need for a trade remedy system that could impose antidumping or countervailing duties on unfairly priced or subsidized imports. It suffered from no foreign import competition and ipso facto no unfair trade practices.

The political economy context for this absence of trade law was thirty years of successful experience with import substitution industrialization (ISI) that delivered industrial development at a 6.5 percent rate of growth with low inflation. Although inefficiencies resulting from hyperprotection caused concern in some quarters, there was no recognition until 1976 of the need to develop exports. When the new Commission on Tariffs and Controls on Foreign Trade was established and the idea of joining the General Agreement on Tariffs and Trade (GATT) led to preliminary negotiations in 1979, many nationalist sensibilities were so shocked that this gesture toward international opening became a hot political issue.

As for relations with the United States, the Reciprocal Trade Agreements Program of 1942 had lapsed in 1950. It was not until 1981 that a first and inconsequential formal agreement, the Joint Trade Commission on Trade and Commerce, was established.[7] Even with the devastating crisis of 1982 raising doubts about the viability of Mexico's industrial development model and putting liberalization on the policy agenda, resistance to abandoning state dirigisme was considerable. The Ministry of Commerce's National Program of Industrial Promotion and Foreign Trade—which proposed liberalizing as little as possible—expressed the private sector's unwillingness to liberalize and bureaucrats' reluctance to give up their power. Once President Miguel de la Madrid insisted in 1985 that liberalization was to be the government's official policy and Mexico engaged in a sweeping program of economic modernization, structural adjustment, and linkage with the world economy through trade, foreign investment, and the transfer of technology, something analogous to a political avalanche took place, with changes throughout the system sweeping old obstacles into oblivion and putting official prices, import permits, and foreign investment limits on the endangered species list.[8]

In November 1985, the president instructed the secretary of commerce to resume negotiations with GATT, and by August of the following year Mexico officially joined the international trade order. This first step was far from bold, but the timid beginning indicated a direction of change. Mexico eliminated official prices but limited its participation in tariff liberalization to 373 out of 8,143 import categories affecting some 16 percent of its imports. It bound its maximum tariff to 50 percent, down from 100 percent. These concessions mostly affected intermediate goods not made in Mexico and excluded the key sectors of agriculture, automobile, electronics, and pharmaceutical products, where performance requirements were imposed in the spirit of the still functioning ISI model. The idea at the Ministry of Commerce was to minimize commitments in light of the forthcoming Uruguay Round, but the landslide, having begun, proved hard to stop.[9] In December 1987, import liberalization was accelerated: a total of 7,500 (90 percent) import categories were fully liberalized, with a maximum tariff of 20 percent and an average rate of 16 percent.[10]

In this period, with trade conflicts rising on the U.S. border, a pattern was established in which change at the multilateral level alternated contrapuntally with change at the bilateral level. With a devalued peso stimulating Mexican exports, U.S. protectionist actions against these products caused Mexico to sign the Bilateral Understanding on Subsidies and Countervailing Duties with Washington in April 1985. Mexico obtained the benefit that proof of injury would be required for U.S. producers threatening Mexican exports, but membership in GATT had eliminated neither peak import tariffs in Mexico's main U.S. market nor protectionist measures against Mexican exports.[11] The trading arrangement between the two countries amounted simply to the exclusion of the in-bond zone from either country's trade barriers, making the maquiladoras a miniature legal order created by intergovernmental agreement. Trade authorities at the Mexican Ministry of Commerce and Industrial Development (SECOFI) knew they would have to make more changes but delayed acting as a strategic decision to get reciprocal concessions from the United States when it came to the next round of real negotiations.[12] The 1985 understanding was followed by the Framework Agreement on Trade and Investment negotiated with Washington in 1987, which was succeeded by the Mexico-U.S. Understanding Regarding Trade and Investment Facilitation Talks in 1989.[13]

These initial exchanges of concessions in each other's system were the precursor of the ultimate adoption in the wake of the negotiation of both NAFTA and the WTO of a complete antidumping and countervailing duty regime that was to accompany a broad new set of investor rights.

Mexico was still a trade-law virgin in 1986 when it introduced its first antidumping and countervailing duty law two months before signing on to the GATT. The Foreign Trade Act (implementing article 131 of the constitution) was relatively rudimentary and unsophisticated, with just two articles constituting the legal framework for subsidies.[14] This law was elaborated in November 1986 under the Regulations Governing Unfair International Trade. A year and a half later the antidumping regulatory framework was expanded as a consequence of Mexico signing the Agreement in Implementation of Article VI of GATT, the antidumping code from the Tokyo Round. (Mexico still did-n't sign the GATT subsidies code because of its own substantial subsidy system.)

Observers can only note wryly that the wholesale adoption by Mexico of an aggressive trade protectionist system violated not only the spirit of a free trade area but also the neoliberal principle underlying it, namely, the need for markets to be allowed to favor the highest possible levels of competition in the interest of getting for the consumers the lowest possible priced goods. The greatest change in Mexico's legal system was the adoption of the most retrograde aspect of the so-called advanced countries' legal order, which constitutes a costly barrier to entry encouraging collusive activity and perversely stopping competition by price.[15] "I rue the day," regrets one practitioner, "that Mexico finds itself having to adopt U.S. antidumping laws as the benchmark for its competition policy . . . since antidumping is a non-tariff barrier in the grossest form."[16]

The paradoxes of antidumping continued in that NAFTA—in order to scotch any possibility that a supranational trade order might develop on the European model—had left the bulk of dispute settlement to ensuring the three member states properly implemented their own trade remedy laws. Because Mexico did not have laws on antidumping or countervailing duties, it agreed to import a complete legal microstructure—and on the Canadian-U.S. common law model—in order for it then to be enforced. In creating its new trade regime, Mexico also had to respond to the virtually simultaneous agreements incorporated in the WTO.

The constitutional framework for the NAFTA-mandated antidumping regime was article 28 of the constitution concerning subsidies,[17] article 73.X giving Congress authority to legislate on commercial matters, and article 131 empowering the executive to negotiate tariffs.[18] These articles were not changed.

The legal order, however, had to be adjusted. The 1993 Foreign Trade Law (FTL) made amendments to articles 60 and 68 of the FTL concerning administrative procedures and articles 97 and 98 concerning file determinations.[19] These were legislated to implement NAFTA alongside the NAFTA Implementing Decree.[20] From January 1995, the GATT subsidies code of 1994, article 1, was part of Mexican law and was far more precise than the Foreign Trade Law article 37 that in consequence had to be amended. Introducing an antidumping and countervailing duty regime involved changing more than one law. Statutes considered to be part of the antidumping and countervailing duty legal framework are the Law of Amparo, the Federal Judicial Power Organic

Law, the Federal Tax Code, the Income Tax Act, the Customs Act, and the Federal Public Administration Organic Law.

Farther down the political scale, the administrative order had to be adjusted. FTL regulations were promulgated, as was a SECOFI bylaw of April 1993 concerning access to information and participation in dispute settlement.[21]

The process of adjusting its law to NAFTA's and the WTO's norms subjected Mexico to surveillance from both bodies. "When Mexico adhered to the Antidumping Code, this issue, as well as others, was subject to scrutiny by the GATT Committee on Antidumping Practices, as it reviewed the compatibility of Mexican unfair trade law with GATT and its code. After two years of analysis, in April 1990, the committee determined that Mexico's statutes did not require amendment."[22]

Whereas only importers at first had the right to judicial appeal, as a consequence of NAFTA the right to appeal or challenge a trade determination was extended to all of the interested parties in an antidumping or countervailing duty proceeding.[23] However, whatever passing grade Mexican trade law may have received from its GATT review, it was considered inadequate by Canadian and U.S. trade negotiators when NAFTA's rules were being written. "Mexico was obligated to make significant, substantive revisions to its antidumping laws and regulations in order to implement the binational process."[24] Twenty-one changes to Mexico's administrative procedure were specified in NAFTA's text.

These changes introduced due process provisions so that interested parties could participate fully in all stages of investigations. Worth noting especially were the requirements for the publication of the administrative and final determinations and for the investigating authority to maintain an administrative record that would constitute the basis for its final determination—two concepts foreign to the Mexican legal system.[25] Twenty of the twenty-one stipulated changes were made, the one exception considered to be in conflict with Mexico's constitutional order.[26]

Importing the antidumping and countervailing duty regime into Mexico caused changes to be made in its legal, judicial, and administrative orders without changing its constitutional order. In confirmation of this, a Mexican Senate report concluded that NAFTA was congruent with the Mexican constitution. Indeed, "When drafting Chapter 19, the Mexican negotiators were particularly careful in observing strict compliance with the individual guarantees and rights established in the constitution."[27] For their part, Canada and the United States were concerned that the Mexican appeal system based on the notion of *amparo* (injunction) might interfere with the trade panel process and insisted that a new mechanism safeguard the panel review system from this;[28] but as Beatriz Leycegui points out, no signatory can guarantee that its courts will not challenge a trade agreement's constitutionality.

As a result of the combined influence of the continental and multilateral negotiations, there is a high level of harmonization among the three continental partners. "Because the U.S. and Canadian laws have also adopted the GATT terminology and methodology, the concept of export price and the methods for calculating it in the three NAFTA countries are analogous."[29] Similarly, the definition of price discrimination in FTL article 30 is consistent with GATT's antidumping code article 2. Article 31 (the three methods of calculating the normal value of merchandise from market economies) is "in congruence with international practice and particularly U.S. practice."[30]

Because Canadian and U.S. law also incorporate GATT rules, the result is a Mexican legal and administrative order for antidumping and countervailing duties that is very similar in terms of the period subject to investigation, the economic factors considered, causal relations between injury and imports, the determination of injury provisions (Antidumping Code article 3, Subsidies Code article 15), and the definition of domestic industry (Antidumping Code article 4, Subsidies Code article 16). Conformity reaches down to the very questionnaires used by SECOFI that are similar to those used in the U.S. system.[31]

Mexico could not introduce a new administrative order in a vacuum. Its regulatory framework for administrative procedures being both dispersed and incoherent with every administrative law having its own procedures, it had to reform its administrative procedure system, bringing in the Federal Act of Administrative Procedures in 1994.[32] As the process of regulatory reform continued, additional changes were introduced to broaden its scope. On March 23, 2000, the Mexican Senate passed amendments to this law in response to "four main concerns: to increase transparency in the drafting of regulations by the executive branch; promote public participation in the regulatory process; provide citizens' legal certainty regarding the enforcement of procedures and regulatory requirements; and ensure that the benefits resulting from new regulations outweigh their costs."[33]

From Theory to Practice: The Actual Experience of Mexico's Trade Remedy Law

A trade remedy system exists primarily to give national producers protection against what is deemed unfair foreign competition in their own market. As defined by the WTO and NAFTA agreements, Mexico's regime was made as transparent and predictable as its partners had demanded. It was also made liable to binational appeal through NAFTA chapter 19's dispute settlement process that had been designed not to be a supranational judicial order in any way similar to the European Court of Justice. On the contrary, the rules spelled out in chapter 19 simply allowed private parties—typically a company or industry whose exports had been targeted with antidumping or countervailing duties—to trigger an appeal process. This took the form of a binational panel whose mandate was to review whether the final determination made by SECOFI had properly followed the prescriptions of Mexican law. In effect, while Mexico's new antidumping and countervailing duty regime gave it a defense against unfairly competing U.S. or Canadian exports, chapter 19 gave the U.S. or Canadian exporters a counteroffensive tool with which to call into question the validity of any such defensive action they believed had been invalidly taken.

The best example so far of successful U.S. exploitation of this right is the Cut to Length Steel Plate case that caused considerable upset in the Mexican legal community.[34] The NAFTA panel remanded SECOFI's final determination, declaring it illegal and null because several officers conducting the investigation lacked jurisdiction, thus violating article 238.1 of the Federal Tax Code (Código fiscal de la federación [CFF]). According to the CFF article 238, one of the standards for review by the Federal Taxation Court (FTC) is the competence of the officials concerned. SECOFI challenged the panel's view of its own competence, arguing that it only had powers under NAFTA 1904(8) to remand a decision for reconsideration. Two of the three panels argued, however, that NAFTA gave them the same jurisdiction as the FTC, the court that they were replacing, which had the power to review administrative agency determinations.[35]

The legal uproar raised by the debate over a NAFTA panel's competence over Cut to Length Steel Plate, which was seen as an application of U.S. concepts to Mexican judicial proceedings, was mitigated somewhat by a parallel panel investigating the antidumping duty imposed on U.S. flat-coated steel products.[36] In this case the panel considered itself an arbitrator whose jurisdiction was limited by NAFTA and Mexican law. In short its authority was not the same as the court it replaced. It did not believe it had jurisdiction to declare a challenged determination null. Although it considered that one SECOFI official was without jurisdiction and therefore his actions were illegal, and although it ordered changes in the determination concerning one of the complainants, it upheld SECOFI's final decision.[37]

In a third early case, Polystyrene and Impact Crystal, there was another controversy over the extent of the panel's jurisdiction to consider whether SECOFI had exceeded its own jurisdiction.[38] Ultimately, the panel deferred to SECOFI, and the political issue raised by this problem abated. (Unlike the United States but like Canada, the same agency carries out the investigation into dumping and determines the injury. Some question the legitimacy of SECOFI acting in both capacities, claiming that this creates distortions in the process.)

Trade law is not simply a matter of defending home markets. It can also be a strategic tool to gain access to a competitor's market. In the case of the Mexican antidumping duties imposed on U.S. apple exports, the nature of the solution—a suspension agreement that established a reference price for U.S. apples in the Mexican market in exchange for U.S. Department of Agriculture removal of barriers to Chihuahua apples entering the U.S. market—suggests that the original antidumping action had an element of strategic arm wrestling about it.[39]

Once one understands that NAFTA is more about "managed" than about "free" trade, then chapter 19 dispute settlement can be seen as another tool available to exporting producers, competing national producers, and their respective governments in a continual quest to improve their relative positions. The long and complex case of High Fructose Corn Syrup is an exemplar of this reality. If the Mexican government's objective was to increase its sugar exporters' share of the U.S. market, then its antidumping determination against U.S. exports of high fructose corn syrup was a pawn in the strategy. When the United States called for a chapter 19 panel to review SECOFI's final determination, Mexico showed how it had learned from the master to play the new trade game by exploiting its right to appoint the fifth panelist to the panel and then delaying that appointment. Not surprisingly, the United States responded to this stalling tactic by showing off its mastery of trade dispute strategy. It managed to launch not only a NAFTA chapter 19 appeal against Mexico's antidumping duties but also a panel at the WTO as well, thereby aiming to reduce Mexico's leverage in stalling the original case. As Luis de la Calle made clear, Mexico preferred a settlement to a continuing confrontation, although the Mexican government was itself under pressure from sugar workers to launch a chapter 19 action against U.S. restrictions on Mexican sugar exports.[40] Unfortunately, since much of the dispute revolved around private letters exchanged between the NAFTA negotiators, Mickey Kantor and Jaime Serra Puche, it is not possible for the public to know what legal case Mexico had to stand on.

In an antidumping duty applied to Mexican tomato exports following a surge of produce in the wake of the peso devaluation, the United States applied a 201 safeguard duty under GATT article XIX. Intergovernmental negotiations produced a so-called suspension agreement in October 1996 that bound Mexican growers to sell their produce at a predetermined price in the U.S. market.[41]

However true it may have been that Mexico had "quite a lot to learn from Canada and the United States and other countries about how to defend itself in foreign trade related matters," it has been a fast learner.[42] Mexico is now the second most active user of antidumping in the world after the United States.[43] In the related field of food standards, it followed a U.S. announcement that three Mexican food-processing plants were in violation of U.S. food safety regulations by disqualifying seventeen U.S. plants from shipping meat and poultry to Mexico (no matter that none of the Mexican inspectors who inspected the U.S. plants spoke English).[44] This tit for tat was not just giving the message that Mexico can play hardball too; it demonstrated how quickly Mexico had internalized the U.S. political culture of trade war.

NAFTA chapter 11 gives NAFTA-area corporations an extremely broad right to challenge a government ruling that "expropriates" its assets and to submit the case to binding international arbitration. This innovation adds a significant option to Mexico's judicial order, for it gives corporations based in Canada and the United States the right to challenge a Mexican government regulation jeopardizing their profits.[45] In the first of the three chapter 11 cases brought against Mexico, its victory in the Desona case suggests that NAFTA, in the words of the panel decision, will not "allow investors to seek international arbitration for mere contractual breaches. Indeed NAFTA cannot possibly be read to create such a regime which would have elevated a multitude of ordinary transactions with public authorities into potential international disputes."[46]

Americanization

In assessing its significance for the Mexican political order, it was intuitively persuasive to argue that chapter 19's panel process would "be an instrument for change in the Mexican legal framework regarding countervail and antidumping legislation and procedure since . . . this aspect of Mexican law will now be subject to scrutiny by the international panels." NAFTA's dispute mechanism would "aid domestic reformers to accomplish their goal of making the Mexican legal process more transparent and comparable in certainty to the Canadian and U.S. systems."[47] Support for this hypothesis is rooted in the fact that Mexico had no such system and that the new one it installed was essentially "made in the U.S.A." Prior to NAFTA, it had virtually no experience in international trade disputes, whether binational panels or international arbitration panels.[48] As a result, very few law firms had experience or even professional expertise in this field. Law faculties offered no courses in antidumping, international trade, conflict of law, or enforcement of foreign judgments. Mexico began "to be inspired by U.S. statutes in these areas and, as a result there is an Americanization of Mexican law."[49] Even the fact that this gap is being filled by cram courses and seminars now being offered at UNAM and SECOFI to bring lawyers, students, and judges up to speed on trade law supports the Americanization thesis.[50]

Two factors caution us to qualify the argument. First, chapter 19 has been a considerable disappointment. It has not provided definitive and noncontroversial solutions. Solutions have not been particularly expeditious, although the number of days to reach a decision has fallen from 1,362 to 435. It has turned out to be very expensive and not a deterrent to initiating trade remedy actions. It has created neither certainty nor predictability as far as exporters' access to other NAFTA markets is concerned. And it is itself the cause of further intergovernmental tensions.[51] Hence, it may suffer a loss of institutional momentum in relation to other dispute settlement venues.

There has been great difficulty in establishing a consensus about the panels' status and scope. It has proved difficult to find qualified panelists, several of whom have had to withdraw because of alleged conflicts of interest, thereby slowing the process. There is even disagreement about the profile of a proper panelist, the United States preferring judges who are likely to defer to U.S. trade agency rulings. Canada and Mexico prefer trade experts who will be more rigorous in applying domestic law and more zealous in overturning what are often highly politicized decisions in the United States. Language differences have caused important problems, and not only in slowing down proceedings by requiring translation of documents and interpretation during meetings. More fundamentally, differences between English and Spanish languages express profound differences between the two systems.

Second, although NAFTA negotiators tried to ensure that Mexico's antidumping and countervailing duties law and practice would follow common law standards and so be removed from the Mexican judicial order, chapter 19 panels are mandated nevertheless to act as would a Mexican court of appeal. The rub is that a Mexican court would necessarily operate according to the tenets of Mexican legal culture that in many respects are different and in some cases unique. For instance:

- Mexico's civil justice system limits the damages that can be recovered. The United States allows unlimited damages, including punitive damages.
- In Mexico, the parties in a case do not serve each other; it is the duty of the court to give notice.
- An injunction is not available in Mexico where damages are irreparable; in the United States it is the preferred remedy.
- Mexican civil law uses an inquisitorial procedure as opposed to the adversarial procedure of U.S. common law.
- In Mexico, trial evidence is presented as documentation in front of judges who themselves question witnesses.[52]
- Hearings are held only to resolve questions of evidence; judges may make decisions about evidence without questioning the parties.[53]
- In Mexico, the jury does not play a part in adjudicating civil disputes; in the United States, the jury is integral to the adjudication process.
- Mexico allows civil disputes to invoke criminal sanctions.
- Mexican legal practice is not specialized—completely different from the elaborate division of labor in the U.S. legal profession.[54]
- In the Mexican tradition, articles of law are interpreted in relation to the entire jurisprudence.
- Mexico does not have the concept of administrative practices; it relies on legislative histories.[55]
- A judicial precedent is much more difficult to establish; for this to happen, the Mexican Supreme Court has to decide the same point in five consecutive separate cases.[56]
- Two basic principles of Mexican law—*motivación* from article 14 of the constitution, and *fundamendación* from article 16—have no meaning to common law practitioners.
- The law of amparo has a similar stature to habeas corpus in the common law. It is the instrument to provide remedy against the

> final decision of all judges, all laws, and even administrative authorities.[57] Although NAFTA 1905 was written to safeguard against the use of amparo and NAFTA 1904:11 was meant to preclude judicial review of panel decisions, Mexicans—as Americans—are unlikely to accept that their right to appeal has been abrogated.[58]

In the words of one practitioner, "We are a different civil system, we have a different set of laws, and we think differently."[59]

Given these substantial differences among the NAFTA countries' legal systems and judicial orders, it remains unclear what the long-term impact in adopting antidumping and countervailing duty laws and procedures will be, whether at Mexico's national level or the continental level of NAFTA's judicial development. The four chief possibilities would seem to be:

1. A complete Americanization of those aspects of Mexican law that deal with NAFTA's trade tensions might result. This would imply a final severing of the links between trade law and the rest of the Mexican legal order and so the development of a dual judicial order.
2. At the other extreme, there could be a Mexicanization of antidumping and countervailing duty practice, a kind of Montezuma's revenge in which the foreign system is integrated into the fabric of national judicial practice.
3. Somewhere in between there could be the development of an arbitration culture separate from the national along the trail already blazed by chapter 11. Resort to mediation, arbitration, and such bodies as the International Convention on the Settlement of Investor Disputes (ICSID) could help the integrated business culture of North America develop its own trade law, which could lead to another possible outcome: the development of a continental judicial order.
4. Parties to binational panels in Mexico have already cited cases from U.S. antidumping history.[60] "Although NAFTA was set up to prevent such a development, there are panels citing other panel decisions to some of the decisions or determinations that they make. Some panels are already indicating that they are relying on the reasoning or determinations that were made by prior panel. From that perspective it could be said that we can see the beginning of a NAFTA jurisprudence."[61] Such cross-citing is

> normal for the common law's legal culture. In the Mexico antidumping case against Guatemala, the WTO panel even cited the reasoning of the CUFTA softwood lumber case.

There are persistent problems in finding qualified panelists, as indicated by NAFTA member states' failure to create the thirty-person permanent roster as required by NAFTA. Resultant pressure from within the legal community to establish a NAFTA tribunal would considerably move forward the development of a continental legal order. A more powerful stimulus to constructing a continental legal order would be formally to grant panel decisions the precedent-forming power that they are now adopting informally. With *stare decisis,* panel precedents would become a matter of course, as they are at the WTO level.

The Dance of the Dialectic: Trade Liberalization Meets Neoliberalism

For all its complications, the antidumping and countervailing duty regime is relatively self-contained. The first analytical challenge is to observe how successfully a corpus of foreign legal practice could be transplanted. More subtle, complex, and therefore difficult to analyze is the relationship between pressures from without and forces acting from within to change already existing aspects of the Mexican political economy.

In principle it should be possible to establish the nature of any specific economic sector at the moment when the PRI regime shifted to its neoliberal path. Its liberalization-from-above program could be contrasted with the from-below resistance, on the one hand, and the from-without forces on the other. Among these latter factors, one can distinguish between the openly politicized, direct U.S. government pressure expressing the demands of its private-sector interests and the more legalistic requirements embedded in the continental and global regimes of NAFTA and the WTO.

Although the following discussion will adopt this simple model for heuristic, expository reasons, we need to bear in mind two important caveats. First, what we conceptualize as a from-within and from-above force—the ideological commitment of the PRI leadership in the mid-1980s to a neoliberal counterrevolution—can itself be understood partly as a from-without force. Because the young technocrats of the generation that took over programmatic direction of the PRI regime had learned their paradigm in the leading graduate schools of the United States, and because of a globalized consensus diffused among the elites of the non-Soviet world in the wake of Thatcherism and Reaganism, it is somewhat simplistic to consider the de la Madrid/Salinas counterrevolution to be an entirely internal phenomenon.

A further difficulty with the notion of from-above forces is that it obscures the differences within the system's elites. A program of reform that offers a prescription in the national interest may also play a role in a power struggle within the ruling party. Introducing the question of elite interests also obscures the distinction between internal and external factors. One device currently used by ruling groups to block their internal enemies—whether dinosaurs within their own party or opposition politicians seeking to unseat them—is to sign international agreements that create norms that are supraconstitutional, committing the state in ways that are virtually irreversible, however much distress they cause to dispossessed peasants, unemployed workers, or bankrupted debtors.

The second caveat is that analytical shorthand conceals further conceptual difficulties. "Market forces" can be seen as pushing for change as if they were disembodied—as indeed they seem to be when a new technology creates tremendous pressure to change an existing regulatory system. The "market's need" may mean the economy's projected demand for a certain amount of electric power. It may also express pressure by aggressive foreign transnational corporations to exploit their market dominance at home by capturing market share abroad. But a need is never objective. Mexico's "need" for a low-cost, efficient telecommunications infrastructure can also be articulated as the pressure by potential local partners wanting to form alliances with foreign telecom providers and dislodge the monopoly grasp of Telmex.

Having recognized the unfortunate simplifications that a brief overview unavoidably commits, let us plunge into the analysis, keeping in mind our fivefold typology of a political order's principal components: depending on the particular sector of the economy, the changes produced by the dialectical dance between trade liberalization and neoliberalism have concentrated in one or another of the constitutional, legal, administrative, judicial, and coercive orders. We will proceed in order of rising levels of external intrusiveness from agriculture and manufacturing through the energy utilities to banking, ending with telecommunications and the associated issues of intellectual property rights.

Agriculture

Amending article 27 of the Mexican constitution in 1992, affecting land tenure norms to promote both foreign and domestic private capital participation in agriculture, was a fundamental reversal of the revolutionary tradition of land distribution, which guaranteed peasant holdings in *ejido* communities. Having taken this radically preemptive initiative, the government took another gamble when negotiating NAFTA by agreeing to eliminate in principle its protectionist regime for the production of Mexico's food staples.[62] Having conceded the principle of liberalization, however, Mexico held out for maximum protection of its farmers, negotiating separate agreements with Canada and the United States that gave the longest transition (fifteen years) to zero-tariff protection for the most sensitive products—corn and beans grown by subsistence farmers.

NAFTA, of course, not only affected Mexico's regulatory order in protecting its farmers from U.S. and Canadian exports over the transition period; its counterpart stipulations generated a continental regulatory order governing the access of Mexican agricultural exports to the U.S. and Canadian markets that—perhaps not surprisingly—gave the longest transition period to those products, such as avocados, most politically sensitive to lower-priced Mexican competition. Given the use of food and health regulations to control the import of foodstuffs, NAFTA's committee on sanitary and phytosanitary (SPS) measures has allowed the United States and Mexico to progress in the development, adoption, and enforcement of SPS measures while letting each country maintain the protection it deems necessary.[63]

Manufacturing

The industrial counterpart to restrictions on foreign ownership in landholding achieved by the Mexican Revolution was the series of measures taken to limit foreign ownership in specific industrial sectors by President Manuel Camacho in 1944 that culminated in President Luis Echeverria's Law to Promote Mexican Investment and Regulate Foreign Investment in the 1970s. The accompanying Calvo doctrine, which disenfranchised foreign investors and rationalized a policy of nationalist capitalist autonomy, kept Mexico from signing a bilateral investment treaty with the United States or accepting the investment protections offered by ICSID.[64]

When the collapse of the Mexican banking system during the 1982 crisis demonstrated that the economy's system of financial intermediation was incapable of channeling national savings into industrial development, the only alternative appeared to be attracting large quantities of foreign capital to finance the modernization of Mexico's manufacturing, infrastructure, and public utilities. These perceived "market needs" prompted a number of changes in the foreign investment regime that preceded the disciplines Mexico accepted in that area when it signed NAFTA. The Foreign Investment Commission (CNIE) was empowered in 1989 to waive restrictions deemed in the public interest, opening for foreign participation areas previously reserved for domestic capital.[65] In 1989, CNIE was authorized to give automatic approval for investment projects in "unrestricted industries." When foreign investment met guidelines to promote foreign trade and create jobs outside the major cities, it was allowed up to 100 percent control.[66] Also in 1989, the National Securities Commission and the CNIE authorized foreigners to buy equities issued by Mexican firms, albeit without voting rights. An empirical indicator of this loosening of foreign investment controls was that the CNIE approved 98.4 percent of the projects it reviewed from 1989 to 1993, the year that the restrictions of the 1973 law were abolished in response to the NAFTA commitments.

Hoping to restore Mexico's credibility with international investors by convincing them that its domestic policy reforms were irreversible, and fearing that a multilateral agreement at GATT was not in the offing, Mexico agreed to investment provisions in NAFTA chapter 11 that gave foreign investors a higher standard of protection than even ICSID provided.[67]

Rights of Canadian and U.S. investors to national treatment and freedom from performance requirements as a condition of establishment required, of course, the eradication of those microeconomic policies that had constituted Mexico's ISI model.

However committed PRI's technocrats may have been to neoliberalism's doctrines, they could not ignore the entrenched interests of Mexican corporatism's most powerful fiefdoms—the automobile and textile sectors. Mexico's Automotive Industry Decree, as modified over the years since 1962, with its complex provisions concerning export performance and national content production, was to be attenuated by NAFTA, not eliminated. In five- to fifteen-year stages, Mexican auto manufacturers were to have: increasing entitlements to import parts, components, and vehicles, with specified shares of the Mexican market; reduced requirements for value added; removed restrictions on foreign ownership for auto parts; internal sales of maquiladora production in the Mexican economy; and even eliminated export restriction on used cars.[68]

These provisions required legislative changes. The rules of origin that accompanied the automotive industry regulations required changes in Mexico's administrative order, particularly its customs officials' administration of cross-border shipments to monitor the sliding scale of North American content for cars (reaching 62.5 percent in 2002), parts (60 percent), and other vehicles (60 percent). Given the crucial role played by customs officials in enforcing rules of origin, the three countries agreed to work out uniform regulations regarding the interpretation, application, and administration of the rules of origin that they would then entrench in each system of national law, focusing particularly on the exporting country issuing certificates of origin for their qualifying export goods.[69]

Whether this "excessive protection for a regional industry"[70] was the key factor attracting major foreign investments in the Mexican automobile industry by Mercedes-Benz, BMW, and Honda to build vehicles with North American auto parts for the continent, it is certain that NAFTA caused a direct change to the legal and administrative orders affecting auto manufacturing.[71] Textiles were another heavily administered system of continental protection established in NAFTA by powerful rules of origin and a complex array of tariff rate quotas.

Energy Utilities

In its NAFTA negotiations, Mexico was least willing to alter its controls in the third pillar of the Mexican Revolution—the oil and gas industry—which was considered strategic to the whole economy, if not sacrosanct in the political system.[72]

Electricity

The private producers of electricity had been regulated since 1933, and since 1937 the Comisión Federal de la Electricidad (CFE) had been a nationally owned utility. Ultimately, electricity had been made a national sector by the 1960 constitutional amendment of article 27.[73] With the anticipated growth of demand exceeding Mexico's capacity to generate electricity, calls for more foreign investment had, by 1992, already led to changes that opened power generation to foreign participation of 49 percent (or more, if authorized as a benefit to the Mexican economy). Private investors could now construct electricity generating plants and power conduction lines and networks. With NAFTA chapter 6 and the resulting amendments to the Law for Public Service of Electric Power, along with its implementing regulations, foreign investors could now own and operate electric generation facilities for industrial consumers and sell their excess power to the CFE.[74]

With projected needs for forty 350-megawatt power plants over the twelve years following 1995,[75] NAFTA appears to have opened the door for loosening regulations to encourage more foreign participation in electricity generating facilities not only for the use of the investor but also cogeneration and independent power production.[76] State firms may now negotiate cross-border supply contracts between suppliers and end users. CFE can negotiate purchases and sales with independent power producers in the United States, and foreign suppliers can sell to the CFE, which keeps its monopoly on transmission and distribution under open, competitive bidding rules.[77]

The dialectic between forces from within and forces from without can be seen in the subsequent proposal by President Ernesto Zedillo in February 1999 to amend article 27 of the constitution in order to reform the electricity sector, privatizing it into several generation and distribution firms, establishing a national transmission firm, and adding an independent regulatory entity to operate the transformed system. Although the proposal stalled in Congress, President Fox, who had talked a lot about the need to open the sector and allow more private investment, plans to introduce a similar proposal himself.

Oil

Because article 27 was the "most significant outcome of the Mexican revolution," embodying its cry for economic independence and proclaiming the destruction of vested interests, with the nation declared as the direct owner of the *propiedad raiz* (land, water, and subsoil minerals) and the rights of society prevailing over the rights of individuals, Mexico's free trade interlocutors were obliged to accept major reservations in NAFTA that protected the petroleum industry as a state enclave (NAFTA annex 602.3).[78]

PEMEX had been formed in 1938 to operate properties expropriated from the foreign oil companies. Even though PEMEX remains the sole owner of the petroleum industry exploiting these resources, the sole supplier, and the only trader of oil and gas, NAFTA nevertheless reinforced the trend toward opening the petroleum industry that had already begun in 1989 when the Petrochemical Resolution declassified some petrochemicals, making them eligible for foreign investment and loosening the list protected from outside control from twenty to five.[79]

Although Mexico's constitutional, legal, and administrative order seems to have been the least affected by NAFTA in the petroleum industry, U.S. pressure to gain foreign investment rights in exploration and exploitation, the economy's need for greater supplies for internal use and export revenue, and the changes that have already been made in chipping away at PEMEX's monopoly suggest that article 27—which has already been amended fifteen times—is vulnerable to further alteration. A harbinger of such change came in 1997 when a new legal framework was established for natural gas production, distribution, and sale to residential and commercial customers.

Undermining PEMEX's monopoly from another side is the system's contemporaneous antitrust regime. The Ley Federal de Competencia Económica created in December 1992 the first effective competition authority, the Comisión Federal de Competencia (CFC), which was designed on the basis of Canadian, European, and U.S. models with a "high priority to interact with international counterparts in order to develop standards compatible with international standards and to establish a prominent role for the CFC in the globalization process."[80]

The CFC's challenge to PEMEX's misuse of its overwhelming market power at the service-station level would be misunderstood if it were taken to be the result of NAFTA's 1501(1) injunction that parties shall "adopt or maintain measures to proscribe anti-competitive business conduct and take appropriate action with respect thereto." It is, rather, a result of internormativity within the epistemic community of antitrust policymakers whose work has ensured that "national laws tend to converge towards best practices."[81]

Banking

If the story of trade liberalization in oil is one of successfully plugging the dike's leaks, the story of banking is that of the dike being swept away in a tidal wave. While the dike, in the first example, was solidly constructed on the basis of historical trauma and national action, the second was weakened from constant leveling and rebuilding. In the financial crisis of 1982, President Portillo changed the constitution to make banking another state monopoly, nationalizing all but two of the banks that had themselves been a major cause of the economy's financial collapse.

Given the crucial role financial institutions play for neoliberal theory in achieving economic efficiency by allocating and pricing capital, the Salinas administration began deregulating the financial sector to enhance its efficiency and to attract investment. It deregulated deposit and lending rates, ended credit allocation, removed restrictions on the kinds of business in which financial institutions could engage, strengthened prudential regulation (loan classification and capital adequacy guidelines were made consistent with those of the Bank of International Settlements), and amended the constitution to permit, once again, private ownership of the banks.[82] In 1990 the Ley de Instituciones de Crédito and the Ley para Regular las Agrupaciones Financiarias created a universal banking model with limited foreign investment quotas. When most commercial banks were privatized in 1992–1993, the new owners demanded protection from foreign competition because of the high prices they had paid. As the government itself wanted to keep a national payment system in domestic hands, it approached this part of the NAFTA negotiations defensively. As a result, it made minimal concessions at the micro level, though it was more accepting of major change at the macro level. Although NAFTA provided national treatment, procedural transparency, prudential and safeguard measures, plus a dispute mechanism for trade and investment in banking, investment, and securities institutions, it nevertheless restricted foreign ownership of banks, keeping strict market share limits on U.S. and Canadian acquisitions. This created a dual banking system with foreign-controlled entities subject to clear limitations and Mexican-controlled banks free of such limitations.[83]

At the macro level, one could debate whether Mexico had retained the autonomy of its banking system with article 1410, which allowed it to take reasonable measures to maintain the integrity of its financial system. This presumably would have allowed measures such as those implemented in Chile imposing reserve requirements on short-term capital flows.[84] Alternatively, NAFTA's article 2104.2(a), on the balance of payments, allowed Mexico to impose capital controls under emergency conditions provided that it consulted with the International Monetary Fund (IMF) and was put under the IMF's article 8 surveillance regime. Because article 8 imposes extreme austerity, analyst Timothy Canova argues that Mexico had given up the right established by the Bretton Woods agreement article 6, allowing states to restrict capital transfers. Chapter 11's definition of "investment" to include private debt and equity securities means that Mexico has "surrendered virtually all controls on hot money capital flows."[85] These provisions are not written in Mexican law. They are elements of the NAFTA order for the continental regime applying specifically to Mexico.

The expectation that the three signatories would preserve their "distinct national approaches to regulation" and, through article 1403, retain autonomy with respect to stabilization, monetary, credit, and exchange rate policies proved short-lived.[86] The liberalization of financial institutions that Mexico had instituted prior to NAFTA provided the mechanism for the capital flight that precipitated the crisis in 1994–1995—the most severe in a history studded with such disasters—and the consequent collapse of the financial system. Having withstood U.S. and Canadian pressure for opening up its banking system, Mexico was now forced to accelerate its financial institutions' liberalization while suffering the indignity of having its oil export revenues held as collateral against the $51 billion bailout that allowed it to restore its financial system's functioning.[87]

Far more than NAFTA, the exchange rate crisis led to very substantial changes in the financial system's legal order. With the government's Fondo Bancaria para Protección al Ahorro taking over thirteen banks along with much of their bad debt, the government proceeded to eliminate barriers to foreign ownership of banks and to allow foreign takeovers of troubled institutions exempt from NAFTA-specified limits. Its administrative order was also affected: a bailout condition attached to the World Bank's Financial Sector Restructuring Loan was Mexico's adopting accounting provisions closer to international standards to make the banking commission's monitoring and supervision of national bank solvency more transparent.[88]

Telecommunications

Mexico's telecom reform preceded its negotiation of NAFTA by a considerable margin based on the twin logics of privatizing the state monopoly and establishing a regulatory regime to facilitate competitive entry of new firms. Encouraging competition was deemed a crucial means to achieve the end of attracting efficient industries requiring a high-quality communications and data-transmission infrastructure.[89] In 1989, Mexico opened telecommunications to foreign participation and a year later privatized Telmex, which was allowed to maintain its monopoly of international and long distance telephone calls.[90] While the

Federal Competition Commission began to regulate competitiveness in 1993, Telmex resisted the breakup of its monopoly power. With frequencies for the mobile service market allocated by auction, Bell Atlantic moved into this sector.[91]

In the NAFTA negotiations, Mexico was almost as reluctant to open up telecommunications as petrochemicals. Nevertheless, NAFTA established a gradual opening. Article 1302 provided that public telecommunications networks and services were to be nondiscriminatory for firms in enhanced, value-added, and intracorporate telecommunications. This only represented a small change in the telecommunications market, but it was a stepping-stone toward further liberalization.[92] In 1995, the Federal Telecommunications Law established a regulatory system by creating the Federal Telecommunications Commission (COFETEL) to implement the new regulations for the sector and give out licenses.[93] Consistent with the NAFTA commitments, new regulations for long distance telephone in 1997 withdrew the monopoly enjoyed by Telmex.[94] The U.S. firms MCI and AT&T established joint ventures that rapidly gained 30 percent of the long distance market.[95] In July 1998, local telephony was liberalized by the auction of seventy-seven licenses for mobile phones. Although NAFTA article 1304 required the signatories' mutual recognition of their regulatory test data and technical standards for attaching equipment to public networks, and although NAFTA's Telecommunications Standards Subcommittee developed such standards, Telmex has been resisting pressure to provide its competitors with services.[96] Paradoxically, the privatized Telmex has enough political and economic strength as a private monopoly to frustrate the liberalization goals of the same government that created it. COFETEL has proven unequal to the task.

As a result of its NAFTA commitments and those made in the WTO's telecommunications agreement, Mexico has been under considerable pressure from the U.S. government on behalf of its major telecom companies, which complain of unfair competition because of Telmex's market dominance. With MCI grieving about "Telmex's escalating pattern of anti-competitive abuse" and about COFETEL's incapacity to curb noncompetitive behavior,[97] the United States asked Mexico for consultations at the WTO on its regulatory practice on July 27, 2000, alleging that Telmex's refusal to remove existing restrictions on international traffic between private carriers and to supply its competitors with dedicated lines for Internet and business services violates the WTO Reference Paper.[98] Conflict between national, continental, and global norms was complicated when a Mexican court ruled against

COFETEL and in favor of Telmex—a judgment that the United States insisted did not release Mexico from its trade agreement obligations.

On a related issue, Mexico's commitment at the WTO to allow international simple resale (which would allow firms to bypass Telmex lines with private lines) did not specify a date for introducing new regulations. This omission allowed Mexico to stall on Telmex's behalf.[99] Although NAFTA obliges Mexico to recognize U.S. and Canadian certification bodies on the grounds of national treatment by January 1, 1998, Mexico did not in fact recognize U.S. certification bodies.[100]

Not being able to get the full benefit expected from its trade agreements, the United States has resorted to other levers. The FCC fined the U.S. subsidiary of Telmex $100,000 as punishment for its parent not supplying MCI's Avantel and AT&T's Alestra with private phone lines.[101] On both sides of the border, interests are conflicted. Beyond a certain point, the United States is reluctant to get involved in its corporations' battles over the interpretation of the rules affecting product safety test data and attaching equipment.[102] In Mexico there are also interagency problems, with the Secretariat of Communications and Transport (SCT) opposing SECOFI's positions.

Intellectual Property Rights

Most relentless of all has been U.S. pressure to exploit the concessions it won in NAFTA concerning intellectual property rights. These rules and disciplines, more stringent than those contained in any previous international agreement, required Mexico to overhaul not only its law and regulations but also its judicial and enforcement institutions.

Well before NAFTA, the 1991 Law for the Promotion and Protection of Industrial Property opened most areas of science and technology for patenting with twenty-year terms. The 1994 Industrial Property Law simplified the administrative measures to facilitate the granting of patents.[103] Mexico's 1997 copyright law was challenged by the United States as a violation of NAFTA article 1714, on "expeditious remedies and procedures."[104] Following continuing pressure from its industry, the United States prevailed on Mexico to make its copyright periods consistent with NAFTA: twenty years for patents, fifteen years for industrial designs, ten years for trademarks and trade names, fifty years for sound recordings, and fifty years beyond the life of the author of computer software programs and databases.[105]

Altering the legal and administrative order in compliance with international obligations does not necessarily mean that practice changes in a system. Mexico's judicial capacity to enforce the law was weak. Raids and seizures of pirated tapes, for instance, were rare, court rulings few, penalties minimal, and delays in pressing criminal cases extensive.[106] The issue was the enforcement of NAFTA intellectual property rights to stop piracy.[107] NAFTA legitimized tough arm-twisting by the United States, which used the agreement as an instrument in its hegemonic pressure. Mexico promised to show the United States its draft regulations in light of threats from Washington to name Mexico as a priority country under section 301 of its trade law.[108]

The Mexican government ultimately announced the National Crusade Against Crime and Delinquency in November 1998, proposing legal reforms to federal criminal procedure laws, reclassifying copyright infractions as criminal violations and piracy as serious economic crime, increasing penalties from six months to six years for copyright infractions, and increasing fines by a factor of ten. In the domain of enforcement, it provided increased funds for agencies to fight piracy and increased the 1999 budget to $15 million, three times that of 1998, to allow 7,200 company inspections per year compared to the 1,800 carried out in 1996.[109] This "crusade" reflected close U.S. oversight following congressional review of the draft regulations.[110]

Conclusion

The prime identifiable effects of NAFTA and the WTO on Mexico can be understood as direct, indirect, or contingent:

- The direct effects are the changes Mexico made to its political order so as to comply with its external commitments.
- The indirect effects are those resulting from subsequent demands, threats, and requests made by its NAFTA partners anxious to exploit the concessions won in their negotiations.
- Contingent effects may be triggered at any time when some national law, regulation, or procedure is decided to be in violation of a member state's NAFTA or WTO commitments.

Two instruments that were billed as contingent levers for Canadian and U.S. pressure on the Mexican system have proven as ineffectual as their designers actually intended. The North American Agreement on Labor Cooperation (NAALC) and the North American Agreement on

Environmental Cooperation did not require change in Mexico's formal political order. Rather, they were to increase pressure on Mexico to enforce the existing provisions of its constitutional, legal, and administrative order so that its workers' rights would be protected in reality and its environmental norms be applied in practice. The NAALC is a statement of intentions that sets up formalistic and bureaucratic procedures that are weak, ineffective, and in practice incapable of forcing Mexico to apply its labor laws.[111] Although observers are divided in their assessments of these two side agreements' effects, it appears reasonable to infer that "recent increases in Mexican budgets for environmental infrastructure and enforcement of laws and regulations would almost certainly not have come about if NAFTA had not provided the impetus."[112]

Although our focus has been almost exclusively on the Mexican political order as the object—having to change as the result of outside pressure to conform to its new continental and global trade obligations—these agreements must be seen as also extending Mexico's political order because they give that country rights in the political economies of its partner states. Canada and the United States have obligations under NAFTA to open their markets to specific Mexican products according to a clearly identified timetable. The WTO establishes further norms of behavior to which they are obligated to comply in their treatment of Mexican products and investors. If they fail to comply, then both NAFTA and the WTO, as continental and global legal orders in their own right, provide mechanisms to have misbehaving members conform.

Mexico's use of chapter 19 panels against U.S. antidumping actions has been active but unsuccessful. Given the almost century-long U.S. experience in developing a sophisticated trade law jurisprudence, it was perhaps to be expected that Mexico would lose each of the cases that it initiated, whether porcelain on steel cookware,[113] Portland cement,[114] oil country tubular goods,[115] or fresh-cut flowers.[116] The panels all deferred to the U.S. agency, finding the original antidumping duties to have been properly determined according to U.S. trade law.

Beyond the narrow—if deep—domain of antidumping, Mexico has shown it can use NAFTA's general dispute settlement mechanism to good effect. In two cases, chapter 20 has proven of some assistance in dealing with U.S. violations of the basic NAFTA agreement.

In January 1998, Mexico won a chapter 20 ruling against the U.S. imposition under WTO rules of a 201 safeguard duty against Mexican broomcorn brooms. The panel argued that the U.S. Department of Commerce had not effectively given "reasoned conclusions on all issues of law and fact" as required under NAFTA's Article 803.3(12). What was justified under the WTO was no longer valid under NAFTA. When the United States refused to withdraw its duties, Mexico retaliated by imposing duties on a range of U.S. exports. Finally, on November 11, 1998, the United States withdrew its safeguard.[117]

Trucking has been a messier issue, because it is more politically charged. Although rationalized in terms of protecting the U.S. public from dangerous Mexican vehicles and drivers, the U.S. violation of its NAFTA agreement to open its border to cross-border trucking was widely regarded as a political response to the Teamsters Union's fear of low-wage competition for its members. Following years of U.S. administrative stonewalling in the face of its protests, Mexico initiated a chapter 20 dispute process in August 1998.[118] In a clear demonstration that NAFTA dispute settlement is not the expeditious process its defenders had anticipated, a panel was constituted for this action only in December 1999. Meanwhile, the United States had been pressuring Mexico to improve the safety of its trucks by deploying more trained police for inspections, establishing automated truck safety data exchange, and ensuring government oversight of carrier compliance.[119]

At the same time, the United States has bolstered its tenuous position by linking the truck question to another of its transportation industry's goals: getting expanded deregulated access to the Mexican market for U.S. express couriers. The chapter 20 dispute is but part of the complex overall U.S.-Mexico transportation issue. Even though 80 percent of U.S.-Mexico trade is conducted by land, there is a long way to go before bilateral transit problems have been smoothed out. Mexicans have different administrative procedures and customs practices: even the forms used by trucking companies as truck bills become cause for contestation delaying cross-border transporting of goods.[120]

Although Mexico is more a rule taker than a rule maker in the global trade system, it has nevertheless shown an interest and capacity for using the new multilateral regime at its disposal to further its interests proactively, whether in working out judicial interpretations of existing norms or in contributing legislatively to the negotiation of new trade norms. In working out a subsidy code during the Uruguay Round, it suggested that environmental subsidies should be green-lighted within carefully specified limits. It was a party with the European Union in the U.S. film case against Japan, disagreeing with the U.S. argument.[121] With Ecuador,

Guatemala, Honduras, and Panama, it associated itself with the United States against the European Union in the bananas case.[122]

Besides triggering a panel at the WTO to fight a Guatemalan antidumping duty against its exports, it is arguing in the current round of WTO negotiations for extending the transition period for implementing trade-related investment measures for third world countries.[123] The obligations enshrined in the WTO are both more comprehensive than NAFTA's and more potent. The disputes handled through the WTO's dispute body are more expeditiously resolved and more authoritatively applied than under NAFTA.

For its part, NAFTA is a supraconstitutional order with less heft. We have already seen that the development of a continental trade jurisprudence has been hobbled by the difficulty of finding panelists to staff a dispute, the trade panels' inability to use previous judgments as precedent, and the national sovereignty principle entrenched in antidumping and countervailing duty law. There are weak signs of a continental polity emerging. The negotiation of SPS and telecommunications standards in NAFTA working groups shows some autonomous normative capacity, and the harmonization of customs procedures to handle rules of origin and other cross-border matters suggests some minuscule supranational heartbeat.

After reviewing the various impacts that NAFTA and the WTO have had on Mexico's political order, it is difficult to conclude that they are malevolent factors whose radical reform or abolition—"fix it or nix it" was the most pertinent of the slogans inspiring antiglobalization demonstrators in Washington in April 2000—offers hope for solving Mexico's problems. Indeed, those pressing for corrections of the Washington consensus in the post-Seattle period of globalization may do better to work for transnational alliances that try to shift norms and rules at both the national and international levels. For if the opponents of neoliberalism have anything to learn from its successes in such countries as Mexico, it is that reform from within is not feasible without being linked to reform from without. As Mexico's economic system continues to evolve, pressure for change will undoubtedly continue from both sources.

Notes

Research for this chapter was carried out under a Killam Senior Research Fellowship provided by the Canada Council and a fellowship at the Woodrow

Wilson International Center for Scholars. It profited greatly from the research assistance of Olga Palacios and the comments of Luz María de la Mora, Maria Teresa Guttierez-Haces, and Marjorie Griffin Cohen.

1. There are very good reasons for not considering globalization to be new at all because rates of foreign investment and trade as a proportion of GDP were as high a century ago as they are now. Nevertheless, *some* features of today's globalization, such as the world-embracing and regionally limited trade agreements, are justifiably described as new.

2. Interview with Luis de la Calle, Washington, D.C., February 1997.

3. Article 133 of the Mexican constitution was derived from article VI(2) of the U.S. Constitution, article 104 (concerning disputes over treaties signed by Mexico) from article III(2).

4. Christopher J. Mailander, *Reshaping North American Banking: The Transforming Effects of Regional Market and Policy Shifts* (Washington, D.C.: Center for Strategic and International Studies, 1999), pp. 16–17.

5. Jorge A. Vargas, "Enforcement of Judgments and Arbitral Awards in Mexico," *United States–Mexico Law Journal* 5 (1997): 140.

6. Luis F. Rubio, Cristina D. Rodriguez, and Roberto V. Blum, "The Making of Mexico's Trade Policy and the Uruguay Round," in Henry R. Nau, ed., *Domestic Trade Politics and the Uruguay Round* (New York: Columbia University Press, 1989), p. 167.

7. Gustavo Vega and Luz María de la Mora, "Mexico's Trade Policy: Financial Crisis and Economic Recovery," in Kevin Middlebrook and Eduardo Zepeda, eds., *Confronting Development: Assessing Mexico's Economic and Social Policy Challenges* (Palo Alto: Stanford University Press, 2003).

8. Rubio et al., "The Making of Mexico's Trade Policy," p. 172.

9. Vega and de la Mora, "Mexico's Trade Policy," p. 4.

10. Rubio et al., "The Making of Mexico's Trade Policy," p. 186.

11. Rogelio Ramirez De la O, "The North American Free Trade Agreement from a Mexican Perspective," in Steven Globerman and Michael Walker, eds., *Assessing NAFTA: A Trinational Analysis* (Vancouver, British Columbia, Canada: Fraser Institute, 1993), p. 61.

12. Beatriz Leycegui, "A Legal Analysis of Mexico's Antidumping and Countervailing Regulatory Framework," in Beatriz Leycegui, William B.P. Robson, and S. Dahlia Stein, eds., *Trading Punches: Trade Remedy Law and Disputes Under NAFTA* (Washington, D.C.: National Planning Association, 1995), p. 44.

13. On the Framework Agreement, see Rubio et al., "The Making of Mexico's Trade Policy," p. 173.

14. Leycegui, "A Legal Analysis of Mexico's Regulatory Framework," p. 43.

15. Gabriel Castaneda Gallardo, "Antitrust Enforcement in Mexico 1993–1995 and Its Prospects," *United States–Mexico Law Journal* 4 (1996): 19–34.

16. David Amerine, in Jimmie V. Reyna, Eduardo David Garcia, and David Amerine, "Practice Before U.S.-Mexico Binational Panels Under Chapter 19 of NAFTA: A Panel Discussion," *United States–Mexico Law Journal* 5 (1997): 73–82.

17. Leycegui, "A Legal Analysis of Mexico's Regulatory Framework," p. 44, n. 10.

18. Ibid., p. 68, n. 11.

19. *Diario Oficial de la Federación*, July 27, 1993.

20. *Diario Oficial*, December 22, 1993.

21. On the former, see *Diario Oficial*, December 30, 1993.

22. Leycegui, "A Legal Analysis of Mexico's Regulatory Framework," p. 73, n. 73.

23. Ibid., p. 74.

24. Jimmie V. Reyna, "NAFTA Chapter 19 Binational Panel Reviews in Mexico: A Marriage of Two Distinct Legal Systems," *United States–Mexico Law Journal* 5 (1997): 66.

25. Ibid.

26. "NAFTA provides that determinations issued as a result of judicial, administrative, or panel review shall be applicable to other interested parties, to the extent they are relevant so that all parties benefit. This is the only one . . . that was not incorporated into the new statutes, because of incompatibility with Mexico's entire domestic legal scheme." Leycegui, "A Legal Analysis of Mexico's Regulatory Framework," p. 66.

27. Ibid., p. 60.

28. Ibid., p. 62.

29. Ibid., p. 69, n. 32.

30. Ibid., p. 69, n. 26.

31. Ibid., p. 73, n. 78.

32. *Diario Oficial,* August 4, 1994; Leycegui, "A Legal Analysis of Mexico's Regulatory Framework," p. 72, n. 67.

33. Citation from letter to the author by a SECOFI official, August 1, 2000; *Diario Oficial,* April 19, 2000; see also www.cde.gob.mx.

34. Mex 94–1904–02.

35. Gustavo Vega-Canovas, "Disciplining Anti-Dumping in North America: Is NAFTA Chapter Nineteen Serving Its Purpose?" *Arizona Journal of International and Comparative Law* 14 (spring 1997).

36. Mex 94–1904–01.

37. Vega-Canovas, "Disciplining Anti-Dumping in North America."

38. Mex 94–1904–03.

39. Luz María de la Mora, "Unpacking NAFTA: Progress, Problems, and Potential" (unpublished paper, January 31, 2000), p. 52.

40. *Inside U.S. Trade,* August 21, 1998.

41. de la Mora, "Unpacking NAFTA," p. 51.

42. Gabriel Castaneda Gallardo, "Antitrust Enforcement in Mexico," pp. 19–34.

43. Stephen J. Powell, in Michael W. Gordon et al., "Agricultural Disputes: Mexican Tomatoes to Florida and Washington Apples to Mexico," *United States–Mexico Law Journal* 6 (1998): 138.

44. *Inside U.S. Trade*, January 7, 2000.

45. Ramirez De la O, "The North American Free Trade Agreement from a Mexican Perspective," p. 78.

46. *Inside U.S. Trade*, November 12, 1999.

47. Steven Globerman and Michael Walker, "Introduction," in Globerman and Walker, eds., *Assessing NAFTA*, p. xxiv.

48. Jorge A. Vargas, "Enforcement of Judgments," pp. 137–148.

49. Ibid.

50. Reyna et al., "Practice Before U.S.-Mexico Binational Panels," pp. 80–81.

51. Vega-Canovas, "Disciplining Anti-Dumping in North America."

52. Hope H. Camp Jr., "Dispute Resolution and U.S.-Mexico Business Transactions," *United States–Mexico Law Journal* 5 (1997): 85–99.

53. Eduardo David Garcia, in Reyna et al., "Practice Before U.S.-Mexico Binational Panels," p. 75.

54. Ibid.

55. Reyna, "NAFTA Chapter 19 Binational Panel Reviews in Mexico," p. 70.

56. Ibid.

57. Vega-Canovas, "Disciplining Anti-Dumping in North America."

58. Ibid.

59. Beatrice Prati, "NAFTA: Its Legal Effects—Broad Strokes: A Mexican Perspective," *Canada–United States Law Journal* 23 (1997): 113.

60. Reyna et al., "Practice Before U.S.-Mexico Binational Panels," p. 80.

61. Ibid., p. 82. See also General Accounting Office, "U.S.-Canada Free Trade Agreement: Factors Contributing to Controversy in Appeals of Trade Remedy Cases," GAO/GGD-95–175BR, (1995), cited in Reyna, "NAFTA Chapter 19 Binational Panel Reviews in Mexico," p. 65, n. 3.

62. Sidney Weintraub, "The North American Free Trade Agreement as Negotiated: A U.S. Perspective," in Globerman and Walker, eds., *Assessing NAFTA*, p. 11.

63. de la Mora, "Unpacking NAFTA," p. 27.

64. Ewell E. Murphy Jr., "NAFTA Revisited: Seeing NAFTA Through Three Lenses," *Canada–United States Law Journal* 23 (1997): 74–75.

65. Claus von Wobeser, "El régimen legal de la inversión extranjera en el TLCAN and sus efectos en los flujos de capital hacia México," in Beatriz Leycegui and Rafael Fernandez de Castro, eds., *Socios naturales? Cinco anos del Tratado de libre Comercio de América del Norte* (México, D.F.: Instituto Tecnológico Autónomo de México, 2000), p. 231.

66. Ibid.

67. de la Mora, "Unpacking NAFTA," p. 6.

68. Jon R. Johnson, "NAFTA and the Trade in Automotive Goods," in Globerman and Walker, eds., *Assessing NAFTA*, pp. 116–117, and Ramirez De la O, "The North American Free Trade Agreement," pp. 73–74, 118–120.

69. Peter Morici, "NAFTA Rules of Origin and Automotive Content," in Globerman and Walker, eds., *Assessing NAFTA*, p. 238.

70. Ramirez De la O, "The North American Free Trade Agreement," p. 73.

71. Vega and de la Mora, "Mexico's Trade Policy," p. 20.

72. Weintraub, "The North American Free Trade Agreement as Negotiated," p. 7.

73. Ewell E. Murphy Jr., "Back to the Future? The Prospects for State Monopoly," *United States–Mexico Law Journal* 1, no. 3 (1995): 54.

74. William D. DeGrandis and Michael L. Owen, "Electrical Energy Legal and Regulatory Structure in Mexico and Opportunities After NAFTA," *United States–Mexico Law Journal* 3 (1995): 61.
75. Ibid., p. 67.
76. de la Mora, "Unpacking NAFTA," p. 22.
77. Ibid.
78. Murphy, "Back to the Future?" p. 55.
79. G. C. Watkins, "NAFTA and Energy: A Bridge Not Far Enough?" in Globerman and Walker, eds., *Assessing NAFTA*, p. 213.
80. Castaneda Gallardo, "Antitrust Enforcement in Mexico," pp. 19–34.
81. Eleanor M. Fox, "The Antitrust Laws of the United States and the Ley de Competencia of Mexico: A Comparative Review, 1992–1994," *United States–Mexico Law Journal* 4 (1996): 18.
82. Organization for Economic Cooperation and Development (OECD), *Regulatory Reform in Mexico* (Paris: OECD, 1999), p. 23.
83. Mike Lubrano, "Foreign Investment in the Financial Sector of Mexico," *United States–Mexico Law Journal* 6 (1998): 81–86.
84. Timothy A. Canova, "Banking and Financial Reform at the Crossroads of the Neoliberal Contagion," *United States–Mexico Law Journal* 7 (1999): 111.
85. Ibid., p. 99.
86. John F. Chant, "The Financial Sector in NAFTA: Two Plus One Equals Restructuring," in Globerman and Walker, eds., *Assessing NAFTA*, p. 181.
87. Sidney Weintraub, *NAFTA at Three* (Washington, D.C.: Center for International and Strategic Studies, 1997), p. 63.
88. Mike Lubrano, in John Rogers et al., "Restructuring of Mexican Financial Services and the Application of Chapter 14 of NAFTA," *United States–Mexico Law Journal* 7 (1999): 67.
89. Ramirez De la O, "The North American Free Trade Agreement," p. 76; OECD, *Regulatory Reform in Mexico*, p. 79.
90. de la Mora, "Unpacking NAFTA," p. 39.
91. OECD, *Regulatory Reform in Mexico*, p. 80.
92. de la Mora, "Unpacking NAFTA," p. 39.
93. OECD, *Regulatory Reform in Mexico*, p. 81.
94. de la Mora, "Unpacking NAFTA," p. 40.
95. OECD, *Regulatory Reform in Mexico*, p. 80.
96. de la Mora, "Unpacking NAFTA," p. 41.
97. *Inside U.S. Trade*, February 11, 2000.
98. *Inside U.S. Trade*, September 18, 1998.
99. *Inside U.S. Trade*, April 2, 2000.
100. *Inside U.S. Trade*, March 12, 2000.
101. *Inside U.S. Trade*, February 11, 2000.
102. *Inside U.S. Trade*, September 18, 1998.
103. de la Mora, "Unpacking NAFTA," pp. 33–34.
104. *Inside U.S. Trade*, May 16, 1998.
105. *Inside U.S. Trade*, June 12, 1998.
106. de la Mora, "Unpacking NAFTA," p. 35.

107. *Inside U.S. Trade,* September 4, 1998.
108. *Inside U.S. Trade,* November 27, 1998.
109. de la Mora, "Unpacking NAFTA," p. 35.
110. *Inside U.S. Trade*, May 15, 1998.
111. Maria Teresa Guerra and Anna L. Torriente, "The NAALC and the Labor Laws of Mexico and the United States," *Arizona Journal of International and Comparative Law* 14 (spring 1997).
112. Weintraub, "The North American Free Trade Agreement as Negotiated," p. 27.
113. USA-95–1904–01.
114. USA-95–1904–02.
115. USA-95–1904–04.
116. USA-95–1904–05.
117. de la Mora, "Unpacking NAFTA," p. 50.
118. *Inside U.S. Trade,* August 31, 1998.
119. Ibid.
120. Boris Kozolchyk, "Highways and Byways of NAFTA Commercial Law: The Challenge to Develop a 'Best Practice' in North American Trade," *United States–Mexico Law Journal* 4 (1996): 56.
121. *Inside U.S. Trade*, April 18, 1997.
122. *Inside U.S. Trade*, September 22, 1998.
123. *Inside U.S. Trade*, January 28, 2000.

9

The Challenges to Rural Mexico in an Open Economy

Kirsten Appendini

When the modernization program of the agricultural sector was launched at the beginning of Carlos Salinas's presidency in 1990, it meant just that—modernization—with the overall aim of improving welfare and justice in the countryside.[1] Within the spirit of neoliberal discourse, this goal could be achieved only by increasing production and productivity in the agricultural sector. This was to be attained by establishing clear property rights, ending decades of ambiguity concerning the security of land tenure in order to attract investment, securing efficient resource allocation, and ultimately restructuring agricultural production to operate competitively in an open economy. A profound program of institutional and economic reform was carried out during the 1990s, changing the institutional framework for policy implementation and legislation of the land tenure system. Underlying the discourse of modernization, the peasantry, who constitute the bulk of rural producers, were to become efficient or perish.[2]

After more than a decade of reform, however, agricultural performance has not realized the expectations set by the neoliberal agenda of the administrations of Carlos Salinas de Gortari or Ernesto Zedillo; neither have peasants and the rural population in general seen any improvement in their livelihoods. Through the first two years of the Vicente Fox administration (the president was elected in July 2000), we have seen a continuation of neoliberal policies and no political will to change the agenda toward the countryside. And in the meantime, we have seen two important peasant mobilizations: by grain producers in the northwestern region, and by sugarcane producers.

Agriculture is thus submerged in crisis, and Mexico's rural population continues to endure widespread poverty. The challenges for rural

Mexico remain as harsh and complex at the beginning of the twenty-first century as they did in 1990.

In this chapter, I will briefly describe the current situation of rural Mexico and underline the transformation of the countryside. The focus will be on agriculture and how the peasantry is faring in the context of an open economy, halfway through a tariff liberalization process under the North American Free Trade Agreement (NAFTA).[3]

Next I will examine how peasants are dealing as unequal partners with the challenges of an open market, focusing on one of the most problematic groups: corn producers. The efforts of Mexico's staple food producers to cope with changing rules of the game and to defend their role as farmers provide an example of how Mexican peasants are constantly struggling for survival and for a recognized space within the countryside, which is deeply rooted in Mexico's culture and history.

Facts and Figures on Rural Mexico

During the 1990s, Mexican agriculture did not perform well. The rate of growth of agricultural gross domestic product (GDP) was well below the growth of the overall economy from 1990 to 1999—1.2 percent compared to an overall growth of 2.8 percent.[4] By 1997, the agriculture sector contributed only 5.3 percent of total GDP; in 2001 it was 4.7 percent. The policy designers of the modernization program had not hesitated to underscore that modernization meant narrowing the gap between agriculture's contribution to GDP and the percentage of the labor force devoted to agricultural activities, suggesting that this gap was a drain on productivity. However, by the end of the 1990s, 22 percent of the Mexican labor force was still involved in agriculture.[5]

Structural changes on the better agricultural lands have been slow to take place and are in no way as straightforward as that prescribed by orthodox development economics. For example, fruit and vegetable production, which was expected to boom with Mexico's entry into NAFTA, has increased but not crowded out basic crops on irrigated land.[6] Corn still predominates agricultural production, accounting for 39 percent of harvested area in 1998. Rather than a restructuring of basic crops in favor of export crops, shifts may be taking place within broad groups of products, for example, when one tradable is substituted for another.[7]

Neither are there spectacular signs of private investment flowing into agroindustry. Land transactions at the national level following the removal of restrictions on land markets by the 1992 liberalization of land tenure legislation also seem to be moving at a slow pace.[8] Land transactions within the *ejido* sector mainly take place at the local level among members of the community, particularly among kin, and are not registered formally. Only 5 percent of *ejidatarios* (cooperative landowners) have registered the sale of their land since the PROCEDE program began in 1993.[9]

According to empirical evidence from a national ejido survey undertaken in 1997, land transactions have mainly taken the form of rent. From 1994 to 1997, there was a 22 percent increase in rental transactions among ejido households; however, only a small number of households were engaged in these transactions (19 percent, as compared to 15 percent in 1994). Large farmers were more likely to rent land, whereas small farmers leased their land, showing a trend toward the compacting of cultivatable areas. Less than 5 percent of ejido households were involved in ownership transactions.[10]

In all, the loss of profitability in agriculture, restrictions and risks in entering export crop markets, a lack of a sectoral policy and financial resources to embark on an aggressive restructuring of cropping patterns, technological change, and market penetration are some of the reasons for the weak response to institutional reforms.

In addition, response to institutional reform implies a selective process that is highly exclusive. The impact of reforms on the rural population does not give an optimistic picture. Aggregate data show that poverty increased from 1989 to 1996. Whereas 49 percent of rural households were considered poor in 1989, 53 percent were poor in 1996 and 25 percent were in extreme poverty (compared to 23 percent in 1989).[11] There is a high incidence of poverty in marginal rural areas. Of the 4.6 million households categorized as living in extreme poverty (21 percent of total households in Mexico), 75 percent are in localities with less than 500 inhabitants.[12] Hence, the problem of exclusion has increased during the modernization decade, as agricultural as well as nonagricultural activities in the countryside did not offer the opportunities for improvements in income and welfare predicted by technocrat policymakers.

In spite of the gloomy picture of agricultural performance, the countryside has not remained stagnant. Within different regions, communities, and social groups, the forces of change take on diverse responses as people adjust and reconstitute their livelihoods at the individual, household, and community levels in varying and complex ways. Hence, the interaction of macroeconomic and institutional change within the local and regional contexts has increased the heterogeneity of the Mexican countryside as territory and people adapt to transformation and changing rural space.

The main trend is the increasing importance of nonagricultural activities, which in many regions are changing the income sources of rural households as well as the rural landscape. Hence, one could argue that modernization is taking place in the countryside but not within the context of agricultural activities.

Nonfarming occupations, whether wage work or self-employment in crafts, microenterprise, petty trading, or services, are spreading, underlining a trend for households to rely less on farm activities for monetary income. Surveys in the ejido sector show that during the 1990s nonfarm income for rural households has become more important. In 1994, 46 percent of ejido household income derived from nonfarm activities, increasing to 55 percent in 1997.[13] Wage labor is the most frequent strategy adopted. Forty-seven percent of ejido households were involved in the off-farm labor market in 1997, compared to 48 percent in 1994; however, self-employment saw an increase to 24 percent in 1997 from a mere 9 percent in 1994.[14] This confirms that the diversification of income sources—a characteristic of peasant households for several decades—became accentuated in the 1990s. It also shows that wage work does not seem to be an answer to peasants and their families. The rate of growth in self-employment may well indicate that rural households are facing constrained labor markets, in which minimum real wages in 1999 were only 65 percent of wages in 1990.[15]

Community case studies also point to the importance of nonfarm income. For example, in such isolated communities as in the highland forests of the Sierra de Juárez in Oaxaca, nonfarm income (excluding forestry) accounted on average for about 53 percent of monetary income in the households surveyed. Nonetheless, agriculture is an important subsistence activity, and all households report expenditure on agriculture, subsidized by nonfarm income and family labor.[16] In cases from Michoacán, household monetary income from nonfarm sources ranged from 54 to 80 percent.[17]

Even so, agriculture is not disappearing. In 1997, 20.8 percent of the total economically active population was occupied in agricultural activities (compared to 23 percent in 1990). In small communities (up to 2,500 inhabitants), 62.5 percent worked in agriculture; in localities with 2,500–15,000 inhabitants, the percentage was 27.9.[18]

Women have notably increased their participation in agricultural employment, mainly as wage workers. Agroindustry in particular is in demand for female workers in packing plants, as well as in the fields for cutting and picking, primarily employing migrants, often ethnic minorities.[19] In some regions, women's wages are now an important income source for rural households. Seventy percent of the workers in packing plants and greenhouses for mangos and avocados in Michoacán and for flowers in Morelos—all export crops—were women. It is well documented that women have for decades been entering jobs as a flexible labor force, often interpreted as a desirable trait in the process of emancipation. However, this is controversial, because rural women face dead-end jobs, and they struggle with low wages, long working days during peak seasons, and poor working conditions.[20]

Migration is another important trend in the countryside. In particular, international migration is increasing, making remittances an important component of total income for many rural households. A 1994–1997 World Bank ejido study that included data from 1,342 households in a panel survey shows that migration within Mexico has decreased, whereas households engaged in migration to the United States have increased from 3 percent to 8 percent. For the overall sample, 45 percent of all ejido households have a family member who has migrated to the United States, and 80 percent of households have a family member residing outside the community. Migration differentiates by age and sex: young men are the main migrants, but the migration of women is increasingly rapidly.[21]

In 1998, the estimated flow of remittances to Mexico was around $5.6 billion, according to the Banco de México. One out of ten households in localities of less than 2,500 inhabitants receive remittances (an estimated 37 percent of the total flow).[22]

Migration and a decrease in fertility have changed the demographic composition of rural localities. From 1990 to 1995, rural population grew at a rate of 1 percent. Fertility rates in the twenty-to-thirty-four age group were slightly lower than for urban women in the period 1992–1996.[23] Hence, there is an aging of the rural population. The average age of ejido heads of households is fifty-two.

In some communities and regions, the "classic" developmentalist concern of population pressure on land and other resources—with the consequence of decreasing productivity and environmental degradation—has been turned around. Labor scarcity may now be a concern and may influence decisions on cropping patterns as well as cultivation practices in subsistence agriculture and even environmental practices.[24]

To draw further on the communities in the Sierra de Juárez, Oaxaca, there are cases in which migration has undermined the population of those of working age (both male and female) in some communities. The use of soil and space has changed so that the options offered given by a range of agroecological diversity, from mountain highlands to deep ravines, have been abandoned and economic activity is located only on plateaus near villages.[25]

At the national level, labor-intensive practices in agriculture have been abandoned and inputs that imply monetary costs have dropped, both with impact on yields, as confirmed by ejido households nationwide from 1992 to 1994.[26]

The increasing presence of nonfarm activities can also be assessed at the community and regional levels. A variety of economic activities such as manufacturing is gaining hold in the countryside. This is not a new process; for example, a thriving garment industry has consolidated in the Altos de Jalisco since the 1980s. In Tangamandapio and Moroleón, Michoacán, workshops set up by women within their households are today a flourishing industry, exporting to the border states of the United States.[27] Contracting and subcontracting for making bits and pieces of different manufactured goods offer extended employment in many rural regions. Some of these arrangements follow the best example of sweatshop practices, others the form of established formal factories. Among them are the *maquila* industry that has expanded toward inland Mexico and the countryside. Such is the case of the region of San Juan del Río and Tequispuiapan in the central state of Querétaro in which manufacturing industry grew rapidly in the 1990s, changing the regional labor market by hiring local/rural labor. Rural communities are becoming sites of residence as household members commute daily to the factories.[28]

The trends of change in the Mexican countryside pose a challenge concerning rural development in general, which encompasses not only agriculture but also the promotion of economic activities that will create opportunities for employment, thereby increasing income and conditions for better livelihood for the rural population, whether peasants, wage workers in industry, or self-employed in nonfarm activities, at the individual and community levels. This challenge also implies improving public infrastructure in communications, transport, health, and education.

The second challenge is that agriculture should not be neglected—notwithstanding heterogeneous trends in economic diversification and changes in the occupation and use of rural space. To promote the consolidation of an agricultural sector is consistent not only with the agroecological configuration of the countryside but also with the social structure and with the historic and cultural heritage of rural Mexico. From a socioeconomic perspective, this consolidation encompasses a rural project that recognizes the heterogeneity of agriculture and the agrarian structure, giving space to both entrepreneurs and family farms and a variety of agriculture, livestock, and forestry.[29] Within agriculture, it includes a space for specialization in high-value crops such as fruits and vegetables, traditional export crops such as coffee and sugarcane, as well as basic food crops such as corn. A rural strategy also needs to embrace environmental concerns and provide an institutional framework to support such a model in the context of an open economy. The remaining discussion of this chapter will be concerned with some of these issues, mainly focusing on the peasantry and corn production.

The Challenges for Rural Mexico: An Agriculture with Peasants

Small and medium-sized farming households constitute the social backbone of rural Mexico in a historically heterogeneous agrarian structure in which entrepreneurial farming has accounted for only a small proportion of farm units, although it has been located on the best lands (irrigated) and often engaged in the more dynamic crops and livestock raising, having benefited from agricultural policies.[30] During the latter years of the inward-oriented development model (the 1960s up to 1982), agricultural stagnation rooted in a polarized agrarian structure was confronted with propeasant policies supporting basic food production through the extension of publicly subsidized green-revolution technology, thus creating a modern subsidized strata of peasants, particularly within the ejido sector.[31] This model was abruptly interrupted with the debt crisis in late 1982 and thoroughly blamed by the Programa de Modernización (Modernization Program) of 1990 for low productivity and costly agriculture.[32]

Ten years after the Modernization Program, there are more than 4 million farm households in Mexico. The agrarian structure consolidated under agrarian reform has not changed radically with the opening-up of the ejido to privatization, as already mentioned. All told, 51.4 percent of rural territory is under the regime of ejido or *comunidad* (collective property of communities). There are approximately 3.5 million ejido and *comunero* (commune) households, most of which possess a small amount of land: 50.1 percent have plots of five hectares or less, 25.6 percent have plots of five to ten hectares, and 24.7 percent have more than ten hectares.[33] Though nonfarm income is increasing for rural households, land is still an important productive asset. In 1997, farm income accounted for 45.2 percent of total income for ejidatarios with five to ten hectares and for more than 57 percent for those with ten hectares or more.[34] That means that for roughly half of the ejido peasants (1.7 million), land is a productive asset and farming should be a potential activity.

Cropping patterns also show that basic crops predominate in agriculture. This is due partly to the agroecological constraints; 73 percent of cropping acreage is rain-fed land, and much is considered marginal because of dry climate and/or erosion.[35]

Switching to high-value crops has physical constraints. Even if investment in irrigation was to be expanded, the availability of water is a problem, as are environmental hazards due to the use of pesticides in fruit and vegetable crops.[36] Hence, climate and low labor costs do not guarantee a successful export agroindustry. Physical and environmental constraints must be taken into account. But market concerns are important as well; even if—production aside—processing, storage, and transport facilities and managerial skills were upgraded in order to be more competitive, access to the U.S. market is not unlimited. Under NAFTA, Mexican fruit and vegetable exports are seasonally regulated by changing tariffs and remain complementary to Florida and California producers, under a phasing-out period of liberalization.

Hence, the argument for a diversified and domestic market–oriented agriculture has a sound basis. I will now underline this by looking closer at corn. An estimated 2.5–3 million rural producers are engaged in cultivating corn, the basic food staple in Mexico. Seventy-four percent of producers are located on rain-fed land—associated with peasant agriculture—whereas 26 percent are on irrigated land.[37]

A dual pattern of corn agriculture emerged during the 1990s due to an ambiguous price policy that favored the relative price of corn when agricultural commodities were starting to be liberalized. The policy diminished the risk of corn-cropping versus more tradable commodities and provided incentive for entrepreneurial farmers to grow maize, especially on irrigated land. This policy was later reinforced with the direct-subsidy program known as Procampo (Programa Nacional de Apoyo Directo al Campo, or Direct Rural Support Program), initiated in 1994, giving the right to receive direct payment to farmers who were or had been engaged in cultivating basic crops.[38] Production of corn grown on large or entrepreneurial farms located on irrigated lands increased by 11.4 percent from 1990 to 1998 (compared to 1.3 percent on rain-fed land).[39] Irrigated corn acreage doubled in the ejido sector between 1994 and 1997, whereas it remained stagnant on rain-fed land.[40]

About 72 percent of rural households engaged in producing corn are in the ejido sector, contributing to 62 percent of national output.[41] Forty-six percent of maize farmers mainly cultivate for self-consumption. Corn producers have been caught in the squeeze of liberalization: real prices have decreased continuously from 1987 while the withdrawal of subsidies on the production side has increased the costs of cultivation. Despite official rhetoric, direct income support from Procampo has not compensated for the price-cost squeeze. The real income of a peasant producer on rain-fed land with average yields (2.5 tons per hectare) has been falling constantly and was half that of a decade before, as shown in Figure 9.1.

Corn production has been sustained due to strategies followed by different groups of producers: subsistence farmers, entrepreneurial farmers, and former modernized-subsidized farmers. The first two strategies—entrepreneurship and subsistence—have been analyzed to some extent and presented as the trend of corn agriculture in a polarized and dual model.

As mentioned above, corn production on irrigated land has increased. New areas, such as in the state of Sinaloa, switched to corn production when relative prices and a secure market made a rent-seeking strategy profitable for high-yielding land using technology similar to farmers in the irrigated valleys of the U.S. Pacific Northwest.[42] Entrepreneurs formerly engaged in sorghum and wheat production, as well as in horticulture for export such as tomatoes, found corn production more viable. They were soon (1993–1994) to be compensated by Procampo when able to apply for the direct income subsidy as having been engaged in basic crops.

The subsistence peasant strategy has, on the contrary, been able to withdraw from the market and grow corn only for self-consumption. In the ejido sector, the increasing costs of fertilizers and energy, a lack of credit, and the like led to a strategy in which investment in cultivation,

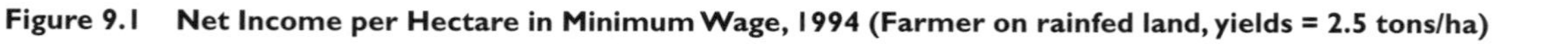

Figure 9.1 Net Income per Hectare in Minimum Wage, 1994 (Farmer on rainfed land, yields = 2.5 tons/ha)

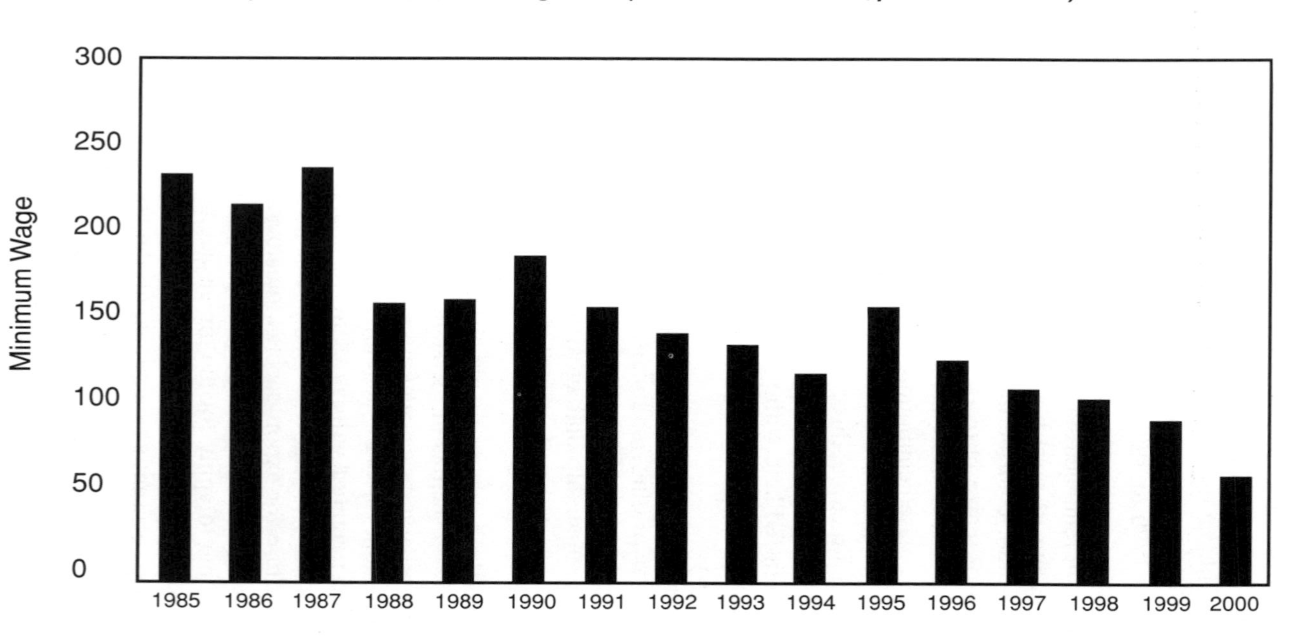

Source: Kirsten Appendini, *De la milpa a los tortibonos la restructuració de la politica a limentaria en México* (Mexico: Colegio de México, 1992).

such as purchased inputs and labor, was minimized. Market surplus decreased, and corn was destined for self-consumption within the household both for food and fodder.[43]

In some regions and among poorer households, this meant a return to the *milpa* system and the abandonment or minimizing of green-revolution technology.[44] In many regions, particularly in the central highlands, fertilization is absolutely necessary because the practice of leaving land fallow has been abandoned for decades. This trend was again reverted in 1994–1997 when use of chemical fertilizers and high-yielding seeds by ejido households returned to the proportions of 1990.[45]

Raising livestock became a strategy for corn producers, integrating corn and livestock production. In the first half of the 1990s, it was the larger ejido households that returned to this strategy. But by 1997, 48 percent of the ejido households owned cattle (compared to 44 percent in 1994), and the average size of cattle herds had increased from 5.7 to 6.7 per household).

It is difficult to estimate the number of peasant producers engaged as surplus producers who contribute to the domestic market. An important part of the former modernized-subsidized corn producers is located in the states of Jalisco, Mexico, Chiapas, and Michoacán, which contribute to 38.4 percent of national output, mainly of white corn.[46]

According to the ejido survey of 1994, 28.3 percent of corn producers were net sellers, representing the market-oriented households. In 1994, Conasupo, the state marketing agency for grains, received 52 percent of the sales of this group.[47] This group of corn producers has been under the most stress as support for production, credit, and, later, marketing was withdrawn. Little has been reported in the literature on how these producers have coped with changes and adjusted to the free market. Rather, success stories of peasants coping in an open economy have been related to potential export crops, such as organic coffee in Oaxaca and fruits and vegetables in Chiapas[48] or the less successful farmers' organizations in Michoacán.[49]

I will now draw on two cases of former modernized-subsidized corn producers who have been coping with the changing rules of the game in regard to institutional reforms and NAFTA. These producers have focused their efforts on organizing to market their products and to purchase inputs rather than on cultivating.

Until the mid-1990s, surplus-corn peasants sold their crops through Conasupo, which mediated production and consumption of basic food staples through a complex food-subsidy system for more than thirty years.[50] This was also true for entrepreneurial farmers. Selling crops to Conasupo assured a stable outlet with a secure price and, in many years, access to associated programs for marketing crops like PACE (Programa de Apoyo a la Comercialización Ejidal, or Support Program for Ejido Marketing).

When Conasupo withdrew from most crops—except corn and beans—in 1990, the security of markets and good relative prices was an incentive for risk-averse entrepreneurs, which explains the shift to maize on irrigated land in Sinaloa. But changes were in sight, and it was clear that Conasupo was slowly withdrawing from the countryside and concentrating in the large surplus areas. By 1998, Conasupo purchased 12 percent of domestically marketed crops, down from 23 percent in the peak period of 1993–1994. Sinaloa became the main supplier to Conasupo while the agency retired from peasant producing regions such as the states of Jalisco and Mexico.

The dismembering of Conasupo was a difficult and negotiated process. From the start of the modernizing program, there were clear signs that corn producers were to be left to enter the free market in the near future within the context of falling prices and increasing imports. This was a serious challenge: peasants not only lacked experience in marketing their products; they also needed technical and financial support for beginning such a venture.[51] It also became apparent that corn producers not only lacked technical and financial support in the context of falling real prices and future liberalization of corn imports within NAFTA; they also faced deliberate policy decisions by Mexico's Trade Ministry that undermined the producers. In 1996, 1998, and 1999, years in which corn production was at a historical high of 18 million tons, a total of 8.3 million tons of corn imports free of tariffs above the tariff-free quota established by NAFTA was authorized.[52] By this, the protection given to Mexican corn producers under NAFTA was de facto, canceled by dumping corn on the Mexican market in detriment to domestic farmers.[53]

Peasants and their organizations throughout the country were aware of the upcoming changes and the need to confront them. Peasants have a rich organizational experience in Mexico, rooted in the struggle for land since the 1910 revolution, under the ejido regime of local governance, and in struggles for access to productive resources, technology, and better marketing conditions.[54] This social capital has proven to be a resource with much more potential than the individual potential of the modernizing efficiency discourse.

In the mid-1990s, staple food producers, primarily corn and bean, as well as producers of other main crops such as sorghum, wheat, and other products, founded the National Association of Commercialized Farming Companies (Asociación Nacional de Empresas Comercializadoras Campesinas, or ANEC), an association for the marketing of their crops.

ANEC was based on local and regional peasant organizations throughout the country and drew heavily on previous experience dealing with Conasupo and its affiliate, Boruconsa, that handled storage facilities, as well as with the technical support of personnel from the state agency.[55] ANEC's first strategy was to take advantage of the slow phasing-out of Conasupo/Boruconsa by organizing producers in groups for collectively selling the corn harvest in their communities. In this way organized producers were able to bargain better for benefits other than price, such as bonuses for better quality (measured by humidity), bonuses under the PACE program, provision of sacks, and in some cases financial support for the organization to purchase from local members with credit from government programs such as FONAES (Fondo Nacional de Empresas de Solidaridad, or National Fund for Solidarity Businesses).

Later, organizations supported by ANEC began to venture into the free market, selling directly to the corn industry, the flour industry, Maseca (which produces items using corn and flour), and the oil industry (such as Arancia in Jalisco), taking over some of the regional space of a market that was formerly controlled by Conasupo and competing with the import of corn to which industry now had direct access. ANEC has also become partner in SIACOMEX, a firm for selling grains, which can handle commercialization directly for the association's members. Negotiating financial support for local and regional organizations is also a key commitment of the association, relying not only on increasingly scarce public programs but also on private banks, using innovative means such as *financiamiento prendatario* (getting loans with stored grain as guarantee). As an association, ANEC has also negotiated compensatory payments to its members through Aserca (Apoyos y Servicios a la Comercialización Agropecuaria, or Support Services for Agricultural Marketing), which is not accessible to individual small and dispersed producers.[56]

ANEC has also supported its members in the acquisition of infrastructure, mainly in dealing with Boruconsa and Andsa (Almacenes Nacionales de Depósito, or National Deposit Warehouse) in the transfer of storage facilities and warehouses to local organizations.[57] Other activities of ANEC are directed at giving technical advice and capacity-building in marketing and financing skills.

As of 2000, ANEC represented 220 producer organizations with 62,300 members in 4,458 ejidos and communities covering 665,800 hectares. Sales of grain amounted to 968,000 tons of corn, 420,000 tons of sorghum, 100,000 tons of wheat, and 45,000 tons of beans. The collective enterprises were present in twenty-two states of the country. Regional and local organizations owned 110 storage facilities with a capacity of 1 million tons under closed buildings. ANEC has also become partners with two other major enterprises—a construction firm (ICA) and the flour industry (Minsa) in major grain storage facilities acquired from the formerly state-owned enterprise Andsa in major metropolitan cities. Organizations within ANEC were able to sell major volumes of grain to the food industry such as Minsa and Maseca (corn flour), as well as the cornstarch industry, and were venturing to directly sell to the traditional tortilla industry in towns and cities that formerly depended on subsidized quota provisions by Conasupo.[58]

Another experience is that of Comagro (Comercializadora Agropecuaria de Occidente), a social-sector enterprise formed in 1992 by peasant organizations in the corn-producing region of Jalisco.[59] By 1992, the base organizations that founded the enterprise had organizational experience in acquiring inputs and selling corn collectively. Comagro was created in the wake of institutional reform and privatization with the 1990 dismantling of Fertimex, the parastatal enterprise that had distributed fertilizers throughout Mexico at subsidized prices for several decades. After a long and complex struggle with regional private interests, Comagro was able to obtain seven Fertimex distribution centers in Jalisco and two in Michoacán and Querétaro (out of twenty-five distribution centers in Jalisco, nine went to private interests and sixteen to peasant organizations).

In these endeavors, Comagro drew strong support from groups within the state apparatus that were sympathetic to collective and social-sector participation in the privatization process. That enabled the enterprise to negotiate for not only the fertilizer but also credit from Banrural (the public rural bank), and other programs such as Solidaridad (the aid program started by Salinas for those still in poverty) and the like. This was particularly so during the Salinas government. With the 1994 economic crisis and the Zedillo administration, this support stopped. Comagro then consolidated its links to private industry, a process that had been initiated in parallel. In 1994, the enterprise bought shares in an agroindustrial plant belonging to Maseca, providing a direct market for corn output of its members. By 1996, Comagro was Maseca's main supplier of corn in the region. In 1995, Comagro entered a joint venture with Mitsubishi in the fertilizer distribution business; the Japanese firm gave financial support, and Comagro provided the distribution channels for urea and agricultural inputs produced by the transnational corporation. Coping with a changing institutional framework, negotiating and juggling state support, and then consolidating ties with the private sector after 1994, Comagro is today a consolidated collective enterprise at the regional level. Comagro is primarily involved in the distribution of fertilizers to its members in the region and collective sales of corn to the food industry. In 1996, Comagro had twenty-nine member organizations and extended its operations throughout Jalisco, Nayarit, Colima, and, to a lesser extent, Michoacán and Querétaro.

These two examples of enterprise based on peasant organizations show that the collective efforts are viable and have a role to play in the Mexican countryside. In both cases, the enterprises emerged in the context of receding state support. To a larger extent, Comagro drew from the experience and resources of heterogeneous interest groups within the public sector, particularly the Ministry of Agriculture and Conasupo, that envisioned a future project with room for both the private and social sectors within an agricultural industry that would be increasingly reliant on its own resources and less so on the state.

ANEC also drew on a learning process with Conasupo/Boruconsa. However, by the end of the Salinas administration, and certainly during the Zedillo government, goodwill toward public policies for collective or social endeavors within the modernization process was reduced. As these two cases show, peasant organizations have been able to carve out their projects and survive in a privatized market in a very unfavorable policy context for domestic grain producers.

ANEC has had less impact on basic grain policy, even though the association is strongly committed to joining with other major peasant organizations in defending the interests of its constituencies in national forums such as the Congress and the Ministries of Agriculture and Trade in order to promote an agricultural policy in the interest of domestic production and in compliance with the rules established under the free trade agreements, for example, respecting the import tariffs for corn, as mentioned above.

Conclusion

The challenge for rural Mexico is to maintain the diversity of its social and economic landscape. The peasants' struggle of the early twentieth century changed the social and economic structure of rural Mexico, entrenching the peasantry in the economic and social fabric of rural society. Their livelihoods have been under constant stress and change. Mexico's rural population has adapted, resisted, and reconstructed its livelihood according to the specific circumstances of local and regional contexts, ethnicity, and gender and according to the predominant policy paradigms.

In that process, peasants have been semiproletarized, subsumed, modernized, subsidized, made migrants and poverty-ridden, excluded, and included in the sweep of national development projects. At the turn of the twenty-first century, they exist on the rural stage as producers as well as wage workers, migrants, and microentrepreneurs, both as individuals and as collective agents. Although the challenge to rural change is an overall development in which part of the rural population will be engaged increasingly in nonfarm activities, the challenge to agriculture is to preserve a space for small and medium producers in order to promote an articulate and socially sustainable rural development process with room for agricultural production both for export and for the domestic market—the latter in order to provide food security in terms of quantity and quality of basic foods. In the case of food producers, this means recovering a food policy that is concerned with peasants and small farmers who cultivate the white corn needed for the main food staple in Mexico. A space for family farms within agriculture is also linked to issues of defending biodiversity and, in the case of corn, the richness of biogenetic material.

The institutional framework for supporting such endeavors is strongly embedded in the organizational experience of Mexico's peasants, but the environment for such efforts has been challenged by policymakers under the Modernization Program. It is thus a major challenge to shift the emphasis of policymakers to recognize the potential of Mexico's peasantry as an organized and productive agent and to reconstruct a proper institutional environment that supports peasant farmers with credit, technical assistance, marketing skills, and bargaining power in order to defend the interests of rural Mexico.

Notes

1. Programa Nacional de Modernización para el Campo (PROMOCAM), Secretaría de Agricultura Recursos Hidraúlicos (SARH), "Programa Nacional de Modernización para el Campo, 1990–1994," *Comercio Exterior* 40, no. 10 (México, D.F.: Banco Nacional de Comercio Exterior, 1990).

2. There is a vast amount of literature on the impact of neoliberal reform in Mexico. For an overview of rural institutional reform, see Kirsten Appendini, "Changing Agrarian Institutions: Interpreting the Contradictions," in W. Cornelius and D. Myhre, eds., *The Transformation of Rural Mexico: Reforming the Ejido Sector* (La Jolla: Center for U.S.-Mexican Studies, University of California–San Diego, 1998); for a discussion of the modernization discourse, see H. Krause Hansen and K. Appendini, "Economic Integration and the Construction of the Efficient Peasant, " in Bislev and Appendini, eds., *Deficient Institutionality: European and North American Integration* (London: Macmillan, 1999); for a discussion on the intrinsic failure of the neoliberal technocratic policies, see R. García Barrios, "Free Trade and Local Institutions: The Case of the Mexican Peasants," in Bislev and Appendini, eds., *Deficient Institutionality.*

3. According to the agreement, tariffs on all commodities within zero to fifteen years starting in 1994 will be phased out progressively. Vulnerable products such as Mexican corn fall under the longest tariff schedule of fifteen years.

4. The exception was 1995, when the agricultural sector grew by 1 percent while economic crisis plunged the economy to a growth rate of –6.2 percent.

5. Data from INEGI, *Encuesta Nacional de Empleo* (Aguascalientes: INEGI, 2000); and Hernández Laos, Garro, and Lamas, cited by Alejandro Mohar Ponce, "La nueva institucionalidad rural: El caso de México," FAO Report, n.d., available at www.fao.org/Regional/prior/desrural/reform/estudios/mexico.pdf.

6. Export crops, fruits, and vegetables are mainly grown on irrigated land, which accounts for 27 percent of the agricultural land in Mexico.

7. For example, agave is being planted on former horticultural lands in southern Jalisco (personal communication by M. Nuijten, Mexico City, July 2000); according to results of a 1997 survey carried out in the ejidos, changes were region-specific, and changes in crop patterns took place mainly in the Gulf region and the North Pacific. World Bank, *Mexico Ejido Reform: Avenues of Adjustment—Five Years Later* (Main Report, Discussion Draft Document, February 1999).

8. Article 27 of the constitution was modified in 1992 to allow for privatization of ejido and communal lands, which are under the agrarian reform regime and constitute approximately half of agricultural land, 25 percent of pastures, and 80 percent of forest lands.

9. Programa de Certificación de Derechos Ejidales y Titulación de Solares Urbanos/Program for the Certification of Ejido Land Rights and the Titling of Urban House Plots (PROCEDE) gives certificates of land boundaries and rights to ejidos, comunidades, and to individual ejidatarios. The program

began in 1993 and to date has covered 70 percent of agrarian communities with regularized plots covering an estimated 63 percent of ejidatarios and comuneros with agrarian rights. Hector Robles Berlanga, "Tendencias del campo mexicano," *Estudios Agrarios* (México, D.F.: Revista de la Procuraduría Agraria, Procuraduría Agraria, 1999).

10. World Bank, *Mexico Ejido Reform,* pp. 22–24.

11. Mohar, "La nueva institucionalidad rural," p. 28, citing CEPAL, *Panorama social de américa latina,* 1998.

12. John Scott, "Experiencias exitosas de combate a la pobreza rural: Lecciones para una reorientación de las políticas," *Estudio Rimisp-FAO* (Final Report, July 1999), p. 27.

13. World Bank, *Mexico Ejido Reform.*

14. Ibid., p. 11.

15. Based on minimum salary data in Poder Ejecutivo Federal, *V Informe de Goberno, Anexo* (september 1999), p. 58.

16. R. García Barrios et al., "Estrategias de ingreso en los hogares rurales para el alivio de la pobreza e interacciones con las instituciones locales: Caso México," a report to FAO/SDAR by CRIM/UNAM/CRUCO/UACH (Morelos, Mexico: unpublished, 1999).

17. Communities are Paso del Muerto and Cheranatzicurin in 1996. Beatriz de la Tejera, *Instituciones onómicas comunitarias y el proceso de modernización en el campo: un estudio comparativo en la Meseta Purépecha* (Ph.D. thesis, Instituto de Enseñanza e Investigación en Ciencias Agrícolas, Instituto de Socioeconomía Estadística e Informática, Especialidad en Economía, Colegio de Posgraduados, Montecillo, Texcoco, Edo. de México, Mexico, 1997).

18. INEGI, *Encuesta nacional de la dinámica demográfica 1997 panorama sociodemográfico Estados Unidos Mexicanos* (Aguascalientes, México, D.F.: INEGI, 1997).

19. Sara M. Lara Flores, *Nuevas experiencias productivas y nuevas formas de organización flexible del trabajo en la agricultura mexicana* (México, D.F.: Procuraduría Agraria/Juan Pablo Editores, 1998).

20. K. Appendini, M. L. Macías, and B. Suárez, *¿Responsables o gobernables? Las trabajadoras en la agro-industria de exportación* (México, D.F.: El Colegio de México, 1997).

21. World Bank, *Mexico Ejido Reform,* p. 15.

22. Mojar, "La nueva institucionalidad rural," p. 30.

23. INEGI, *Encuesta Nacional;* the census has determined that areas with 2,500 inhabitants and more are urban.

24. R. García Barrios and L. García Barrios, "Environment and Technological Degradation in Peasant Agriculture: A Consequence of Development in Mexico," *World Development* 18, no. 11 (1990).

25. García Barrios et al., "Estrategias de ingreso."

26. A. G. Gordillo de Janvry and E. Sadoulet, *Mexico's Second Agrarian Reform: Household and Community Response* (La Jolla: Ejido Reform Research Project, Center for U.S.-Mexican Studies, University of California–San Diego, 1997).

27. Fiona Wilson, *De la casa al taller* (Michoacan, México: El Colegio de Michoacan, 1990).

28. Unión de Esfuerzos para el Campo, A.C./El Colegio de México 2000 (UDEC), *Proyecto Tesquisquiapan: Estudio regional: Conclusiones preliminar* (unpublished document, May 2000).

29. There is a recent amount of literature focusing on peasant producers and organizations' efforts to integrate in the market of export crops. See Luis Hernández, "Cafataleros: del adelgazamiento estatal a la guerra del mercado," in J. Moguel, C. Botey, and L. Hernández, eds., *Autonomía y nuevos sujetos sociales en el desarrollo rural* (México, D.F.: Siglo XXI Editores, 1992); R. Marsh and D. Runsten, "Del traspatio a la exportación: potencial para la protección campesina de frutas y hortalizas en México," in S. Lara Flores and M. Chauvet, eds., *La inserción de la agricultura mexicana en la economía mundial, Volume I: La sociedad rural mexicana frente al nuevo milenio* (México, D.F.: INAH, UAM, UNAM, Plaza y Valdes Editores, 1996); Lois Stanford, "Ante la globalización del tratado de libre comercio: el caso de los meloneros en Michoacán," in S. Flores and Chauvet, eds., *La inserción de la agricultura mexicana.*

30. Kirsten Appendini, *De la milpa a los tortibonos: La restructuración de la política alimentaria en México* (México, D.F.: El Colegio de México, 1992); Cynthia Hewitt de Alcántara, *La modernización de la agricultura mexicana, 1940–1970* (México, D.F.: Siglo XXI Editores, 1978).

31. Appendini, *De la milpa*; R. H. Robles García Barrios, N. McCarthy, and E. Ericksson, "Vulnerabilidad y recursos institucionales autóctonos de los campesinos pobres en el medio rural reformado: El caso del manejo colectivo de pastizales," in S. Zendejas and P. De Vries, eds., *Las disputas por el México rural. Transformaciones de prácticas, identidades y proyectos* (Michoacán, México, D.F.: El Colegio de Michoacán, 1998).

32. Krause Hansen and Appendini, "Economic Integration."

33. Robles Berlanga, "Tendencias del campo mexicano."

34. World Bank, *Mexico Ejido Reform.*

35. Erosion is estimated to affect 70 percent of cultivable land in Mexico. The main causes are due to rain in tropical regions of the south and to salinization in irrigated land (10 percent of surface) and semiarid climate in the north. Comisión para la Comisión Ambiental (CCA), "Estudio temático 1. El maíz en México. Algunas implicaciones ambientales del Tratado de Libre Comercio de América del Norte," in *Evaluación de los efectos ambientales del Tratado de Libre Comercio de América del Norte* (Montreal, Canada: CCA, 1999).

36. Public investment in infrastructure in irrigation has decreased in real terms, as has the acreage of new irrigated land. CCA, "Estudio temático 1."

37. Mohar, "La Nueva Institucionalidad rural."

38. Appendini et al., *¿Responsables o gobernables?*

39. Secretaría de Agricultura y Ganadería (SAGAR), *Situación actual y perspectiva de la producción de maíz en México 1990–1999,* n.d., available at www.SAGAR.org.mx.

40. World Bank, *Mexico Ejido Reform*, p. 28.

41. Mohar, "La nueva institucionalidad rural."

42. In 1990, only 236,000 tons of corn were grown in Sinaloa. Output increased to 1.7 million tons in 1993 and 2.1 million tons in 1998.

43. De Janvry et al., *Mexico's Second Agrarian Reform.*

44. The *milpa* system refers to the plot of land on which maize or corn is cultivated. Maize or corn is often cultivated in association with other food crops such as beans and squash.

45. World Bank, *Mexico Ejido Reform.*

46. SAGAR, *Situación actual y perspectiva de la producción de maíz.*

47. De Janvry et al., *Mexico's Second Agrarian Reform.*

48. Marsh and Runsten, "Del traspatio a la exportación."

49. Stanford, "Ante la globalización;" Lois Stanford, "Examining the Social Dimensions of Agricultural 'Organization': The Case of the Avocado Industry of Michoacán," paper presented at the workshop The Transformation of Rural Mexico: Building an Economically Viable and Participatory Campesino Sector, organized by the Center for U.S.-Mexican Studies, University of California–San Diego, and CIESAS-Occidente, Guadalajara, Jalisco, April 16, 1997.

50. Appendini, *De la milpa.*

51. In Mexico, the corn market was highly segmented. Large farmers and surplus peasant producers sold to Conasupo. Peasants with small or irregular marketing surplus sold to local or regional merchants. Until the early 1990s, Conasupo was the only provider of grain to the food industry, producing tortillas, maize flour, oils, starch, and other products and controlling both the domestic market and imports. Private grain merchants controlled the rural market, mainly grain for animal consumption. Appendini, *De la milpa.*

52. The quota for corn imports free of tariffs established in NAFTA began at 2.5 million in 1994 and is to increase by 0.3 percent each year until the final phasing-out in fifteen years. Corn came under the longest protection period negotiated. By 1999, the import quota free of tariff was 2.9 million tons. From 1994 to 1999, 23.7 million tons of corn were imported, eight tons above the quota. By not applying the permitted tariff, Mexico lost a fiscal income equivalent to $1.9 billion for corn imports only, equivalent to one year of support to the agricultural sector through the two main programs: Procampo and Alianza para el Campo! (Estimated by *ANEC Boletín,* August 2000, based on data from SECOFI, Bacomext, INEGI, and Banco de México).

53. ANEC, *Boletin ANEC,* various issues, 1994–2000, available at www.laneta.apc.org/anec/.

54. J. Fox and G. Gordillo, "Between State and Market: The Campesinos' Quest for Autonomy," in W. A. Cornelius, J. Gentleman, and P. H. Smith, eds., *Mexico's Alternative Political Future* (La Jolla: Center for U.S.-Mexican Studies, University of California–San Diego, 1989).

55. Information on ANEC is based on its biweekley *Boletin ANEC* and on interviews with Victor Suárez, general director of ANEC.

56. Aserca is a public agency established in 1989 that mediates between the market and basic crop producers through a system of compensatory payments based on negotiation case by case.

57. Andsa was the major state-owned grain storage facility at the points of consumption, also privatized.

58. Information based on personal communication by Victor Suárez, director of ANEC, Mexico City, June 2000.

59. The information on Comagro is based on T. Legler, *Filling the Void: The Case of Comagro*, paper presented at the Second Congress of the Canadian Association for Mexican Studies, Mexico City, November 10–13, 1996.

10

Economic Reform and Development: What Have We Learned?

Gustav Ranis

This chapter briefly reviews what I believe we have learned about reform and development over the past few decades and subsequently relates that review to the changes I see in Mexico since I last spent a year there some three decades ago. It concludes with what I believe are that country's current opportunities and problems.

What Have We Learned?

What have we learned? Perhaps the most important lesson of the past several decades is that we have learned to qualify and amplify our development objectives, moving from growth to a broader view of development that not only encompasses the elimination of both private and public income poverty but also extends to an analysis of how growth relates to human development, the basic quality of life. This is not to say that earlier generations never worried about development—in contrast to pure growth—in the third world, but we have managed to substantially advance this discourse in terms of defining the relationships among the various objectives and in terms of reaching the basic understanding that income is really a means to an end rather than an end in itself.

We do not, of course, claim that we have *the* answer to what particular countries like Mexico ought to include in any further reform package in order to move toward the achievement of this broader view of fundamental societal objectives. There currently exists a general agreement that at least some portions of the old "Washington consensus" should be preserved, notably at the macro level. This is especially true of fiscal and monetary stability, even if we do not accept the mechanical notion that there is some minimal acceptable inflation rate that needs to be tolerated. More important, when it comes to the micro level, focusing on structural changes and their sequencing, there exists a great diversity of opinion, with country differences dominating; no one, certainly not outsiders, should claim to have the truth by the beard, so to speak. Reform packages clearly have to be very country-specific, depending on the initial conditions and the inevitably heavy hand of history; they need to be nuanced; and, most important, they need to be reached via a true domestic consensus and in a decentralized fashion.

This also implies that old-fashioned conditionality is out the window even if this is not yet fully recognized in Washington. Conditionality will only work if it is really "self-conditionality." This means that we need to abandon the ritual dance engaged in by the international financial institutions (IFIs) with the countries in the past. Development was and continues to be a domestic affair; foreigners can be helpful only at the margin and only if they are fully respectful of local priorities and willing to be more passive and responsive rather than eagerly pushing on a string in order to move money.

Success also requires that the role of the state, which has been put on the back burner of late, be brought back. This is not in terms of returning to a closed economy, or an import substitution–type of regime, or even of an industrial policy of trying to pick winners but as still the main instrument for building the institutions necessary to help markets function better. This goes beyond the market-friendly intervention terminology and extends to land reform, regulatory changes, financial reforms, the creation of research and development institutions useful for directly productive activities, and, most important, the government's contribution to the improved health and education of the population. Clearly, it is now understood that systems have to move from getting prices right to getting institutions right. We need to understand much better the complementarity between markets and institutions, including the importance of the rule of law and of an independent judiciary; how regulatory functions are performed; how social safety nets are constructed; and how important it is to harness civil society to the overall development effort.

This also means that the state itself needs to be analyzed and disaggregated. We need to know whether, in a particular case, it is an honest traffic cop or whether it has its own, independent, sometimes nefarious agenda. Moreover, is the system sufficiently decentralized? We know, of course, that decentralization may take two forms: vertical or horizontal. The vertical variety has been much discussed in terms of fiscal and administrative devolution or lack thereof. The horizontal version deals more with whether or not power has devolved from the executive branch to the legislature and to an independent judiciary at various levels of government. Both dimensions need careful and, in many ways, complementary attention.

We also have learned something about the complicated relationship between development and democracy. We are reasonably certain that continued development ultimately requires a lot of decentralized decisionmaking that (as in the cases of Taiwan and Korea and, most probably, in the future case of China) will ultimately promote political democracy to go along with the sequential strengthening of economic democracy via participation. But we are still less sure whether democracy promotes development unless we accept that narrower version, that is, participatory or economic democracy, as opposed to insisting on the broader Westminster version focusing on multiparty systems, voting behavior, and abiding by poll results.

I believe we have also learned that natural resource abundance, along with foreign capital for the asking, represents a two-edged sword. It may cause so-called Dutch disease, not only in the narrow sense of affecting the exchange rate adversely (thus making it difficult for a country like Mexico to export its labor-intensive products while simultaneously leading to the neglect of agriculture) but also in terms of affecting the overall decisionmaking process. This extended version of the Dutch disease—or, as some people would put it, the case of an income effect overcoming a substitution effect—argues that the flow of additional resources tends to take the pressure off decisionmakers and politicians and permits them to avoid making policy changes, especially painful ones. It raises a moral hazard problem similar to that accompanying implicit or explicit loan guarantees that we have seen at work in the context of the Asian financial crisis of the late 1990s.

I think we have also learned that cross-country regressions to explain growth, adding more and more variables, including ethnic diversity, temperature, and the kitchen sink, are not really likely to advance our understanding of what makes for development. In these regressions, as has been pointed out by others, indeed only the investment rate seems to be robust as we add and subtract variables. Neither is the assumption of convergence likely to hold except among neighbors, such as the members of the European Union or states of the United States.

Perhaps the biggest payoff, in my opinion, continues to emerge from comparative longitudinal country study research that stays within a particular typology, for example, a labor-surplus Latin American country like Mexico, or a small Central American country like Costa Rica, or a human resource–deficient African country like Chad, or a labor-deficient land-surplus country like Kazakhstan. The so-called new growth theory—all the rave but a few years ago—has not, in my view, panned out. To its credit, it has appropriately refocused our attention on externalities, especially on education and research and development, in an effort to try to endogenize technology change and thus help explain the absence of diminishing returns to investment. But to date it has shown little empirical content and recorded even less policy impact to be weighed in its favor.

We have also learned that in countries with substantial agricultural sectors, we simply must permit that sector to play its critical historical role. If we do not, then its contribution to the development process will be nullified in its savings, technology, and labor-supply aspects. The complementary role of agricultural and nonagricultural activities is likely to be necessary for developmental success from both a growth and a distributional perspective. In other words, balanced growth in the rural areas remains a large part of the answer; too exclusive a fascination with the more exciting and visible international and trade dimensions of development can be dangerously misleading. Indeed, anything that is overdone can become grotesque and counterproductive. This is emphatically not to say that trade does not represent an important handmaiden of development—only that it is not a leading sector or an engine of the process. Even if Jeffrey Sachs might disagree, I believe that domestic balanced growth in tandem with an increasing outward orientation remain critical for developmental success.

The old-fashioned discussion concerning the role of government versus markets should be put aside. We need government interventions that accommodate rather than obstruct markets. Using Simon Kuznets's terminology, if the colonial past has left a system with inadequate "organic nationalism" or cohesive cement, the newly independent government has to provide its synthetic equivalent without, however, overstretching its (usually limited) organizational, fiscal, and technical capacities. What we are clear about is that the worst outcome is one of alternating private sector– and public sector–friendly policies, yielding the equivalent of the well-known stop-go phenomenon in terms of interventionist and more market-oriented policy mixes alternating with each other as exogenous shocks occur or finance ministers change.

With respect to exchange rate policies, we have also learned, largely as a consequence of recent financial crises, that two extremes seem to work best, that is, either an exchange rate policy that comes close to dollarization (or at least a currency board) or moving toward a floating exchange rate system with minimal interventions. In that sense we have come to realize that Robert Mundell is right and that it is quite impossible to achieve all three objectives: capital mobility, a fixed exchange rate, and being in charge of one's independent national monetary policy. More and more countries have consequently been driven to the extremes: giving up any independent monetary policy, as in Argentina, or pursuing a floating rate with free capital movements while retaining an independent monetary policy, as in recent-vintage Mexico.

Moving on to what we have learned about negotiations on trade—regional or global—the whole process, of course, suffers from the original sin of the reciprocity concept that countries should be willing to open themselves to increased imports without reciprocity from the point of view of rational economic analysis. However, from the point of view of political economy, we know that this position has long ago been sacrificed. In terms of the global versus regional approaches to trade liberalization, two-thirds of world trade is now governed by arrangements typified by the European Economic Community and the North American Free Trade Agreement (NAFTA), which on paper seem quite acceptable as long as the external tariffs of such groupings are not raised and they are open to new members.

From the point of view of developing countries, however, the World Trade Organization (WTO) approach, or global liberalization, is much to be preferred, especially in the case of relatively small nations that are likely to be trampled when the large elephants fight. But in either case, trade liberalization can provide an important advantage, especially to labor-surplus developing countries, although, of course, the key may well be whether or not textiles are part of any deal or are deleted from the liberalization package. Even under the Uruguay Round of negotiations, when the commitment was made to end the Multi-Fiber Agreement, giving way to tariffs that would then ultimately be brought down, this agreement is so back-loaded that developing countries have the right to be skeptical about what will actually happen by the year 2005. In any case, computable general equilibrium models, which are used to provide quantitative evaluation of effects of government policy, show very large potential gains, in the hundreds of billions of dollars, for developing countries, including in Latin America, especially if we assume that current levels of unemployment and underemployment can be mopped up in the course of trade liberalization. A particular advantage for developing countries, not previously realized, is in the services arena, especially in construction and some of the knowledge industries, which are now not only recognized as constituting important traded goods but also growing faster than trade in commodities.

One dimension of trade negotiations, which we have come to understand better in recent years, is whether the "special and differential" treatment enjoyed by developing countries is really good for them. Once considered a great advantage as part of the import-substitution syndrome, the current view is that, though it may be necessary for a very short period of time at an early stage of development, it should not be extended too long. In other words, developing countries like Mexico can do better by participating in multilateral liberalization on a generalized WTO basis than by utilizing special and differential treatment options in its various manifestations.

I think it is generally agreed by now that the effort by developed countries to include environment and labor conditions as side agreements to trade negotiations in an effort to harmonize domestic policies in these areas across the board makes very little economic sense across different stages of development and endowment levels. When dealing with environment as a global good, side payments from rich to poor countries make sense; but the effort to view low wages or otherwise differential conditions of labor markets as unfair competition, threatening a race to the bottom, very quickly becomes a subterfuge for protectionist interests. The movement of labor by incorporation into traded commodities and services is really the main way to relieve the pressures of illegal immigration that are building up in Western Europe, Japan, and the United States.

Relevance to the Mexican Economy

Although I do not claim to have been a close observer of the Mexican economy over the past three decades, let me take the plunge and make some assertions as to which items from the above listing of things we have learned may be especially relevant for the Mexican economy. I do this with the benefit of some historical perspective, as I spent a year (1970–1971) at the Colegio de México and subsequently wrote a piece in *Demografía y Economía* entitled "Is the Mexican Miracle Turning Sour?" The article questioned the validity of the then-current euphoria reflecting more than thirty years of sustained growth at nearly 6 percent, coupled with relative political stability, the absence of inflation, and a fixed exchange rate. Today, thirty years later, I am tempted to raise the question, Is the Mexican economy finally "turning sweet"?

With respect to changing societal objectives, I suggested then that Mexico needed not to dethrone the gross national product but to pay much more attention to the distributional aspects that have resulted from the nature of the particular growth path it had chosen. Realistically, little can be done fiscally about an unfavorable income distribution, but much can be done by changing the structure of the economy. Until recently, Mexico had been a kind of enclave economy, with natural resource exports financing a relatively narrow, capital-intensive, and inefficient industrial sector. Land reforms initially gave Mexico an advantage over other countries in Latin America. However, these reforms were not sufficiently well thought through and created a series of incentive problems on the *ejido* land that—together with the bad distribution of irrigation—led to the relative neglect of a large part of the heavily populated southern states.

Moreover, Mexico historically followed the typical political economy pattern of development over time. The initial upturn (the 1960s to 1973), given favorable terms of trade, ushered in the so-called growth with stability era, with levels of protection probably increasing, deficits kept in check, the exchange rate fixed, and capital inflows largely related to traditional exports. However, once the post-1973 downturn occurred, and in order to maintain growth in the face of deteriorating terms of trade, domestic spending was increased in an effort to replace foreign exchange earnings by the creation of additional domestic purchasing power. This, coupled with the realization of larger than expected oil reserves, meant a breakdown of all fiscal and monetary restraint, with foreign investors competing to come in on what looked like excellent investment opportunities. The money supply increased from 25 percent in 1974 to 60 percent in 1982; the budget deficit reached as high as 14 percent of gross domestic product (GDP), and, with velocity increasing, inflation reached 90 percent in the 1980s. Foreign debt rose fivefold between 1973 and 1976, and when the oil price reversal came in the early 1980s, the debt burden became quite intolerable and Mexico felt it had to defend its exchange rate with import controls.

After 1986, in the presence of an external upturn, caused largely by oil prices recovering, spending was initially kept under control. However, by the early 1990s, Mexico experienced a major crisis. Foreign capital, which had come in large volumes with the expectation of major oil exports, now turned around precipitously and moved out. Once again, the domestic expansion of monetary and fiscal policy was used to make up for the shortcomings in export earnings and foreign capital inflows. This time, however, because Mexico had joined the General Agreement on Tariffs and Trade in 1986 and NAFTA in 1994, it did not return to the syndrome of import controls plus delayed large-scale devaluation but instead adjusted prices earlier—if admittedly not very adroitly. Consequently, Mexico did not repeat the 1979–1982 experience, which represents a fundamental change for the better: I believe the old political economy cycle has been broken in a fundamental way. Even though a crisis did occur, the response permitted a softer landing than had historically been the case.

The *maquiladora* factories along the U.S.-Mexico border have remained an increasingly important escape valve for Mexico's labor surplus throughout the period, with foreign investment roughly doubling every decade and employment rising by 50 percent. It should also be noted that Mexico has come to rely more on direct investment and is less dependent on portfolio capital, which helped avoid the massive flight of capital experienced in Asia. Meanwhile the trade-to-GDP ratio went from 0.2 in 1983 to 0.6 in 1998. Moreover, in spite of the relatively high price of oil today, manufactured goods currently amount to 90 percent of total exports. Thus, Mexico has a much lower dependence on natural resource exports and, therefore, a decreased vulnerability to Dutch-disease problems.

There has been, moreover, much institutional construction and various other reforms put in place to support trade liberalization in pursuit of a more generalized export expansion. In 1985, tariffs were reduced to a maximum of 20 percent, and items covered by license were reduced from 90 percent to 20 percent. In 1993, more favorable regulations governing foreign direct investment were promulgated. With respect to agriculture, reforms of the ejido system, though incomplete, were promulgated. Conasupo, the state marketing agency for grains, which had provided unequal sales access to large and small farmers, was dismantled in 1999. Tortilla and other subsidies were eliminated. Although levels of investments in research and development and in education remain inadequate, the trade-growth nexus of mutual reinforcement is increasingly in evidence.

However, the medium and small-scale industrial sector still remains largely out of the loop, partly because it is starved for credit. The most recent financial crisis made most observers realize that capital-market liberalization should not move too far ahead of banking reform, which continues to be a problem. However, even though the economy is by no means immune from future crises, I believe there is a good chance that the historical stop-go pattern has been broken for good, along with the dominance of a one-party system virtually merged with the state.

Domestic savings rates have risen from 14 percent to 20 percent, and direct productive-sector investment has been increasing steadily since 1996, averaging 18 percent, this time of the private-sector, not the public-sector, variety. However, in spite of PROGRESA, a government program to increase education, health, and nutrition expenditures, public-sector human development–oriented outlay remains deficient. As was strongly emphasized in the recent electoral campaign, adequate educational investments at the secondary and especially the vocational levels are still inadequate.

In fact, a major remaining weakness—related also to the nonparticipation of medium and small-scale, especially rural, industry—is the still highly unequal distribution of income, as well as the associated lack of satisfactory progress on poverty alleviation and human development. Mexico's Gini coefficient, at 0.54, is one of the highest in the world and remains a real challenge. Given respectable income growth, this clearly reflects a relatively poor performance in poverty alleviation and human development. Poverty rates, however measured, are somewhere in the 20 percent range, although incomes among the self-employed and farmworkers are probably not fully recorded. It is probably no exaggeration to state that fully one-third of Mexico's workers are either unemployed or underemployed even at this point, and even after a relatively successful 5 percent annual growth performance during much of the 1990s. Labor market reforms, which move toward plant-level negotiations and thus promise greater labor market flexibility, are in the works but have not yet yielded results. Decentralization of the public sector, either of the vertical or horizontal variety, has been much talked about but not yet implemented; this also remains a serious problem. Fifty percent of federal tax revenues now go to local bodies on a relatively unrestricted basis. The possibility of actually transferring tax powers to local bodies, which would provide a real boon to rural industry, has not yet been explored. It has only recently been recognized that poverty alleviation cannot be an afterthought but needs to be part of Mexico's overall development strategy.

The relationship between growth and human development, of course, runs in both directions. For a given level of per capita income we know that the lower the poverty level, or the better the distribution of income, the more resources are bound to be allocated by households to human development–oriented goods (e.g., education, health, and nutrition). It should also to be noted that the higher the level of female education, and the higher the proportion of the wife's contribution to total family income, the larger the allocation of expenditures to human development–related goods at the same level of family income.

In summary, much remains to be done, especially with respect to the distribution of income and the human dimensions of development. However, the prospects for continued progress are much improved because the stop-go policies of the past have become constrained by Mexico's membership in WTO and NAFTA, as well as by the more competitive domestic political system that has been so amply demonstrated since the 2000 presidential election. A closer interaction between economic and political development is very much in evidence already and can be counted on to give Mexico a better chance to enter the virtuous cycle between sustained growth and the achievement of equally sustained progress in human development.

PART 3

Mexicans Abroad

11

Building Transnational Ties: Mexicans in the United States

Stephen Pitti

Due to the large number of emigrants living and working in the United States, Mexico has long existed *en el extranjero* (outside) of its geographic boundaries. Today more than 15 million residents of Mexican descent live in the United States, of whom more than 7 million were born in Mexico. The July 2000 elections and the historic victory of Vicente Fox drew considerable new attention to that population, in part because immigrants had their first opportunity to elect a U.S.-based delegate to the national Congress. Polling stations in northern Mexico attracted *votomigrantes* (migrant voters) from across the border, and the three major presidential candidates attempted to outshine one another in proposals regarding migration and border enforcement. Francisco Labastida, the candidate of the Institutional Revolutionary Party (PRI), announced that he would create new jobs to discourage out-migration but that he also believed it

> *indispensable atender a quien ha emigrado del país, creando para legalizar sus papeles, para propiciar que haya emigración temporal durante 6 meses o periodos parecidos, protegidos por la ley, defender los derechos de los mexicanos, temporalmente emigrantes, y consolidar un régimen que permita que sus derechos sean defendidos, que no se violen los derechos a un buen salario, que tengan acceso a buena vivienda y a buena morada, que se les faciliten todos los trámites allá y además mantener las relaciones educativas, culturales, de tal manera que no se pierda el contacto con los mexico-americanos.*[1]
>
> [. . . is essential to assist those who have emigrated from the country, creating mechanisms to legalize their documents, to allow for temporary migration protected by the law for six months or similar periods, to defend the right of Mexicans as temporary emigrants, and to consolidate a regime that defends their rights, that their rights to a

> good salary are not violated, that they have access to good housing, that they are able to have access to services while maintaining educational and cultural relations in such way that they do not lose contact with Mexican Americans.]

Democratic Revolutionary Party candidate Cuauhtémoc Cárdenas similarly emphasized protecting the human rights of *mexicanos* living in the United States and their "efforts to keep alive their cultural identity and native languages," whereas Fox argued for greater ease of movement across the U.S.-Mexico border similar to the system developed by the European Union. In addition to suggesting that the Mexican government might help train more of its citizens to work as gardeners in the United States, Fox criticized the U.S. Border Patrol for violating the human rights of Mexican transmigrants.[2]

From their homes in the United States, citizens of Mexico therefore had a great deal to think about in the months leading up to the July elections, and an untold number crossed the border to vote, some driving for hours to Tijuana and other border cities from distant locations in the United States. The results of that contest caused excited discussions within many immigrant communities, even as the election itself evidenced a new governmental recognition of the growing transnational linkages between Mexican immigrants in the United States and their home communities.[3] The demographic growth of the ethnic Mexican community in the United States since 1970 has increased the significance of those transborder connections, and as a number of social scientists have argued in recent years, immigrants have been able to forge stronger linkages home because of "the ready availability of air transport, long-distance telephone, facsimile communication, and electronic mail," technological changes that seem to be hallmarks of the worldwide information economy.[4]

Although the character and extent of Mexican immigrants' transnational linkages have no doubt developed with the availability of these technologies, such connections have certainly not appeared out of nowhere, and in this chapter I will argue for the importance of understanding contemporary Mexico within its long history of transborder migrations. The historian Devra Weber correctly notes that "current migrations are more recent manifestations of a very old process than a fundamentally new phenomenon," and others have recognized for decades that mexicanos' complex relationship to the country of their birth raises questions about the solidity of the political boundary dividing the United States and Mexico.[5] As one pioneering immigrant scholar argued in 1978, the historical movements of Mexican transborder migrants have called into question the permanency of that international boundary line, reminding scholars and policymakers that national subjects will "devise ways of breaking through" political boundaries "frozen" decades before by nation-states.[6] The origins of Mexicans' transnational practices go as far back as the middle of the nineteenth century, when the U.S.-Mexican War of 1846–1848 established a new international boundary line between the two countries that divided families and threatened economic networks established decades before. In places like southern Texas, residents of one side of the Rio Grande found themselves traveling into another country on visits to aunts and uncles living across the waterway. Patterns of repatriation began during this era, too, and historian David Montejano estimates that half of San Antonio's ethnic Mexican population left that city by 1856, many to relocate in Mexico.[7]

In this chapter I also highlight the contemporary and historical importance of economic networks linking Mexico and the United States. From their homes in the United States, Mexicans began struggling to maintain established economic ties to Mexico soon after the formation of the new international boundary line in 1848. María Amparo Ruíz de Burton, for one, an elite resident of the San Diego area who had grown up in Baja California and married a U.S. Army lieutenant in Alta, California, found herself embroiled in costly but unsuccessful legal efforts by the 1870s to retain her family's ranch on both sides of the border.[8] Although mexicanos residing in the Southwest at the conclusion of the U.S.-Mexican War were offered U.S. citizenship under the Treaty of Guadalupe Hidalgo (1848), the signers of that agreement did not anticipate that new groups of Mexican citizens would soon travel north to work in what had become the U.S. Southwest. To the surprise of observers in both nations, new migrations of Mexicans since the California gold rush made the international *frontera* (border) an open zone of economic contact between mexicanos and U.S. citizens, a "greater Mexican" space in which new labor systems would develop by the early twentieth century.

Finally, I advance two additional arguments about Mexican migrations to and from the United States. First, I emphasize the role of national governments in shaping transnationality and argue that those migrations have not simply emerged as individual economic responses independent of state interventions. Second, I suggest that Mexican migrations have created new cultural practices and visions of the Mexican community that transcend the boundaries of either Mexico or the United States. In fact, it seems clear that a nascent "transnational social field" began to be established in that region in the decades after the U.S.-Mexican War, particularly near the frontera as a set of transnational economic and cultural practices developed from cross-border familial networks—the persistent labor force participation of immigrants in the United States, the recurrent hostility of many U.S. residents toward the permanent settlement of Mexican immigrants, and the public policies designed by both U.S. and Mexican government officials. In more recent years, mexicanos have fashioned communities in the United States that participate "on a routine basis in a field of relationships, practices, and norms that include both places of origin and places of destination."[9] In the concluding section of this chapter, I address the formation of the new political visions emerging from Mexican transnationality.

The Political Economy of Transmigration

Along with working people, capital and commerce have moved back and forth across the U.S.-Mexico border for more than a century, and current moves to "integrate" the two national economies under the North American Free Trade Agreement (NAFTA) have clear antecedents. In 1848, for instance, the state of Tamaulipas instituted a free-trade zone with Texas to allow for the easier movement of goods across the Rio Grande, a policy that one member of the Mexican Chamber of Deputies celebrated by emphasizing that

> smuggling ceased to exist because there was nothing left to encourage it. Goods sold in Brownsville lost their appeal because they could be purchased in Mexico at the same or even lower price. Before the advent of the Free Zone, poverty, depression, and low spirits prevailed on the right bank of the Rio Bravo, but afterward there was activity, well-being, and progress. Mexican businessmen used to cross into the United States to make their purchases and then avoided paying ever-rising tariffs in Mexico; after the Free Zone they had no need to spend their fortunes in American establishments or to defraud the Mexican treasury.
>
> With equality in commerce, truly a necessary thing in that part of the nation, emigration of Mexicans to the United States ceased, poverty ended, and a state of well-being was reestablished.[10]

Under Porfirio Díaz, the national government of Mexico maintained a free-trade zone along the entire border from 1885 until 1905, during which many parts of northern Mexico witnessed massive investments by U.S. capitalists in mining, railroads, and agriculture. Those developments employed local Mexicans in new emerging sectors and made it difficult for many villages to remain independent of the wage-labor economy. Even more important, the establishment of new trans-border links between U.S. and Mexican capitalists had the effect of encouraging mexicanos to travel to the United States to seek work. In historian Miguel Tinker Salas's formulation, as "Americans looked south" to invest in new industries across the border, "Mexicans went north" for jobs in the United States.[11] Those interrelated processes of U.S. capital investment in Mexico and Mexican labor migration to the United States continued into the late twentieth century. Douglas Massey and Kristin Espinosa have argued,

> The provisions of NAFTA . . . help to bring about the social and economic transformations that generate migrants. The integration of the North American market will also create new links of transportation, telecommunication and interpersonal acquaintance, connections that are necessary for the efficient movement of goods, information and capital, but which also encourage and promote the movement of people—students, business executives, tourists and, ultimately, undocumented workers.[12]

The shape of working-class Mexican immigration to the United States and the interdependence of the two national economies developed significantly during the era of the Mexican Revolution, when hundreds of thousands of Mexicans began to move north across the international boundary. Mexico still lives with the effects of those transformations today. Agricultural, mining, and other extractive industries in the U.S. border states attracted thousands of mexicanos to the United States, and labor contractors employed by those industries commonly visited settlements in Mexico in search of prospective employees. Often faced with grave economic pressures, towns in both the northern and central states watched large groups of their residents depart en masse for California, Arizona, Texas, Colorado, and the Midwest. The historian Lawrence A. Cardoso notes,

> By the eve of World War I, big, irrigated cotton and sugar beet farms covered the river valleys of the Southwest. These farms had become like plantations and required large numbers of cheap, unskilled, migratory laborers. Railroads were in constant need of track crews to keep their rolling stock in proper order, and the mining industry continued to employ thousands of workers in pick and shovel work and in smelting work.[13]

During these formative years, migrations totaled at least 50,000 from 1900 to 1910, approximately 220,000 in the following decade, and some 460,000 from 1920 to 1930. Enticed by the availability of new jobs, Mexicans began to establish patterns of "chain migration" to Chicago and even more distant locations. Many of the regions that sent residents to the United States during those early decades continued to be major immigrant-sending communities for most of the remaining years of the twentieth century.[14] By the 1980s, one investigator would therefore discover that in the town of Aguililla, Michoacán,

> Almost every family had members who were or had been abroad; the local economy depended heavily on the influx of dollars; and many of the area's small farming operations continued only because they were sustained by migrant remittances . . . few abandon the municipio forever. Most people stay in the United States relatively briefly; almost all of those who stay longer continue to keep in touch with the people and places they have left behind, and even those who have been away for many years quite often return.[15]

As residents of Aguililla and other locales in Mexico have long known, movements across the U.S.-Mexico border were not simply one-way travels, and many immigrants insisted on returning to their hometowns whenever possible. Circular migration characterized these travels, and as early as 1903, when Mexican track workers in Los Angeles went on strike against the Pacific Electric Railway Company, a key complaint was that their contractors had threatened to cancel workers' "free trip home" to Mexico.[16] Thousands again insisted on returning to the Mexican *patria* (homeland) in the summer of 1917 when rumors circulated in the United States that immigrants would be drafted and sent to Europe as cannon fodder in the war effort. "During the first five days of June [1917]," one historian notes, "5,451 repatriates streamed across the border; by June 11 another 4,000 had left the United States. Through the remainder of June and July the daily count of returning workers continued to mount."[17] Between 1919 and 1926, as well, at least 489,748 returned to Mexico, and during the nativist early 1930s more than 1 million immigrants chose to repatriate in the hope of "a viable alternative to a life and an economy gone sour" in the United States.[18] Perhaps the most dramatic instance of massive repatriation during the twentieth century began in June 1954 with Operation Wetback, an effort by the U.S. Border Patrol to deport undocumented Mexicans or scare them into repatriating on their own.

More than 60,000 in Texas set out "voluntarily" for Mexico within the first month of the program, and the U.S. Immigration and Naturalization Service later claimed to have apprehended more than 1 million other illegals during that year.[19] As that major event in U.S.-Mexican relations made clear, mexicanos have not always chosen to return to Mexico and instead were forced by state agencies to travel south across the border in enormous waves over the course of the twentieth century, even as thousands of others moved in the opposite direction.

Despite the prevalence of repatriations and deportations, Mexicans have been critical to the economic growth of the United States for decades as mostly low-wage workers in a racially segregated economy. Agents of the U.S. Border Patrol often recognized the near impossibility of stemming the arrival of job-seekers from Mexico and the demand for them in the United States. As one official admitted in 1987,

> Illegals are a fact of life in California agriculture. Growers depend on them. They work harder than legals and they stick with the work. If politicians were concerned about illegals, they would give us the staff to make a difference. Right now all we do is harass a few workers and harass a few growers. We don't stop the use of illegals. Workers return in three to five days. They're gone on Friday and back on Monday. It's the norm. We scare them a little and cost them a lot. That's all.[20]

By the late 1920s, in fact, Mexicans already represented approximately 75 percent of both California's farm labor force and Texas's unskilled construction labor force, more than half of the Southwest's sugar beet laborers, 60 percent of the region's mineworkers, and perhaps as much as 90 percent of local railroad track crews. U.S. government agencies generally supported the formation and segmentation of this Mexican workforce in later years by crafting new contract labor programs that sent Mexicans north to fill low-wage occupations.

Mexican officials did little to stem out-migration during the early twentieth century, and some even expressed hope by the 1920s that temporary work in the United States might transform the Mexican peasantry living "in relatively inferior stages of development" into more "modern" types with forward-looking perspectives on consumption and production. As the influential Mexican social scientist Manuel Gamio saw it, stints in the United States might serve as a sort of school for the emerging Mexican nation-state:

> Although the [Mexican] immigrant often undergoes suffering and injustice and meets many difficulties [in the United States], he undoubtedly benefits economically by the change. He learns the discipline of modern labor. He specializes. He becomes familiar with industrial and agricultural machinery. He learns about scientific intensive agriculture. He observes and learns about the transformation of raw material into industrial products. He becomes a laborer of the modern type, much more efficient than before. Could all the immigrants return to Mexico, they would do much to make of it a great industrial and agricultural country.[21]

Ideologies of modernization continued to justify increased outmigration, as others in Mexico hoped after World War II that their compatriots who labored temporarily in the United States would import an improved understanding of U.S. technology and agricultural practices that would in turn improve the patria.

Laboring in the U.S. economy remained an economic survival strategy for working-class Mexicans during the early twentieth century, and remittances helped many later migrants to develop local agriculture and small businesses in their home communities. By 1926, when Manuel Gamio began to research the recently arrived communities of mexicanos in the United States, he therefore found compatriots wiring home money from forty-six U.S. states. The amount of those money orders had risen from just over 5 million pesos in 1919 to more than 16 million in 1927; most found their way to the states of Michoacán, Guanajuato, and Jalisco, yet funds had also traveled via Western Union to every Mexican state except Quintana Roo.[22] Although tracing more recent remittances is difficult, Wayne Cornelius has estimated that they totaled some $3 billion in 1975; Manuel García y Griego and Francisco Giner de los Rios tabulated approximately $1.8 billion in 1984; and other estimates suggest that the remittances of transborder migrants today are $2–4 billion per year.[23] During the 1990s, many state governments in Mexico (including Guanajuato under the leadership of Vicente Fox) also began to encourage those capital flows by providing matching funds for dollars sent to local public works projects.[24]

Not everyone in Mexico has agreed on the value of emigration to the United States, of course, and many have long criticized it as a sign that the Mexican government has been using the U.S. labor market as a "safety valve" instead of developing more effective internal programs of national economic growth. Vicente Fox leveled a similar charge at the PRI in his 2000 campaign, and the Mexico City newspaper *La Jornada* recently editorialized,

> *Las preocupaciones por la posibilidad de que disminuyan los fondos que los mexicanos emigrados envían a sus comunidades deberían asustar a todos. En efecto, ellas se acomodan sin más al hecho de que el país se haya convertido en exportador de seres humanos y creador de tragedias rurales en nuestro suelo y, en vez de pensar en cómo frenar las migraciones, sólo se inquietan por los flujos monetarios que las mismas originan o pueden dejar de originar. Esta idea del mercado de brazos, sangre, cerebros, sólo centrada en la monetarización de las desgracias humanas y del deterioro de los suelos y la producción nacionales, ve a los emigrantes como productores de remesas en divisas y revela una gran insensibilidad humana y social o, en muchos casos, incluso cinismo.*[25]
>
> [The concerns over the possibility that the funds that emigrated Mexicans send to their communities may diminish should frighten everyone. In fact, these concerns are reconciled based on the mere fact that the country has been converted into the exporter of human beings and the creator of rural tragedies on our land, and instead of thinking about how to restrain migration, the only worry is about the monetary flows that the migrants themselves create or are able to stop creating. This idea of a market of arms, blood, brains, only centered on the monetarization of the human suffering, the deterioration of the land, and national production, sees emigrants as producers of remittances and reveals a large human and social insensitivity, even cynicism.]

Critics of emigration today often emphasize that mexicanos have crossed the border into the United States in part because of their own government's activities. During the late nineteenth century, the dismantling of the communal *ejido* system of landholding and massive efforts in both countries to build national transportation networks encouraged many early migrants to leave their home communities.[26] Often traveling first to local cities, Mexicans moved north and south across the frontera with increasing ease as a result of those new rails and highways, and their settlements boomed in places like El Paso as a result of the integration of U.S. and Mexican transportation systems.[27] Subsequent state-driven agrarian reforms in Mexico also shaped migration patterns to the United States. In the 1930s, President Lázaro Cárdenas's *reparto agrario* (agrarian distribution) divided what had been large individual landholdings into smaller plots, a change that apparently helped to reduce out-migration in some locations by requiring that individuals who wanted to keep their new plots stay and maintain them in production.[28] Thirty years later, however, state-sponsored programs of agricultural modernization often had the opposite effect. In Altamira, Jalisco, and other towns, the introduction of new crops, machinery, and insecticides during the "green revolution" of the 1960s increased costs of production, led to the decline of sharecropping in the area, and "created the conditions for mass migration" from that community and others.[29] In more recent years, neoliberal structural adjustments implemented in Mexico have also exacerbated many people's need to travel abroad for work. Mexico's "increasing incapacity to integrate its growing population into formal employment" during the 1980s and 1990s helped to lower real wages to the point that those who remain in Mexico can expect only to "earn about a fifth to a quarter of the wages earned by inhabitants of the United States."[30]

Permanent Settlement and Contract Labor

In addition to economic restructuring in both countries, immigrant transnationality has been shaped by the reception in the United States of Mexican immigrants as a racial group and a labor force. Employers have often been extremely influential in that regard. Although often supporting the arrival of greater numbers of mexicanos, many hoped during the twentieth century that those immigrants would return eventually to Mexico and would remain transnational "sojourners" instead of permanent settlers north of the border. Employers commonly explained their need for "nonwhite" Mexican workers before World War II with a self-serving racial logic, and those supporting the arrival of low-wage Mexican workers were often quick to assure restrictionist politicians that mexicanos would not remain in the United States for long. Many declared that population to be naturally suited for farm labor under the hot sun, for example, and others announced their need for Mexican immigrants because "we have no Chinamen; we have not the Japs. The Hindu is worthless; the Filipino is nothing, and the white man will not do the work."[31] In the midst of congressional immigration debates in the 1920s, proponents of increased migration argued that Mexicans' interest in returning to their homeland made them an ideal low-wage workforce, and some even suggested that Mexicans' biological instinct prompted them to flock back across the border on a regular basis and remain "birds of passage." Assertions of Mexican cultural inferiority were common. The grower S. Parker Frieselle characteristically offered his guarantee "that the civilization of California would never be built on a Mexican foundation," and the federal government's Dillingham Commission argued in 1911 that "while the Mexicans are not easily assimilated, this is of no very great importance as long as most of them return to their native land after a short time."[32]

For most of the twentieth century, U.S. labor unions generally expressed either hostility or disinterest toward Mexican immigrant workers. Concerned in large part that those new low-wage laborers would be used as strikebreakers or would be hired before white Americans, the American Federation of Labor (AFL) led the way in arguing for immigration restrictions during the 1920s. Although many of the left-wing unions that affiliated as the Congress of Industrial Organizations (CIO) showed far greater interest in involving mexicanos in their organizations as members and leaders during the 1930s and 1940s, the following decades witnessed a resurgence of restrictionist sentiment among many labor organizations in the U.S. Southwest. By the mid-1960s, the United Farm Workers, headed by Mexican Americans such as César Chávez and Dolores Huerta, vehemently argued that rural civil rights were imperiled by the arrival of new immigrants. In more recent years, a number of prominent African American civil rights leaders have similarly contended that mexicanos contribute to the impoverishment of their community by taking much-needed jobs. Recent efforts by the AFL-CIO (and, in particular, the Service Employees International Union and the Hotel Employees and Restaurant Employees International Union) to organize Mexican immigrants are startling reversals, then, of the dominant restrictionist trend in twentieth-century U.S. labor politics.

Widespread opposition to the permanent settlement of Mexicans in the United States by U.S. labor unionists and others, combined with the Mexican government's concern about the civil rights of undocumented Mexicans, encouraged the creation of temporary contract labor programs between the two countries during the twentieth century. Faced with labor shortages during World War I, U.S. employers first persuaded the federal government to exempt Mexican agricultural, railroad, mining, and construction workers from restrictions barring the entry of illiterate immigrants. From 1917 to 1921, U.S. employers applied to either the United States Employment Service or the Bureau of Immigration for Mexican workers, and with the U.S. government's permission contracted some 72,000 workers at the border during those years. U.S. officials did little to monitor the program, and employers were expected to provide adequate housing and wages and to pay the costs of immigrants' return to Mexico—demands that became a loose model for developing a similar contract labor system in 1942.[33] Designed once again to fill wartime labor shortages in the United States, the Emergency Labor Agreement (known as the Bracero Program) set out to organize more carefully the movement of those contracted mexicanos to the United States and back. Designed almost exclusively for agricultural workers, the program reflected the bargaining leverage of Mexican officials vis-à-vis the United States, as officials from Mexico City successfully demanded that workers be given a written contract; that both national governments be involved in overseeing the administration of the program; that the U.S. government pay for the costs of *braceros'* transportation to their worksites; and that instances of "racial discrimination, of the type in which Mexicans were turned away from 'white' restaurants and public facilities or sorted by color on buses" would be grounds for barring braceros from working in a given community.[34]

Over the course of the agreement's twenty-two-year history, nearly 5 million contracted Mexican workers labored in the United States under its terms and established new traditions of migration to the United States. Derided in some quarters for importing "shock troops" for U.S. agriculturalists who only wanted to lower farm wages and avoid unionization, the program was continually renewed (at times against the wishes of the Mexican government) until activists in the United States successfully blocked its passage in 1964. The certified workers who arrived under the aegis of the program often complained that their working and living conditions were inferior to what they expected from the contractual guarantees, and many thousands "skipped out" of their contracts to become undocumented workers and thereby avoid the abuses of the program. Those who did so lost wages, however, as the agreement required that a portion of each paycheck be distributed only upon the worker's return to Mexico. (Many former braceros living in both the United States and Mexico have recently come forward to claim that they never received those savings, and a leader of the movement to reimburse those aging workers claims to have been kidnapped by Mexican government agents in March 2000.)

Despite significant allegations of graft in the handling of bracero earnings, the agreement illustrated both governments' clear intent to stop Mexicans' permanent settlement in the United States in favor of institutionalizing seasonal migrations. For that reason, the program remained open only to Mexican men over the course of its long history and relied on a hope that the permanent residence in Mexico of women and children would also discourage workers from skipping out on their contracts. As the sociologist Pierrette Hondagneu-Sotelo has argued, the program effectively ensured that Mexico would absorb the social costs of reproducing the low-wage agricultural labor force in the United

States by demanding that Mexican society support those emigrants during the off-season.[35]

Although other contract labor programs have developed since the conclusion of the Bracero Program in 1965, the vast majority of Mexicans who have arrived in the United States since then have crossed the border without legal documentation. After the end of the Bracero Program, descriptions of life in the United States by returning mexicanos prompted new groups of prospective emigrants to seek out the support of kin north of the border in order to reduce the costs and risks of making the trip. Movement between the two countries has remained attractive to many because of cross-border familial ties and new economic pressures on local households. Recent migrations include far more single women and children than the male-dominated movements of the 1950s and 1960s. One immigrant explained that leaving his home in Oaxaca and going to the United States

> was a matter of following the tradition of the village. One could even say that we're a village of wetbacks. A lot of people, nearly the majority, have gone, come back, and returned to the country to the north; almost all of them have held in their fingers the famous green bills that have jokingly been called "green cards"—immigrant cards—for generations. For several decades, Macuiltianguis—that's the name of my village—has been an emigrant village, and our people have spread out like the roots of a tree under the earth, looking for sustenance. My people have had to emigrate to survive.[36]

In addition to those migrant networks established by decades of movements during the twentieth century, recent restrictionist public policies have had the often unintended effect of encouraging rather than discouraging immigration to the United States. For example, migrants have been able to rely on family reunification provisions of the 1965 U.S. Immigration Act to legalize their status north of the border, and though the 1986 U.S. Immigration Reform and Control Act (IRCA) was intended to limit the arrival of new waves of immigrants, "the 2.7 million migrants (mainly Mexicans) who were legalized under IRCA made the transnational community stronger for undocumented workers by becoming more stable sources of social support" for Mexico's prospective emigrants.[37] In recent years, the 1996 Welfare Act and public policies such as Proposition 187 in California have encouraged record numbers of mexicano immigrants to begin the process of naturalization, and it seems that increased rates of U.S. citizenship may in turn provide kin with even greater stability for new migrations from Mexico into the United States.

The persistence of undocumented migration between Mexico and the United States has also prompted new calls by governors of several U.S. border states for a guest-worker program modeled on the Bracero agreement, and publications such as *Business Week* have supported such a change by claiming that "as long as the U.S. needs more workers and Mexicans need more jobs, the problem of illegal immigration won't go away."[38] President Vicente Fox has vowed to oppose such an agreement, however, and some prominent Mexican American and other Latino political activists have also opposed those proposals, arguing that they signal efforts to revive an exploitative system and to allow farmworkers to continue working in poverty. The most influential Latino lobbying organization in Washington, D.C., the National Council of La Raza (NCLR), declared,

> Latino farm laborers are America's hardest working, least compensated and least protected workers. NCLR and the rest of the Latino community cannot allow them to be subjected to the disrespect and mistreatment that this legislation would engender. H.R. 4548 would lower wage rates, eliminate housing requirements, and let unscrupulous employers continue to exploit foreign farmworkers. Instead, Congress should be seeking to improve the lot of farmworkers already in the United States who, because of employer practices, continue to suffer from double-digit unemployment rates, stagnant wages, poor working conditions and substandard housing.[39]

Despite such objections, guest-worker programs seem to have captured the interest of many in the United States as a way to avoid the social costs of supporting low-wage immigrant workers on a year-round basis, and U.S. policymakers have shown little public support for allowing workers to move themselves freely back and forth across the border. In recent U.S. debates about immigration, Mexicans' "illegal" transnational movements have fueled the wrath of restrictionists who have argued that mexicanos fail to assimilate, to support local merchants in the United States, and to pay adequate taxes, thereby draining the nation of its wealth and threatening its national insularity. As proof that Mexicans have little interest in adapting to life as permanent residents of the United States, restrictionists complain that too few become U.S. citizens, and even recent U.S. defenders of liberal immigration policies such as Peter Salins have cautioned that the United States ought to admit immigrants with higher naturalization rates.[40] Others in the United States have conducted extensive cost-benefit analyses to determine whether Mexicans pose a net gain or loss for the national economy. Although those studies often vary wildly in their conclusions about immigrants' impact on social services, the local tax base, and the U.S. unemployment rate, some politicians have effectively used the cost-benefit debate to galvanize support for increased border militarization against Mexican immigrants deemed too expensive for the United States to admit.[41]

In addition to concerns about immigrants' economic impact, opposition to the arrival and permanent settlement of Mexicans in the United States has been shaped by other factors that have recently determined the course of U.S. politics. In a time of increased racial hostilities, anti-Mexican sentiments have played a fundamental role in U.S. discussions of illegal migration. Echoing earlier racist arguments from the 1920s against Mexican immigrant transnational movements, for example, journalist Peter Brimelow, in his polemic *Alien Nation*, argued in 1995 that ongoing immigration threatened the "racial hegemony of white Americans" and that "it is simply common sense that Americans have a legitimate interest in their country's racial balance. It is common sense that they have a right to insist that their government stop shifting it."[42] The founder of the Federation for American Immigration Reform similarly emphasized in the late 1980s that irresponsible Latin American immigrants would avoid birth control, have large families, and pose a threat to non-Latinos in the United States. "Can *homo contraceptivus* compete with *homo progenetiva* if borders aren't controlled?" he asked, concluding that "those with their pants up are going to get caught by those with their pants down" if large-scale immigration from Latin America were to continue.[43] In national elections, parallel arguments opposing the arrival of Mexicans have carried weight among U.S. voters as the presidential campaigns of Patrick Buchanan showed, and vigilante violence against Mexican immigrants is now on the rise, particularly in Arizona.[44]

Others in the United States have recently feared Mexican transmigration as a manifestation of immigrants' disinterest in accommodating to mainstream U.S. politics. Some have predicted that separatist Mexican immigrants would make the U.S. Southwest another Lebanon, whereas others have warned that their *reconquista* (reconquering) of the territory presents the possibility "that in the next generation or so we will see a kind of Chicano Quebec take shape in the American Southwest."[45] Articles in the mainstream press have suggested that violence might result from Mexicans' transnational orientation, as a 1992 account made clear:

> Poor enclave communities not only make it easier for homeland values and languages to persist, but they also possess the potential, particularly during bad economic times, for resentment-driven violence, such as the rioting in the Mount Pleasant district of Washington, D.C. in the spring of 1991 or the devastating April–May 1992 Los Angeles riots. One-third of those apprehended in Los Angeles for looting were illegal Hispanic immigrants.[46]

These sentiments had antecedents earlier in the twentieth century, when U.S. observers worried that political radicals who moved easily between the two countries would also import dangerous ideologies. Such fears prompted the *Los Angeles Times* to warn its readers during World War I that German agents were posing as Mexican immigrants, and a local journalist noted ominously that "if the people of Los Angeles knew what was happening on our border, they would not sleep at night."[47] Similar anxieties about communist agitators in the United States during the Cold War prompted parallel concerns about Mexican transnational practices, and Senator Pat McCarran of Nevada warned of Russian spies disguised as farmworkers while the Immigration and Naturalization Service (INS) expressed new fears about "the crescendo of communism with its devious schemes of infiltration."[48] But anxieties about Mexican transnational practices seem to have risen in more recent years, and some non-Mexican residents of the United States have argued that immigrants' "almost religious" devotion to their hometowns and the Mexican patria threatens the ideal of the American melting pot. In 1994, for example, many non-Mexicans in California protested sharply at the sight of ethnic Mexican residents proudly marching against the passage of Proposition 187, an initiative designed to restrict immigrants' access to welfare and other social services in the state. As Philip Martin notes, those protests "were marked by large numbers of Hispanic students walking out of high school to protest Proposition 187. In the opinion of many Proposition 187 opponents, these protests were counterproductive; the Mexican flags students waved reportedly convinced many undecided voters to support Proposition 187."[49]

Finally, fears of Mexican criminality have long shaped restrictionist movements in the United States as well. Many in the United States have worried that a recognizable criminal element has lurked within Mexican immigrant communities for nearly a hundred years, as an open U.S.-Mexico border has seemed to allow fugitives to plunder freely in the Southwest. During the early twentieth century, police in Los Angeles and other parts of the United States bemoaned the movement of apparent fugitives to and from Mexico, and the U.S. popular press often contended during the 1950s that mexicanos were importing illegal marijuana that would corrupt American youth.[50] More recently, U.S. observers have argued that Mexican immigrants pollute U.S. society by importing other sorts of danger. As commentators have turned increasing attention to the smuggling of illicit drugs across the U.S.-Mexico border, policymakers in the United States have justified the multibillion-dollar war against drugs and drug traffickers as an effort to stop unsanctioned movements between the two countries. Although calls to end drug smuggling in northern Mexico have centered on its effects on the democratic press and the bribing of public officials, pronouncements in the United States have labeled smugglers a national security threat demanding a military response. In 1990, one U.S. official announced, "We are engaged in something akin to a guerrilla war along the border against well-entrenched and well-organized trafficking groups," and efforts to turn the region into a militarized zone have had critical effects on Mexican migration patterns to the United States.[51]

These border wars have created new hazards for arriving Mexicans and have prompted an outcry from organizations such as Amnesty International and the American Friends Service Committee, which are concerned about human rights abuses at the international boundary line. Significant dangers first emerged in that region with the establishment of the U.S. Border Patrol in May 1924, a government agency that has prompted bitter jokes that Mexicans can boast a police force of their own in the United States, but dangers escalated when the INS annual budget tripled from $1.5 billion to $4.2 billion between 1993 and 1998.[52] The physical dangers now facing immigrants have dramatically escalated with the construction of new fences and military surveillance technologies in high-density crossing regions, developments that have pushed migrants to take ever greater risks by traveling through far less hospitable terrain in efforts to cross the frontera. As more immigrants asphyxiate in desert heat or drown in dangerous rivers, the price of hiring a *coyote* (immigrant smuggler) as a guide has risen at a pace commensurate with the rising death rates at the border. Recent estimates suggest at least 1,000 fatalities among border-crossers between 1993 and 1997.[53] Although such well-publicized dangers seem not to have led to an actual reduction in emigration from Mexico, the military buildup has discouraged undocumented immigrants already in the United States from attempting to return to the patria on visits. Many low-wage immigrant workers who hold only seasonal jobs now feel compelled to stay year-round in the United States, where they encounter new hardships during long periods of unemployment and poverty between their seasonal paychecks.[54]

Through it all, citizens of the United States have continued to profit from the labor of Mexican immigrants, and both countries continue to live with the long history of transnational migrations. Taking employment that few citizens of the United States find attractive, mexicanos have occupied "a large number of low-skilled, so-called bad jobs that do not pay enough to sustain a middle-class standard of living" in the United States. Laboring in occupations "shunned by most young native-born workers entering the labor force," Mexicans have continued to work in jobs that "involve arduous manual labor, or at least menial and highly repetitive tasks."[55] As communities in Mexico have become "nurseries and nursing homes for wage-laborers in the United States," the racial division of labor has solidified in the United States since the conclusion of the Bracero Program.[56] More vulnerable in the workplace after the establishment of employer sanctions against hiring undocumented immigrants in 1986, most have become ineligible for federal welfare benefits in recent years as well. These developments have meant greater poverty and instability for Mexican immigrants, and though many experienced real economic mobility in the United States during the 1940s and 1950s, "in recent years, Mexican immigrants have tended to enter the . . . bottom of the economy—and to stay there."[57]

Cultural Connections

Economic dynamics and government policies have long shaped the position of Mexicans in U.S. society and motivated residents to migrate between Mexico and the United States, yet they do not begin to account for the meanings that mexicanos have given to those movements and their experiences in the United States. Along with labor markets, cultural practices in greater Mexico have become increasingly transnational in recent years, and the activities of migrants have been instrumental to these developments. As in the construction of transborder economies, the U.S. and Mexican governments played a crucial role in those cultural transformations by establishing high-tech infrastructures that have allowed immigrants to stay in close contact with their home communities and thereby nurture thoughts of home. Telephone service, for example, has given migrants more regular and, at times, immediate access to information about their kin, to their local government representatives, and to knowledge about the economic pressures facing Mexican households; and the Internet now offers about 100 newspapers from Mexico online to readers on both sides of the frontera. Cross-border contacts have changed life in Mexico for many, and new words derived from English have made their way into local Mexican parlance. Rural residents of Oaxaca, for instance, have come to speak of *pizzeros* (pizza makers), *bosbois* (busboys), and *la main* (Main Street) in distant U.S. towns such as Poughkeepsie, New York, where many former neighbors now work.[58]

As a result of strong familial and other linkages between Mexico and the United States, northward emigration has captured the imagination of Mexicans on both sides of the international border, and popular culture has often reflected that interest.[59] Popular religious practices have changed as a result of transmigration, with Mexican immigrant Catholics organizing annual tours in U.S. cities of important religious images from shrines in Mexico. According to sociologists Jorge Durand and Douglas S. Massey,

> A replica of the Virgin of San Juan de los Lagos, for example, leaves Jalisco each year to visit churches in San Antonio, Los Angeles, Chicago, and other cities with large emigrant communities. . . . The arrival of the Virgin is celebrated with special novenas and masses, and devotees pack the church and fill the altar with candles and a variety of votive objects.[60]

At the same time, emigrants who return to Mexico commonly leave devotional offerings in Catholic churches in thanksgiving for safe passage to and from the United States. Along with those *retablos* left in religious shrines, jokes and other cultural texts produced by Mexican immigrants represent something of a "hidden transcript" that charts the social costs of Mexico's twentieth-century development. Many of those narratives highlight the difficulties confronting immigrants in the United States, and at least one quip told by mexicanos clearly lampoons the difficulty of low-wage work in the United States as well as immigrants' ongoing preoccupations with returning to Mexico with high earnings:

> A man who has been to the United States returns to Mexico and tries to convince his compadre to join him there by telling him all kinds of stories about the opportunities that await them north of the border. "In fact," he says, "in the United States you can walk down the streets and just pick the money right off the trees." Convinced by the exaggerations, the friend agrees to come with him.

> As soon as they cross the border they see a dollar bill on the ground. When the more experienced man reaches down to pick it up, the newcomer grabs his arm and says, "Hey, don't bother picking that one. Let's just go to the other end of the orchard and work our way back to the border!"[61]

Another joke relies on phonetic confusion to accentuate the anti-Mexican racism that has long given shape to many transnational experiences:

> Two compadres go to work in the United States. After working for some time in the States they return to Mexico to their hometown. All their friends and relatives want to hear about the United States; they want to know how the people are, what language they speak, about the freeways and buildings, etc. One compadre eggs on the other, "You tell them!" The other says, "No, you tell them!" Finally one of the men says, "O.K. I'll tell you. To begin with, let me tell you, California is a very saintly land. All the towns in California bear saints' names: San Isidro, San Diego, San Clemente, Santa Ana, Los Angeles, San Francisco—all saints' names. Well it was such a saintly land, such a Christian land that they called my compadre 'Son of a Bitch' [San Ofabitch] and they called me 'Son of a Gun'! [San Ofagun]."

In addition to drawing attention to the problems immigrants encounter in the United States, popular culture also keeps alive the hope of a political response to the difficult material conditions experienced there. *Corridos* (ballads) sung in the United States have therefore documented U.S. employers' abuses of immigrants as they remember mexicano efforts to form unions and other political organizations in response. As the scholar María Herrera-Sobek notes, many of these songs have also emphasized "the perception by many undocumented workers that the U.S. Immigration and Naturalization Service . . . was closely allied with U.S. farmers, agribusinesses, and police." In relating how one immigrant came unwittingly to be used as a strikebreaker, for example, "El corrido del ilegal" began:

> *Andando yo en la frontera*/As I was walking along the border
> *Ya me cargaba el hambre*/I was already burdened by hunger.
> *Dicen que el hambre es canija,*/They say that hunger is unrelenting,
> *Pero es más del que ya le ande.*/But it is even more painful to the hungry one.
> *Me pasé al otro lado.*/I crossed over to the other side.
> *Tuve que hacerla de alambre.*/I had to cross the wire fence.
> *A los poquitos momentos*/In a few moments

Me agarra la inmigración./The immigration officer caught me.
Me dice, "Tú eres alambre." /He said to me, "You are illegal."
Le contesté, "Sí, señor." /I answered, "Yes, sir."
"De eso no tengas cuidado," /Don't worry about it,
"Tal vez tengas tú razón." /"Perhaps you are in the right."
"Si tú quieres trabajar,/"If you want to work,
Nomás que no seas Chavista,/As long as you're not a Chavista,
Yo mismo te he de llevar/I myself will take you
A manos del contratista./To a contractor.
Le estamos dando la chanza/We are giving an opportunity
A todos los alambristas."/To all the wire jumpers."[62]

While "El corrido del ilegal" clearly highlights the role of government agents in shaping migration patterns, other songs have been even more explicit about the potential costs of living in the United States and the difficulty many have faced in trying to return to Mexico. One of the most famous and influential *conjunto* (ensemble, group) recordings of the late twentieth century, a 1985 production by the Northern California group Los Tigres del Norte, expressed just that sentiment. Popular in both the United States and Mexico, the Los Tigres composition "La Jaula de Oro" (The Gilded Cage) effectively thematized common concerns about "work, the state, and its ideology of democracy, and the importance of history" in giving voice to a widespread sentiment that compared living in the United States to being trapped in a "gilded cage," surrounded by wealth but trapped nonetheless.[63] As literary critic Ramón Saldívar translates the lyrics,

So here I am well settled
In the United States.
It's been ten years since
I crossed as a wetback.
I never applied for papers;
I'm still an illegal.
I have my wife and children
Whom I brought when they were small,
But they no longer remember
My beloved Mexico,
Which I never forget
And to which I cannot return.
What good is money
If I'm like a prisoner

In this great nation?
I weep when I think of it,
For even if the cage is gilded,
It's no less a cage.

[Spoken in Spanish]: "Listen, my son, would you like to return to live in Mexico?"

[Spoken in English]: "What you talkin' about, Dad? I don't wanna go back to Mexico. No way, Dad!"

My children don't speak to me.
They've learned another language
And forgotten their Spanish.
They think like Americans;
They deny that they are Mexican
Even though they share my color.
From work to home,
I don't know what is happening to me.
Even though I'm a family man,
I hardly venture out on the streets
For fear that
I'll be found and deported.
What good is money
If I'm like a prisoner
In this great nation?
I weep when I think of it,
For even if the cage is gilded,
It's no less a cage.[64]

Like the narrator of "La Jaula de Oro," many other Mexican immigrants in the United States have struggled for decades to maintain the Spanish language and the cultural traditions they had known prior to their emigration, convinced that they would one day return to Mexico. This has been a critical feature of Mexican cultural practices en el extranjero. Rather than meaning simple assimilation into U.S. society, migration from Mexico has often meant the development of new cultural and political affiliations in the United States. New perceptions and debates about the meaning of national identity and the expectations of patriotism have emerged, and some immigrants have become much more attentive to their Mexican national identity during their stays in the United States than they had been in Mexico. Already worried during the postrevolutionary period about forging a stronger sense of *mexicanidad* out of "many Mexicos," Manuel Gamio therefore wrote optimistically in 1931 that out-migration would help strengthen the Mexican nation because immigrants

> learn immediately what their mother-country means, and they always think of it and speak of it with love. Indeed, it can be said that there is hardly an immigrant home in the United States where the Mexican flag is not found in a place of honor, as well as pictures of national Mexican heroes. Love of country sometimes goes so far that very often altars are made for saints and flag or hero, or both, giving patriotism thus an almost religious quality.[65]

In later years, songs poking fun at those who seemed to have failed to remember the *patria* and who had become *agringado* (whitened) have been common. Some before World War II laughed that

> *En Texas es terrible*/In Texas it is terrible
> *Por la revoltura que hay;*/How things are all mixed up;
> *No hay quién diga "hasta mañana,"* /No one says "until tomorrow,"
> *Nomás puro "good bye."* /It's nothing but "good-bye."
> *Y "jau-didi-dú fren,"* /And "howdy-dee-do my friend,"
> *"En ayl sí yu tumora,"* /"And I'll see you tomorrow";
> *Para decir "diez reales"* /When they want to say "diez reales"
> *Dicen "dola yene cuora."* /They say "dollar and a quarter."[66]

In a similar process of politicizing cultural maintenance and asserting the cultural unity of the patria, Mexican writers describing the experiences of their compatriots laboring in the United States have also encouraged immigrants to avoid assimilation and remain focused on returning to Mexico. Dozens of movies produced in twentieth-century Mexico and seen in both countries treated the same themes. The first of its kind in 1922 characteristically dramatized "the cruel realities of what it is like to be Mexican in the United States," narrated an emigrant's encounter with a racist foreman, and concluded with the hero's happy return to his homeland for the sake of "true love and . . . a proper path of life." More recent cinematic efforts have often also emphasized that "no good awaits [Mexicans] in the United States" and have urged the repatriation of mexicanos.[67]

Appealing to immigrant audiences, the Spanish-language press based in the United States has played a somewhat different and more complex role vis-à-vis immigrant transnationality. On the one hand, it has been instrumental in efforts to retain the Spanish language and Mexican cultural practices in the United States for more than a century.

Purveyors of information about Latin America to communities throughout the United States, journalists have frequently urged local residents to consider themselves "*México de afuera*"—a Mexican national community living outside that country's national boundaries that would look to return "home" at the earliest opportunity. On the other hand, immigrant journalists have also taken leading roles in organizing civil rights campaigns rooted in the U.S. context that have become agents of "Americanization."[68] During the 1930s, for example, the celebrated radio announcer Pedro J. González argued forcefully over the airwaves for an end to the deportation of Mexican citizens, and Spanish-language newspapers in Los Angeles urged residents to recognize that because their labors had contributed to the "colossus of the north" they deserved the same opportunities accorded white Americans. Then and now, journalists have been among the most politically influential members of immigrant communities, working in an important institution that has helped immigrants to mediate their transnational and local concerns. Founded in 1926, Los Angeles–based *La Opinión* remains the most important ethnic Mexican newspaper in the United States today with more than 600 employees and 500,000 readers.[69]

In addition to struggling to define their relationship to both the Mexican patria and the United States, immigrants have long expressed an active interest in identifying with particular regions of Mexico, the *patrias chicas* (small homelands) that they have called home. Chain migrations of family members and friends have shaped that allegiance, and many had banded together with *paisanos* (fellow countrymen) from their own home states or towns by the 1920s when the state of Michigan became widely known as "Michoacán del norte" in recognition of the number of residents from that area of Mexico. Passionate concerns about the patria chica have since found even more fervent expression in the United States, and the 1990s witnessed a dramatic upsurge in the formation of hometown clubs in the United States. More than 1,500 in number today, those associations of U.S. residents from Zacatecas, Jalisco, and other states stage beauty pageants, raise funds for civic improvement in Mexico, gather together for weekend soccer leagues, and conduct similar activities throughout the United States. More recently, those organizations have become politically active in new ways, joining with the AFL-CIO in June 2000 to lobby for a general amnesty for undocumented immigrants. Efforts to legalize their stays and become U.S. citizens may seem a surprising outcome of movements to celebrate Mexican national pride, but one hometown club leader explained that "we're all affected by this problem [of anti-immigrant sentiment and limited access to social services], one way or another. Everyone has friends or family members who are undocumented. The support for this idea is unanimous."[70]

Conclusion

Those new cooperative efforts between Mexican immigrant organizations and the U.S. labor movement point to an important future site of transnational political struggle in the United States. The U.S. labor movement has floundered since the 1940s under leaders who showed little interest in organizing agricultural or service workers and devoted few resources to recently arrived Latin American and Asian immigrants, but new migrants may revive that moribund institution. The recent ascendance of new national leadership to the AFL-CIO has changed both the rhetoric and priorities of the labor movement. In February 1999, the Service Employees International Union in Southern California won a union election of 74,000 home health-care workers (many Latino immigrants) in Los Angeles County. One of the most significant union victories in the United States since the 1930s, that struggle has already pushed other labor organizations to attempt to make inroads among ethnic Mexican workers. Still, local chapters intent on involving mexicanos at times face overwhelming odds, including the fear of many that political involvement might lead to deportation by the INS. Moreover, non–U.S. citizens continue to be ineligible for many jobs in public-sector employment, where many energetic union efforts have developed.

Although the future of these union efforts remains cloudy—and the AFL-CIO's enthusiasm for mexicanos may change if U.S. unemployment rates surge—immigrants continue to bring creative new tactics to their political organizing efforts in the United States. For example, Latino janitors attempting to unionize in Los Angeles during the early 1990s created the superhero "Mopman" modeled on Mexico's "Superbarrio," a masked wrestler who had articulated the concerns of the poor in the aftermath of the 1985 Mexico City earthquake. As a new "transnational working-class hero" in California, Mopman inspired energetic union campaigns over the following decade that culminated in victories for the "janitors for justice" campaign in 1999 and 2000.[71] New indigenous political movements among migrant Oaxaqueños and other indigenous agricultural laborers have changed the face of politics in Mexico as well. Living and working in the U.S. context, many people increasingly see their common cause with other indigenous peoples, losing their sole focus on home villages and crafting regional responses critical of the Mexican state. As Carole Nagengast and Michael Kearney have shown, this has meant new forms of "ethnic" identification in the border region where "ethnicity . . . has become the basis for political activism and a means of defending themselves socially, economically, and politically."[72] New forms of ethnicity have also developed among U.S.-born Mexican Americans as a result of Mexican transmigration. Although Mexican Americans have taken an active interest in immigration matters for decades, prominent U.S. citizens of Mexican descent have taken influential roles in international debates about guest workers, the negotiation of the NAFTA accords, and the future of U.S.-Mexico relations, whereas artists and writers have articulated new social visions that respond to the presence of transnational migrants. Mexican American political organizations such as the Hermandad Mexicana Nacional and the Southwest Voter Registration Education Project have also led efforts to encourage mexicanos to naturalize as U.S. citizens. In the view of many, discouraging immigrant transnationality will both protect Mexicans' civil rights and increase the political clout of Mexican Americans at the ballot box.

How will Mexican immigrants in the United States continue to imagine and forge transnational familial, economic, and political ties in the coming years, and how will the Mexican state, Mexican-American organizations, and local U.S. politicians in turn seek to shape those efforts? In a time of greater militarization of the U.S.-Mexico border, new calls in both countries for a guest-worker program, and decreasing economic opportunities for many Mexican immigrants in the United States, the future of the transnational past seems at once unclear and ever more important, more possible thanks to high-tech communications networks, and yet more dangerous because of increased Border Patrol expenditures. What is clear is that the challenges facing Mexico today are abundantly evident en el extranjero—among Mexican citizens living outside of the geographic boundaries of that nation. The historical movements of working-class Mexicans back and forth between the two countries have certainly created deeply entrenched practices of "autonomous migration" reflected in popular culture and structured by state agencies on both sides of the border. In the near term, new discussions in both Mexico and the United States must seek to recognize the complexity of those transnational migrant networks and to resolve the troubling human rights abuses that face Mexican migrants in the early twenty-first century.

Notes

1. See www.labastida2000.org.mx and the *Los Angeles Times*, June 11, 2000.
2. See www.fox2000.org.mx and *Migration News*, July 2000.
3. *Los Angeles Times*, July 4, 2000, and July 1, 2000.
4. Alejandro Portes, Luis E. Guarnizo, and Patricia Landolt, "The Study of Transnationalism: Pitfalls and Promise of an Emergent Research Field," *Ethnic and Racial Studies* 22, no. 2 (March 1999): 223.
5. Devra Weber, "Historical Perspectives on Mexican Transnationalism: With Notes from Angumacutiro," *Social Justice* 26, no. 3 (fall 1999): 40.
6. Ernesto Galarza, "The Reason Why: Lessons in Cartography," *Rural America* (September 1978).
7. David Montejano, *Anglos and Mexicans in the Making of Texas, 1836–1986* (Austin: University of Texas Press, 1987), p. 29.
8. Lisbeth Haas, *Conquests and Historical Identities in California, 1769–1936* (Berkeley: University of California Press, 1995), p. 79.
9. Frank Roberts and Fernando Lozano-Ascencio, "Transnational Migrant Communities and Mexican Migration to the U.S.," *Ethnic and Racial Studies* 22, no. 2 (March 1999): 239; Nina Glick Schiller, Linda Basch, and Cristina Blanc-Szanton, "Towards a Transnationalization of Migration: Race, Class, Ethnicity, and Nationalism Reconsidered," *Annals of the New York Academy of Sciences* 645 (1992): 1–24.
10. C. Perales, "Why the Border Needs the Free Trade Zone," in Oscar J. Martínez, ed., *U.S.-Mexico Borderlands: Historical and Contemporary Perspectives* (Wilmington, DE: Scholarly Resources, 1996), pp. 99–100.
11. Miguel Tinker Salas, "Sonora: The Making of a Border Society, 1880–1910," in Martínez, ed., *U.S.-Mexico Borderlands: Historical and Contemporary Perspectives*, p. 88.
12. Douglas S. Massey and Kristin E. Espinosa, "What's Driving Mexico-U.S. Migration? A Theoretical, Empirical, and Policy Analysis," *American Journal of Sociology* 102, no. 4 (January 1997): 991–992.
13. Lawrence A. Cardoso, *Mexican Emigration to the United States, 1897–1931* (Tucson: University of Arizona Press, 1980), p. 45.
14. Gerardo Necoechea Gracia, "Customs and Resistance: Mexican Immigrants in Chicago, 1910–1930," in John Mason Hart, ed., *Border Crossings: Mexican and Mexican-American Workers* (Wilmington, DE: Scholarly Resources, 1998), pp. 185–208.
15. Roger Rouse, "Mexican Migration and the Social Space of Postmodernism," in David G. Gutiérrez, ed., *Between Two Worlds: Mexican Immigrants in the United States* (Wilmington, DE: Scholarly Resources, 1996), p. 252.
16. Edward J. Escobar, *Race, Police, and the Making of a Political Identity: Mexican Americans and the Los Angeles Police Department, 1900–1945* (Berkeley: University of California, 1999), p. 38.
17. Cardoso, *Mexican Emigration to the United States*, p. 50.
18. Manuel Gamio, *Mexican Immigration to the United States* (New York: Dover Publications, 1930, 1971), pp. 8–9; Francisco E. Balderrama and

Raymond Rodríguez, *Decade of Betrayal: Mexican Repatriation in the 1930s* (Albuquerque: University of New Mexico Press, 1995), pp. 2, 122. On Gamio, see also Arthur Schmidt, "Mexicans, Migrants, and Indigenous Peoples: The Work of Manuel Gamio in the United States, 1925–1927," in Ingrid E. Fey and Karen Racine, eds., *Strange Pilgrimages: Exile, Travel, and National Identity in Latin America, 1800–1990s* (Wilmington, DE: Scholarly Resources, 2000), pp. 173–178.

19. Kitty Calavita, *Inside the State: The Bracero Program, Immigration, and the I.N.S.* (New York: Routledge Press, 1992), p. 54.

20. Miriam J. Wells, *Strawberry Fields: Politics, Class, and Work in California Agriculture* (Ithaca: Cornell University Press, 1996), pp. 66–67.

21. Gamio, *Mexican Immigration to the United States*, pp. 49, 57.

22. See Yuji Ichioka, *The Issei: The World of the First Generation Japanese Immigrants, 1885–1924* (New York: Free Press, 1988), p. 73.

23. Jorge Durand and Douglas S. Massey, "Mexican Migration to the United States: A Critical Review," *Latin American Research Review* 27, no. 2 (1992): 12.

24. Fernando Lozano Ascencio, *Bringing It Back Home: Remittances to Mexico from Migrant Workers in the United States,* trans. Aníbel Yáñez (La Jolla: Center for Mexican Studies, University of California–San Diego, 1993), p. 70; *Migration News*, July 2000.

25. *La Jornada*, June 18, 2000.

26. George J. Sánchez, *Becoming Mexican American: Ethnicity, Culture, and Identity in Chicano Los Angeles, 1900–1945* (New York: Oxford University Press, 1993).

27. Mario García, *Desert Immigrants: The Mexicans of El Paso, 1880–1920* (New Haven: Yale University Press, 1981); Ricardo Romo, *East Los Angeles: History of a Barrio* (Austin: University of Texas Press, 1983), pp. 125–126.

28. Durand and Massey, "Mexican Migration to the United States," p. 29.

29. Douglas Massey, Rafael Alarcón, Jorge Durand, and Humberto González, *Return to Aztlán: The Social Process of International Migration from Western Mexico* (Berkeley: University of California Press, 1987), p. 60.

30. Enrique Dussel Peters, "Recent Structural Changes in Mexico's Economy: A Preliminary Analysis of Some Sources of Mexican Migration to the United States," in Marcelo M. Suárez-Orozco, ed., *Crossings: Mexican Immigration in Interdisciplinary Perspective* (Cambridge: Harvard University Press, 1998), p. 61.

31. Mark Reisler, "Always the Laborer, Never the Citizen: Anglo Perceptions of the Mexican Immigrant During the 1920s," in David G. Gutiérrez, ed., *Between Two Worlds: Mexican Immigrants in the United States* (Wilmington, DE: Scholarly Resources, 1996), p. 35.

32. United States Congress, House Committee on Immigration and Naturalization, *Seasonal Agricultural Laborers from Mexico Hearing*, 69th Congress, 1st Session, 1926, p. 24, quoted in Balderrama and Rodríguez, *Decade of Betrayal*, pp. 19–20.

33. Cardoso, *Mexican Emigration to the United States*, pp. 47–48.

34. Manuel García y Griego, "The Importation of Mexican Contract Laborers to the United States, 1942–1964," in Gutiérrez, ed., *Between Two Worlds*, p. 52.

35. Pierrette Hondagneu-Sotelo, "Women and Children First: New Directions in Anti-Immigrant Politics," *Socialist Review* 25, no. 1 (1995): 169–190.

36. Ramón "Tianguís" Pérez, *Diary of an Undocumented Immigrant*, trans. Dick J. Reavis (Houston: Arte Público Press, 1989), p. 12.

37. Douglas S. Massey, Luin Goldring, and Jorge Durand, "Continuities in Transnational Migration: An Analysis of Nineteen Mexican Communities," *American Journal of Sociology* 99, no. 6 (May 1994): 1494, 1515–1516; Néstor Rodríguez, "The Battle for the Border: Notes on Autonomous Migration, Transnational Communities, and the States," in Susanne Jonas and Suzie Dod Thomas, eds., *Immigration: A Civil Rights Issue for the Americas* (Wilmington, DE: Scholarly Resources, 1999), pp. 34–35, 37–38.

38. *Business Week* June 5, 2000, p. 6.

39. National Council of La Raza, "Press Release," July 26, 2000.

40. Balderrama and Rodríguez, *Decade of Betrayal*, p. 20; Peter D. Salins, *Assimilation American Style* (New York: Basic Books, 1997).

41. Raul Hinojosa and Peter Schey, "The Faulty Logic of the Anti-Immigration Rhetoric," *NACLA Report on the Americas* 29 (November–December 1995): 18–23; Susan González Baker, Robert G. Cushing, and Charles W. Haynes, "Fiscal Impacts of Mexican Migration to the United States," in Frank D. Bean, Rodolfo O. de la Garza, Bryan R. Roberts, and Sidney Weintraub, eds., *At the Crossroads: Mexican Migration and U.S. Public Policy* (New York: Rowman and Littlefield Publishers, 1997), pp. 145–176.

42. Peter Brimelow, *Alien Nation: Common Sense About America's Immigration Disaster* (New York: Random House, 1995), pp. 122, 264.

43. Quoted in Susan González Baker, "Demographic Trends in the Chicana/o Population: Policy Implications for the Twenty-First Century," in David R. Maciel and Isidro D. Ortiz, eds., *Chicanas/Chicanos at the Crossroads: Social, Economic, and Political Change* (Tucson: University of Arizona Press, 1996), p. 16.

44. See www.buchanan.org.

45. David M. Kennedy, "Can We Still Afford to Be a Nation of Immigrants?" *Atlantic Monthly,* November 1996, pp. 52–68; David Montejano, "On the Question of Inclusion," in David Montejano, ed., *Chicano Politics and Society in the Late-Twentieth Century* (Austin: University of Texas Press, 1999), p. 4.

46. *National Interest* (summer 1992): 45.

47. Romo, *East Los Angeles*, p. 106.

48. Calavita, *Inside the State*, pp. 49–50.

49. Philip Martin, "Proposition 187 in California," in Darrell Y. Hammamoto and Rodolfo D. Torres, eds., *New American Destinies: A Reader in Contemporary Asian and Latino Immigration* (New York: Routledge Press, 1997), p. 328.

50. Escobar, *Race, Police, and the Making of a Political Identity* p. 33.

51. Calavita, *Inside the State*, pp. 2–3.

52. Philip L. Martin and J. Edward Taylor, "Poverty Amid Prosperity: Farm Employment, Immigration, and Poverty in California," *American Journal of Agricultural Economics* 80, no. 5 (1998): 1008–1015.

53. Karl Eschbach, Jacqueline Hagan, Néstor Rodríguez, Rubén Hernández-León, and Stanley Bailey, "Death at the Border," *International Migration Review* 33, no. 2 (summer 1999): 430–454.

54. Peter Andreas, "Borderless Economy, Barricaded Border," *NACLA Report on the Americas* 33, no. 3 (November/December 1999): 14–23.

55. David Lopez and Cynthia Feliciano, "Who Does What? California's Emerging Plural Labor Force," in Ruth Milkman, ed., *Organizing Immigrants: The Challenge for Unions in Contemporary California* (Ithaca: Cornell University Press, 2000), p. 37; Wayne A. Cornelius, "The Structural Embeddedness of Demand for Mexican Immigrant Labor: New Evidence from California," in Suárez-Orozco, ed., *Crossings*, p. 134.

56. Roger Rouse, "Mexican Migration and the Social Space of Postmodernism," in Gutiérrez, ed., *Between Two Worlds*, p. 252.

57. David G. Gutiérrez, *Walls and Mirrors: Mexican Americans, Mexican Immigrants, and the Politics of Ethnicity* (Berkeley: University of California Press, 1995), p. 321.

58. Alison Mountz and Richard A. Wright, "Daily Life in the Transnational Migrant Community of San Agustín, Oaxaca, and Poughkeepsie, New York," *Diaspora* 5, no. 3 (winter 1996): 405, 414.

59. José Macías, "Informal Education, Sociocultural Expression, and Symbolic Meaning in Popular Immigration Music Text," *Explorations in Ethnic Studies* 14, no. 2 (July 1991): 15–31.

60. Jorge Durand and Douglas S. Massey, *Miracles on the Border: Retablos of Mexican Migrants to the United States* (Tucson: University of Arizona Press, 1995), p. 64.

61. José R. Reyna and María Herrera-Sobek, "Jokelore, Cultural Differences, and Linguistic Dexterity: The Construction of the Mexican Immigrant in Chicano Humor," in David R. Maciel and María Herrera-Sobek, eds., *Culture Across Borders: Mexican Immigration and Popular Culture* (Tucson: University of Arizona Press, 1998), p. 207.

62. María Herrera-Sobek, *Northward Bound: The Mexican Immigrant Experience in Ballad and Song* (Bloomington: University of Indiana Press, 1993), pp. 187–188.

63. Ramón Saldívar, "Transnational Migrations and Border Identities: Immigration and Postmodern Culture," *South Atlantic Quarterly* 91, nos. 1–2 (winter/spring 1999): 217–230.

64. Translated in Saldívar, "Transnational Migrations and Border Identities," pp. 221–222.

65. Gamio, *Mexican Immigration to the United States*, p. 128.

66. Herrera-Sobek, *Northward Bound*, p. 109.

67. David Maciel and María Rosa García-Acevedo, "The Celluloid Immigrant: The Narrative Films of Mexican Immigration," in Maciel and Herrera-Sobek, *Culture Across Borders*, pp. 155–156, 196.

68. Sánchez, *Becoming Mexican American*, p. 249.

69. Robert B. Kent and Maura E. Huntz, "Spanish-Language Newspapers in the United States," *Geographical Review* 86, no. 3 (July 1996): 446–457; Nicolás Kanellos, "A Socio-Historic Study of Hispanic Newspapers in the United States," in Ramón Gutiérrez and Genaro Padilla, eds., *Recovering the U.S. Hispanic Literary Heritage* (Houston: Arte Público Press, 1993), p. 111.

70. *Migration News*, July 2000.

71. Devra Weber, "Historical Perspectives on Transnational Mexican Workers in California," in Hart, ed., *Border Crossings*, pp. 209–210; www.seiu.org; *Los Angeles Times*, April 13, 2000, April 20, 2000, and April 26, 2000.

72. Carole Nagengast and Michael Kearney, "Mixtec Ethnicity: Social Identity, Political Consciousness, and Political Activism," *Latin American Research Review* 25, no. 2 (1990): 62.

12

Campaigning for Change: Reinventing NAFTA to Serve Migrant Communities

Robert L. Bach

Since January 2001, the administrations in Mexico and the United States have had the opportunity to dramatically improve bilateral relations. In many ways, the relationship between the two countries has reached a level of cooperation unsurpassed in modern history. Across a broad array of issues, the neighbors share common goals and pursue similar strategies. However, several areas of public dispute reflect historically entrenched, difficult dilemmas. One of the most difficult involves large-scale cross-border migration. Without bold new approaches, the migration issue and border affairs in general will continue to strain the relationship.

Fortunately, the administrations of Ernesto Zedillo and Bill Clinton made progress in laying the groundwork for a transformation in policies that affect border and migration issues. Though embracing the need for joint approaches to long-term security, free trade, open investment, and application of the rule of law, they also acknowledged that these fundamentals would be insufficient. In May 1997, the two presidents signed the Joint Statement on Migration that committed both governments to working together to design a comprehensive new vision for the future of the border area. Subsequently, they exchanged private letters calling for a sustained, open-ended discussion that has led to a new framework for managing migration.

The administrations of Vicente Fox and George W. Bush today have an opportunity to take up this charge more formally and publicly than their predecessors. A good start would be for the administrations to accelerate and strengthen the initiatives launched during the Zedillo-Clinton years. All remain incomplete and unstable. Both administrations will also need to confront entrenched economic interests and political assumptions if they are to progress toward the breakthrough envisioned by the Zedillo-Clinton statement. Prominent among the views that must be confronted are the goals, objectives, and priorities embedded in the North American Free Trade Agreement (NAFTA).

NAFTA-inspired strategies for managing exchange of goods (trade) or people (immigration) become less effective and even counterproductive the more integrated the cross-border regional labor market becomes. They reproduce tired notions of immigration policy that remain a primary stumbling block to developing a new vision of the bilateral relationship. President Fox's visit to Canada and the United States in August 2000 to initiate a dialogue over more visas and "open borders" faltered because it placed so much emphasis on established views and ventured so little to address the unmet human needs that accumulated during NAFTA's first decade. His reception in Canada and the United States, which was a polite but firm rejection of the idea of open borders, was a friendly reminder that solving the underlying economic, social, health, education, and law-enforcement problems in the region is as important as strengthening the benefits of physical integration through cross-border exchanges.

President Fox's September 2000 proposal to establish a free-trade zone from Panama to Mexico also missed a key opportunity, repeating the fallacy underlying NAFTA. The problem is not free trade or even migration per se. Rather, trade liberalization creates unequal conditions that stimulate migration in the absence of conscious and effective investments to meet household needs in employment, education, health, and housing in the communities that send as well as those that receive migrants. Nothing in NAFTA's current framework—even if it is extended into Central America—offers new terms and conditions for workers and their families who must bear the consequences of extending labor markets across international borders. Persistent illegal migration and repetitively stale migration policies are manifestations of the weak and exploitative foundations of regional free-trade regimes. The way forward requires the reinvention of NAFTA and its rules for integration to meet the social and human needs of communities on both sides of the border.

Beyond NAFTA

NAFTA's heritage lies deep in the structural adjustment policies imposed by the International Monetary Fund (IMF) in response to

Mexico's massive foreign debt in the 1980s. As a model of fiscal responsibility, these policies slashed government expenditures, weakened public regulation, and opened the country to foreign goods, services, and capital. The guiding vision was to trade more and spend less.

Within its own terms, NAFTA has delivered what it was supposed to. For almost a decade, Mexico has enjoyed dramatic increases in direct foreign investment in equipment and property, and trade has accelerated to both Canada and the United States. Especially in northern Mexico, the number of *maquiladora* plants and workers has increased dramatically. For instance, more than 500,000 Mexican workers now make parts and assemble vehicles for eight of the world's largest automakers. Central Mexican states, including Guadalajara, Guanajuato, and Puebla, have also become an export zone for sophisticated electronic products. Financial liberalization has brought additional benefits. It has begun to open up Mexican business practices, challenging the traditional reliance on extended families, personal friendships, and government contacts, and it has sparked a move toward professional management and foreign ownership. As more and more U.S. and Mexican companies work together, many executives now consider their companies to be North American corporations rather than of a particular nationality.[1]

NAFTA has also certified the commitment of both governments to the IMF's dictates, which included embracing an economic ideology that celebrated the marketplace even in full recognition of its accompanying widespread social, economic, and political displacements. For example, NAFTA proponents point to Mexico's commitment to market liberalization during the 1994 peso crisis. On the day Mexico announced its final payment on the U.S. loan to help recover from the devaluation, President Clinton declared that the situation would have been much worse in the absence of NAFTA. "This is a remarkable turnaround," the president said.

> Following its 1982 financial crisis, it took seven years—seven years—for Mexico to return to the private financial markets. This time, it took seven months. After the 1982 crisis, Mexico imposed prohibitive tariffs, and U.S. exports fell 50 percent, not recovering for seven years. This time, Mexico continued to fulfill its NAFTA commitments, and our exports are already 11 percent above pre-crisis levels.[2]

Of course, NAFTA's model of regional integration was never Mexico's alone. NAFTA formalized a model of economic partnership in which both the United States and Mexico became deeply and perhaps inextricably intertwined in a common economic future. President Clinton recognized this interdependence during the Mexican financial crisis in 1994: Mexico's difficulties were now also U.S. problems. The U.S. loan to Mexico aimed to prevent the destabilization of Mexico and any loss in the sales of goods and services that generated jobs for U.S. workers. "Two years ago, helping our friend and neighbor in a time of need was quite controversial," the president said.

> Some said that we should not get involved, that the money would never be repaid, that Mexico should fend for itself. They were wrong. Today the American people can be proud that we did the right thing by Mexico and the right thing for the United States, and the right thing to protect global prosperity.[3]

The negative consequences of NAFTA, however, like other free-trade regimes spawned by structural adjustment policies, are generating a growing and increasingly articulate opposition. Neither the U.S. nor Mexican administration should ignore the substantive arguments arising from the mounting challenge to the current terms of globalization and regional integration schemes. The criticisms have deep roots in social and economic conditions that have long generated opposition to NAFTA. These include concerns that NAFTA would consolidate and legitimize structural adjustments policies, deeply damage the social infrastructure, exacerbate income inequality, leave the impoverished with less help and fewer alternatives, and destroy the public's ability to defend itself against the impacts of trade liberalization. NAFTA-led reforms have fulfilled each of these predictions. For example, they have concentrated economic power—fifty major companies now account for one-half of Mexican exports, and twenty major corporate groups control more than three-fifths of national economic output. Small Mexican companies face nearly insurmountable financing costs; traditional farming continues to shed excess workers; and labor-intensive sectors, including agriculture and light industry, cannot compete internationally. Labor laws remain mostly unchanged, and income inequality—already one of the deepest in the world—has increased.

In this context, President Zedillo may have been a bit intemperate when he dismissed protesters who gathered at the World Trade Organization meetings in Seattle and Davos to demonstrate against the impacts of trade liberalization. He called them a "peculiar alliance" of self-appointed representatives of civil society, environmental and labor groups, and the extreme left and right trying "to save the people of developing countries from development."[4] "They seem determined," he wrote, "to ignore the fact that, frequently, the alternative for those workers is extreme rural poverty or a marginal occupation in the urban informal sector of the economy, where hardly any labor rights can be made effective."[5]

Other Mexican leaders, however, have recognized the fundamental flaw in NAFTA's strategy. In late 1999, Jesús Silva-Herzog, former Mexican ambassador to the United States, described this flaw as follows: "Mexico forgot the warning to avoid dogma or economic extremes. . . . Economic growth must be attained to meet Mexico's social needs."[6] He argued that the strategies formed after the economic crises of the early 1980s, which inspired NAFTA, could not accommodate population growth, new entries in the labor force, and mounting pressures for emigration to the United States. Then, as now, the issue was not and should not be confined to an argument about growth or no growth, jobs or no jobs, more or fewer visas. The fundamental issue is what type of growth and what kinds of alternatives can different regional integration approaches generate for workers and their impoverished communities.

Other leaders, even those who fully supported NAFTA, have also recognized its structural limitations and have begun to press for a different strategy. For example, President Clinton, who signed NAFTA into law, expressed reservations about NAFTA-like regimes. He acknowledged that free markets often develop unevenly and incompletely, creating the need to find ways to allow everyone to participate in the development process.

This focus on broad-based participation and benefits is perhaps the primary difference between a new vision of regional integration and that of NAFTA originally envisioned by the administrations of President Carlos Salinas de Gortari and President George H.W. Bush. For example, President Clinton's speech in Brazil focused on expanded education opportunities as the primary mechanism to enhance participation and advancement. He did not attempt to explain how current inequalities, poverty, and ignorance in Brazil would diminish over time as economic growth created new job opportunities. NAFTA proponents, however, frequently invoke these latter arguments. He also did not advocate the acceptance of illegal child labor or youthful illiteracy, even though there was a "market niche" for it in the expanding economy. In contrast, advocates of unauthorized and temporary contract work routinely advance such apologetic arguments about labor-market niches stretching across the U.S.-Mexico border.

Rather, President Clinton's message was that education is essential to, not in conflict with, trade and development because it creates alternatives to seemingly inevitable conditions. Education represents just one of many institutional foundations of economic growth that support the well-being of those fortunate enough to gain access to the market and, especially, of those excluded and bypassed who hope one day to also benefit.

Opponents of the structural flaws of NAFTA understood from the outset the need to invest in the institutional foundations of development to encourage broad-based participation. The Chiapas rebellion, timed to start on the same day NAFTA went into effect, was, of course, the most dramatic display of opposition. Although hardly indicative of widespread opposition to regional integration, the rebellion at least alerted everyone to the reality that not all communities wanted to be part of a NAFTA model that embraced, rather than challenged, exclusion, oppression, and inequality.

The original Salinas-Bush version of NAFTA also set the parameters of policy options on cross-border affairs, including migration. It accepted in silence the nature of structural adjustments, the huge displacements, and the chaos and hardships that were predicted for the Mexican economy, its labor markets, and low-wage workers. It accepted the social consequences for poor families and the intrinsic pressures within the framework that made it unlikely that many households could sustain employment and family life inside Mexico. It embraced as "inevitable" the belief that Mexico's surplus labor supply was born of demographic growth and relatively anemic levels of job growth. Therefore, the only alternative that workers had for the misery of isolation commonly found in the pre-1980 period was to succumb to the insatiable U.S. demand for cheap additional workers and to move northward, as President Zedillo noted. Even if migration reaches its maximum in fifteen to thirty years before it begins to decline, as some researchers project, these workers and their families must endure the inequalities of the NAFTA period and the consequences of extending the labor market hundreds and thousands of miles.

Monitoring NAFTA

Early opposition to NAFTA pushed the Clinton administration to negotiate side agreements covering labor and environmental standards. The side agreements provided mechanisms for resolving complaints about labor or environmental conditions and for organizing debate about widely perceived intrinsic problems with regional integration. The side agreements also limited public debate by focusing on resolving specific complaints rather than the structural problems of the regional economy. In turn, the side agreements reduced the political heat on NAFTA's early performance and helped to garner the support of some labor and environmental groups during the fight for congressional approval of NAFTA.

Opposition to the migration-related aspects of NAFTA could have been quite strong. Both governments agreed during the negotiations that regional economic integration—even under the most optimistic growth scenarios—would continue to generate high levels of unmanageable migration to the United States for decades. Yet neither government believed it had sufficient political support to openly and transparently confront issues of migration. Even an attempt to craft a side agreement could have raised public concerns and scuttled all NAFTA negotiations. The failure to reach an agreement left both governments, and those living on both sides of the border, without an institutional mechanism or even a forum to address the predictable problems of cross-border migration.

Tragically, the worst fears of those who shied from confronting the immigration issue came true. Without a side agreement, the migration issue exploded across the stage of public debate. In 1994, California governor Pete Wilson whipped up popular opposition to Mexican immigration in his bid for reelection. His efforts stimulated other governors to sue the federal government to recover the education, health, and law-enforcement costs associated with immigration. His efforts also led California voters to pass Proposition 187, which became the symbolic centerpiece of attacks on the rights and well-being of immigrants. The public controversy opened the way for overt opposition to NAFTA itself. Pat Buchanan's "America First" campaign drew increasing support by calling on the federal government to seal the U.S. borders to goods and, especially, to people.

Matters worsened when TV cameras recorded police officers in Riverside, California, assaulting several Mexican citizens. Tensions between the two governments intensified even more when the U.S. Congress passed the Illegal Immigration Reform and Immigrant Responsibility Act of 1996 shortly thereafter. The law incorporated much of the California-inspired anti-immigrant sentiment into intensified enforcement efforts.

Realizing that these tensions threatened the underpinnings of regional cooperation and the overall bilateral relationship, the Zedillo and Clinton administrations embarked on wide-ranging discussions of shared concerns. Both sides specifically increased their institutional attention and priority to border affairs. The new effort focused on the Binational Commission, an annual gathering of cabinet-level officials from both governments. The two administrations also embarked on creating a series of problem-solving mechanisms, largely organized informally along the border. Where the Salinas-Bush administrations had failed, Zedillo-Clinton officials set out to craft their own de facto side agreements on migration to provide a way to organize a response to the growing number of problems.

De Facto Migration Side Agreements

Despite the rocky start, the Zedillo-Clinton administrations developed these initial contacts into an unprecedented working relationship that helped the two governments manage several difficult incidents at the border. The relationship matured through a series of statecraft initiatives, involving formal memoranda of understanding, communiqués, protocols, joint statements, and novel joint public appearances addressing border problems. The meetings established trust among officials from both sides, and, more important, they became ad hoc mechanisms for addressing complaints, doing informally what the NAFTA side agreements were supposed to do.

The de facto side agreement meetings produced statements and communiqués on many issues, including efforts to protect the human rights of migrants, implement safe and orderly procedures for the repatriation of migrants, and combat cross-border smuggling. In the immediate aftermath of Proposition 187, the two administrations agreed to several cooperative measures set forth in the Zacatecas Accord, the first in what became a series of agreements on joint or complementary activities. They included expanded border crime-prevention units, joint efforts to eliminate illegal pedestrian port and lane runners in San Diego, and coordinated tactics to close access to the flood tunnels in Nogales used to carry contraband into Mexico and illegal immigrants into the United States.

Over the years, these de facto side negotiations evolved beyond specific operations and began to take shape around three broad goals. First, these meetings reinforced Mexican efforts, begun years before, to expand consular activities inside the United States. Whether the long-term outreach increased service to the expatriate community or, as some researchers have argued, attempted to prevent embarrassing political demonstrations against the Institutional Revolutionary Party (PRI), the expansion of consular involvement in matters of immigration law enforcement fit Mexico's overall diplomatic strategy.[7] The harshness of the 1996 U.S. immigration law, the rapid increase in enforcement incidents involving Mexican citizens, and a rising number of violent encounters between Mexican immigrants and border officers pushed the Mexican consulates to establish regular contact with officials of the U.S. Immigration and Naturalization Service (INS) and attempt to change some of the enforcement practices. Mexican secretary of foreign relations Rosario Green described her government's actions as follows:

> Unfortunately . . . we regularly hear of new incidents where migrants find their rights violated. We will continue to demand the protection of the human and labor rights of all Mexican nationals, regardless of their migratory status and we will continue to strengthen our capacity to provide protection through our consular network in the United States. Mexico has the largest consular network in the world, with 42 offices in the United States: we are determined to make it the most effective. The administration of President Zedillo regards this question as one of its highest priorities.[8]

Perhaps the most important outcome of this consular activity was a formal memorandum in which the INS and Mexico's secretary of foreign relations established so-called interior consultative mechanisms. Mechanism meetings became the most frequent and routine venue for the discussion of complaints, including the exchange of information about INS enforcement operations and problem incidents. Within these mechanisms, the two governments also signed safe and orderly repatriation agreements, although several U.S. border officials resisted their implementation.

Second, the routinization of liaison meetings among officials gave each side an opportunity to explain its overall perspective on the migration issue. The dialogue helped to prevent gross misunderstandings. Yet they also became opportunities to "win" the inclusion of specific wording in the postmeeting communiqué that gave recognition to a particular perspective. The latter became increasingly important because each side used the announcements in their respective media to demonstrate progress on tough and politically volatile issues. For the United States, the meetings were opportunities to inform Mexican officials about the growing number of border enforcement operations and to explain the rationale behind the largest buildup of U.S. immigration enforcement in decades. For Mexican officials, the meetings became increasingly defensive. They tried to demonstrate to the Mexican media that despite the number of border incidents a cooperative, rather than antagonistic, approach with the United States was paying off.

The Zedillo administration also used the meetings of the Binational Commission to influence U.S. public opinion on issues related to border enforcement. The Mexican government worked hard to generate supportive discussions and analyses among sympathetic researchers and advocates in the United States, reaching out specifically to proimmigration think tanks, even though they resisted including their own nongovernmental organizations in the migration debates. The government especially put great political stock in pushing for a study of migration to help change the debate from a focus on law enforcement to the inevitability of the migratory flow based on the nature of the labor market.

In the end, the political purposes of the binational study far exceeded its scientific value. Within binational scientific communities it certainly was not news that migration could be viewed as a comprehensive economic, social, and historical phenomenon. It was also not news in policy circles. More than a decade before, another group, the Ascencio Commission, had concluded that the migration flow was structural and that only increased trade would serve, over the long term, to reduce migration pressures.

However, the binational study took on significance for the Zedillo administration as a way to counter the arguments of Proposition 187 and the growing emphasis on immigration enforcement in the United States. In a series of public presentations of the research results—all taking place in the United States—senior Mexican officials used the study's results to reinforce the thesis that the cross-border migration flow was inevitable. No significant effort was made to use these occasions to open discussion on alternative development strategies or to question the terms and conditions of NAFTA itself.

Finally, and perhaps most important, the two administrations made the greatest strides and took the largest risks by encouraging local government officials along the border to solve problems locally. Some of these efforts were formally organized through the border liaison mechanisms, which were long-standing working groups designed to foster dialogue about local border issues. These and other more informal local initiatives generated joint problem-solving approaches that were novel. In San Diego, for example, a stellar combination of Mexican consular officials, local INS immigration officers, and the U.S. Attorney for Southern California created what could have become a model of a local cross-border law-enforcement partnership. Their actions drew broad-based support from the law-enforcement and community leaderships of both Tijuana and San Diego. The partnership defused problems when they occurred, improved public safety programs, established cross-border criminal prosecutions, and pressed for improvement in traffic management at the ports of entry that were vital to the binational regional economy. These joint actions went beyond complaint mechanisms and for several years pointed to new directions in forging true cross-border institutions. Unfortunately, both governments let the San Diego initiative and, with it, an important model of border transformation falter and, in the end, actively undermined the cooperative efforts.

All along the border, these local meetings and working groups provided a much-needed opportunity for discussion and dispute resolution. Yet these activities have not advanced beyond the limitations that appear intrinsic to all side agreements, including the formal procedures on labor and environmental issues. Many of the complaint mechanisms have become ritualistic and have taken on the tone and character of formal binational diplomatic exercises rather than down-to-earth problem-solving operations. The ritualism drove many of the more energetic and creative problem-solvers to avoid the meetings and reinforced their reliance more on interpersonal trust and cooperation than on institutional effectiveness and procedures. Even the periodic gatherings of national leaders spent more time drafting communiqués than on carrying out much of the hard work. Past efforts to institutionalize the liaison gatherings have pushed joint action even farther from problem-solving activities. Ironically, under a stated goal of opening up discussions to local communities, these efforts have made the encounters less effective and actually reduced the substantive participation of communities directly engaged in improving conditions along the border.[9]

Side agreements—whether formal or de facto—do not hold the promise of establishing a new institutional framework for regional integration. They remain rooted in their original frame of reference, focused on the disputes that the Salinas-Bush NAFTA model did not address. In that sense, the agreements have tried to be ameliorative, not transformational, and under persistent pressure are likely to fail even in their original purpose.

Moving Forward

The next step for both administrations clearly is to strengthen efforts toward regional integration. Turning backward in the hopes of overcoming the problems caused by nearly a decade of full-paced integration is no longer possible. Yet moving forward requires both governments to acknowledge the full extent of unmet human needs and the social and economic costs that are structurally embedded in NAFTA-style regional development models. A full accounting of the costs and benefits of NAFTA goes beyond efforts to calculate, then redistribute, the advantages of cross-border flows to communities on either side of the border. Transborder market integration produces numerous unpaid bills—economically, socially, and politically—and places the burden of paying them disproportionately on low-income communities on both sides of the border.

The U.S.-Mexican dialogue should now focus on the creation of alternatives. For example, policies that recognize the assets and needs of migrant-sending communities should focus efforts on creating more opportunities at home for workers to stay and live in dignity. The goal should be to expand alternatives in sending communities so that the decision to migrate expresses a real choice among household members and not the compulsion of market discipline and demographic inevitability. In the context of these alternatives, the conditions and rules under which citizens of both the United States and Mexico move back and forth across the border to work, visit, and live would, and certainly must, dramatically improve.

The following section offers four proposals to stimulate debate on alternatives to current conditions underlying the migration flow. Both governments can undoubtedly generate many more proposals once the task is no longer just to find ways of extending the current framework but to begin meeting the needs of both Mexican and U.S. low-income communities.

Proposal 1: National Program of Alternatives to Emigration

Mexican society has tackled seemingly inevitable population trends before and been very successful in creating economic, social, and cultural alternatives. Several decades ago, the Mexican government launched an impressive national campaign to reduce the rate of population growth. In similar fashion, the Mexican government should launch a national campaign that is committed to eliminating unauthorized migration between the two countries. The government would have to openly acknowledge its responsibility—politically, socially, and economically—to those who cannot find jobs and are compelled to move northward to secure a livelihood.

The Mexican national campaign could include special initiatives to increase employment alternatives, generate work opportunities for everyone in the household, and, especially, expand social investments in housing, education, and consumption that much of the migration northward now funds informally. These initiatives will undoubtedly develop binationally with U.S. participation and could require a combination of programs that would increase, not decrease, legal migration. They should certainly expand travel opportunities and accelerate local cross-border movements that are already normal realities of border life.

The Fox administration would also do well within the context of a national campaign to trade in the economic determinism of prevailing views of Mexican migration and begin to examine emigration as a political process as well. President Fox recently took a good first step in connecting the rise of democracy in Mexico and the opportunity to move beyond current debates about migration popular on both sides of the border. An increasing number of scholars are beginning to question PRI-led efforts over decades to deny the political foundations of the northward emigration. By focusing on emigration as a popular response to the absence of democratic opportunities, the Fox administration could shift the policy and planning discussion from simply trying to change public opinion in the United States to providing its own citizens opportunities to express their underlying claims within the Mexican system.

Finally, this new national campaign could also extend enforcement of the rule of law to the migration arena, protecting individual rights and defending community desires and opportunities. The Mexican government should dramatically increase efforts to enforce Mexican law against illegal trafficking of persons across its northern border. It should also assist individuals who are stranded or caught in these trafficking networks to return home and find safe livelihoods.

Proposal 2: A U.S. Labor-Market Campaign

The George W. Bush administration should also reassess its strategy of encouraging labor export from Mexico. Until now, U.S. foreign policy has passively accepted the view that migration from Mexico was an escape valve essential to maintaining the political and social stability of its southern neighbor. Yet as democracy deepens in Mexico, the United States should shift its understanding of large-scale emigration as an obstacle to necessary economic and social changes in the Mexico countryside and in the low-wage regional economy in general.

The problem, of course, is that the United States has its own deeply ingrained interests in the structural adjustment policies that gave birth to NAFTA. Efforts to reform the regional development framework to address human needs will require the United States to aggressively move against some of the most characteristic features of this impoverished transborder labor market. These efforts could take several forms, although none can have much of an effect on its own. The following examples are only a few elements of a broad-based U.S. labor-market campaign that would complement the Mexican initiative proposed earlier.

First, if either administration truly seeks to gain sufficient credibility to reinvent NAFTA to respond to human needs, they must together attack the dreadful conditions of farmworkers in both the United States and Mexico. Agricultural labor conditions are such embarrassing examples of the fatal flaws of current regional integration schemes that even liberal advocates have virtually conceded the raw realities of farmwork.

The fundamental issue is, of course, the wage paid to farmworkers. In the past, campaigns to increase wages have fallen on deaf ears or have been squarely opposed by producers who threatened to pass along the price increases to consumers through higher food prices. Yet since the early 1990s the declining wages of farmworkers have subsidized consumers at a time when the incomes of most middle-class consumers have risen significantly. In short, the consumption of the urban middle class continues to be subsidized by the impoverishment of farm laborers both in the United States and Mexico.

The time has come for the cost of agricultural production to compensate farmworkers for poor working conditions, rather than making the workers' families absorb them through depressed consumption. These reforms should significantly reduce the burden on individual farmworkers who bear the cost of moving hundreds and thousands of miles and making the illicit crossing into the United States to make the U.S. farm-labor market function.

As in Mexico, economic reforms of the magnitude needed in U.S. farm-labor markets will not succeed unless they are organized as part of a substantial political, social, and cultural campaign. Although these campaigns should be national in scope, the time is especially ripe for corporate leaders in California's new economy sectors to become involved in reforming the conditions of agricultural workers. Agriculture and its depressed labor conditions remain perhaps the most prominent examples of the old economy. Their persistence challenges the goal of many new corporate leaders to build a Californian community that works for all state residents. New-economy entrepreneurs have the opportunity—and the self-interest—to lead an enlightened campaign that creates cooperative strategies to improve wages and living standards of all low-wage workers in the state. Agricultural conditions, however, will remain a continuous thorn in their side unless their efforts specifically target reforms in rural California.

Second, both governments need to acknowledge the full costs of the regional labor market and find ways to compensate low-wage workers and their families through a variety of mechanisms that increase social wages. Unfortunately, migrant-sending governments and apologists for NAFTA's costly impacts have become enamored with the significance of remittances as a source of development funds in the Mexican countryside. Clearly, the ability of a Mexican worker to gain employment and use the earnings to increase household consumption is a welcome step forward. Work pays, whether in Mexico or the United States. So-called *migradollars,* however, should not become *milagrodollars*—miracle dollars that are treated as the investment spark to overcome the extreme difficulties and costs of a transnational labor market.

The meager savings of immigrants should be available first and foremost to support family consumption, including the vast unmet social needs in education, health care, and improved child and family development. And if they truly exist, such savings should help support the building of a public infrastructure to meet immediate and necessary household and community needs. Mexican families should not have to use access to U.S. earnings to compensate for a lack of credit opportunities at home and the failure of the state to provide for physical infrastructure. A direct challenge for the Fox administration is to accelerate banking reforms far sooner than envisioned. But even that will not be enough.

The social wage attached to jobs held by immigrant workers in the United States must be radically reconsidered. If the true costs of Mexican immigration are realized in the poverty of the Mexican countryside, then employment in the United States should compensate for the costs of sustaining a decent standard of living not only for the worker while he or she is resident in the United States but also for their families in Mexico. For this to happen, health care systems would have to become transnational, crossing the international border to properly reflect the needs and conditions of their clients.

The social wage for immigrant workers should also contribute to education investments in Mexico. Every day, Mexico loses investments in the education, skills, and health of its youth as they leave for the United States because they are unable to find employment at home. In turn, with each passing year, U.S. schools face the increasing costs of absorbing and educating these children. The two governments should increase public investments in education and health in migrant-sending and -receiving communities to minimize the disruptions in child education from migration.

Third, the United States should launch another legalization program similar to the amnesty conducted under the 1986 Immigration Reform and Control Act. Unlike before, however, no one should pretend that such a program resolves the migration problem. The need for a new amnesty has less to do with immigration per se than with the conditions and standards of the transborder labor market. During a time when many low-wage immigrant workers have lost real income or increased their earnings at a far slower rate than other workers, a legalization program would help stabilize these workers and increase their likelihood of being able to organize to improve their conditions. Without these specific labor-market improvements, a separate immigration-only amnesty program could be counterproductive. It would legitimize a cyclical pattern that already underlies the original NAFTA framework, which allows for long periods of illegal migration to be followed by periodic amnesties, as if the latter were reparations for the years of economic and personal hardship and exploitation.

Proposal 3: Border Infrastructure

Nowhere are the inherent weaknesses of NAFTA more prominent than in building physical and social infrastructure along the border. The de facto side agreements discussed above work well within the diplomatic logic of formal relations among states. As complaint mechanisms, they also fit well into the organizational mandates and cultures of the U.S. Department of State and the Mexican Ministry of External Relations. However, these agreements are woefully inadequate in managing the increasing integration of foreign and domestic dimensions of transnational commerce, labor, and community.

If private corporations increasingly consider themselves North American enterprises, then governments must respond with regional institutions. Though such institutions challenge every principle rooted in sovereign political systems, the place to make progress could be at the border, where the integration, as well as the needs and benefits, are greatest.

Working together, the United States and Mexico should move rapidly to improve border infrastructure, especially at the ports of entry, to facilitate the exchanges that fuel border economic development. During the past few years, the two governments have demonstrated the value of dedicated commuter lanes—first in San Diego, then in El Paso—as an infrastructure project with clear transborder benefits. However, both governments need to bring infrastructure improvements up to a scale that matches the enormously expanding needs. This cannot be achieved simply by arithmetic increases in port projects.

Instead, the governments should launch a borderwide infrastructure campaign that would rival the U.S. interstate highway system. The NAFTA corridor initiative is a start, but it still falls far short of future needs. Financing a transnational transportation system is much more of a challenge than creating an interstate highway network. Early in the Clinton administration, Congress rejected an effort to pass legislation to establish a border-crossing fee. The primary reason was that border communities believed, with some justification, that the federal government would use the federal fee in ways that only partially served the needs of the communities from which the money was collected. The mistake, however, was not in the concept but in its formulation.

Before fees are collected, the two governments should establish several cross-border port authorities modeled on a modernized version of the regional transportation authorities that several states have created within the United States. As transnational authorities, they would be able to raise money in international credit markets and allocate investments to improve the infrastructure capacity of the border without interference from either Washington or Mexico City. A transborder infrastructure trust fund, managed through these cross-border port authorities, could also ensure that the fees collected from local communities remained in the border area. These financial innovations, or other similar ones, would provide the much-needed investment for the border, which is quickly becoming the critical crossroads of the rapidly integrating NAFTA region.

Proposal 4: Enforcement Partnerships

Improving border infrastructure also calls for a substantial transformation of policing efforts in communities on both sides of the border.

Cross-border partnerships in law enforcement could be the single most important short-term initiative of both new administrations, especially if the Fox administration proceeds with its plans to reform the attorney general's office and the national police. As in the economic realm, the two governments need to work together on several immediate initiatives to establish their credibility.

First, the administrations should agree on the comprehensive design and implementation of a public safety campaign that suppresses violence along the entire border. Some of the border violence is directed at law enforcement personnel. In Nogales, for example, armed assaults against U.S. immigration officers have significantly increased since the mid-1990s. In Tecate, members of Mexico's Grupo Alpha have been attacked and at least one officer killed. In San Diego, both governments have had to intervene to stop cross-border drive-by shootings and to prevent potential retaliation.

The dangers of illicit trespassing across the border can also be dramatically reduced through cooperative action. Despite critics' disbelief, the U.S. Border Patrol has shifted its tactics and deployment of agents to reduce the risks to migrants' lives on numerous occasions. If the officials are working as true partners, then joint tactics can solve many border safety problems. Unfortunately, these efforts usually ended up limited to micromanagement of issues such as the availability of water jugs in Border Patrol vehicles, placements of warning signs, and the wording of public service announcements. The efforts have also simply been neglected. During a period when the INS has found millions of dollars to spend on consultants to draw organizational charts in hopes of forestalling its own reorganization, the Border Patrol has had to continuously fight to obtain even the $100,000 a year that was begrudgingly devoted to the Border Safety Initiative.

Second, both governments should seize the opportunity to expand efforts to carry out joint cross-border investigations designed to destroy the infrastructure of smuggling and trafficking organizations, especially those who target women and children. Although current efforts have been very modest, the results have been dramatic and, if brought to scale, could have a profound impact on the safety of the border. Joint progress in targeting smuggling could also make it possible for the Border Patrol to progressively transform its block-and-tackle defensive posture into a broader-based and more effective investigative strategy.

Third, a new law enforcement initiative should extend far beyond the piecemeal initiatives with which the two governments experimented in the early and mid-1990s. The governments should join forces to create nothing less than a regional cross-border criminal justice system. The goal would be to focus binational resources and tactics on combating the sources and consequences of crimes that use border-crossing for profit and deception.

A major innovation in the cross-border criminal justice system would be to change the U.S. strategy of deportation. The legitimate desire to reduce the likelihood of felony recidivism as well as the costs of incarceration inside the United States is simply not achieved by physically removing the immigrant felon. It also does little to solve the criminal justice issues that face both the United States and Mexico.

The testimony of INS officials before Congress as well as criminology research in general have shown that removing felons physically does little to change the chances of repeat behavior. In the case of immigration, recidivism is often twofold: a deported felon remigrates illegally to the United States and then often commits another crime. The administrations should begin serious work on resolving the revolving door. They could begin with a joint program against youth crime, including a focus on the transnational youth gangs that now operate simultaneously in both countries. Other cooperative activities would certainly involve sharing criminal justice information and evidence, undertaking joint prosecutions, and connecting data systems to maximize the ability to identify and arrest a felon in either country. The two governments could also draw on the full force of prevention and prosecution strategies to reduce the incidence and intensity of violent cross-border crimes and to construct a comprehensive approach to law enforcement that seeks to prevent problems rather than simply to grab and remove the criminals that cause them.

Conclusion

The Zedillo-Clinton era has left Mexico and the United States positioned to make significant advances toward transforming the binational regional labor market. This transformation goes beyond demographic destiny, open trade, and increased border enforcement and seeks to change the structural underpinnings of NAFTA. Policy discussions should now focus on conscious efforts to democratize the rules that govern the transborder economy and community, responding to the interests of migrant-sending and -receiving communities to create alternatives to the current chaotic labor market. They should force the debate to move beyond efforts that address problems by exporting or importing temporary solutions.

President Fox has openly voiced the quiet longing of the Zedillo administration—to convince the United States to expand the number of visas available to Mexican citizens who want to work in the United States. Unfortunately, he has not yet expressed an understanding that progress toward a future of more open borders requires solving the problems of NAFTA, not expanding them with a greater exchange of the same kind.

Mexico already has an unprecedented and unique place within U.S. immigration policy, which includes high levels of legal immigration, the existence of border-crossing cards, and relatively recent amnesty for millions of illegal immigrants. Even the much-maligned temporary work programs available to Mexican citizens have substantially increased in the last few years. The question for U.S. immigration policy is not whether there should be more visas or fewer but whether the degree of physical integration under NAFTA has reached a sufficient level to support entirely new rules for labor exchange and population movement in general.

Currently, the United States administers most of the cross-border movement as part of a global immigration framework that treats all countries the same. Perhaps as part of the overall reforms proposed earlier, the three NAFTA partners should consider delinking selected cross-border labor-market movements from the legal framework of more general immigration policies. Such a change would certainly constitute the type of breakthrough that many NAFTA reformers desire. Yet such a fundamental change in the legal frameworks would be much more likely to occur if substantial progress to dramatically improve the conditions of low-income communities on both sides of the transnational networks was already evident.

The challenge facing both regimes, however, is more about democracy than it is about labor markets or visas. No democratic country in the world enables, as Mexico does, such a large unauthorized movement of its people across a friendly neighbor's borders. If it is true that no democratic country ever has a famine because a free people do not tolerate such misery, then perhaps a corollary is that no democratic country would permit so many of its citizens to face the perils present in the U.S.-Mexican transborder labor market. At the very least, it would not do so without taking heroic steps—as partners with its neighbor—to solve the problems that force people to flee their homes.

President Zedillo and President Clinton have already committed each government to work together to formulate a new approach to cross-border migration and social and economic development for the entire region. The challenge that remains is for both nations to acknowledge that NAFTA is not yet that approach. A new vision must seek to overcome the past—not simply to extend it.

Notes

The perspective and opinions expressed in this chapter are the author's sole responsibility and do not necessarily represent the official views of agencies with which the author has been or is currently affiliated.

1. Pacific Council on International Policy, "Mexico Transforming," *New Perspectives Quarterly* 17, no. 2 (spring 2000).
2. White House Press Office.
3. Ibid.
4. Ernesto Zedillo, "Against Globaphobia," *New Perspectives Quarterly* 17, no. 2 (spring 2000): 4.
5. Ibid., p. 6.
6. Interview reported in *UC Mexus News,* winter 1999, p. 8.
7. Alejandro Portes, "Conclusion: Towards a New World—The Origins and Effects of Transnational Activities," *Ethnic and Racial Studies* 22, no. 2 (March 1999): 474. Robert C. Smith, "Mexican Immigrants, the Mexican State, and the Transnational Practice of Mexican Politics and Membership," *LASA Forum* 24 (summer 1998): 20–21.
8. Rosario Green, text of speech released by the embassy of Mexico, Washington, D.C.
9. Formal gatherings of cross-border groups, rather than stimulating local participation, have replaced substance with form. The same outcome has occurred recently under the Canada-U.S. Partnership initiative along the U.S.-Canadian border. Rather than facilitating cross-border cooperation, these efforts have added yet another level of bureaucratic overlay.

PART 4

CONCLUSION

13

Toward a New Partnership with Mexico

Joseph S. Tulchin and Andrew D. Selee

Mexican politics and society have been rapidly transformed since the early 1980s. The postrevolutionary political and economic model, which had survived with modifications for more than five decades, featured a single governing political party dominated by an all-powerful president and a development model that was predominantly state-led and protected national industry. The economic crises of the 1980s and 1990s drastically reshaped this model. Falling wages and rising inflation fueled existing demands for greater political openness and strengthened political and social organizations opposed to the government. National leaders looked outward to find new sources of capital and embarked on an export-oriented development strategy. Millions of Mexicans were drawn northward to the United States in hopes of better opportunities for employment.

By the end of the 1990s, the remnants of the one-party system had collapsed, replaced by a more plural and competitive one. The relationship among the various institutions of government—civilian and military; federal and state; executive, legislative, and judicial—were in a period of redefinition. Demands around indigenous rights and gender equality had moved to the forefront of public debate. Mexicans in the United States played an even more important part in the social and political lives of their home communities as well as those in their adopted homes abroad. Macroeconomic stability had been restored, and Mexico's economy was increasingly integrated with that of its neighbors to the north—Canada and the United States. Despite this, inequality had increased and average wages had stagnated. The overall picture was one of hope, a sense that Mexico had survived a period of tumultuous change and had emerged stronger, more plural, and more stable.

However, questions remained on how to consolidate democracy and achieve development with equity.

These vast political, economic, and social changes taking place in Mexico, along with the growth of economic and social ties across the border, have helped set the stage for a much deeper bilateral relationship with the United States. In this chapter, we look at the way that these changes in Mexico are affecting the bilateral relationship between Mexico and the United States, and we venture a few thoughts on the potential for closer partnership between the two countries in the years to come.

A History of Asymmetry and Mistrust

Throughout most of the nineteenth and twentieth centuries, Mexico and the United States considered their proximity to each other as a liability. The shared history has included a major war, which concluded with the transfer of a third of Mexico's territory to the United States in 1848, and repeated U.S. military incursions in the nineteenth and early twentieth centuries. Until recently, the contours of Mexican nationalism were defined, in large part, as resistance to U.S. encroachment. Throughout most of the twentieth century, Mexico's government pursued a foreign policy strategy that prioritized ties with other developing countries and emphasized the nation's autonomy of action in the international system, often opposing U.S. actions abroad. In multilateral agencies, such as the United Nations and the Organization of American States, Mexico often set itself against initiatives that might commit Mexico to cooperation with the United States or in which Mexico might find itself subjected to U.S. hegemony.

At the same time, the U.S. government saw Mexico as a problematic yet essential neighbor. During the Cold War, the United States valued the Mexican government's stability and sought to maintain some leverage with Mexico as a bulwark against Soviet intervention in the hemisphere (especially in Central America). The U.S. government avoided criticizing the one-party state in Mexico throughout most of the 1980s and 1990s, even as it adopted "democracy" as a banner elsewhere in the hemisphere, so as not to undermine the stability of the regime.[1] Overall, however, Mexico did not figure particularly high in the priorities of the U.S. foreign policy establishment outside of its role in maintaining subregional stability. The U.S. government treated migration as a matter of domestic policy, which the Mexicans found demeaning.

The Mexican economic crises of the 1980s substantially redefined this relationship. Rising interest rates and falling oil prices sent Mexico's economy into a tailspin, leading ultimately to a major devaluation of the peso and to massive capital flight.[2] The United States and the multilateral banks responded with a series of loans that managed to keep Mexico afloat throughout the 1980s. Meanwhile, the Mexican government, starved for foreign capital to cover its debts and pressured by the multilateral banks, implemented a series of structural adjustment programs that reduced the size of the state, opened the economy to foreign investment, and liberalized trade.

In 1990, President Carlos Salinas de Gortari decided to negotiate a free trade agreement with the United States and Canada as a way to attract additional capital. Although he originally had hoped to pursue a multilateral trade strategy, he found that neither the Europeans nor the Japanese were willing to enter into trade pacts with Mexico.[3] The negotiations for the North American Free Trade Agreement (NAFTA) created immediate credibility for Mexico among international investors, and as a result foreign investment and trade flows increased dramatically. The implementation of NAFTA in 1994 reinforced these tendencies.[4]

The cumulative effects of the opening of the Mexican economy meant a dramatically increased economic relationship with the United States. In 1999, Mexico became the second biggest trading partner of the United States. Today it accounts for 10.3 percent of U.S. imports and 12.3 percent of exports, levels that catch the attention of the private sector and even the most inward-looking member of the U.S. Congress. For Mexico the change has been even more dramatic. Foreign trade made up only 11–13 percent of gross domestic product (GDP) in the early 1980s, but by 1996 it represented more than a third of GDP, making Mexico one of the most open developing economies in the world. Whereas in 1980 64.6 percent of Mexico's exports were with the United States, this had risen to 88.1 percent by 1999.[5] Meanwhile, foreign direct investment in Mexico, which had increased modestly in the 1980s from $2.1 billion to $2.6 billion per year, quadrupled between 1990 and 1998 to $10.7 billion per year.[6] U.S. investment in Mexico made up more than 60 percent of this amount.[7]

The Mexican government's commitment to pursue closer economic ties with the United States and the degree of economic dependence this created led to a gradual change in Mexico's foreign policy in the 1990s with regard to its northern neighbor. Economic liberalization produced new goals in Mexican foreign policy, including a more economic-centered approach, a move toward pragmatism, and an emphasis on closer coordination with the United States.[8] The Mexican government continued to stake out positions contrary to those of the U.S. government with regard to Cuba and on key votes at the United Nations, but it largely avoided major foreign policy confrontations with the United States.[9]

U.S. policy toward Mexico changed substantially as well. In the 1980s and 1990s, the United States began to give Mexico a higher priority in its foreign policy agenda than it had in previous decades on a number of fronts. Mexican and U.S. leaders met a total of seventeen times for bilateral summits during the 1990s, compared to only twelve times in the 1980s and eight times in the 1970s.[10] More significant, these summits were not photo opportunities or postcard sessions; they were working meetings that included virtually every cabinet secretary in the U.S. government. During the 1995 peso crisis, the U.S. Treasury put together a $50 billion rescue package to stem capital outflow from Mexico and keep the government solvent to meet its financial obligations. This response was much quicker and considerably more comprehensive than the U.S. response during the 1982 crisis, and it was made despite considerable opposition in Congress. This reflected a new understanding in Washington of the importance of Mexico as a trading partner and the role of its economic health for stability in the hemisphere.

Nonetheless, throughout the 1990s recurrent conflicts about migration and drug trafficking marred smooth relations between the two countries. To some extent, this reflected divergent perceptions of the issues by the two governments. Most politicians in the United States considered both problems to be the result of poor law enforcement in the sending countries and argued that the fault lay on the supply side outside the United States, not on the demand side for labor and drugs within the United States. This policy was used in dealing with other countries sending immigrants or exporting drugs to the United States as well. Although this approach created good press for U.S. politicians, it achieved little in the way of reduced migration and drug flows, and it irritated Mexico and other countries as well.[11]

Mexican migration to the United States increased rapidly in the 1980s and 1990s as economic crises and increased poverty drove Mexicans to search for work in the north, where the economy always seemed to demand more and more cheap labor. The administration of President Bill Clinton, pressured by anti-immigrant sentiment in California and elsewhere, reacted by tripling the budget of the Immigration and Naturalization Service (INS), from $1.4 billion in

1992 to $4.3 billion in 2001, and by doubling the number of Border Patrol agents.[12] Although the INS calculates that Mexicans make up 54 percent of undocumented immigrants, more than 96 percent of those arrested as undocumented immigrants were Mexican.[13] And though the renewed efforts to control illegal immigration through increased border enforcement failed to stifle the flow of migrants, it did redirect migrants into areas that were more dangerous for crossing. This led to an increase in the deaths of migrants, reaching almost 500 in 2000 alone.[14] The increased border enforcement also appears to have broken the cyclical migration flows between the two countries, as Mexicans who came to the United States for the harvest season decided to stay in the United States rather than risk not being able to cross again next season.

During the 1990s, drug shipments through Mexico, particularly of cocaine, increased dramatically. This increase was driven by a successful U.S. campaign to close down drug-shipment routes through the Caribbean and South Florida in the 1980s. The Colombian cartels partnered with the much smaller Mexican cartels to open new transshipment routes.[15] In the early 1980s, little cocaine passed through Mexico, but by 1989 the U.S. Drug Enforcement Agency reported that 30 percent of cocaine traffic to the United States passed through Mexico. By 1992 that number had risen to 50 percent, and it oscillated between 50 percent and 85 percent for the rest of the 1990s.[16] Various U.S. government estimates put the total value of the profits generated by the Mexican cartels at $7–10 billion per year, slightly more than the annual revenues of Mexican oil.[17] These moneys were—and continue to be—highly corrosive to Mexico's political system because they create possibilities for wide-scale corruption of political, judicial, and law-enforcement officials. Moreover, drug enforcement strategies appeared to have succeeded only in shifting transshipment points and breaking a few large cartels into many smaller ones without reducing supply.

Nothing was as symbolic of the recurrent conflicts in U.S.-Mexico relations throughout the 1990s as the drug certification program, first enacted by the U.S. Congress in 1986, which required the U.S. State Department to certify the compliance of other countries in U.S. drug control efforts every year. This program irritated Mexican government officials and the Mexican public at large, who wondered how the country that was the primary market for narcotics could judge their efforts in combating drug trafficking. In several years, the U.S. Congress considered decertifying Mexico, which would have led to a range of economic sanctions. Although this never occurred, it created a profound, recurring irritant in the relationship and showed the disjuncture between the increasing commercial interdependence of the two countries and the fragility of cooperation in other areas.

Toward Partnership

With the inaugurations of Presidents George W. Bush and Vicente Fox, bilateral relations have entered a new stage. This is partly a reflection of the specific interest that these two presidents have shown for the relationship between the countries. Each has given considerable attention to the relationship despite some criticism from members of their own parties. As a former governor of Texas, President Bush is familiar with Mexico and has a long history of involvement in U.S.-Mexican issues. As a former governor of the state of Guanajuato, one of the areas of greatest migration to the United States, and as a former Coca-Cola executive, President Fox knows the United States well and has been eager to engage the neighbors to the north. This mutual interest—and the chemistry between the two leaders—has been essential to the decisions of each to make the relationship a priority. However, three additional contextual factors have also helped drive the relationship forward and have created momentum for greater engagement across the border in years to come.

First, the interdependence between the two economies has grown exponentially since the signing of NAFTA in 1994. As noted previously, Mexico exports 88 percent of its goods to the United States and receives around 12 percent of U.S. exports. The volume of trade between the countries has almost tripled since the signing of NAFTA.[18] Equally important, the signing of NAFTA led to the creation of numerous task forces, bilateral consultative groups, and annual meetings among leaders from both countries to address a range of issues, including commerce, law enforcement, migration, and economic development. NAFTA has been a catalyst for increasing official and unofficial contacts among government officials, business leaders, and civil society organizations on both sides of the border.[19] The bilateral relationship is more dense than it has ever been and less dominated by government-to-government contacts.

Second, the growth of the Mexican population in the United States has made the bilateral relationship a question of domestic politics in both countries as well. The Latino population in the United States—two-thirds of which is of Mexican origin—grew almost 60 percent in the 1990s to represent 12.5 percent of the total population. In several states, including California, Texas, New Mexico, Arizona, Colorado, Nevada, and Illinois, the population of Mexican origin is an especially influential sector of the electorate.[20] By the end of the 1990s, leaders in both the Democratic and Republican parties began looking more actively for ways to court Latino voters who they saw as a key swing vote in local and national elections. Promoting better relations with Mexico and legalizing Mexican workers in the United States became popular strategies to attract voters of Mexican descent.

At the same time, the Mexican government has increasingly sought to court Mexicans in the United States because of their economic power—remittances from Mexicans living in the United States contribute over $6 billion annually to the Mexican economy—as well as the likelihood that they would soon be allowed to vote in Mexican elections by absentee ballot.[21] This began somewhat in the 1990s, but under the Fox administration there has been a concerted effort to reach out to Mexicans in the United States with frequent presidential visits to Mexican communities in the United States and a new special office that serves as an ongoing liaison.

Third, the democratic transition in Mexico has led to a reassessment of Mexico's foreign policy and a new approach that stresses international engagement. Previous administrations were fearful of U.S. intervention and cautious that other countries might criticize authoritarian elements in the Mexican political system. As a result, foreign policy was primarily based on a strict interpretation of state sovereignty and sought to avoid international entanglements that might compromise Mexican sovereignty or allow others to criticize Mexico's internal politics. With the advent of a more democratic order, the current administration has stressed that Mexico should couple respect for sovereignty with active engagement in world affairs, including in regimes to protect human rights and promote democracy. The Mexican government has sought to balance active engagement with the United States on bilateral issues, with an even more active agenda within multilateral agencies, including the United Nations (UN) and the Organization of American States. In 2001, Mexico won a nonpermanent seat on the UN Security Council, which it assumed in January 2002 with a public declaration that it would use its new position to actively participate in discussions on international governance. The Mexican government has also sought to play a bridging role between North America and Latin America, with active engagement in the Colombian peace process and other issues of hemispheric security. As a result, the United States increasingly has come to see Mexico as a critical partner in achieving stability and development in a hemisphere often plagued by uncertainty.

These factors, coupled with the special interest that the leaders of both countries share for the bilateral relationship, suggest that the relationship between Mexico and the United States is likely to continue to deepen. The deepening will not occur without tension. For Mexicans, historical distrust about U.S. interventionist tendencies will not disappear overnight, whereas some in the United States still question Mexico's ability to be a dependable partner. The countries have different legal, political, and cultural traditions that must be understood by each other. The GDP of the United States is eighteen times that of Mexico.[22] Profound asymmetries remain in the amount of attention each country gives to the other.

The terrorist attacks in the United States on September 11, 2001, highlighted the difficulties implicit in the bilateral relationship. President Fox and Foreign Minister Jorge Castañeda both quickly expressed Mexican solidarity with the United States and their support for the U.S. response to the attacks. Many Mexican politicians, however, expressed concerns about the U.S. response and criticized President Fox's endorsement of U.S. efforts. Polls showed that many Mexicans were highly skeptical of the U.S.-led war on terrorism. For many Mexicans, the U.S. attack on Afghanistan seemed to echo earlier invasions of Mexico and other countries around the world and give evidence of continuing hubris.

At the same time, Mexico seemed to drop off the map of U.S. policy and public opinion. Only a few days before, President Fox had visited Washington for a week of meetings that made headlines in major U.S. newspapers. President Bush had introduced him at one meeting by stating that the United States has "no more important relationship in the world than the one we have with Mexico."[23] The framework of a bilateral migration agreement seemed likely by year's end. Only a week later, U.S. foreign policy was focused almost exclusively on the Middle East, and public sentiment had turned against immigration once again. President Fox's subsequent visit to the United States in October barely warranted a byline in the major papers.

This sudden shift in the bilateral relationship does not appear to be permanent. Mexico is once again emerging as a key U.S. foreign policy priority—though clearly secondary to crisis management in the Middle East. The Mexican government has been persistent in trying to restart negotiations on migration and other issues on the bilateral agenda and has continued to express solidarity with U.S. efforts on terrorism. The same factors that made the relationship a priority before September 11 are still important: the presence of millions of Mexicans and Mexican Americans in the United States; the constant and growing trade between the countries; the links among people, business groups, local governments, federal agencies, and civil society organizations; and the desire to seek stability and development in the hemisphere. What happened in the relationship after September 11 underscores the multiple challenges that the two countries confront in developing a closer and more equitable relationship and the asymmetries that complicate the task.

These challenges can be overcome only by time and the concerted effort of national leaders—both those in government and those in society—determined to forge a new era of cooperation. The key to a successful bilateral relationship will be the level of mutual trust and respect between the two countries that can be generated and sustained. All of the issues ahead are sensitive. All of them require compromise. To accomplish any of these goals requires sustained cooperation between the two countries—a partnership. The partnership must be built on a foundation of mutual respect and trust, which are the result of careful efforts by governments, private corporations, civil society organizations, the media, and individuals. The future is ours to build.

Notes

1. Two studies do a good job of tracing U.S. support of the one-party regime: Sergio Aguayo, *Myths and [Mis]Perceptions: Changing U.S. Elite Views of Mexico* (La Jolla: Center for U.S.-Mexican Studies, University of Califonia–San Diego, 1998); and Jacqueline Mazza, *Don't Disturb the Neighbors: The U.S. and Democracy in Mexico, 1980–1995* (New York: Routledge, 2001).

2. Mexico had borrowed liberally from international creditors during the late 1970s based on the rising price of oil and the plentiful supply of low-interest credit. When credit became more expensive and of a shorter maturity in 1981 and the price of oil plummeted, Mexico did not implement policies to adjust to the new situation. Fear of a devaluation led to capital flight and exacerbated the crisis. In 1982, the Mexican government was finally forced to devaluate, leading to further capital flight and a series of ill-advised emergency policies. See Nora Lustig, *Mexico: The Remaking of an Economy* (Washington, D.C.: Brookings Institution Press, 1998), pp. 3–4.

3. The Europeans were concerned with Eastern Europe and unable to look westward at the time; Japan was leery about doing anything in what they perceived as the U.S. sphere of influence. See Peter H. Smith, *Talons of the Eagle: Dynamics of U.S.–Latin American Relations,* 2nd ed. (New York: Oxford University Press, 2000), p. 328.

4. Enrique Dussel Peters, *Polarizing Mexico: The Impact of Liberalization Strategy* (Boulder: Lynne Rienner Publishers, 2001), pp. 118–119.

5. Not surprisingly, Mexico's exports to the European Union dropped from 15.3 percent to 3.8 percent in the same period, and exports to Asia dropped from 5.3 percent to less than 1.5 percent. Trade figures for Mexico and the United States are from International Monetary Fund, *Direction of Trade Statistics* (Washington, D.C.: IMF, 1987, 1991, and 2000). Figures for trade as a percentage of GDP are from Guadalupe González, "Foreign Policy Strategies in a Globalized World: The Case of Mexico," in Joseph S. Tulchin and Ralph H. Espach, eds., *Latin America in the New Interational System* (Boulder: Lynne Rienner Publishers, 2001), p. 155.

6. Dussel Peters, *Polarizing Mexico*, pp. 118–123.

7. Ibid., p. 119.

8. González, "Foreign Policy Strategies in a Globalized World," p. 162.

9. Ibid., pp. 163–172.

10. Mexican embassy in Washington website: www.mexicoembassy.org. Accessed March 11, 2001.

11. This led one observer to remark: "In the case of the U.S.-Mexico border, signaling a commitment to deterrence and projecting an image of progress toward that goal has been more politically consequential for state actors than actually achieving deterrence." Peter Andreas, *Border Games: Policing the U.S.-Mexico Divide* (Ithaca: Cornell University Press, 2000), p. 9.

12. Wayne Cornelius, *Death at the Border: The Efficacy and "Unintended" Consequences of U.S. Immigration Control Policy, 1993–2000.* University of California–San Diego, Center for Comparative Immigration Studies *Working Paper* No. 27, November 2000, p. 2. Smith, *Talons of the Eagle*, p. 306.

13. Immigration and Naturalization Service, "INS Releases Updated Estimates of U.S. Illegal Population," News Release, February 7, 1997. INS, "FY 2000 INS Removals Show Slight Increase," News Release, December 20, 2000.

14. On the outcome of the law enforcement strategy, see Smith, *Talons of the Eagle*, p. 306. The number of deaths of Mexican migrants calculated by the INS is 369 for 2000; the Mexican government's figure is 491, according to University of Houston researchers Jacqueline Hagan and Nestor Rodriguez. University of Houston, "UH Researchers Establish Link Between Border Deaths and U.S. Immigration Policy," News Release, February 14, 2001.

15. Guadalupe González, "Drug Trafficking as a Bilateral Issue," in Andrew Selee, ed., *Mexico in Transition*, Woodrow Wilson Center Reports on the Americas no. 1 (Washington, D.C.: Woodrow Wilson Center Press, 2001).

16. Peter Smith, "Semiorganized International Crime: Drug Trafficking in Mexico," in Tom Farer, ed., *Transnational Crime in the Americas* (New York: Routledge, 1999).

17. Andreas, *Border Games*, p. 60; Smith, "Semiorganized International Crime," p. 196.

18. The total volume of trade rose from $89 million in 1993 to $274 million in 2000. IMF, *Direction of Trade Statistics* (Washington, D.C.: IMF, 1997, 2001).

19. Jorge Dominguez and Rafael Fernandez de Castro make this point eloquently in *The United States and Mexico: Between Partnership and Conflict* (New York: Routledge, 2001); see esp. pp. 73–74.

20. The Latino population, mostly of Mexican origin in these states, makes up 32.4 percent of the population in California, 32 percent in Texas, 42.1 percent in New Mexico, 25.3 percent in Arizona, 17.1 percent in Colorado, 19.1 percent in Nevada, and 12.3 percent in Illinois. In certain major cities, the Latino population represents a particularly significant part of the population, including Los Angeles (46.5 percent), San Antonio (58.7 percent), Houston (37.4 percent), and Chicago (26 percent). These data from 2000 U.S. Census, available online at www.census.gov.

21. In 1999, an Inter-American Development Bank study calculated that remittances were worth $6,795 million to the Mexican economy. *Remittances to Latin America and the Caribbean: Comparative Statistics* (Washington, D.C.: Multilateral Investment Fund, Inter-American Development Bank, May 2001). Similarly, the International Monetary Fund calculated remittances at $6,573 million in 2000. IMF, *Balance of Payments Statistics Yearbook*, Part 1: Country Tables (Washington, D.C.: IMF, 2001).

22. GDP ratio from the World Bank, *World Development Indicators Database,* July 2000, available at www.devdata.worldbank.org.

23. Kevin Sullivan, "U.S. Relations Change Suddenly for Mexico," *Washington Post,* September 21, 2001, p. A32.

Selected Bibliography

Aguayo, Sergio. *1968: Los archivos de la violencia.* México: Grijalvo-Reforma, 1998.

———. *Myths and [Mis]Perceptions: Changing U.S. Elite Views of Mexico.* La Jolla: Center for U.S.-Mexican Studies, University of California–San Diego, 1998.

Andreas, Peter. *Border Games: Policing the U.S.-Mexico Divide.* Ithaca: Cornell University Press, 2000.

Arnson, Cynthia, and Raúl Benítez Manaut, eds. *Chiapas: los desafíos de la paz.* Mexico City: Miguel Angel Porrúa, 2000.

Bailey, John, and Roy Godson, eds. *Organized Crime and Democratic Governability: Mexico and the U.S.-Mexico Borderlands.* Pittsburgh: University of Pittsburgh, 2000.

Bean, Frank D., Rodolfo O. de la Garza, Bryan R. Roberts, and Sidney Weintraub, eds. *At the Crossroads: Mexican Migration and U.S. Public Policy.* New York: Rowman and Littlefield, 1997.

Becerra, Ricardo, Pedro Salazar, and José Woldenberg. *La mecánica del cambio político en México.* México: Cal y Arena, 2000.

Camp, Roderic Ai. *Generals in the Palace: The Military in Modern Mexico.* New York: Oxford University Press, 1992.

———. *Citizen Views of Democracy in Latin America.* Pittsburgh: Pittsburgh University, 2001.

Castañeda, Jorge G. *Utopia Unarmed: The Latin American Left After the Cold War.* New York: Knopf, Random House, 1993.

———. *Perpetuating Power: How Mexican Presidents Were Chosen.* Trans. Padraic Arthur Smithies. New York: New Press, W. W. Norton, 2000.

Castro Soto, Gustavo E., and Ernesto Ledesma Arronte, eds. *Siempre cerca, siempre lejos: las fuerzas armadas en México.* Mexico City: CENCOS, CIEPAC, Global Exchange, 2000.

Chalmers, Douglas A., Carlos M. Vilas, Katherine Hite, Scott B. Martin, Kerianne Piester, and Monique Segarra, eds. *The New Politics of Inequality in Latin America: Rethinking Participation and Representation.* Oxford, UK: Oxford University, 1997.

Chand, Vikram. *Mexico's Political Awakening*. Notre Dame: University of Notre Dame Press, 2001.

Cook, Maria Lorena. *Organizing Dissent: Unions, the State, and the Democratic Teachers' Movement in Mexico*. University Park: Pennsylvania State University, 1996.

Cordera, Rolando, and Alicia Ziccardi. *Politicas sociales al fin del milenio: decentralización, diseño y gestión*. Mexico City: Miguel Angel Porrúa, 2000.

Cornelius, Wayne A. *Mexican Politics in Transition: The Breakdown of a One-Party-Dominant Regime*. La Jolla: Center for U.S.-Mexican Studies, University of California–San Diego, 1996.

———. *Death at the Border: The Efficacy and "Unintended" Consequences of U.S. Immigration Control Policy, 1993–2000*. Center for Comparative Immigration Studies Working Paper No. 27. La Jolla: University of California–San Diego, November 2000.

Cornelius, Wayne A., and Ann Craig. "Houses Divided: Parties and Political Reform in Mexico." In Scott Mainwaring and Timothy R. Scully, eds., *Building Democratic Institutions: Party Systems in Latin America*. Stanford: Stanford University Press, 1995.

Cornelius, Wayne A., Todd A. Eisenstadt, and Jane Hindley, eds. *Subnational Politics and Democratization in Mexico*. La Jolla: Center for U.S.-Mexican Studies, University of California–San Diego, 1999.

Cornelius, Wayne, and David Myhre, eds. *The Transformation of Rural Mexico: Reforming the Ejido Sector*. La Jolla: Center for U.S.-Mexican Studies, University of California–San Diego, 1998.

Cosio Villegas, Daniel. *El sistema político mexicano*. México: Joaquín Mortiz, 1972.

Dominguez, Jorge, and Rafael Fernandez de Castro. *The United States and Mexico: Between Partnership and Conflict*. New York: Routledge, 2001.

Dresser, Denise. *Neopopulist Solutions to Neoliberal Problems: Mexico's National Solidarity Program*. La Jolla: Center for U.S.-Mexican Studies, University of California–San Diego, 1991.

Durand, Jorge, and Douglas S. Massey. "Mexican Migration to the United States: A Critical Review." *Latin American Research Review* 27, no. 2 (1992): 12.

Durand Ponte, Victor Manuel. "The Confederation of Mexican Workers, the Labor Congress, and the Crisis of Mexico's Social Pact." In Kevin Middlebrook, ed., *Unions, Workers, and the State in Mexico*. La Jolla: Center for U.S.-Mexican Studies, University of California–San Diego, 1991.

Dussel Peters, Enrique. *Polarizing Mexico: The Impact of Liberalization Strategy*. Boulder: Lynne Rienner Publishers, 2001.

Fox, Jonathan. "The Difficult Transition from Clientelism to Citizenship." *World Politics* 46, no. 2 (January 1994): 151–184.

———. *Assessing Binational Civil Society Coalitions: Lessons from the Mexico-U.S. Experience*. Chicano/Latino Research Center Working Paper No. 26. Santa Cruz: University of California–Santa Cruz, April 2000.

González, Guadalupe. "Foreign Policy Strategies in a Globalized World: The Case of Mexico." In Joseph S. Tulchin and Ralph H. Espach, eds.,

Latin America in the New Interational System. Boulder: Lynne Rienner Publishers, 2001.

———. "Drug Trafficking as a Bilateral Issue." In Andrew Selee, ed., *Mexico in Transition*. Woodrow Wilson Center Report on the Americas No. 1. Washington, D.C.: Woodrow Wilson Center Press, May 2001.

González Casanova, Pablo. *La democracia en México*. México: Era, 1965.

Gutiérrez, David G., ed. *Between Two Worlds: Mexican Immigrants in the United States*. Wilmington, DE: Scholarly Resources, 1996.

Harvey, Neil. *The Chiapas Rebellion: The Struggle for Land and Democracy*. Durham, NC: Duke University, 1998.

Hernández Díaz, Jorge. *Etnicidad, poder y nación*. Oaxaca, Mexico: Universidad Autónoma Benito Juárez de Oaxaca, 1993.

Klesner, Joseph. "Electoral Competition and the New Party System in Mexico." Paper presented at the Annual Meeting of the American Political Science Association, San Francisco, August 30–September 2, 2001.

Lamas, Marta, A. Martínez, M. L. Tarrés, and E. Tuñón. "Building Bridges: The Growth of Popular Feminism in Mexico." In Amrita Basu, ed., *The Challenge of Local Feminisms: Women's Movements in Global Perspective*. Boulder: Westview, 1995.

Le Bot, Yvon. *Subcomandante Marcos: El sueño zapatista*. Mexico City: Plaza and Janes, 1997.

Levy, Daniel, and Kathleen Bruhn. *Mexico: The Struggle for Democratic Development*. Berkeley and Los Angeles: University of California Press, 2001.

Leyva Solano, Xochitl, and Gabriel Ascencio Franco. *Lacandonia al filo del agua*. Mexico City: CIESAS, 1996.

Lorey, David E. *The U.S.-Mexican Border in the Twentieth Century*. Wilmington, DE: Scholarly Resources, 1999.

Lujambio, Alonso. *El poder compartido*. México: Oceano, 2000.

Lustig, Nora. *Mexico: Remaking of an Economy*. Washington, D.C.: Brookings Institution, 1998.

Lustig, Nora, and Miguel Székely. *México: Evolución económica, pobreza y desigualdad*. Washington, D.C.: Inter-American Development Bank, Economic Commission for Latin America and the Caribbean, and the UN Development Program, 1997.

Martínez, Oscar J., ed. *U.S.-Mexico Borderlands: Historical and Contemporary Perspectives*. Wilmington, DE: Scholarly Resources, 1996.

Massey, Douglas S., and Kristin E. Espinosa. "What's Driving Mexico-U.S. Migration? A Theoretical, Empirical, and Policy Analysis." *American Journal of Sociology* 102, no. 4 (January 1997): 991–992.

Mazza, Jacqueline. *Don't Disturb the Neighbors: The U.S. and Democracy in Mexico, 1980–1995*. New York: Routledge, 2001.

Meyer, Lorenzo. "La crisis del presidencialismo mexicano. Recuperación espectacular y recaída estructural, 1982–1996." *Foro Internacional* 36, núm. 1–2 (1996): 11–30.

Middlebrook, Kevin. *The Paradox of Revolution: Labor, the State, and Authoritarianism in Mexico*. Baltimore: Johns Hopkins University Press, 1995.

Mizrahi, Yemile. "The Fox Administration After One Year in Power." *Mexico*

Policy Bulletin No. 3. Washington, D.C., Woodrow Wilson Center, February 2002.

———. "Veinte años de descentralización en México: un proceso de arriba hacia abajo." In Philip Oxhorn, Joseph Tulchin, and Andrew Selee, eds. *Decentralization, Civil Society, and Democratic Governance.* Unpublished manuscript.

Pastor, Robert A. *Towards a North American Community: Lessons from the Old World for the New.* Washington, D.C.: Institute for International Economics, 2001.

Pastor, Manuel, and Carol Wise. "State Policy, Distribution, and Neoliberal Reform in Mexico." *Journal of Latin American Studies* 29, no. 2 (1997): 419–456.

Rubin, Jeffrey W. "Decentering the Regime." In Joe Foweraker and Ann L. Craig, eds., *Popular Movements and Political Change in Mexico.* Boulder: Lynne Rienner Publishers, 1990.

———. *Decentering the Regime: Ethnicity, Radicalism, and Democracy in Juchitán, Mexico.* Durham, NC: Duke University, 1997.

Scherer, Julio, and Carlos Monsivais. *Parte de guerra: Tlatelolco 1968.* Mexico City: Nuevo Siglo-Aguilar, 1999.

Selee, Andrew, ed. *Mexico in Transition.* Woodrow Wilson Center Report on the Americas No. 1. Washington, D.C.: Woodrow Wilson Center Press, May 2001.

Smith, Peter H. "Semiorganized International Crime: Drug Trafficking in Mexico." In Tom Farer, ed., *Transnational Crime in the Americas.* New York: Routledge, 1999.

———. *Talons of the Eagle: Dynamics of U.S.–Latin American Relations.* 2nd ed. New York: Oxford University Press, 2000.

Tello Diaz, Carlos. *La rebelión de las Cañadas.* Mexico, D.F.: Cal y Arena, 1995.

Tuñón, Esperanza. *Mujeres en escena: de la tramoya al protagonismo (1982–1994).* Mexico: Miguel Angel Porrúa, PUEG, Ecosur, 1997.

Ugalde, Luis Carlos. *The Mexican Congress: Old Player, New Power.* Washington, D.C.: Center for Strategic and International Studies, 2000.

Weintraub, Sidney. *NAFTA at Three.* Washington, D.C.: Center for International and Strategic Studies, 1997.

Womack, John Jr., ed. *Rebellion in Chiapas: An Historical Reader.* New York: New Press, 1999.

Zebadúa, Emilio. *Breve historia de Chiapas.* Mexico: Colegio de Mexico and Fondo de Cultura Economica, 1999.

The Contributors

Kirsten Appendini is professor of economics at El Colegio de México.

Robert Bach is currently a senior fellow at the Inter-American Dialogue in Washington. Previously he served as director of the Global Inclusion Program at the Rockefeller Foundation and as executive associate director of the Immigration and Naturalization Service.

Raúl Benítez is a professor at the Universidad Nacional Autónoma de México. He has served as Mexico's associate national security adviser and has been a visiting scholar at Columbia University and the Woodrow Wilson Center.

Ilán Bizberg is professor of International Relations at El Colegio de México and has been a public policy scholar at the Woodrow Wilson Center.

Katrina Burgess is the William R. Rhodes Post-Doctoral Fellow at the Thomas J. Watson Institute for International Studies at Brown University while on a two-year leave from her position as assistant professor of political science in the Maxwell School of Citizenship and Public Affairs at Syracuse University.

Jorge Castañeda is Mexico's secretary of foreign relations. He is a professor at the Mexican National Autonomous University and has been a visiting scholar at Columbia University and the Carnegie Endowment for International Peace.

Stephen Clarkson is professor of political economy at the University of Toronto and has been a fellow at the Woodrow Wilson Center.

Carlos Elizondo is director of the Centro de Investigación y Docencia Económicas and a columnist for Mexico's influential newspaper *Reforma*.

Marta Lamas is editor of *Debate Feminista* and director of the Grupo de Información en Reproducción Elegida.

Manuel Pastor is professor of Latin American and Latino Studies at the University of California–Santa Cruz and director of the Center for Justice, Tolerance, and Community.

Stephen Pitti is assistant professor of history and American studies at Yale University.

Gustav Ranis is director of the Center for International and Area Studies and the Frank Altschul Professor of International Economics at Yale University.

Andrew Selee is senior program associate in the Latin American Program of the Woodrow Wilson Center and directs the center's Mexico Project.

Rodolfo Stavenhagen is a professor at El Colegio de México, special rapporteur of the UN Human Rights Commission for the rights and liberties of indigenous people, and president of the Commission for Monitoring and Follow-up of the San Andrés Accords.

Joseph S. Tulchin is director of the Latin American Program of the Woodrow Wilson Center. He taught at Yale University and was director of international studies at the University of North Carolina at Chapel Hill.

Carol Wise is associate professor of international relations at the University of Southern California. Previously she was associate professor of Latin American Studies at the Paul H. Nitze School of Advanced International Studies of Johns Hopkins University and a research fellow at the Carnegie Endowment for International Peace.

Index

About the Book

As electoral politics in Mexico have become more open and democratic, the country's economy also has been thoroughly restructured and new ideas about government, state-society relations, and Mexico's place in the international system have taken hold. *Mexico's Politics and Society in Transition* explores these interrelated trends. Offering fresh perspectives on the contemporary problems on the Mexican agenda, the authors cogently discuss the politics of change, the challenges of social development, and the realities of building a productive, mutually beneficial U.S.-Mexico relationship.

Joseph S. Tulchin is director of the Latin American Program at the Woodrow Wilson International Center for Scholars. **Andrew D. Selee** is senior program associate in the Latin American Program.